Technology and Innovation Management in the Age of Gen AI

Technology and Innovation Management in the Age of Gen AI

Third Edition

SANJIVA SHANKAR DUBEY
Professor and Dean
Executive Education and Hybrid Program, IILM Lodhi Road
Former Dean Academics, BIMTECH, Greater Noida
Former IBM Consulting Principal and Asia Pacific Executive

PHI Learning Private Limited
Delhi-110092
2025

In fond memory of ***Shri Asoke K. Ghosh*** *(October 1942 – February 2024), Founder Chairman and Managing Director of PHI Learning, whose vision endlessly inspires.*

The Legacy Continues....

Published by Pushpita Ghosh, PHI Learning Private Limited, Rimjhim House, 111, Patparganj Industrial Estate, Delhi-110092 and Printed by Multi Colour Services, I-45, DLF Industrial Area, Sector-32, Faridabad, Haryana-121003.

₹795.00

TECHNOLOGY AND INNOVATION MANAGEMENT IN THE AGE OF GEN AI, Third Edition
Sanjiva Shankar Dubey

ISBN-978-93-5443-954-4 (Print Book)
ISBN-978-93-5443-791-5 (e-Book)

The export rights of the book are vested solely with the publisher.

To

My Parents

Late Vidyawati Dubey and Late Sidheshwar Dubey

Contents

Foreword

by Dr. Raj Ramesh

We are living in a moment of profound technological change, where generative AI is emerging not as a passing trend but as a transformational force that will redefine how organizations operate, compete, and create value. From my vantage point of artificial intelligence, enterprise architecture, and digital transformation—disciplines that guide leaders in navigating complexity and building organizations that are both resilient and innovative—it is clear that generative AI has the capacity to fundamentally reshape organizations. It is not limited to gains in efficiency or automation; rather, it reaches into the deepest layers of creativity, strategy, and decision-making.

This book, *Technology and Innovation Management in the Age of Gen AI* by Professor Dubey, is both timely and comprehensive. Prof. Dubey not only presents AI as a tool but also explores the broader ecosystem required for successful adoption. Technology alone is never enough. For generative AI to deliver a sustainable impact, organizations must align their strategy, embrace cultural change, assess risks, and establish robust governance. Leaders must think not only about what AI can do, but also how it integrates with people, processes, and values.

Prof. Dubey shares examples across industries, from healthcare to finance to education, to illustrate practical applications of how generative AI accelerates innovation. These case studies provide leaders with a deeper understanding of the challenges and opportunities. Yet as he points out, this shift must also account for ethical dilemmas and global inequalities, where fairness, transparency, and governance play critical roles. Still, the future looks immensely promising. When embraced thoughtfully within a framework of strategy, culture, and responsibility, generative AI can unlock possibilities that redefine competitiveness and spark further human creativity.

What makes this book unique is the way it brings together these perspectives in a structured and accessible manner. From practical applications to ethical considerations, from innovation frameworks to organizational readiness, it provides a holistic roadmap for anyone considering how to introduce generative AI into their organization. Whether you are an executive, an innovator, or simply curious about the future of work, you will find valuable insights here.

Generative AI is not just shaping the tools we use—it is redefining the foundations of competition and collaboration in the digital age. That is why this book is a must-read for leaders who want to stay ahead of change and harness AI responsibly to build the organizations of the future.

Dr. Raj Ramesh
Author, TEDx Speaker and Consultant
Strategy Consultant NASA Jet Propulsion Laboratory
www.drrajramesh.com youtube.com/c/rajramesh

Foreword

Dr. Harivansh Chaturvedi

Technology and Innovation Management is a key emerging discipline in the areas of management and technology. We have seen massive enrichment and exponential growth in business performance through technology and innovation. The same is happening in the public services and social sector now. The potential of using technology and innovation to enrich each of these areas is immense. In our personal lives too, staying connected through social media and mobile apps has permeated all across. New technology interventions, like driverless car, Drone for home delivery or using robotics for precise and complex medical surgery has become a near reality.

But it is also well-known that not every company which has taken to new technology and innovation route has succeeded in equal measures. For every successful Google there are hundreds of start-ups or new product launches which have never ever succeeded. The problem lies not in any technology or innovation approach, but the absence of adopting sound management process to make it a success. This brings us to the conclusion that serendipity is not the only method for new technology and innovation, but there has to be a proactive approach adopted by corporations to establish well-proven practices in this field. They need people who are trained in the methods of Technology and Innovation Management, and who can execute the best practices around this discipline. This book on Technology and Innovation Management by Prof. Sanjiva Shankar Dubey comes at an appropriate time when corporate leaders are eagerly willing to join hands with youngsters with cutting-edge insights of technology and zeal to implement Innovative Management practices at their work place.

Consequently, higher education institutes of management and technology will have to increase focus on subjects that enable students to understand and deploy technology for innovation purposes. A book on this subject by someone who is not only a well-known practitioner of technology and innovation but also a rich contributor in academics, is a welcome arrival.

I know Prof. Dubey for over a decade now while he was serving at IBM as its Asia Pacific Executive. His passion for teaching and grooming youngsters have seen him at BIMTECH campus as visiting faculty and industry advisor. During this period he has authored eight books while being in full time industry career, which shows his deep commitment to creating and disseminating knowledge. Now he is with IILM as Dean, and earlier with BIMTECH as Dean Academics. His research efforts of several years backed up with over three decades of experience has taken shape in the form of this book.

I wish to congratulate Prof. Dubey and extend my best wishes for the success of this book.

Dr. Harivansh Chaturvedi
Director General IILM, Lodhi Road
Former Director
Birla Institute of Management Technology (BIMTECH)

Preface

The foundational principles of Technology and Innovation Management (TIM) have long guided organizations through periods of technological change, emphasizing strategic alignment, efficient processes, and continuous innovation. These core tenets remain profoundly relevant in the contemporary business landscape. However, the advent and rapid proliferation of Artificial Intelligence (AI), and particularly Generative AI (Gen AI), necessitate a fundamental re-evaluation and significant expansion of these established concepts. AI is not merely another technological advancement; it represents a transformative force that is reshaping nearly every facet of business operations, strategic planning, and societal interaction. This revised edition aims to provide a cutting-edge understanding of managing technology and innovation in this new, AI-driven era.

The accelerating pace of AI adoption presents a significant challenge to traditional strategic planning and operational cycles. Data indicates that the workplace adoption of generative AI has been as swift as that of the personal computer, and its overall adoption has surpassed both personal computers and the internet in speed. This unprecedented velocity of technological diffusion implies that the conventional, often slower, strategic planning cycles are no longer adequate for maintaining competitive relevance. Instead, organizations are compelled to embrace more agile and continuous approaches to TIM, prioritizing rapid learning, experimentation, and adaptation over rigid, long-term forecasts. The compressed timeline for technological evolution means that the window for establishing competitive advantage, whether as a first-mover or a fast-follower, is considerably narrower, intensifying the pressure on firms to forecast, acquire, and implement new technologies with unprecedented speed and precision.

The Transformative Power of Generative AI: A New Paradigm

Generative AI, a subset of AI, stands at the forefront of this technological revolution. It possesses the unique ability to learn from existing data and then create entirely new, realistic content that reflects the characteristics of its training data without merely replicating it. This capability marks a significant departure from earlier forms of AI, which primarily focused on classification, prediction, or optimization. Gen AI's creative capacity spans diverse domains, including the generation of text, images, video, music, speech, software code, and even complex product designs and scientific hypotheses.

This generative capability fundamentally alters how innovation occurs within organizations and how businesses create value. The ability of Gen AI to rapidly generate novel concepts and solutions suggests a profound shift in the innovation paradigm. It moves beyond simply optimizing existing processes or enhancing efficiency (which were the primary benefits of earlier AI forms) to truly augmenting human creativity and enabling autonomous ideation. This implies a future where innovation is less about human ingenuity operating in isolation and more about a symbiotic relationship between humans and AI. This collaboration has the potential to democratize creative processes, making advanced design and content generation accessible to a broader range of individuals and teams. However, it also raises complex questions regarding intellectual property, the nature of original work, and the evolving role of human creators in the innovation lifecycle.

Continuing with the additions (Chapter 12—Innovation Driving Industry 4.0 and Fourth Industrial Revolution, Chapter 13—Design Thinking for Innovation) and revisions of the existing chapters in the Second Edition, the book now in its *Third Edition* has undergone comprehensive review in the light of AI's amplifier effect on creativity and innovation.

Four new Chapters 14, 15, 16 and 17 have been added in the new edition. In addition, each of the earlier chapters has been revised considering the impact of the most pathbreaking development of our times, Generative AI. In the new Chapter 14, it considers the macro view impact of Generative AI on Businesses. This is followed by Chapter 15, which discusses the Impact of Gen AI in Innovating Processes, Models, and Targets for business. The next Chapter is 16. Describes the examples across the industry of Generative AI Adoption.

The book sums up in Chapter 17 with Strategic Adoption Frameworks for Generative AI to help enterprises adopt the new technology efficiently, effectively and responsibly. For students, this chapter is "Do-How" for Gen AI adoption, something that is missing from most discourse.

While core principles of Technology and Innovation management remain strong as ever, the newer technology (such as Gen AI) gives us opportunities to continue the innovation processes further and stronger.

Sanjiva Shankar Dubey

Preface to the First Edition

Technology is all-encompassing and all-permeating in business as well as in our daily lives. In the recent past, world has witnessed dramatic changes in the business landscape, rapid rise of new products and companies leaving behind a trail of disruption. New companies from nowhere have sprung surprises to the established ones, in some cases decimating them to footnote. As consumers, we welcome all these changes. For instance, the ease with which we are now able to conduct our daily routine whether it is to stay in touch with our friends or family, seek medical assistance or just entertainment, is all due to innovative offerings by upcoming entrepreneurs. These are the results of harnessing newer technology for innovative outcome. This phenomenon has also challenged established management principles, because new technology led innovation has a better approach to deal with the current issues being faced by the world. Authorities sought help of Unmanned Aerial Vehicle (UAV), commonly known as a drone and data analytics to locate stranded tourists in flood raved Himalayas. Be it the precise prediction of weather or saving a life of patients with rare form of cancer using analytical model by arriving at an accurate diagnosis and leading to proper treatment, is an innovative use of technology.

Surprisingly, not every new technology innovation succeeds or every start-up becomes a billion dollar enterprise in a few years. There are many that do not survive beyond a few months after highly publicized launch! The track record of established old-economy players in embracing technology led innovation is equally dismal. They wake up when the opportunity is nearly at its last leg and pay a heavy price for their inaction.

The question does arise as to why it happens? There are myriad factors, such as lack of preparation and understanding how technology evolves, when to grab it, when to invest in R&D, new product introduction, leadership and finally managing an effective innovation agenda for the business. In a few words, this happens due to lack of understanding concepts, principles and practices of **Technology and Innovation Management.** We need to expose this subject to our budding management and technology major students. Managers already in the job may require re-tooling with these concepts.

A course on Technology and Innovation Management is mandatory for all students who are going to join the industry in near future from B-Schools (MBA/PGDM), Engineering institutes (BTech/M Tech) and institutions providing programs for government and public services. Leading institutes across the globe have already introduced this subject and most will follow soon. This book is a humble attempt to provide students and faculty a rich compendium of cutting-edge issues and best practices approach to understand and imbibe the subject of **Technology and Innovation Management (TIM).**

This book is written with a practical approach to explain the complex concept in a simple and easy-to-read manner. As a practitioner I have spent over three decades implementing technology led innovation projects across countries for leading corporations. But equally enriching was to teach this subject to diverse cross-section of students (including managers) in leading B Schools in India and Middle-East countries. This book is an outcome of the successful sessions of my TIM Courses with very high student feedback at many institutes of repute where I taught as a Visiting Professor. The sole aim of the book is to equip its readers to implement the concepts quickly and effectively before any technology/innovative idea becomes old or irrelevant. The book has well-balanced eleven chapters which ensures that essential aspects of technology and innovation management is covered in depth. A brief summary of their coverage is presented as follows:

Chapter 1 of this book aims to lay foundation of the subject. It starts with defining why technology and Innovation Management has become more important for managers. After explaining concept and meaning of technology, the book covers topics such as impact of technology on society and business, technology topologies, evolution and growth of technology. It then defines the relationship between technology, Innovation and Strategy and presents a conceptual frame work of Management of Technology (MOT). The chapter concludes with explaining the role of Chief Technology Officer (CTO), who is entrusted to drive the technology and innovation process within the enterprise.

Chapter 2 takes the discussion further by bringing deep understanding of Technology Strategy. This covers how to gain competitive advantages through new technologies, hence outlines a need for developing technology strategy of the firm. It then defines the role of technology in product and process development and the role of technology in bringing about Innovation. This chapter argues that Technology and Innovation requires a conducive ecosystems to be built by articulating the role of Government in Technology Development. Briefly it links technology, development and competition and explains the process for managing Research and Development (R&D) and Intellectual Property. The chapter concludes with thoughts around defining Organization's strategic direction.

Chapter 3 elaborates the core principles of technology management, its components and how to choose the right management strategies for technology. By defining Technology Management guiding principles and Technology Management lifecycle it further presents various perspectives of Technology Management. This is a core chapter of the book to build foundation for remaining chapters.

A natural progression on the subject of TIM was to discuss Innovation Management which has been done in Chapter 4. The chapter starts with meaning of Innovation and creativity, sources of Innovation and describes the Innovation Management process. It explains the types and patterns of technological innovation, S-curve and the segment zero principle, and enriches the content by succinctly establishing the meaning of innovation and creativity. This chapter, which is one of key building blocks of the book, further explains the factors that drive innovation and the impact of intellectual property management on innovation. It further dwells on market structures that yield more or better innovations, and on why are some countries rich and some poor. Elaborating further on the innovation ecosystem, it also analyses whether economic regulations are good or bad for innovation. Finally, the chapter tells us the process for choosing the right Innovation projects.

Technology is characterized with its ever-changing, ever-improving and ever-surprising nature. So Chapter 5 deals with methodology to do technology forecasting and assessment. It covers forecasting methods, such as intuitive, extrapolation, growth curves, etc. It explains the methods to trace technological evolution in various contexts, such as industry, organizational and strategic. The chapter then describes various technology monitoring process and how to do technology morphological analysis and draw mission flow diagram. An important decision of making technology choice whether leadership and follower ship is also explained. Further various tools for technology planning, industry technology analysis and tracing trajectories of technology has been explained. The choice of technology acquisition and its timing of entry has been further elaborated with examples and case studies. Technology acquisition also requires working with other companies that leads to forming various alliances, a topic which has been covered in this chapter in detail. Issues, such as domestic versus international alliances, concerns in alliances, mergers and acquisitions has been elaborated at length. Finally, this chapter tells us the strategic reasons for mergers and acquisitions and various types of mergers and acquisitions.

Chapter 6 explains Product and Process Development and role of technology. This starts with defining various stages of the product life-cycle and building understanding of the process of developing new-product ideas. The discussion further elaborates on how companies run new-product development process, which leads to assimilate the role of technology in product development. This chapter lets its readers gain concepts of how to manage New Product Development Teams. An overview of Managing Research and Development (R&D), Intellectual property and protecting Innovation is also presented. Finally, it defines product deployment strategy and approach for process development and role of technology in this process.

Due to increase penetration of ICT across geographical boundaries and to the remotest place of the world, the new ways to conduct business is being attempted through innovative business models. A significant impact of technology and innovation interplay has given rise to such new business models. This is why Chapter 7 focuses on building concepts around technology and business model. This chapter defines business model and explains as to why it is significant in the modern business. It further helps conceptualize different types of business models and how to choose from them. The role of technology in formulating business model and building sustainable business model is further explained. Finally, the chapter discusses how to appraise business models as well as grow and maintain it over times.

Chapter 8 focuses on technology and innovation implementation, a topic that requires deep practical wisdom and experience to bring out success at such endeavours. This chapter outlines the implementation processes that a firm should follow, and describes the responsibility and accountability. The important concept discussed is the selection of timings of technology intervention. Finally, this chapter deals with the methods to measure the success of implementation.

Chapter 9 presents an overview of existing and emerging technology used across industries, especially in the business management area. The content presented in this chapter is necessary for all management students, irrespective of their specialization. Briefly, this chapter covers the essentials of ERP, MIS, DSS, ESS, Data Warehousing/Data Mining, SCM and CRM. This is followed by brief discussion on E-business, E-commerce, B2B, B2C, big data and social media analytics. Finally, it also touches upon Mobile computing, 3D printing, Internet of things and other emerging technologies.

Chapter 10 delves on the human aspects and social issues in technology management. Believing in the axiom that human spirit must prevail over technology and not let it damage the basic fabric of society while trying to improve its function, this chapter describes the issues of integration of people and technology. IT covers the organizational and psychological factors, organizational structure and need to ensure technological change management and maintain Industrial relations. Finally, it prescribes the method for technology assessment and environmental impact analysis.

Chapter 11 covers the relationship of technology and sustainability, and how to ensure that the world's ecological resources are maintained and preserved by technology and not damaged. This chapter is a must read for all technology users as it is likely that they may overlook the sustainability aspect while designing new technology and innovative solutions.

Each chapter of the book ends with a summary that cover what has been covered briefly. Every chapter has case studies, questions and answers, references and stories that help student in gaining deep understanding of the subject.

One can never claim completeness in any intellectual work more so while writing a book on ever-evolving technology and innovation management. But I am fortunate that my colleagues and students have painstakingly reviewed the chapters while it was being written, which has given me confidence of its usefulness and comprehensiveness.

I would be looking forward to feedback and suggestions from all my readers, and would be willing to help with slides, further teaching aids and other tools to enrich the learning process to faculty members. Please write to me on itsm.ssdubey@gmail.com

Sanjiva Shankar Dubey

Acknowledgements

Writing a book on Technology and Innovation Management for me was like, a mountaineer writing his/her experiences while climbing a mountain. While I had wide experience across industry in managing technology and innovation projects, the theoretical foundation has been provided by numerous researchers and academics whose work I have referred to. In short, I just followed the path created by my fellow authors and researchers and added my own understating and experience to it to convert it into a book form. My first acknowledgement and thanks goes to all such individuals whose work have been quoted or just referred to build my own understanding. As rightly said by Sir Isaac Newton "I was also a dwarf who rode on the shoulders of giants to look beyond".

My task of writing was made simpler when I was called upon to teach this course at IIMs, BIMTECH, IMT and several other institutes. The course titles were different but the essence was same. These leading institutes desired that their students must know how to manage Technology and Innovation to be a successful manager. Without which neither these students nor the firms they will work will ever succeed in the technologically charged and innovation enriched world. The inspiration of writing comes from the realization that the current published material is neither comprehensive nor contemporary. This enthused me to take over three years journey to compile my thoughts in a book form. So my deep acknowledgement goes to these institutes for giving me the privilege to teach this subject and students whose inquisitive minds stirred me to think beyond ordinary and seek explanations that were not currently available. My special thanks to Dr. H. Chaturvedi Director General IILM Lodhi Road and Former Director BIMTECH for being a constant sources of encouragement for my writing pursuits and also for agreeing to write the foreword.

By the time this book started to take shape my family has adjusted to my passion, having seen my earlier eight projects. My family comprising wife Vibha, Children Priyamvad, Priya, Devisha, Gaurav and Ayansh (grandchild) have remained supportive, inquisitive and continued to provide inputs when necessary. Priya came out with wonderful cover page design ideas as well.

No human work can ever get accomplished unless God Almighty desires. So to my final humble obeisance to my deity Lord Hanuman ji for getting this work done through me.

Sanjiva Shankar Dubey

Chapter 1

Technology and Innovation Management: Conceptual Foundation

Great is the human who has not lost his childlike heart.

— Mencius (Meng-Tse), 4th century BCE

At the end of this chapter, we will learn:

- Why technology and innovation management has become more important for managers
- Concept and meaning of technology
- Impact of technology on society and business
- Technology topologies: Process technology and product technology
- Evolution and growth of technology
- Role and significance of management of technology
- Relationship between technology innovation and strategy
- Definition of Management of Technology (MOT)
- The conceptual framework for MOT
- Drivers of MOT–Significance and scope of MOT
- Role of Chief Technology Officer (CTO)

1.1 INTRODUCTION

Technology and Innovation Management (TIM) is a multi-disciplinary subject which has attracted a lot of interest amongst business managers, students and management academicians in the recent times. Recent years are full of major breakthroughs leading to economic growths of firms by using innovative technologies to design new products and provide new services or business models. All this has been tapped by entrepreneurs who have captured new business value. The economy itself is being called technology-based and new innovation with the help of technology has enhanced competitive edge for the organisation. Technology without doubt has become all-pervasive and the most useful tool for conducting any business. In the recent times, it has also penetrated in our personal as well as social life. In most cases, the changes brought by technology has helped business, society and individuals. In addition, the role of technology in bringing innovations has also been clearly established.

Technology and Innovation not only gave opportunities to businesses to become global but also subjected them to increased competition from other global firms. Many established, but unprepared firms were truly surprised by the disruptive impact of new technologies leading to serious loss to their market share, and in some cases pushed them to the brink of bankruptcy. On personal and social front, increasing use of technology has eased our lives, and has improved its quality and connectivity with our loved ones. We all like our new gadgets, admire new improved public services and simply love new entertainment opportunities using new technology. However, in some cases, its overuse or misuse has also led to problems that prompts us to exercise caution while using technology, especially, when dealing with strangers, making financial transactions or sharing our personal data online. Our book will cover both sides of the technology, the white and positive side that leads to development of society and business and the dark and risky side about which we should maintain adequate safeguards.

For business managers having a good grasp on Technology and Innovation management is both a necessity for their survival and insurance against obsolescence. In addition, if they are purposefully engaged and relentlessly charged up to adopt new technology for continuous innovation, they can stay ahead of their competitors. Failing to do so may end up in a compromised future of their firms. So they need to continuously understand, imbibe and implement the ever improving technology and to innovate their firms' products and services. In short, in this technology-charged future of the world, every manager must ensure involvement and maintain drive towards innovative use of technology. It is a necessary prerequisite for survival and growth of the firm. It is no wonder that management professionals and academicians have found increased interest in the subject of Technology and Innovation management for their survival and growth. The good news is that newer technology and associated innovation are giving rise to new business models, new products or services, thus creating new opportunities for the world.

Technology and Innovation has become a key strategic driver and differentiator for most firms either old or new to remain competitive in the 21st Century. If we examine some of the recent developments of the hyper growth of some firms, we would realise that it was all due to innovative technologies using which they have launched new products, services and innovative business models. Apple, Google, Pfizer, Wallmart, TCS, Airtel and many others fall under the category of firms whose growth can only be attributed to technology and innovation as a major source of gaining competitive edge. It can, therefore, be summarised that understanding, charting and innovating technology developments on the competitive landscape has become a necessity for all strategists and business planners to make their firms more and more successful in the coming years.

In this book, we will take these two perspectives for understanding the concepts of Technology and Innovation management (Figure 1.1). Our first perspective of TIM would be on the use of technology and innovation in managing and improving business functions and society in general. We all know that no large enterprise and its functions can run without the help of technology which is also an important source of innovation. This perspective will help us understand as to how technology and innovation can be of benefit to commercial business as well as to the society. This perspective, as a user of TIM, establishes its importance for being taught to students of Business Schools as well as to practicing business managers irrespective of their specialisation, functional focus or industry they are working for. For example, if the Indian Postal department starts using more sophisticated technology to manage its functions, it would save millions of

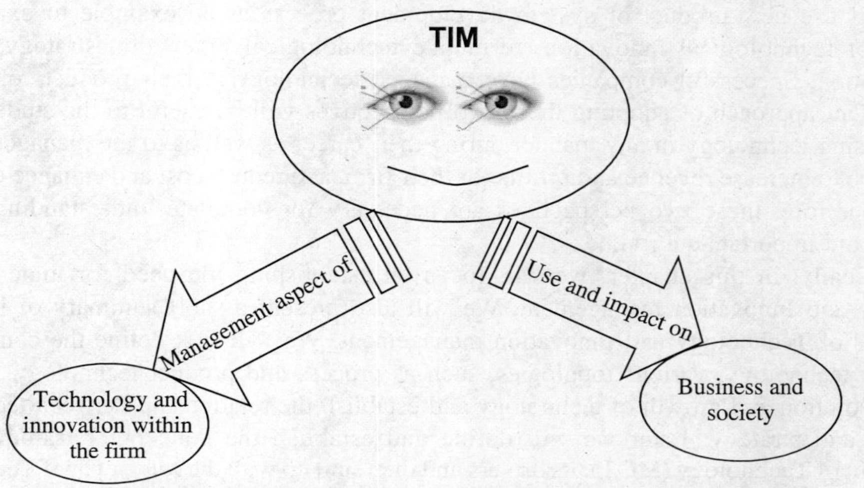

FIGURE 1.1 Technology and Innovation Management: Two Perspectives.

man-hours of masses. The widespread reach of post offices in the rural India is massive opportunity which is not yet been tapped to ensure service delivery of government services and last mile delivery system of burgeoning e-commerce industry.

> ***Student activity:*** *Make small groups of 3-4 students in the class and spend five minutes visualising how the following technologies can lead to new services at post offices especially rural areas. Consider the following technologies:*
>
> - *Wi-Fi*
> - *RFID*
> - *Mounted Digital Tablets or self service kiosk*
>
> *Discuss in the class your ideas. The most innovative one will get suitable reward/appreciation from the faculty.*

Our second perspective will be on how to manage technology and innovation within an enterprise. This perspective will take us through the broad understanding of how to track technology development, understand its various phases and spot the right opportunity to adopt them as part of business process, product, services or business model for the firm. New technologies will keep coming up every other day. Not every technology will be suitable for every business. Yet missing to adopt the most promising one or delaying in adopting will result in missing an opportunity for organisation success. In many cases, failure to remain up-to-date with newer technology has led to organisation failure in the long run.

We will use new product or system development process as an example to explain the dynamics of technological innovation, formulate technological innovation strategy, and its implementation. Successful companies have managed technology in their products of process very well. Our approach of adopting these two perspectives will be useful to the students who would be using technology in any manner during their career as well as to the managers whose job would be to increase revenue and profits for their firm, and reduce cost and enhance customer service. Therefore, these two perspectives are necessary for complete understanding of this interesting and important subject.

Specifically, in this chapter, we will focus on establishing the need for understanding Technology and Innovation management. We will also present a short summary of historical perspectives of Technology and Innovation management. We will first define the concept and meaning of technology, various topologies, such as process and product technology. We will trace the evolution and growth of technology and establish the relationship between technology innovation and strategy. Later we will define and establish the conceptual framework for Management of Technology (MOT), its drivers and then sum up with the role of Chief Technology Officer (CTO).

1.2 WHAT ARE THE MAJOR TAKEAWAYS FROM THE BOOK?

The remaining chapters of the book will primarily focus on the process involved in the development of new technology lifecycle, its impact on innovation for business and society purposes. Subsequent chapters will help building an understanding of the process of technology development and innovation management using new technology for managers and management students. With these inputs, they should be able to assess technology needs for their function within the organisation. Next few chapters will cover issues like technology tracking, development and concept of S–curve as well as its best time and approach for adopting. All these concepts will act as a buildup to adopt and manage technology for the competitive advantage of the firms.

In this book, we will strive to develop an awareness of the range, scope and complexity of issues related to the strategic management of technology and innovation. This will be done by developing a conceptual framework for assessing the technological capabilities of a business organisation and best practices for defining and solving strategic planning issues related to technology and innovations.

Unless technology management strategy is followed up with successful commercial implementation, the firm will not get the desired economic returns. We will, therefore, study both development and implementation as an integrated subject and link with business model and market opportunity. Needless to say, this enquiry would be highly interdisciplinary in nature covering technology as discussed in technical curriculum and its exploitation as in management studies. In this way, the book is relevant to engineering as well as management students. The former looks at the technical (or development) side and the later at exploitation or implementation side of the subject. In fact, the divide has to be bridged between these two sides to gain a comprehensive understanding of this interdisciplinary subject for the advancement of their professional careers.

This book aims to offer a holistic, interdisciplinary and integrated view of the complete technology development management, innovation and implementation process, ranging from technology forecasting, research and development to market considerations. We will emphasise principles and practices related to technological innovation and use new product or system development process as an example to explain the following:

- Dynamics of technological innovation,
- Developing technological innovation strategy, and
- Implementation of strategy.

Our attempt in this book is to dovetail perspectives of organisation, marketing, design, manufacturing and services into a single approach to support new competitive opportunity that may come from new product, new process or developing new markets using technology. By making extensive references to academic research, we will refer to the ground breaking theories, propose practical methods which can be easily deployed, in new product development and technological innovation projects from conceptualisation to realisation.

Finally, we will understand the role people play in managing technology and the challenges required to develop an innovative organisation. We all understand that people play an important role in making any new projects successful, which goes with new technology projects as well. This requires different skills from among the managers to be a change agent, innovative thinker and adviser for profit and revenue.

1.3 CONCEPT AND MEANING OF TECHNOLOGY

The word "technology" has its origin in the two Greek words, namely "technikos", meaning "of art, skillful, practical" and "ology" indicating "knowledge of" or a "systematic treatment of." So technology can be explained as "knowledge of the skilful and practical" for converting something available into something more useful.

The most commonly accepted definition comes from the American sociologist Read Bain[1] who defined technology to include all tools, machines, utensils, weapons, instruments, housing, clothing, communicating and transporting devices and the skills by which we produce and use them. Another definition of technology refers to a class of knowledge about specific product or production technique and sometimes includes the technical skills necessary to use a product or a production technique. Frances Stewart[2] provided a broad definition of technology to include all skills, knowledge and procedures required for making, using and doing useful things. This definition also includes the software of production—managerial and marketing skills, and extended to services—administration, health, education and finance. This view is supported by Smilie [3] who defines technology as "the science and art of getting things done through the application of skills and knowledge". By and large the last definition of Smilie is simple, comprehensive and easy to remember.

[1]Read Bain, American Sociological Review, *Technology and State Government,* Vol. 2, No. 6, Dec. 1937.
[2]Stewart, F. (1977). Technology and Underdevelopment, Macmillan London.
[3]Smilie, I. (1991). Mastering the Machine. *Intermediate London Publications* London.

Some other authors like Chandra and Zulkieflimansyah[4] summarise that technology is a subtle mix of know-how, techniques and tools. They argue that technology in a sense is ingrained in people, their knowledge, skills and routines, just as much as in the tools they use. The physical objects are only the physical manifestation of a particular technology or technologies. Another definition from the business dictionary[5] explains technology as purposeful application of information in the design, production and use of knowledge to produce product or in service. This discourse would definitely give our readers a good understanding of how technology is defined as these definitions and its variations would help understand the deeper issues of how to manage technology and how to use it for innovation.

Technology is generally divided in several major categories as described below:

(a) Tangible, which takes the form of products or models or intangible which refers to methods and processes
(b) High, intermediate and low, depending upon the level of automation and intelligence deployed
(c) Depending upon the industry, technology is categorised as

- Infrastructural and construction
- Transportation including automobile, shipping, railways, pipeline
- Airlines, aerospace
- Oil and gas exploration
- Energy/Power
- Food processing, preservation and research reacted to agriculture
- Environmental protection conservation
- Information and communication
- Manufacturing including discrete, process
- Medical, bio-related and health care

Given these characteristics, one can summarise that technology is the use of knowledge of tools to find a useful product or service for the human being. It is the process that converts systematic knowledge (conceptual, empirical or/and scientific) into useful objects to support human activities. It is a combination of physical objects, social needs, process and procedure. Just having knowledge is not technology but is in its implementation in process or producing a useful product for human benefit.

We all know that the use of science was to understand the behaviour of the nature and consequently devise means and action for the human benefit. Initially, technology was used to convert natural resources, for example, iron ore, solar energy, wind power, etc. into human use. As the human race progressed, technology increasingly made our life easier, enjoyable and entertaining. Advancement such as mobile phone, video calls, internet, etc. has reduced the barriers of communications and the distance between people across the world. However, technology is not without negative effects which are not so welcome and its examples are the use of technology in making atom bombs, weaponry and in all other frauds and crimes.

---

[4]Asia Pacific Management Review (2003) 8(3), 365-407 365 The dynamic of technological accumulation at the microeconomic level : lessons from Indonesia -- a case study Adityawan Chandra* and Zulkieflimansyah**, zul@mucglobal.com.

[5]http://www.businessdictionary.com/definition/technology.html#ixzz2oZhElyET accessed 24 Dec. 2013.

Technology is thus the application of scientific principles for human use which may include theoretical as well as practical knowledge converted into skills to develop products and services and their production and delivery systems. All these put together along with labour, capital, information, material and energy help create a useful product or services.

1.4 ELEMENTS OF TECHNOLOGY

What we normally see is the implementation of technology that comprises scientific principles, use of tools, processes and techniques in the form of a product. Take the case of mobile phone which we use it commonly. The principles of wireless communication were espoused and proved in 1880, when Alexander Graham Bell and Charles Sumner Tainter invented and patented the photophone. Since then several developments in terms of making this principle a commercial success have happened. With digital communication and internet technology coming into play, the mobile communication has found new usage. The latest business model design of pay-for-use, downloading movies, free applications to track location and maps has increased its usability. All this together form what we call it mobile communication technology.

This has been explained in Figure 1.2.

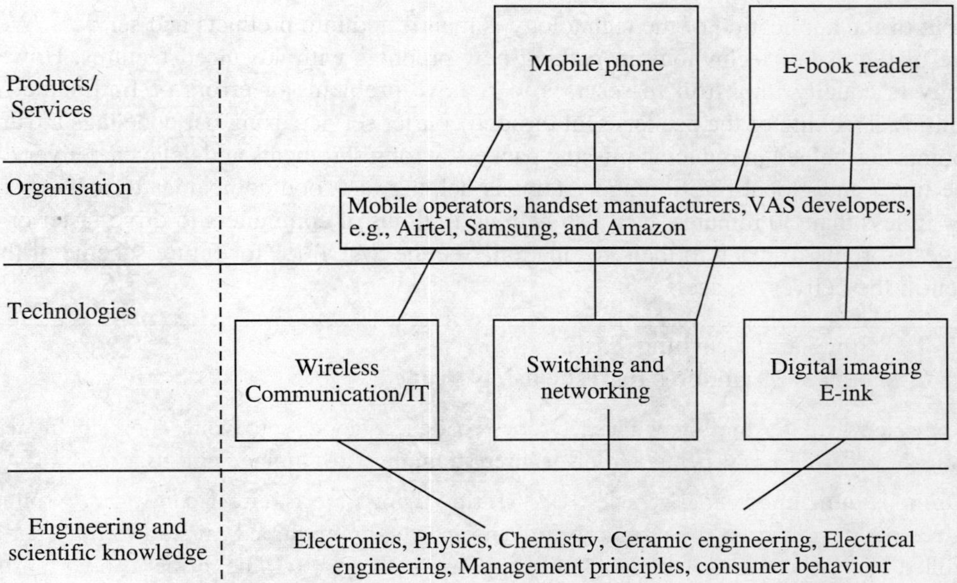

FIGURE 1.2 Relationship of Technologies to Scientific and Engineering Knowledge and to Products Process.

Taking this example as a cue, we can visualise the following elements in any technology:

(a) **Scientific principles and knowledge:** This is a base for any technology and may come from all branches of science, physical, behavioural and at times intuition to forge ahead and discover something new.

(b) **Methods and tools** that covert these knowledge into useful products or services. A good example is the use of principles of X-rays by doctors to see fracture of bones on X-ray images or inserting tiny camera through mouth for examining conditions of the intestine. Remember, we are only considering the machines that do this task, there is yet another set of technology involved in the making of these machines, X-ray plates, etc., which are deployed for producing these machines.

(c) **Organisation:** People and processes are organised to achieve the end products or services. Take the example of air travel and the technology that makes it viable from organisation perspective. The manufacturing technology of the aircraft notwithstanding running a commercial airlines operations requires a number of technologies to support such as ground operations, ticketing, baggage handling, airport operations that includes movement of passengers, security checks, information display, etc. Not only the use but implementation of technology in the field happens through organisation that comprises of people, process and structure. Feedback is provided to the technology designers with problems faced as well as new possibilities from the users to improve it further.

1.5 PRODUCT AND SERVICES

The output of the application of the technology is manifested into products and services. We are all aware of the use of technology in making new products with advanced features. However, technology is equally impactful in services to remove problems or errors or find some more opportunities. Tracking of the packets sent through courier service using bar code tags at various transit points has helped in reducing missing packets, wrong shipments and delayed delivery. Use of online maps and global positioning systems is helping fast food companies to deliver orders precisely in less than 30 minutes. It is also helping millions of commuters to drive faster or take less congested route to reach to their destination. See the SALT 1.1 for future scheme of things to happen in the delivery space.

SALT 1.1 Story and Learning Task
Amazon promises 30 minutes delivery using Drone

A recent news[6] that Amazon will use Drones to deliver goodies to your doorstep in next 30 mins of ordering has generated a lot of interest amongst technology enthusiast.

Drone is unmanned aerial vehicles (UAVs), tiny flying objects, either controlled by pilots using remote devices from the ground or driven on a pre-programmed mission to hit a target controlled by satellite-based navigation system, ground control, etc. The former is used mostly for reconnaissance and surveillance purposes and the later which are typically armed with missiles and bombs, for one off attack. You must have seen them in sci-fi movies or can watch on YouTube. Drone can stay aloft for many hours (Zephyr a British drone, made a world record of flying for over 82 hours nonstop), causes no loss of life as no crew is involved and, above all, cheaper to build. They have been in the news in Afghanistan and Iraq wars where British and US Reaper and Predator Drone controlled via satellite from Nellis and Creech USAF base

[6] www.bbc.co.uk/news/technology-25180906,accessed 27 Dec. 2013.

outside Las Vegas, Nevada made several dramatically successful attacks. The modus operandi is simple, where one person takes control of the object, another operates and monitors the cameras and sensors and the third keeps contact with ground troops and commanders in the war zone. You can visualise that for such a system to be effective and precise, requires enormous ground work, state-of-the-art navigational systems and above all thorough ground intelligence.

So when Amazon, known for disruptive innovative ideas, announced that it will use delivery-by-Drone, it created a flutter in business and technology circle. In reality, this may be an idea ahead of its time, perhaps a good publicity timed perfectly with the Internet's biggest shopping day, Cyber Monday. The possible negatives of Drone include job loss to those in logistics industry, possible chaos in the sky, loss of privacy and unforeseen impact to the environment, etc. But do not brush this idea too soon; even aircraft sketch drawn by Sir George Cayley, a Renaissance genius in 1804, took almost 100 years to get converted into a reality by Wright brothers in 1903. If we translate the pace of technology developments of current times, it could be less than 5 years at the most to see Drones in regular civilian and commercial usage.

Discussion Questions

1. What are the other areas where Drone can be deployed for humanitarian usage?
2. How soon do you think it will be a reality?
3. What are the possible risks of using such unmanned vehicles?
4. What are the precautions society should take while using this technology?

1.6 BRIEF HISTORY OF TECHNOLOGY DEVELOPMENT

Technology has also gone through several stages of growth from historical perspective. In simple terms, making a bow or an arrow is one such example of technology or application of knowledge thousands of years ago when human being used to hunt animals for their sustenance. Since then technology development has passed through several stages, and is categorised as

(a) Stone Age
(b) Bronze Age
(c) Iron Age and
(d) From the last 40–45 years it is called Information Age, Digital Age or Technology Age

During the Stone Age, human beings developed its first shovel from a piece of stone, the Bronze Age saw humans use metal and the introduction of the wheel. It was during the Iron Age that human beings started using harder metals than copper leading to mass manufacturing and transportation. The last century saw the fruits of Industrial Revolution accelerating the pace of human development using technology. Last 50 years, the pace has been further accelerated due to information and other technology development. Some of the technological innovations that have changed the life of people in the last two hundred years are the development of printing press for knowledge dissemination, compass for navigation, especially sea and waterways, paper currency changed the economic world , steel fueled Industrial Revolution, electricity created all-pervasive impact, development of transistors led to semiconductors and computers development, wireless and telegraph made dramatic change in the ways human beings communicated, antibiotics improved health care, steam and automobile engine for transportation and power to name a few.

A noted technology historian[7] has once said that because technology has been considered as a key way to solve problems, we need to be aware of its complex and varied characteristics to use it more efficiently. As the society progresses, its problems have also become complex which need newer and improved solution. This is demand side of the technology development. On the other hand, new technology also presents new opportunities fuelling enhanced needs from the society. Internet, mobile communications and related technologies are example of newer opportunities for small traders to sell their products worldwide, ease of doing business by all and even helping expectant mothers in rural Bangladesh using Mobile apps[8].

1.7 CHARACTERISTIC OF TECHNOLOGY

Technology is a unique human activity that is driven to solve human problems or find opportunities for a better life. It has purpose for betterment and is productive in nature most of the time. The end result of technology is achieved through a deliberate process of application of scientific knowledge to design, develop, manufacture and deliver a product or service that solves human problems and gives something better than the existing. Technological practice includes practice of design, development, construction, manufacturing, planning and management among others. Following are the characteristics of technology:

Need

The first and foremost characteristic of technology is that it arises out of a need or possible opportunity to satisfy a hidden need. We all like to listen to music but are constrained by location and bulky players with limited collection of songs that one can carry on CDs. The i-pad and MP3 players have made it possible to carry/store large number of songs on a compact device. These players now available on mobile handsets are now enabling us access unlimited collection of music available online. These devices have created an opportunity to meet the desire for listening to music on the move. But they are a result of combination of several technologies, such as internet, mobile handset, advanced chip technology, etc. Technological outcome usually are in the form of products and systems that enhance our natural capabilities. Automobile enhances our ability to travel faster, hearing-aids enhance ability of hearing impaired persons, amplifiers enable us to speak to larger audience without stretching our voice and 3D projectors are enabling us to be seen at multiple locations in a real-life like image form. While microscopes allow us to see tiny objects such as bacteria, its distant cousin telescope make us see distant stars and understand about them. The former has been a major breakthrough for medical diagnostics and the later for understanding movement of terrestrial objects.

Appropriateness

Technology should also be appropriate in terms of cost, side effects, risks or possibility of

[7] Thomas Parke Hughes (1923–2014) was an American historian of technology. He was an Emeritus professor of history at the University of Pennsylvania.

[8] http://www.mobilemamaalliance.org/mama-bangladesh, accessed 17 May 2016.

misuse. Nuclear technology was at one time considered an answer to the energy starved world which was concerned due to depletion of natural sources of energy such as coal, oil, etc.; is now found to be risky and lacking appropriateness for various applications. Technology has to always position itself within the social and human context. A technology that can infringe on my privacy, can be dangerous for human lives or can be risky for being misused. Such technology is not appropriate. Would we consider widespread use of camera technology that can see through our cloths an appropriate technology? Any technology that is damaging to the value system of society or environment (and there are many) is not appropriate, no matter how much commercial value they may create. Appropriateness is also related to time and place. Several medicines have been found to be unsuitable at later stages but were hailed as the solution of the human misery when they were discovered. Bore-well for drawing water from the earth was a great technology but overdrawing of water and reckless misuse raise questions of its appropriateness. Use of plastics as carry bags was great novelty till it became menace in cities and started to clog drains and on hills impacting the ecological balance.

Universality

Technology is also characterised with its ability to be universally applicable from one place or person to other. So if the same process, material and human skills will be used, similar products and services can be obtained. It will not be distinguished based on human colour, caste, religion or political affiliation.

Builds on the past achievements

It can also be called **continuously reinventing**. Technology always builds on the past development and comes out with something new. For example, the boundary between the human and machine is getting blurred where intelligent machines, robotics, etc., are performing the task that were hitherto limited for human beings only. At times these have come as a boon to prevent human life from getting into risk, for example, in defusing bombs. Robotics is also used to do certain task that humans may commit errors, for example, precise machining or micro-surgery of critical nature. The capacity and capability of technology is continuously increasing. Speed of aircrafts and their capacity to carry number of passengers have increased manifold over the period of time, computers are known to double their capacity every two years and there are many such improvements which technology has undergone building on its past achievements.

Many be disruptive or totally new

While the capacity, speed and other parameter of a technology get continuously refined, some technologies could be totally disruptive. Digital photography is one such example. In medical research, the role of technology is sometimes breakthrough application. This disruption may happen due to the application of an existing technology to a new or different problem or finding new technology or process for an existing problem. A breakthrough application of technology from defense to medical world was led by former President of India Dr. Abdul Kalam, a renowned Defense Missile technologist. The material used for making missiles and rocket was used to develop calipers (called Floor Reaction Orthosis, FRO) for children suffering from polio. This light weight caliper just weighs 300 grams as against 3 kg when made from normal steel[9].

[9]http://indiatoday.intoday.in/story/spin-offs-from-defence-technology-help-polio-victims/1/293677.html, accessed 27 Dec. 2013.

Driver of social change and driven by social need

Technology also brings in change in the society. The enhanced capabilities not only alleviate the problems of human beings but also present the business opportunities around which the human race is able to enhance its livelihood. Improved high yielding seeds have led to higher produce for the farmers and mobile phones higher business to the vegetable vendors! Increased hauling capacity of trucks has led to lower fuel consumption and better returns to transporters. Traveling by Metro transport system has facilitated women to take up jobs far away from their homes.

The growth of Indian IT/ITes and BPO industry has been facilitated by the enhanced telecom facilities and improved connectivity.

It should be recognised that, on one hand, technology is leading to social change as per technological determinist perspective and, on the other, society is pushing for more developments as per social shaping perspective. When the instances of swine flu, malaria or instances of heart attacks at early age increased scientists and researchers were induced to work on these problems and come out with vaccines, medicines and antidotes wherever possible. With terrorism rearing its ugly head in our daily lives, security-related technology development is likely to take rapid pace. Technology and society are, therefore, intertwined in a complex and often difficult-to-determine ways which cannot be segregated.

Interdisciplinary in nature

This may appear contradictory when we say that technology is interdisciplinary in nature, yet it is also a discipline in its own right. When a new technology development takes place, it draws knowledge and skills from other disciplines; for example, natural science, arts (remember the design of iPhone or wearable mobile sets), mathematics, engineering, etc. So when we study technology management, we have to draw knowledge from other disciplines so that we can utilise them for specific purpose for which the technology is being developed. This requires technologists to collaborate across disciplines, recognise the value of differences between knowledge across domains and draw the similarities from seemingly dissimilarities for achieving a particular objective. Smart Mobile phones provide many features but it also drains their battery faster. We all know that many medicines have side effects yet doctors prescribe them in measured dosages to address a particular disease. Technologists must be sensitive to the unintended consequences and warn people who are less knowledgeable so that they can make a choice. Steel was invented to be used as flexible and wear resistant metal but it is also used for making weapons. Mobile phones, towers are a suspect[10] to impact the life of bees, and cause humans sperm damage, brain tumor, etc. However, as long as their usage is in a controlled limit, our society will accept their usage and look for alternatives that can be less harmful. These thoughts prompt technologists to debate all aspects of the proposed technology and prioritise multiple perspectives and come out with the best alternatives[11].

[10] http://www.ewg.org/cell-phone-radiation-damages-sperm-studies-find, accessed 27 Dec. 2014.

[11] http://technology.tki.org.nz/index.php/Curriculum-support/Explanatory-Papers/Nature-of-Technology/Characteristics-of-Technology/Junior-Primary, accessed 27 Dec. 2014.

1.8 EVOLUTION AND GROWTH OF TECHNOLOGY

The technology evolution and growth is a phenomenon associated with evolution and growth of the human civilisation. On one hand, the human needs (or market forces) allow the technology to be evolved and developed by the researchers. On the other, the technology experimentations and innovations help create new demand. For example, needs of human sufferings pull the research technology to devise new tools and techniques that include replaceable knee joints for patients suffering from arthritis, heart valve and the technology innovation like voice-controlled wheel chairs, etc.

There are several theories of technology evolution and growth and we will examine some of them in this section.

1.8.1 Abernathy and Utterbach (A-U) Model

The first and foremost theory of technology evolution and growth is by Abernathy and Utterbach[12] popularly known as A-U model. It went into several refinements and finally it outlined three phases of growth as discussed here (see Figure 1.3):

(a) **Fluid stage:** At this stage, mostly new product of technology is designed but the process of manufacturing is not well-defined. Both products and processes are subjected to major changes frequently and may alternate designs proliferate. At this stage, market potential is incompletely identified and a lot of trial-and-error takes place at both technical and commercial aspects. This is also a period for relatively high expenditure on Research and Development (R&D).

(b) **Dominant design and transition stage:** At this stage, a dominant design (e.g. Ford's Model T is a good example for automobile and iPad for tablets) starts taking shape after a period of trial and error. This starts providing standards for the rest of the industry to follow. Markets of such products start getting matured. Those companies who have ownership of dominant designs enjoy competitive advantages. The emphasis now shifts for process improvement, performance improvement and marketing of the product for increased volumes. During this period, incremental improvements in the dominant design covering performance, reliability and after-sales service happen. One can identify Korean manufacturer like Samsung showing knack of working in this phase and launching cheaper and feature-rich look alike for Apple products.

(c) **Mature stage:** At this stage, further innovation stops and technology (products or services) and standard designs are produced at mass scale. Changes are resisted as investment is in process and manufacturing equipment has been made and personnel do not want to change their skills and practices. At this stage, others with generic technology but superior performance, cheaper cost, etc., may come in. Chemical industry with synthetic fiber brought in textile industry and electronics displaced mechanical watch industry. Of late, mobile handsets have virtually made camera, laptops, calculators, music players, etc., redundant.

[12]Utterback, J.M., Abernathy, W.J. (1975), A Dynamic Model of Process and Product Innovation, *Omega, The Int. Jl of Mgmt Sci.*, Vol. 3, No. 6, 639–656 and Mastering the dynamics of innovation by JM., Utterback, 1996, Boston, MA: Harvard Business School Press, p. xvii, Figure I-1. Copyright 1996.

Figure 1.3 shows these stages graphically.

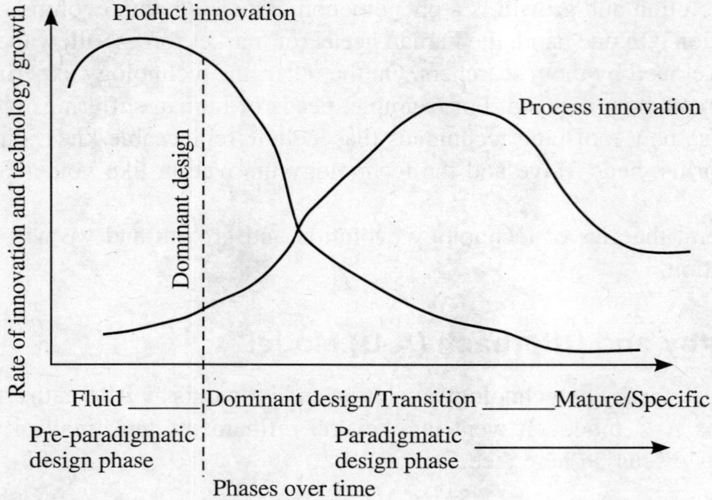

FIGURE 1.3 Technology and Innovation Stages of Development.

1.8.2 Thomas S. Kuhn's Model

Kuhn further refined the curve of technology development stages into two phases as shown in Figure 1.3 are called Pre-paradigm and Paradigm stages.

(i) In the first phase called pre-paradigm stage, no single conceptually accepted innovation is established. Take the case of optics before Newton or aircraft before jet engine.

(ii) In the second phase of paradigm acquisition stage, a dominant design is established and the process innovation takes over, e.g., optics following Newton's Optics. In both cases, either a problem has been solved using a current knowledge, i.e., an existing paradigm or a new breakthrough paradigm has been acquired.

1.9 TECHNOLOGY GROWTH DUE TO SELF-ORGANISING SYSTEM

Yet another perspective of technology evolution has been given in the seminal book of Devendra Sahal[13] who espouses that technology evolution happens through a self-organising trial and error process of learning. He gives example of ants that form and deform their activities according to the roles and responsibilities. Once an idea is laid out, it is improved through a series of improvements and a step-wise technological growth. This is quite frequently achieved by creative symbiosis of two or more previously unrelated technologies (e.g., use of solid state electronics in numarically controlled machines)[14].

[13] Sahal, Devendra, (1981). Patterns of Technological Innovation, Reading: Addison-Wesley.

[14] *Ibid*

SALT 1.2 Mobile Innovation, a Case of Nano Ganesh[15]

Mobile revolution in India has brought people closer. The affordability and vast penetration of network has ensured that even a common man in Indian rural landscape is able to afford a mobile phone. A country where telephone connectivity was available to privileged few has now become so commonplace that it is being touted as one of major technologies that has ushered growth of the economy of the country.

Nano Ganesh is one such innovative use of mobile phone that received several innovation awards[16]. Nano Ganesh is a modem attached to farmers' pumping set which allows farmers to use mobile phones to remotely monitor and switch them on or off. This modem can be attached to any existing electrical starter and motor to power them on or off while the farmer may remain sitting in their homes several kilometres away. Walking to the field in the night may be hazardous. Under the service, farmers have to buy a mobile connection and a mobile modem (Nano Ganesh) which is attached to the starter of the pump set. The farmer then sends a pre-allotted SMS to activate or deactivate the pump. Using the mobile handset, the farmer can remotely switch on and switch off the pump set with the assigned code number.

Discussion Questions

1. Where will you put this innovation on the technology growth cycles?
2. Is there a possibility of further innovation of this product? If yes, what could be those? (Visit the nano ganesh website for further details.)

1.10 IMPACT OF TECHNOLOGY ON SOCIETY AND BUSINESS

Technological progress leads to growth in the society. Technology is used since ages to increase efficiency in generating larger output with lower inputs of energy, labour or wastage of material. It also improves quality of product and variety or leads to totally new products and services. According to Blanchard[17], growth of any country can come from either higher rate of technological progress or adjustment of capital per effective worker. Underdeveloped or developing countries face both these challenges as they can deploy neither more capital per worker nor better technology. The world economy witnessed higher rate of growth of output per capita, from 1950 to 1973, due to rapid technological progress, but not due to high capital accumulation. However, the output slowed down from 1973 due to a variety of reasons, primarily being the decrease in the rate of technological growth[18].

Former UN Secretary General Kofi Annan, in his Millennium Report to the General Assembly, opined that "Freedom from want, freedom from fear, and the freedom of future generations to sustain their lives on this planet" are the three grand global challenges for the 21st Century. We have to see science and technology from the perspective of making this world a better place

[15] http://www.nanoganesh.com/, accessed 30 Dec. 2013.

[16] The application was a Grand Prize winner in the Emerging Markets category of Nokia. Nano Ganesh has been a winner of DST Lockheed-Martin IIGP 2011 program, selected for recognition as a laureate in the Economic Development category for 2011, by The Tech Awards, The Tech Museum at San Jose, CA, USA.

[17] Olivier Blanchard. *Macroeconomics*. 3rd ed., Chapter 12 © 2003 Prentice Hall Business Publishing.

[18] *Ibid.*

to live. It is generally known that the growth of the society has happened due to technological developments. Gerhard Lenski[19], a famous economist and sociologist, has opined in the early 1900s that like all life forms humans have a reproductive capacity that substantially exceeds the necessary subsistence resources in the environment. Lenski concludes that human population tend to grow until they come up against the limits of food production, and then they are checked. The only way the human race can survive is to use technology to decelerate the population growth and conserve the "WEHAB" resources, i.e., Water, Energy, Health, Agriculture and Biodiversity. The role of science and technology for sustainable development of the society is to:

(a) Increase the reduction of population
(b) Sustain and increase agricultural production
(c) Increase efficiency of energy and material usage
(d) Sustain growth of urban population through suitable design with less sacrifice of agricultural or forest land
(e) Prevent degradation to ecosystems and conserve biodiversity
(f) Undertake research in the area of environment, population and social sustainability.

It may be noted that technology just not has "lifestyle" usage but a major impact on the future of the society of which all businesses are an integral part. William Clark[20], a noted scientist, advocates the need of adopting a strategic approach to better mobilise science and technology for sustainability which should be solution-driven for the larger population. He further advocates "Co-production" of usable knowledge through collaboration of users and producers "in place" by engaging global research and innovation *systems.* Active participation of private sectors and incentivising scientist on sustainability projects will help bridging the gap between technology development and society.

All this discussion leads to a new term *appropriate technology* in the context of sustainability and larger social goods. We have discussed that all new technology comes with some negative effect for the society; however, it becomes appropriate when intended positive benefits outweigh its unintended negative consequences. In general, the term "appropriate technology" has been used to include products of scientific or industrial nature as well as lifestyle products covering developments for technologies that promote sustainability, environment protection and low carbon emission. Some more examples of appropriate technology includes renewal energy created from solar, wind or sea waves, green buildings and setting up urban centres that do not consume agricultural and forest land created by making thorough ecological considerations. Appropriate technology ultimately solves problems of society and does not create more problems for the future generations.

---

[19]Gerhard Emmanuel Lenski (born August 13, 1924 in Washington, DC) is an American sociologist known for contributions to the sociology of religion, social inequality and ecological-evolutionary theory.

[20]William C. Clark Professor of International Science, Public Policy and Human Development Center for Science and International Affairs, John F. Kennedy School of Government, Harvard University (william_clark@harvard.edu) Science and Technology for Sustainable Development: Strategic perspectives from an international dialogue. Accessed form the web presentation 27 Dec. 2013.

1.11 TECHNOLOGY TYPOLOGY (FORMS OF TECHNOLOGY)

Technology can be classified in several ways. One of the earlier works of classification of several of technologies was done by Woodward[21] who described three basic forms of technology:

(a) **Unit or small-batch technology:** Used for custom-made products as per customer specifications or making products in small quantities, e.g., ships.

(b) **Large batch/mass production:** Most prevalent method to make large quantities in an assembly line fashion, e.g., automobile.

(c) **Continuous process:** To convert raw materials by process or machine into finished products.

One of the findings of Woodward was that the technology form impacts the organisation design which becomes increasingly complex in the ascending order as it moved from small-batch to continuous process.

Another classification was deduced by James Thompson (1967)[22] who proposed three forms of technology:

- *The long-linked technology* is a primary process with sequential dependence. This is the kind followed in assembly line manufacturing. It is characterised by a high level of standard operations, automation, tools and machines. If we compare Woodward's mass and flow, production technology is aligned to this. One can take chemical process and steel mills as an example in this category.
- *The mediating technology:* Examples of these are services firms like banks, brokerage and all the new age IT based technology which are characterised by a standardised delivery process and the use unique inputs to produce unique outputs. Such service companies deliver unique services to unique clients based on a pre-defined process. These companies use technology to connect with several partners in an exchange to conduct their transactions.
- *The intensive technology*: This is a mix of non-standard process with unique inputs and outputs. Primarily used by experts, this creates unique outcome. Design of equipment, health care, R&D laboratories and project organisations fall under this category.

Thompson's 2 × 2 Matrix had a blank fourth quadrant referred to nonstandard process and standard inputs/outputs. He argued that such a system will be too inefficient to survive or exist. This is shown in Figure 1.4.

---

[21]Woodward, J. (1958), *Management and technology: Problems and progress in technology*, 3.London: HMSO. Penguin Books limited Harmondsworth Middlesex England.

[22]Thompson, James D. (2003) [1967], *Organizations in Action: Social Science Bases of Administrative Theory* (With a new preface by Mayer N. Zald and a new introduction by W. Richard Scott (Ed.), New Brunswick, New Jersey: Transaction Publishers. ISBN 0-7658-0991-5.

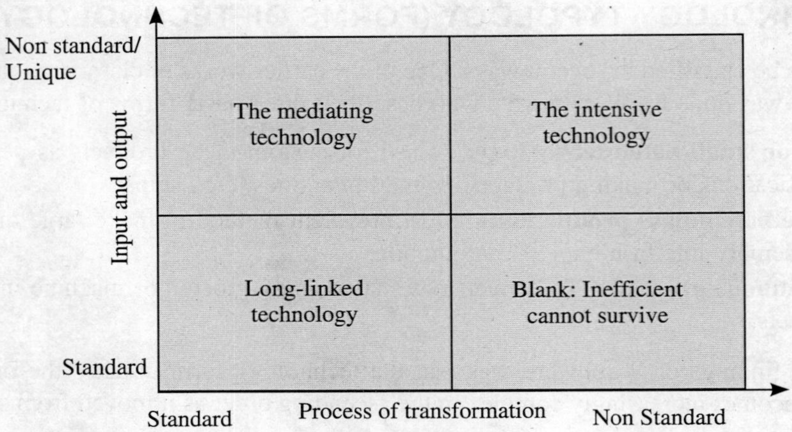

FIGURE 1.4 James Thompson Technology Typology.

Further work on technology typology was done by Charles Perrow who classified them based on knowledge required to operate technology. Perrow's 2×2 matrix as shown in Figure 1.5 is based on task variability and task analysability as the two ordinate and the four combinations are:

1. Routine technology is low variability and high analysability. Traditional manufacturing technologies using assembly lines fall under this category.
2. Craft technology has low variety and low analysability to unpredictable outcomes, examples of which are found in building construction.
3. Engineering typology may have many exceptions and in-depth knowledge is required to perform or use. However, methods are available to solve this problem. It is characterised by high analysability and high variability.
4. Non-routine is characterised high variability but low analysability. Strategic planning, space engineering is one such example.

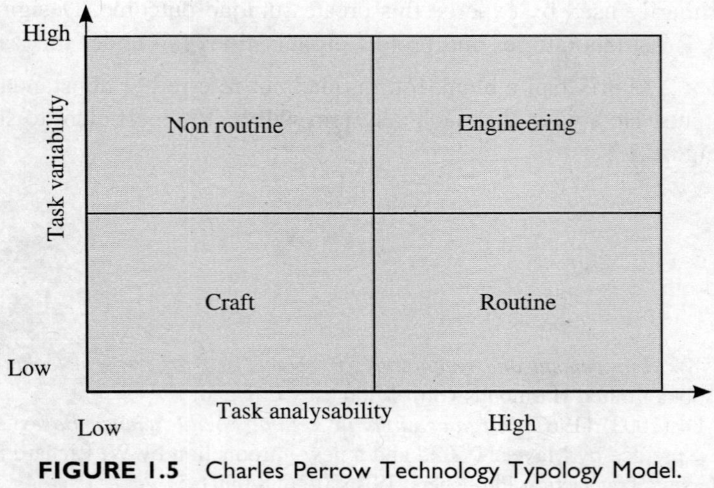

FIGURE 1.5 Charles Perrow Technology Typology Model.

Parrow further analysed the model and improved his 2X2 matrix by analysing the technology typology on the ordinates of coupling and interaction. Based on this, the new typology emerged is shown is Figure 1.6.

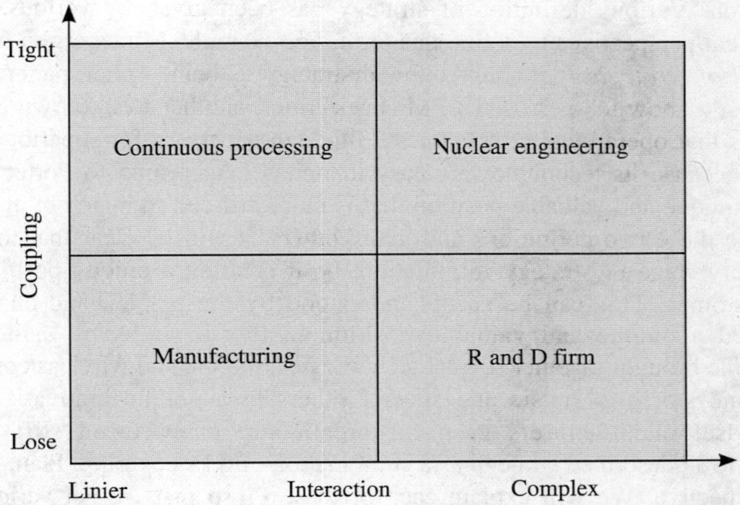

FIGURE 1.6 Charles Perrow Technology Model.

Product and process technology typology: Another perspective of technology typology is to classify them as product or process technology. Technologies that are used in the functioning of the product are called product technologies and those that are used for processes are called process technologies. For example, in an automobile fuel injection technology has eliminated the carburetor used to mix petrol and air to create combustible mixture, this is a product technology. But machining the engine block using numerical control machine tools is a process technology.

In case of product technology, there will be many end-users or consumers of the technology. These are often simpler to understand and have no direct relationship with other technologies. For example, the product technology of a cell phone may completely be different than that of an air-conditioner.

Process technologies, on the other hand, are for intermediate use to produce some product as part of the manufacturing steps. It can also be used for performing any service. A process technology like laser is used for eye-operation, as well as cutting a thick steel slab. Process technologies are used in creating or making other technologies and often are complex than the product technologies.

Interestingly, some technologies can be either product or process depending upon the use they are subjected to. A laser surgical or cutting machine is a product which is also a process technology for eye operations. Mobile phone is a product but when it is used for online order booking or railway reservation, it is part of process technology.

1.12 UNDERSTANDING STRATEGY IN TECHNOLOGY MANAGEMENT CONTEXT

We would like to start with the basic question of the role of technology in strategy formulation and implementation. Various definition of strategy has been given by various authors who encompass divergent perspectives to define this term. For example, Mintzberg in his 1994 book *The Rise and Fall of Strategic Planning*[23] defined strategy as being "plan, pattern, position or perspective" giving a "how to" perspective. Michael Porter, another well-known author, on the other hand, argues that operational effectiveness, although necessary for superior performance, is not sufficient, because its techniques are easy to imitate. According to Porter[24], strategy is about choosing a unique and valuable position that is more difficult to match by the competitor.

If we examine these two definitions and many others, it will be clear that the technology is essential at every stage of strategy formulation, be it creating a unique position or unique value for the customer. This can be easily understood by the Apple hand-phones example which has created a unique and valuable position in this business by using technology appropriately. Apple brought together several technologies, mobile and wireless communication, touchscreen, online stores of music and several others in a unique innovative model that made other handset manufacturers gasp for breath and many faced stiff competition.

Mintzberg in 1987 described strategy as a combination of 5 Ps covering, Plan, Ploy, Pattern, Position and Perspective. We will explain each of these Ps so that we get various ways that strategy of a firm is defined.

The first P stands for strategy as a Plan to achieve the objectives of the firm. This covers various options a firm exercises and undertakes planning to achieve them. This perspective is an essential part of the strategy formulation process. But having a good plan is not enough as no plans can ever be successful unless it is acted upon and for action the firm needs processes, people, skills and various other things.

Mintzberg also describes that strategy should also have the ability to outwit the competitors. For this he chooses another P, Ploy that a firm must adopt to get better of competitors. This may require plotting to disrupt, dissuade, discourage or otherwise influence them. Companies open storefronts at strategic locations, offer huge discounts, run loyalty programmes, etc., to stay ahead of the competition. This P also encompasses patenting key technologies or taking control of intellectual capital. Apple and Samsung have fought bitter wars in the recent times over mobile handset design and have taken each other to courts.

While the first two Ps, plans and ploys are deliberate exercises, yet the strategy is also about a pattern in which the actual outcome happens. This advocates that following a consistent and successful pattern of doing business is also a part of successful strategy. Successful companies depict a pattern in the way they do things, come out with new products or serve their customers.

Strategy is also about delivering value not just creating it. Strategy is a pattern in actions over time; for example, a company that regularly markets very expensive products uses a "high end" strategy. Strategy is also defined as a position that a company wants to achieve that makes it

[23]Henry Mintzberg. Rise and Fall of Strategic Planning Paperback. Free Press; 1st edition (June 29, 2013) ISBN-13: 978-1476754765.

[24]Michael E. Porter, **What Is Strategy?** *Harvard Business Review*, 1 Nov 1996. Prod. #: 96608-PDF-ENG.

unassailable in the particular marketplace by offering unique products or services in those markets. Strategy is also defined as a perspective an organization takes for conducting its business. This covers choices an organisation makes, its patterns of behaviour. A risk taking organisation would try to lead through innovation, acquisition, etc. A risk adverse organisation would like to do more of the same thing.

In short, strategy is just three things:

1. How a firm creates value
2. How a firm delivers value and
3. How it captures value.

As shown in Figure 1.7: What is Strategy?

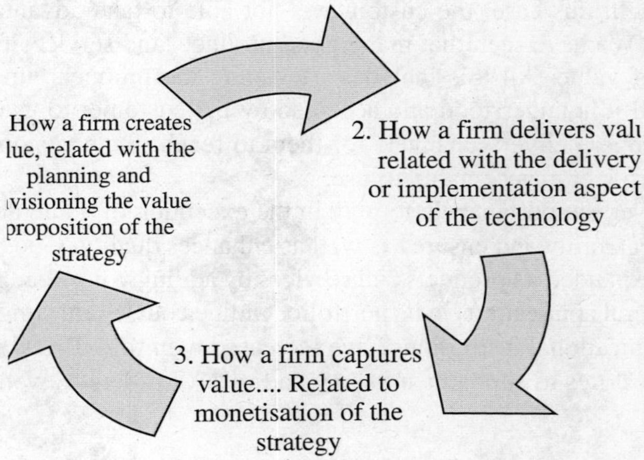

FIGURE 1.7 What is Strategy?

1.12.1 How does a Firm Create Value

Value creation is all about products and services that a firm develops, its ability to make them more and more useful to the customers who choose the firm's products and services over the competition. This also means both functional and perceived (intangible) values such a brand recognition, market repute and standing for quality and reliability. The name of Tata gives an instant recognition of fairness and quality product. It may be premium or the best in the market but is always regarded as priced reasonably and produced with care.

The important question to be asked at this stage is as to how the technology will help in creating value. It may be done through better manufacturing process, less errors and defects and using technology for flawless after-sales services. It also requires to ensure proper mechanism so that the customer accepts the superior value for their advantage. Walkman and cassette players were being used for several decades till Apple brought miniature iPod, a portable media player in 2001. But their sheer look, huge capacity to store songs backed up by their online music store–Tunes, it created a huge success and restored the sagging business of the company. Take the case of fashion apparel maker Zara who has created a short supply chain cycle using technology which ensures that it produces what it sells. New fashion ideas are rolled out quickly before they become obsolete and Zara replenishes the supply to stores every 2 weeks as against few months by other producers. The tight integration of design, planning, merchandising and production in La Coruna enables the company to be flexible and, therefore, able to respond quickly to any market need[25].

1.12.2 How does a Firm Deliver Value

Value delivery refers to how a firm is able to present and share the value to its customer. This refers to the execution perspective. Simply building a better product and services may not determine the success of business unless value is delivered to the customer. A great automobile kept in dirty showroom explained by poorly equipped sales person and lagging after-sales services means poor delivery of value. In this case, the customer is not able to take advantage of the benefits that the product offers. We have seen that many good products and services fail to make a mark due to poor delivery of value. All this includes packaging the products, undertaking the right marketing campaign till it is understood and accepted by the customer to use it. Many products and services require proper delivery channels for them to reach to the customer, the absence of which will make the product unacceptable to use.

Technology has a very important role to play in the execution of value delivery. It brings in cost-effectiveness, repeatability and ensures as well as enhances quality. Google started as search engine and now it has expanded its products and services by adding voice search, context sensitive searches and added several applications in its portfolio. Online courses are similar examples where the value delivery of educational institutions have increased manifold. Brick and mortar retailers have resorted to online stores to supplement, show and receive orders as well as service request from their customers.

1.12.3 How does a Firm Capture Value

The third aspect of strategy is to capture the value. This has reference to the price a customer is willing to pay for the various features and capabilities, apparent as well as perceived value. This perspective refers to monetisation or converting the value into money from the customers. All this requires proper positioning and articulation of the value proposition so that the customer is willing to pay for it. Capturing the value also includes actions around building a brand and superior message for which the customer wants to pay extra. Our sustainable competitive advantage comes from doing all the three right and in each one of these three perspectives technology can help.

It is important that, for the firm's strategy to be successfully executed, the role of technology is properly understood. The value capture perspective covers the business model associated with the firm. There are unique and interesting ways the monetisation is being done by newer firms that is not just the price the customer pays (and in some cases customer uses it free) but the associated ways in which the value is captured. Google search is used by most of us but the value captured by Google (i.e., monetisation) happens through Google Adword, online traffic generation, selling profile data of the people and whole lot of other information related with the Google search.

[25] http://www.forbes.com/sites/walterloeb/2013/10/14/zaras-secret-to-success-the-new-science-of-retailing-a-must-read/, accessed 16 Dec. 2013.

1.13 ROLE OF TECHNOLOGY IN FORMULATING AND IMPLEMENTING STRATEGY OF A BUSINESS

The role of technology spans across both formulation and implementation of strategy. As one can see that technology becomes the common and necessary ingredient to create, deliver and capture value. Taking this thought forward, it is clear that a proper management of technology is necessary to help creation, delivery and capture of value. Erickson, et al.[26] opine that effective management of technology strategy can help a firm gain and sustain competitive advantages, ranging from incremental improvements in product quality or cost, to major breakthroughs that create new market opportunities. Management of technology as per Erickson must, however, be purposeful rather than hopeful or "hands off" and must always be connected with the firm's overall business strategy.

Unfortunately, management of technology is often far remote from the business strategy. Research and development is considered an overhead, and does not churn our new products or services fast enough to beat the competitive pressure. The development and use of technology must be aligned with business strategy. The objective of technology management is to find new opportunities to gain competitive advantage and ward of competitive threat. All this requires a closer coordination with business strategy and technology strategy.

Figure 1.8 describes the relationship between business strategy and technology strategy. It can be seen that, while business strategy drives technology strategy, the reverse is also true where technology strategy starts supporting and enhancing business strategy.

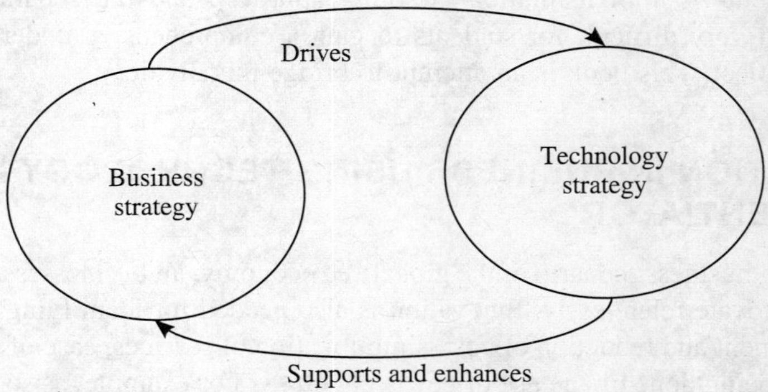

FIGURE 1.8 Relationship between Business and Technology Strategy.

1.14 SIGNIFICANCE OF TECHNOLOGY MANAGEMENT FOR MANAGERS

It is evident that technology helps the organisation to produce better products with higher efficiency and lower cost. Technology management helps to connect the various parts of the organisation such as engineering, research and development production, marketing, financial

[26]Tamara J. Erickson, John F. Magee, Philip A. Roussel and Kamal N. Saad, MIT *Sloan Management Review* Spring 1990, 15 April 1990, http://sloanreview.mit.edu/article/managing-technology-as-a-business-strategy/, accessed 16 Dec. 2013.

management, operations and services to achieve strategic and operational objectives of an organisation through planning, development and implementation of technological capabilities.

Technology is deployed in all types of businesses and ranges from widely used tools for management and effective production, to complex high technology products. Business managers must deal with accelerating technological changes, shortened products and process lifecycles, knowledge as an asset to be managed and interactions with highly qualified scientists and engineers. The diversity and complexity of technologies demand that managers sometimes supervise scientists and engineers whose subject matter knowledge will be beyond their own ability.

In other words, we need to take a broad perspective of organisation, marketing, design, manufacturing and services into a single approach to support new competitive opportunity that may come from new product, new process or developing new markets. In addition to academic theories, we must use practical methods that can be put into direct use for new product development and technological innovation projects from conceptualisation to realiation.

A well-developed technology management strategy without a successful commercial implementation cannot lead to desirable economic returns. Hence, technology development and implementation must be studied as an integrated subject between technology and market opportunity. The complete process is a highly interdisciplinary one, crossing over the conventional engineering college and business school curriculums. Traditionally, engineering students are trained to look at this process from a more technical (or development) viewpoint, whereas business students are asked to learn the management (or implementation) side of the same process. This divided "development-vs.-implementation" training approach and the separation of domain knowledge makes it very difficult for students to gain a comprehensive understanding of this interdisciplinary subject. This book is an attempt to bridge this divide.

1.15 INNOVATION IN BUSINESS USING TECHNOLOGY IS KEY DIFFERENTIATOR

In the ever-changing business scenario of the globalised economy, all businesses are being pushed by customers to innovate relentlessly. Innovation is also needed for identifying newer areas for efficiency improvement and reduction of cost, simplification of services, ease of use, etc. All this can be done and is being done by the use of new technology. For example, as soon as the mobile phones have become affordable, mobile apps are increasingly being used for business purposes.

As a result, technology has become a prime driver for the innovation and new tool for business competitiveness. This is why we need to study Technology and Innovation management in strategic framework so that we can understand its impact in the long run. We will discuss about innovation management in later chapters.

1.16 MANAGEMENT OF TECHNOLOGY (MOT)

Management is defined as a process of business that include organisation and coordination of its activities to achieve its goals. Management deals with resources and its optimal utilisation, and these include men, machines, method, materials and money.

Well known management Guru Peter Drucker (1909–2005) also added tasks such as marketing and innovation to management. Finally, management ensures interlocking of all functions by creating suitable corporate policies to organise, plan, control and direct its four resources men, method, machine and money to achieve the goals and objectives for which the enterprise exists.

Given this definition, MOT is to focus on all activities described above in reference to technology. MOT is, therefore, described as all functions related to planning, organising, optimisation and control of technology. This includes products, processes and services related with technology and all are geared to help organisation achieve competitive advantage. Thus, MOT covers larger aspects that have impact or relationship with:

- Strategy: Role that technology plays in organisation success
- Planning and Forecasting: Identifying relevant technologies for the firm's growth and expansion
- Defining future plan and road map for the technology: Finding the right opportunities to embrace technologies matching with market needs, prioritising their acquisition and management.

Technology management is aimed towards value creation for the organisation using the technology. It also means when to adopt, how to harness and when to discard a technology depending upon the strategic business needs and meeting customer requirements. Finally, technology management is an integrated function that spans strategy formulation, planning, design, implementation, management, optimisation and retrial of technology for products and services that have value to human beings and consequently for the organisation.

1.17 THE CONCEPTUAL FRAMEWORK FOR MANAGEMENT OF TECHNOLOGY

Figure 1.9 presents concise model of technology management.

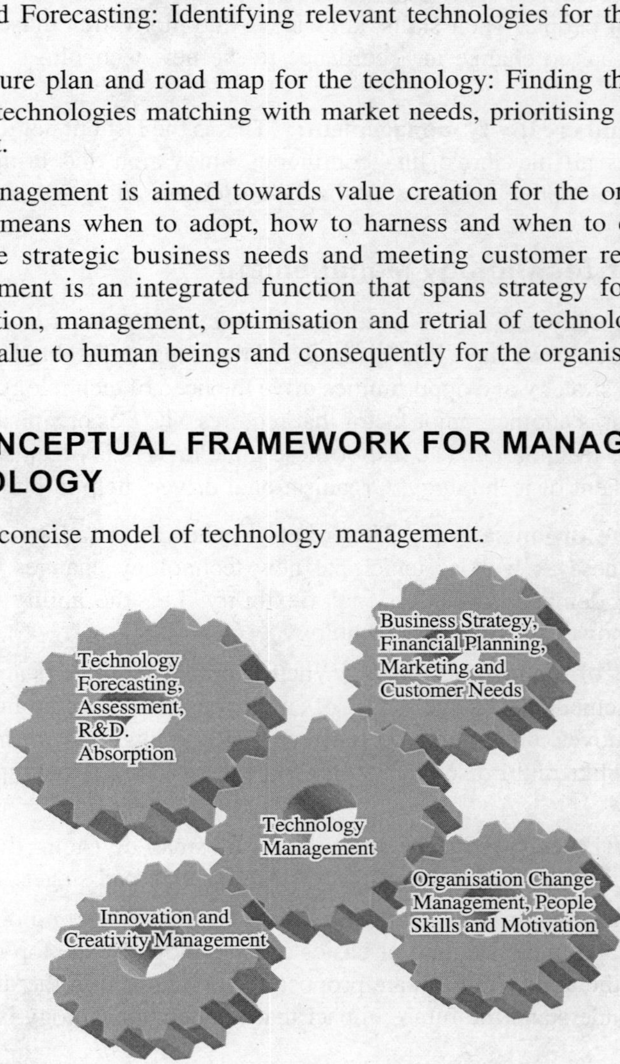

FIGURE 1.9 Conceptual Framework for Technology Management.

This framework has the following elements that form part of technology management:

(a) **Business strategy, financial planning, marketing and customer needs:** This defines the needs and justifies why technology management is needed and what the end objective is in terms of customer value and needs.

(b) **Technology forecasting, assessment, R&D:** Absorption is the second constituent that matches the technology needed to meet the business and customer need objectives. This covers technology forecasting, assessment, selections, buying, R&D and also retiring the technology when the new one comes into use.

(c) **Organisation change management, people skills and motivation:** Since technology has to be adopted by people and applied for people needs, it must ensure change in the mindset of people. Their skills, knowledge and motivation must change with time. Organisation has to change in accordance to the new technology, if it wants to take benefits.

(d) **Innovation and creativity management:** This is the last but not the least component that combines all the above into continuous innovation and brings in organisation creativity into action to create value for the customer and growth for the organisation.

1.17.1 Drivers of Technology Management

Management of technology (MOT) is necessitated due to three major drivers: Business, technology and organisation. We have briefly discussed the impact of technology on strategy of a business. Primarily, the strategy and opportunities drive the need of technology management. The technology development is another major factor that requires MOT as organisation functioning is dependent on the use of technology. The last of these three drivers is organisational drivers that enable proper management of technology. Organisational drivers help in building:

(a) **Agility of the organisation:** This refers to the organisation's ability to balance existing business as well as undertake new technology changes if market changes rapidly. This demands organisational flexibility, i.e., the ability to realign people, process and power for the new technology.

(b) **Cohesiveness of the organisation:** Whether organisation units are able to cooperate across management layers, age groups of employees has good communication practices, easy career moves, integration via placement (R&D aligned with manufacturing) and other features like multi-disciplinary task force teams, long-term employment and skills retention.

(c) **Entrepreneurial culture:** The ability to create small divisions, different budgets for new ideas and promoting some of them till the launch pad stages.

(d) **Active top management:** A good Management of Technology requires active involvement and understanding of basics of technology by the top management. They should have the ability to evaluate proposals, get involved in the discussion and have patience to understand the future impact that the new technology is likely to bring.

1.17.2 Role of Chief Technology Officer

Given all these varied, at times, conflicting as well as contradictory requirements of technology management, organisations need a strong leader. Such a leader should be able to provide direction, management and execution of various projects and programmes, R&D, technology acquisition, transfer and retrial and many other functions. This role is named as Chief Technology Officer (or CTO).

Typically, CTO reports directly to the Chief Executive Officer of the company and is at par with other CXOs, such as Chief of Finance, IT or operations. CTO is responsible to supervise all technology-related services, planning for new technology, R&D, Innovation Management, product development, concept to market or prototype. The CTO is required to stay abreast of new technology development impacting the current as well as future strategies of the firm and a keen observer of how competition is using technology to their advantage. The essential duties and responsibilities include:

(a) Defining technology strategies, standards and policies and suitable measures to understand if these are being implemented properly.
(b) Defining and driving organisational changes necessary to meet a firm's business objectives, while implementing new technology.
(c) Developing and monitoring technology plan, budgets and forecasts.
(d) Establishing technology planning, acquisition, adoption, collaboration, continuous innovation and enhancement.
(e) Managing R&D, new product introduction prototype, concept to market.
(f) Leading implementation and harnessing of new technology.
(g) Reviewing and recommending sun setting (retrial) of exiting technology when it becomes, no longer cost effective.

A Chief Technology Officer (CTO) is a leadership role that must have the following competencies:

- **Technical competencies:** Knowledge of related technologies that are used by the firm.
- **Analytical competencies:** The ability to synthesise multiple sources of complex information, ability to analyse research data; ability to comprehend conclusion based on intuition and experience.
- **Business sense:** To understand the value and impact of a technology based on business acumen.
- **Execution capabilities:** Strong project and programme management skills, planning and organising skills.
- **People-related skills:** People are the key for any innovation and implementations. They need to be motivated and encouraged to perform at their optimum level. Most people assume that CTO is a dry techie type of role but best CTOs are those who have driven their team for superior performance using excellent people management skills.
- **Communication skills:** This includes both oral and written communications that will help in performing his task better.

1.18 UPDATING THE CONCEPT OF TECHNOLOGY: AI AND GEN AI AS PERVASIVE TOOLS

Traditional definitions of technology, such as those by Read Bain or Frances Stewart, broadly encompass tools, knowledge, and procedures used for making, using, and doing useful things. In the contemporary context, AI and Generative AI fit squarely within these definitions, representing sophisticated forms of applied knowledge used to produce valuable products and services. Their defining characteristic, however, is their pervasive nature. Unlike discrete tools or specific processes, AI and Gen AI are increasingly embedded across virtually all business functions and aspects of personal life, transforming from mere "tools" into intelligent, adaptive systems.

This pervasive integration of AI fundamentally blurs traditional technology typologies, such as the distinction between product technology and process technology.For instance, an AI-powered design tool is itself a product, yet it simultaneously optimizes the design process. Similarly, AI can be embedded within physical products to enhance their functionality (e.g., smart devices), optimize complex manufacturing processes (e.g., predictive maintenance in factories), and transform back-office business functions (e.g., HR, finance). This ubiquitous presence necessitates a more fluid and integrated understanding of technology's role, where its impact is seen holistically across the entire value chain rather than in isolated applications. The traditional categorizations, while still useful for foundational understanding, must now be viewed through a lens that acknowledges AI's ability to transcend and redefine these boundaries.

1.19 EVOLUTION AND GROWTH OF TECHNOLOGY: THE AI/GEN AI ACCELERATION CURVE

Models of technology evolution, such as the Abernathy and Utterback (A-U) Model and Kuhn's Model, describe technology development through stages like the fluid stage, dominant design, and mature stage. While these models provide a valuable framework, the unprecedented speed of AI and Generative AI development and adoption significantly compresses these traditional technology S-curves. Generative AI adoption, for example, has been notably faster than both personal computers and the internet. This accelerated pace implies that the "fluid stage," characterized by experimentation and design proliferation, may be considerably shorter. Dominant designs, once established, may also evolve or be disrupted much more rapidly. Consequently, the "mature stage" of a technology is reached and subsequently disrupted at an accelerated rate, demanding continuous reinvention from firms to avoid obsolescence.

The concept of self-organizing systems, as espoused by Devendra Sahal, finds new resonance in the context of AI's autonomous learning capabilities. AI systems, particularly large language models, continuously learn and adapt from vast datasets, leading to rapid, iterative improvements that can accelerate technological growth beyond human-driven cycles. This rapid iteration and evolution mean that companies have less time to react, establish market dominance, or even recover from strategic missteps. The accelerated S-curve for AI technologies necessitates a shift towards highly agile development and deployment methodologies, where continuous monitoring and adaptation are paramount for survival and growth.

1.20 IMPACT OF AI/GEN AI ON SOCIETY AND BUSINESS: OPPORTUNITIES AND CHALLENGES

Technology has always presented a dual nature, offering both immense opportunities for progress and significant challenges. AI and Generative AI exemplify this duality. On the one hand, they present unparalleled opportunities for economic growth, increased productivity, and the emergence of entirely new business models. Projections indicate a massive global economic impact, with AI solutions and services potentially contributing $22.3 trillion to global GDP by 2030, representing approximately 3.7% of the total. McKinsey further projects an annual economic impact of $6.1–$7.9 trillion from AI, with Goldman Sachs predicting that Gen AI alone could boost global GDP by 7% ($7 trillion). This economic expansion is driven by AI's ability to enhance operational efficiency, reduce errors, and accelerate decision-making. Beyond mere optimization, AI allows organizations to transcend traditional process improvements and discover exciting new growth opportunities. The emergence of "AI-native" organizations, built from the ground up with AI at their core, showcases how foundational AI integration can enable new business models that were previously unfeasible.

However, this transformative power is accompanied by significant challenges. The automation capabilities of AI, while boosting productivity, also raise concerns about job displacement. While some foresee AI augmenting human capabilities rather than replacing them, the potential for a "great decoupling" between economic growth and employment growth, as observed in previous technological shifts, is a pertinent concern. AI's ability to automate repetitive tasks and enhance human productivity (e.g., software developers coding 126% more projects per week with AI assistance) suggests a fundamental redefinition of human work and economic value. This necessitates a proactive societal and governmental response that extends beyond traditional labor policies to address broad implications for income distribution, social safety nets, and the very purpose of human activity in an increasingly automated world.

Furthermore, the widespread adoption of AI introduces complex ethical considerations, including potential biases in AI models, issues of privacy and data governance, and the environmental footprint of AI computing. AI servers, for instance, consume significantly more electricity and water than traditional servers, contributing to increased carbon emissions and electronic waste. These challenges underscore the need for responsible AI development and deployment, ensuring that technological progress aligns with societal well-being and environmental sustainability.

1.21 THE EVOLVING ROLE OF THE CHIEF TECHNOLOGY OFFICER (CTO)/CHIEF AI OFFICER (CAIO)

The Chief Technology Officer (CTO) has traditionally been responsible for overseeing technology-related services, R&D, innovation management, and product development within an organization. In the age of AI, this role has expanded dramatically, demanding an even broader and deeper understanding of emerging technologies and their strategic implications. The CTO's responsibilities now explicitly include AI/Gen AI strategy, adoption, governance, and ethical oversight.

The strategic imperative of AI has also led to the emergence of a new C-suite role: the Chief AI Officer (CAIO). The CAIO is specifically tasked with bridging business strategy and AI innovation, ensuring that AI initiatives are aligned with core business objectives and deliver tangible value. The rise of the CAIO signifies that AI is no longer a sub-domain of IT or R&D but a core strategic imperative requiring dedicated, specialized leadership at the highest level. This deepening specialization within technology leadership, however, also presents a potential for new organizational silos if the roles of CTO and CAIO are not effectively integrated. Ensuring seamless collaboration between the CTO (responsible for broader technological infrastructure and strategy) and the CAIO (focused on AI-specific strategy and innovation) is critical for a holistic and unified approach to Technology and Innovation Management, preventing fragmentation and maximizing the strategic impact of AI across the enterprise.

1.22 SUMMARY

In this chapter, we proposed that Technology and Innovation management is a multi-disciplinary subject which will be dealt from two perspectives. The first one is the broad outside world perspective of how Technology and Innovation is impacting business and society and the second is the management aspect of Technology and Innovation within the enterprise. We first laid the conceptual foundation by defining and explaining the meaning of technology. We then elaborated further by examining various elements of technology such as scientific principles and knowledge, method and tools, organisation, and product and services. We also briefly touched on the historical aspect of technology starting from Stone Age, Bronze Age, Iron Age and Information Age and Digital Age which is the current one.

It was important to establish key characteristic of technology such as fueled by need, has to be appropriate for purpose and universally applicable. It should also continuously reinvent or be disruptive and new while being a driver of social change and driven by social need. One of the key principles discussed was that technology management is interdisciplinary in nature. This chapter also discussed the evolution and growth of technology through its different stages such as fluid stage, dominant design and transition stage and mature stage. It was explained that technology growth is also due to its characteristic of being a self-organising system and its impact on society and business was discussed.

The next section of the chapter was to uncover technology typology, i.e., forms of technology from various researchers' perspective to give a broad view. This led to establishing better understanding of strategy in technology management context. This was the basis on which the role of technology needs to be understood as to how it helps a firm in creating, delivering and finally capturing value. This was a natural preamble to define the role of technology in formulating and implementing strategy of a business by describing the interdependent relationship between business strategy and technology strategy.

We then described the significance of technology management for managers. The role of innovation was explained in business using technology as key differentiator. The definition of MOT along with conceptual framework for technology management was given. Further drivers of technology management were also discussed.

The chapter ended with the discussion of the role of CTO, a role which is getting very significant in most organisations which are using technology.

Key Terms: Technology Strategy, Pre-paradigm and Paradigm Stages, Dominant Design, Technology Typology, Management of Technology, Chief Technology Officer

REVIEW QUESTION

1. Identify some major technologies and suggest why they have been developed to solve what all problems of the world.
2. What are the social considerations a technologist must take into account while developing a new technology?
3. Identify growth of any technology and chart out along its growth curve.
4. Identify positive and negative impacts of the following technologies:
   (a) Automobile (b) Mobile Communication
   (c) Internet (d) Social Media
5. What are your suggestions to eliminate some of the negative consequences of these technologies as given in Question 4?
6. Explain various technology typology described by various researchers.
7. What is technology management? Explain its role from the two perspectives adopted in the chapter. **Answer:** Section 1.1
8. Define the conceptual framework of management of technology. What are the drivers of technology management? Also define the role of CTO in brief. **Answer:** Section 1.17

ESSAY QUESTIONS

Question 1: Analyze how the role of the Chief Technology Officer (CTO) has evolved in the age of AI and Generative AI. Discuss the new responsibilities and challenges faced by a modern CTO, including the potential emergence of a Chief AI Officer (CAIO) role.

Hints for Answer: Start by outlining the traditional responsibilities of a CTO (e.g., overseeing technology services, R&D, innovation management, product development). Then, explain how this role has expanded dramatically to include AI/Gen AI strategy, adoption, governance, and ethical oversight. Discuss the emergence of the Chief AI Officer (CAIO) as a new C-suite role specifically tasked with bridging business strategy and AI innovation, requiring dedicated, specialized leadership. Detail the challenges faced by modern CTOs, such as keeping pace with the rapid speed of AI advancements, ensuring ethical deployment, managing change, integrating external AI capabilities, and preventing new organizational silos if CTO and CAIO roles are not effectively integrated.

ASSIGNMENT QUESTIONS

1. Select a company of your choice and track various technology strategy initiatives and present them using various frameworks discussed in this chapter.
2. Take any firm of your choice and identify how value is created by the firm. Find out how the value is delivered and how it is captured.

CASE STUDY

Nokia Sells Handset Business to Microsoft

When the world woke up on 3 September 2013 with the news that Nokia has decided to sell its handset business to Microsoft for $7.2 billion, many could not believe it. Only a few years ago, Nokia was a dominant player of the handset business, much reliable, much adored by its customer, but somewhere it seems to have faltered. With just three per cent of the global smartphone market which is dominated by Apple iPhone and Samsung and challengers like HTC, Micromax, Lava and other low cost manufacturers, this company lost its market cap to one-fifth of what it was in 2007.

Nokia was a clear case of not keeping pace with the technology development. Dual SIM card phones launched by Indian local players like Micromax has already thrown itself out of the lower end of the market. Then came the onslaught form smartphones led by Apple and Android, they just crushed it. Nokia in the past had been a surprisingly adaptive company which kept reinventing itself from paper, electricity, rubber galoshes to focusing only on telecom. Surprisingly, it came up with its first smartphone back in 1996 which was instrumental in building a prototype of a touch-screen and also an Internet-enabled phone. This was a company that spent heavily on research and development (R&D), but it appears that all R&D was not directed towards what customer wanted to have in its products.

Was this due to the fact that Nokia, primarily a hardware company failed to embrace software and realise its potential in the handset business? Was there an organisation dilemma to push software engineers in the forefront in a hardware company? Or they failed to realise that there is no boundary for innovation, hardware and software, marketing and customer care, product and services, strategy and execution, technology and management, all need to simultaneously respond to the changing marketing needs. Some say it is typical reluctance of a giant leader to change the course for something new and exciting. Some say that they were reluctant to embrace openly android platform and continued with their own operating system which was buggy, clunky, and unintuitive to win consumers over. Market is still trying to see the impact of this sell off. Microsoft is purely an enterprise business company and handsets are used by individuals, how this alliance will work is only to be seen in the future.

One thing is sure that in high tech industry one must continue to be innovative and plan the next technology move speedily, decisively and adequately. If you fall behind, consumers will punish you quickly. If you are late and inadequate, then wait for your obituary to be written relatively soon.

Questions

1. What should have Nokia done to face the competitive pressure from iPhone?
2. What is the future of Microsoft and Nokia Combination?
3. Do two wrongs make one right?

ADDITIONAL READINGS

1. Anderson, P. and M. Tushman, 1990, Technological discontinuities and dominant designs: a cyclical model of technological change, *Administrative Science Quarterly* 35:604–633.
2. Christensen, C.M., 1992, Exploring the limits of the technology S-curve, *Part Production and Operations Management Journal* 1:334–357.
3. Rosenberg, N., 1983, *Inside the Black Box: Technology and Economics*, Cambridge University Press, Cambridge, UK.
4. Suarez, F. and J. Utterback, 1995, Dominant designs and the survival of firms, *Strategic Management Journal* 16:415–430.
5. Teece, D., 1986, Profiting from technological innovation: implications for integration, collaboration, licensing and public policy, *Research Policy* 15:285–305.

Chapter 2

Technology Strategy

If you don't have a competitive advantage, don't compete.

— Mencius (Meng-Tse), 4th century BCE

At the end of this chapter, we will learn:

- Competitive advantages through new technologies
- Linking the role of technology in product and process development
- Product development – from scientific breakthrough to marketable product
- Role of technology in innovation
- Role of Government in technology development
- Linkage between technology, development and competition
- Managing research and development (R&D)
- Managing intellectual property
- Defining organizations strategic direction

2.1 INTRODUCTION

Technology is often touted as the source of competitive advantage. Historical wars have been fought and won when the superior machines were used by the winners to defeat the less sophisticated opponents. Many companies were forced to go out of business when a rival launched a superior product or used superior technology to produce a competitive product at a cheaper price, giving the same features or better service. In this chapter, we will first examine if technology has any role to give a firm competitive advantage. If yes, then we will focus on how to deploy technology in achieving competitive advantage for its product or process development. Finally, once the competitive advantage is achieved through technology, can it be maintained and how over the period of time? The last enquiry will need understanding of cultural and human aspects of the enterprise in using technology. If not addressed properly the enterprise may not sustain what it has achieved for long.

In this chapter, we will, therefore, start our enquiry with defining competitive advantages and how they can be gained through new technologies by linking their role in product and process development. We will then define the role of technology in innovation as well as the role of government in technology development for the country to create a techno-innovation ecosystem. We will have to establish a linkage between technology, development and competition along the way and dovetail managing research and development (R&D) and intellectual property to help achieve our objectives. We will then define how an organisation can change its course of strategic direction using technology development, acquisition or partnering.

2.2 WHAT IS COMPETITIVE ADVANTAGE?

A firm is said to have competitive advantage over its rival if its products and services are of greater value perceived by the customer. The perceived greater value can be due to some enhanced features of the product, better quality and/or lower price for the same features. If the price is higher, then it has to be justified by greater benefits, better after-sales services and other features, such as innovative design or brand value. RADO watches have steep prices as compared to their lesser known watch makers but it commands higher price due a combination of factors which include build quality, brand image, unique or limited edition design, etc. On the other hand, Hero MotoCorp. Ltd. sells its motorcycle for higher mileage, resale value and vast service network. It may be noted that the competitive advantage could come from a wide variety of reasons and our effort is to understand that for each such reasons where and how technology plays its role to support them.

2.3 SOURCES OF COMPETITIVE ADVANTAGE

It is a well-known fact that any business has to face competition in the marketplace. Earlier the competition was limited to the geographical boundary of the country or state in which the firm used to operate. But due to globalisation, this is no longer true. Competition can now come up from any firm located in any part of the world which has the desire to expand its market and reach out to new customers anywhere in the world. The role of technology is to help a firm make its products, deliver its services and run its operations. It may seem like everyone may use the same technology sooner or later; hence technology will not offer any superior advantage but in reality it is not true. All banks have the same ATM technology or core banking solution to run the back office but technology savvy banks keep adding superior features faster than their competitors, address issues quickly and always delight their customers using newer technology.

However, the interesting insight about technology is that it is a source of both competitive necessity and competitive advantage. Technology is a competitive necessity because, for doing any task within any function of any business, one needs appropriate use of technology to remain efficient and effective. Technology is also a source of competitive advantage as a firm can develop superior products, services, processes or capabilities using appropriate technology, giving the company a superior position vis-à-vis competitors. The key is in the innovative use of technology by the firm to gain competitive advantage rather than using it only for efficiency enhancement or manpower reduction. A firm is said to have competitive advantage over other firms if it has developed a combination of attributes that allows it to outperform its competitors. For example, the firm may have superior product, lower cost of production, superior quality or captive source of raw material that translates into lower input cost. In addition, it may gain competitive advantage because it has highly trained and skilled staffs that are able to harness new technology better or bring innovative ideas about new products, new features in existing product or improved services. Technology can aid in gaining competitive advantage if it improves the process of manufacturing, distribution and customer service.

Noted management thinker and author, Michael Porter proposed in his well-researched book *Competitive Advantage*[1] three generic strategies by which a firm can gain competitive advantage. We will explain the role of technology in gaining advantages of the following strategies:

(a) **Low-cost leadership:** Those firms that follow this strategy for gaining competitive advantage produce goods or services at the best price. For example, China-based manufacturer especially electronics product makers. All these companies, by adhering to low cost strategy, have become world leading suppliers of leading brands such as Dell, HP, Acer and Lenovo, get their laptops, tablets and desktops. Most home appliances like fans, air-conditioners are manufactured in China and Taiwan as they are produced at lowest cost. Most brands source their products and sell world over. Wall Mart, the retail giant of over 480B USD turnover, also follows the low cost leadership model and uses technologies extensively in its supply chain management to drive the cost down. Remember in all these cases the use of technology following this strategy would be to reduce cost through efficiency improvement. In some cases, superior product is produced using a newer technology at a larger scale. A case in point is of steel industry which has continuously reduced the cost of steel, primarily a commodity through regular improvements in steel making technology. Advanced technology such a LD converters, continuous casting of slabs and billets, thin slab casting continuous annealing, etc., have led to lower cost of manufacturing. In the process, the steel makers of the world discarded older technologies such as BOH process, Ingot making and large rolling mills.

(b) **Differentiation:** The second alternate generic strategy as per Michael Porter is to produce products or services that are truly differentiated and unique. A good example is of the luxury car by the makers of Rolls Royce, among hospitality segment Taj Premium hotels and several designer apparel manufacturers, such as Armani, Prada, etc.

(c) **Focus:** The third strategic alternative as per Porter is to prescribe the firm focus on a few industry or product segments within that industry and specialise in the same. Manufacturers and service provider companies following this strategic choice focus on few specialised products. For example, GE medical systems focuses only on health care industry, there are automobile manufacturers like Tata, who are known for heavy duty all-wheel-drive trucks.

[1]Competitive Advantage: Creating and Sustaining Superior Performance by E. Michael Porter (Author) Simon & Schuster; Export edition (1 January 2004).

There has been several developments and extrapolation of this theory to add other sources of competitive advantage. Some of the additional ones are:

(d) **Attractive price with quality:** Best products or services produced at competitive or attractive price and superior quality keep the firm ahead in the marketplace. Samsung handset falls under this category which are available at slightly lower price with lots of additional features than the much talked iPhone. Walmart in retail is one example that combines both cost and differentiations strategy.

(e) **Innovation:** In the recent times, innovation is regarded as one more source of competitive advantage which is superimposed on the primary sources. iPhone is one such example in this category.

(f) **Efficient and easy to work with customer:** This is yet another source of competitive advantage where the firm is super-efficient and easy to work with. Indigo airlines which in 3 years became the market leader is said to be following this principle of efficient operations, on time arrival and faster turn around of cabin for frequent departures.

2.4 STRATEGIC ACTIONS AND ROLE OF TECHNOLOGY

It may be summarised that competitive advantage helps an organisation to be more profitable than its competitors. It requires proper articulation of a greater perceived value to its customers than its competitors. As discussed, this can be achieved through many ways such as better-quality product or service at a lower price and increasing reach and availability. A firm can gain sustainable competitive advantage if this position is maintained over long term which can help boost its image, valuation and its future earning potential. Irrespective of the strategic choices exercised by the firm, ultimately, they have to be translated into actions. Table 2.1 presents examples of strategies, strategic actions and likely technologies that can support in execution.

TABLE 2.1 Example of Strategies, Actions and Enabling Technologies

Generic strategies	Strategic actions	Enabling technologies
Differentiation	Superior product technology	Product and process technology
Differentiation	Best in class customer service	Increased use of IT, CRM
Lower Cost	Lower costs than competitors	Efficient automation, IT
Differentiation	Better manufacturing technology	Product or process technology
Differentiation	Shorter lead times	CAD/CAM, Supply chain technology
Differentiation	Established brand	Communication technology
Differentiation	Newer innovative design	CAD, CAM, CAE
Focus	Products for niche market or custom made	Research and development, Knowledge management
Cost	Higher margin per item of product or unit of service	Automation

2.5 TECHNOLOGY AS VALUE CREATOR

We have discussed earlier that a firm can distinguish itself if its products or services are more valuable than that of the competitors. In Chapter 1, we defined that the purpose of strategy is to create value, deliver value and capture value. We now see how technology impacts the value creation activity.

Any organisation primarily produces a product or provides services to its customer. For doing this, they need to buy raw material and convert them into final products through a manufacturing process. In the case of service, the organisation applies its skilled resources with necessary equipment to offer services. Now that we have understood broadly what organisations do, we will now look at how technology helps in supporting these activities. Organisations run all these activities in a well-orchestrated sequence which is called business management. Business management comprises several processes which together form organisation's value chain. For example, value chain of a manufacturing organisation will start with purchase of raw material, its storages, further processing, manufacturing and then supplying the finished goods to the customer. Value chain also comprises process which are categorised as support activities such as human resources, sales and marketing, logistics processes for both inbound and outbound nature to name a few. Value chain processes also include service such as after-sales service, on-field maintenance, replacement of faulty parts or fixing any problems during usages.

If we examine closely, we will notice that technology plays an important role at every step of all these processes. In case of manufacturing or logistics processes which involve physical goods, technology is used at every step of running the machine, its sequencing, designing the parts or components or controlling the processes itself. CNC machines, process control computers, robots doing stamping or welding car chassis, automated testing machines, etc., are examples of how closely technology has permeated at every step of any manufacturing process. Further, technology is used in supply chain management and warehousing. The role of technology in these processes is to produce, transport or store goods, cheaper, better and faster.

In case of business processes, the role of information technology in automating and streamlining these processes have led to lower cost, flawless repeatability and absolute precision.

Figure 2.1 shows a generic value chain of a manufacturing enterprise and Figure 2.2 shows a generic value chain for services enterprise.

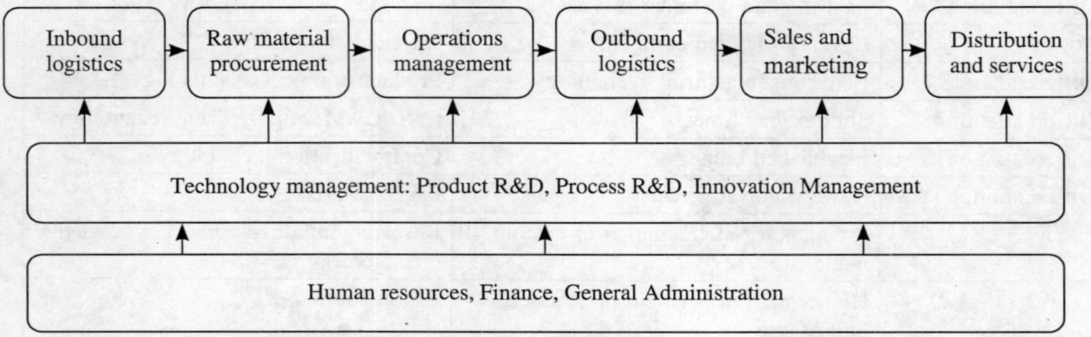

FIGURE 2.1 A Generic Value Chain Example of Manufacturing Firm.

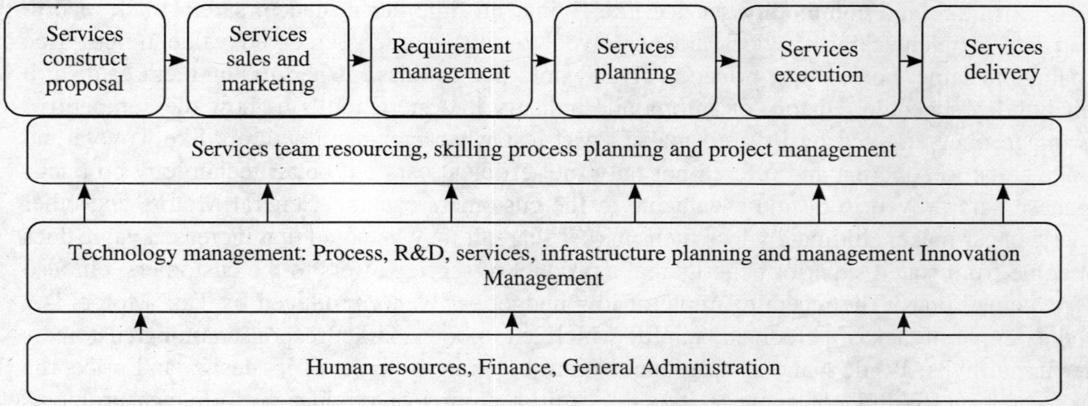

FIGURE 2.2 A Generic Value Chain Example for Services Company.

Broadly, technology has a necessary role to play in automation of value creating processes and bringing in efficiency in the value chain activities of both product manufacturing and in services delivery. All this will lead to lower cost. In short, any value creation activity must be done at a reasonable cost so that a firm can earn its profits.

Pietersen[2] defines competitive advantage as the gap between the value the firm creates and the cost it takes to create the value. For example, Domino's Pizza is able to deliver its pizza at home or offices within 30 minutes of getting an order placed by the customer. This value proposition makes Domino's Pizza unique in the minds of the customer. For maintaining this time, Domino's has to plan for and invest in technology to find less busy routes to reach to the end consumer in the shortest possible time. But if the cost of planning and making sure that the delivery boys reach before the 30 minutes deadline is more than the cost the customer is willing to pay, then the competitive advantage would be lost.

As long as the gap between the value created and the cost of creating the value is higher than that of the competition, then the firm can claim better competitive advantage. If this is not, then the firm will lose money and will become unviable in the long run. Finally, it is not just enough to reduce the cost to increase the gap which according to Porter is inward focus actions. Cost reduction, though necessary in competitive situation, would never be a sufficient condition for winning. The important aspect of extending the value–cost gap is to continuously increase the value as perceived by the customer which comprises the entire bouquet of benefits that the product or services offer.

Understanding value creation

Let us capture some more thoughts on the topic of value creation through some examples. Perceived value would differ from product to product and from one industry to the other. You will see at the end that cost alone is not enough for remaining ahead of the competition if the value perceived is not adequately supported. Let us take a few examples to drive home the point.

---

[2]Willie Pietersen, Strategic Learning: How to Be Smarter Than Your Competition and Turn Key Insights into Competitive Advantage, Wiley; 1st edition (March 15, 2010) ISBN-10: 0470540699.

In a routine and commodity service like flying, on time performance, safety track record, clean and efficient cabin services are perceived to carry higher perceived value if the price remains the same. For a lower price, no flyer would like to miss his/her appointment or disturb their holiday schedule. History of automobile industry in America tells us how the competitive advantage once enjoyed by its auto makers was lost when car manufacturers like Toyota and Honda came to America and offered not only fuel-efficient cars but better technology products. Japanese cars proved to be more valuable to the customers causing General Motors and other American car makers ultimately lose their market share. It may be noted that increased value does not come from stated superior benefits that a product or service offers to the customers, but also the perceived ones. The recent example of low budget car Nano, produced by Tata Motors is a good example of lack of perceived benefits which led to poor market response among customers after initial hype. While Nano as a product is path-breaking in terms of its design and price, the perceived benefits did not enhance its value. Initial reports of product performance problems and low cost image did not enhance a buyer's social image and hence customers did not buy in anticipated volumes. Here the new design and technology did not fail but other factors did which ultimately led to poor response in the marketplace.

2.6 CAN WE GET COMPETITIVE ADVANTAGES THROUGH TECHNOLOGY?

The role of technology for competitive advantage is baffling to many students and researchers. Many claim that technology can be easily replicated and hence can never be a competitive advantage. Nicholas G. Carr in a catchy titled HBR article[3] even proclaimed that technology doesn't matter. While he is referring to information technology in particular, the contempt of technology is fairly evident in his article. Like him, many feel that technology, if available to everyone, can be easily adopted within few months, so can never be a source of competitive advantage. To argue our case of technology as a source of competitive advantage we present here a popular story (see SALT 2.1).

SALT 2.1 Two Friends in the Forest

Two friends were walking in a dense forest and suddenly saw a Leopard looking at them at distance. They got afraid of the animal and one of them started to run. The other friend did not move an inch and remained stand still.

Leopard in its own wisdom moved in some other direction and did not pursue either the one who was running or the one who was standing still.

After a while when both of these friends met, the one who decided not to move asked the other one, "Why did you run, don't you know that Leopard would have outrun you?"

"As long as I outrun you I am safe!" Replied the other.

Discusion Questions

1. How is the story relevant in the context of competition?
2. In order to outrun the competition, what should a firm do?

[3] Nicholas G. Carr. IT Doesn't Matter, May 2003 HBR.

The lesson from this story is that in a competitive situation one should always remain one step ahead of the competition, either in product, services, brand perception or overall benefits. The purpose of the management of a firm is to gain and maintain competitive advantage with respect to its competition. Competitive advantage is gained when the firm creates its products or services that have more perceived value than its rivals. This can be done using a variety of means where relentless use of technology plays a significant role to gain and maintain competitive advantage. This is especially true in technology intensive industries. At the same time, there is hardly any industry which does not use technology extensively. Let us take some examples. Automobile have more features supported by on board computers to manage the engine performance, navigation systems, temperature controls, etc. Even driverless cars are being tried out on pilot basis waiting for commercialisation. So is the case of medical world where robots are deployed to do more precise operations that can not be done through human hands. The list can go long—education, entertainment, retail, transportation, food products; in fact all industries use technology to keep their products and services improving on a continuous basis to remain ahead of competition.

Within the same industry, firms decide to participate along several competitive dimensions such as price, market segments, product quality, technology leadership, distribution channels and customer service. So a company may want to offer a lower cost, less advanced technology products and some other can do just the opposite. Both the firms will use technology in varying degrees for different purposes, the former to reduce the cost of manufacturing and the later for adding more features and enhancing value. But both have to use the latest technology to achieve their strategic objectives, be it cost or superior product. Yet there would be a few still who would not be nimble enough to adopt new technology for their strategic objectives. These firms will be forced to follow the technology path at a later stage with lower returns from the marketplace. Had they followed the leaders soon enough, the story would have been different and if they still further delay then they would be totally rejected by the customers.

Take the case of the retail industry in India, especially, the massive growth of e-retailers in the marketplace who have garnered much larger market share leaving the large format retail store chain owners bewildered so much so that they have started to complain and predict the demise of e-commerce[4]. While the operating results of e-commerce firms, who use technology extensively, may be questioned, the opinion of customer is univocal in terms of higher perceived value as compared with the traditional retail store formats. The convenience of shopping from home at the hours of choice, ability to compare price, cash on delivery, easy exchange policy and many other customer-friendly features make the e-retailers a preferred choice of shopping among younger generation. So instead of crying foul and seeking regulatory protections, the traditional retailers should adopt e-commerce store front quickly. Some have started this attempt and most will follow soon.

Therefore, the need of the hour for firms is to continuously research, track and embrace new technology ahead of the competition and adopt them. In addition, companies should also discard the technology that is no longer effective or serving the purpose of creating value for its customer. This is precisely why technology management as subject is necessary for the students and practicing managers in the industry.

---

[4]http://www.business-standard.com/article/companies/have-biyani-and-friends-slowed-e-retailers-116022201062_1.html, accessed 20 May 2016.

2.7 TECHNOLOGY IMPACT ON MANAGEMENT LAYERS

Let us now examine the impact of technology on various layers of management of a firm. If you look at Figure 2.3, it shows that any organisation will generally have three distinctive management layers such as:

(a) Strategic layer
(b) Tactical layer
(c) Operational layer

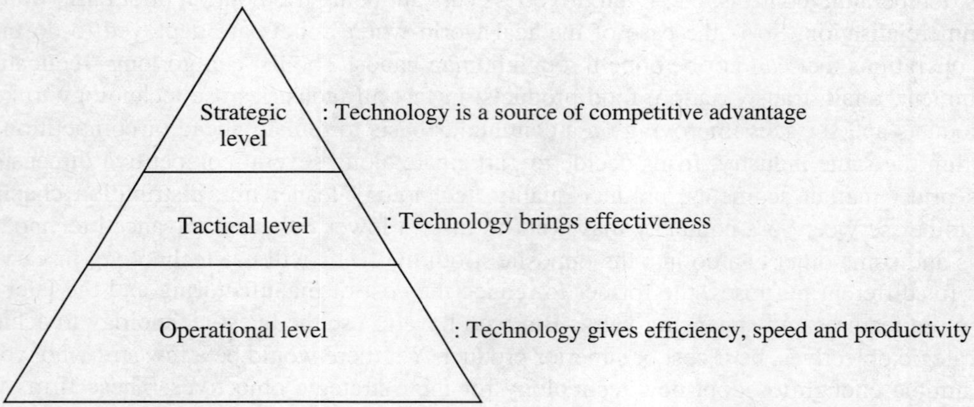

FIGURE 2.3 Role of Technology at Different Management Layers.

The role of technology at the lowest level, i.e., operational level is fairly apparent in most organisation. Technology enables efficiency and automation in task execution, monitoring processes and reporting results. Without using technology and doing all these manually may result in delay, inconsistency, slow speed and waste of resources. A number of industry domain specific technologies are used at this layer. For example, banks would use ATM for cash disbursement, airlines traffic controller use radar and railways automatic signalling to name a few.

At the tactical level, the role of the manager is to bring in effectiveness, i.e., doing the right things. The management role at this layer is to plan, monitor and manage resources. Here the role of technology is to help in better planning and effective utilisation of resources. Using information technology such as ERP, SCM, CRM and many others ensures effective utilisation of resources and better planning leading to competitive advantage. Remember technology becomes a necessity at the lower two stages as no business can function without the aid of technology. Therefore, proper management of technology is anyway necessary at these two lower levels too.

At the strategic level, technology supports the firm's generic strategies such as cost leadership, focus or differentiation. Given the fact that technology can be copied by others quickly, leading firms resort to continuous innovation as an additional source of competitive advantage.

Cakmak and Tas[5] describe the role of information technology in Turkish construction industry and concluded that while cost reduction gives economic benefit leading to focusing in low cost strategy, technology can also be a source of new revenue, thereby producing more benefits. Technology savvy companies have made enormous gains by patenting new research and gaining commercial revenue out of new research, products or processes.

Cool & Dierickx[6], give an interesting example of pharma industry where the firms are categorised into making generic and proprietary drugs. The latter category invests a lot on R&D and comes out with new drugs discoveries and formulations of which they hold the patents of. Consequently, they are able to sell medicines at a higher price as long as the patent can be held by them under their name. These strategic groups of companies take a positioning strategy based on discovering and developing new (blockbuster) drugs which cost enormous amount of money to discover, long gestation time to commercialise, yet it also makes them hugely profitable after successful market launch. Generic companies, on the other hand, do not spend a lot of efforts on new product discovery and, therefore, are forced to produce non-differentiated low margin drugs.

Figure 2.4 shows them in a diagrammatic form.

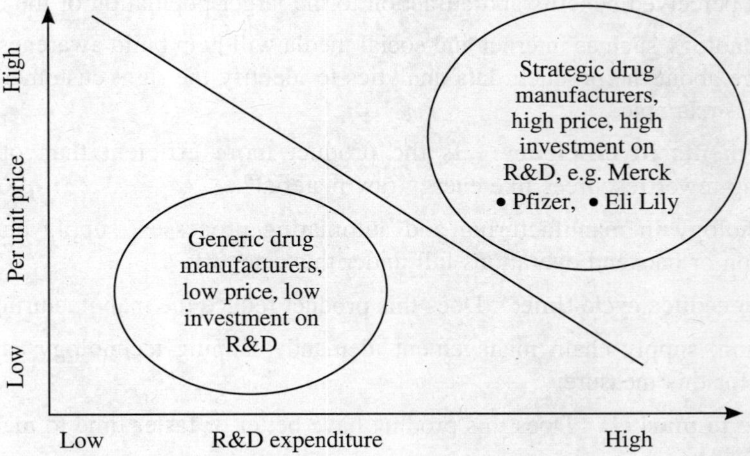

FIGURE 2.4 Strategies Adopted by Global Pharmaceutical Firms.

Remember that for any industry to gain strategic advantage it has to invest in superior products, newer products, better processes through continuous R&D. Unless this approach is taken, the firm will have to compete on cost for which technology will play a reasonable role but not a decisive role.

[5]World Applied Sciences Journal 18 (2): 274-285, 2012, ISSN 1818-4952, © IDOSI Publications, 2012 DOI: 10.5829/idosi.wasj.2012.18.02.744, The Use of Information Technology on Gaining Competitive Advantage in Turkish Contractor Firms Author: Pinar Irlayici Cakmak and Elcin Tas, Istanbul Technical University, Faculty of Architecture, Taskisla, Taksim, Istanbul, Turkey. **Tel: +90 212 2931300, Fax: +90 212 2514895.**

[6]Cool, K. and Dierickx, I. 1993, Rivalry, strategic groups, and firm performance. Strategic Management Journal, 14(1), 47–59.

2.8 LINKING THE ROLE OF TECHNOLOGY IN PRODUCT AND PROCESS DEVELOPMENT

Using the example of pharma industry as described in the earlier section, we can understand the role of technology in product development. Technology helps in not only coming out with breakthrough products in any industry but also creating products which are more marketable. A better product and process of its manufacturing is not easily replicable because the ingrained know-how and do-how is not easily replicable even though you may buy the same machine for producing a product. This combination of technology with process and people of the firm forms the basis of competitive advantage. Process based technologies form core competencies of the firms as they are built over a period of time gradually and cannot be easily replicated by the competition.

Cooper and Kleinschmidt[7] in their seminal article mention the following measures for the success of new product development initiative. Let us see the role of technology by citing a few examples for each of these measures.

- **High market share:** Can the product help increase the firm's market share due to increased perceived benefits and attraction to the larger population of the customers?

  Here technology such as internet and social media will help build awareness, dissimilate knowledge about the product; data analytics to identify the right customer segment can be taken as example.

- **Improvements in efficiency:** Is the product more efficient than others thereby consuming fewer resources like energy raw material?

  All technology in manufacturing and automating processes, supply chain logistics, distribution or backend operations fall under this category.

- **Ability to reduce cycle time:** Does this product reduce the manufacturing cycle time?

  Automation, supply chain management, demand planning technology can be seen as example for this measure.

- **Fast time to market:** Does this product have better or faster time to market?

  CAD/CAM and CAE, design automation, collaborative tools are examples of technology used to support this measure.

- **Profitability:** Is producing product which has better profit margin due to higher benefits perceived by the customer leading to higher price and lower cost?

  Profitability can be increased by reducing cost and increasing margin by adding more value to the product and services. All technologies that help in cost reduction fall under this category. In addition, CRM and technology enabling self-service features can be taken as an example.

- **Opening up new windows of opportunity:** Is it leading to new opportunity for the firm to reach out to new customer segments or industry?

[7] Cooper, Robert G. and Elks J. Kleinschmidt (2000), "New Product Performance: What distinguishes the star products", Australian Journal of Management, Vol. 25, No. 1, 17–45.

Internet has truly revolutionalised access to market for product producing companies especially those which can be digitised. Even physical products can be markets without much cost and new customers can be solicited at distant markets.

- **Technical success:** This refers to introduction of new technology for the product.

New technology introduction has huge potential for market expansion. For example, solar powered vehicles like Tesla have huge market and customer is vying to buy this car as soon as it can be delivered. Companies like Uber, Ola, etc., have shown how mobile app technology can meet the customers need of hiring cabs anywhere any time, thus creating a huge opportunity for cab drivers as well as to these companies.

2.9 ROLE OF TECHNOLOGY IN INNOVATION

Peter Drucker, a renowned management guru has famously opined that ***Marketing and innovation create value, all the rest are costs.*** Innovation is adding new features to a firm's products or services to bring novelty and enhanced benefit to the customer. Innovation is a tool to create value which is helped by the technology. Technology has an important role to play in bringing innovation in not only product but also process and services. By innovation the customer wants something new and of added value.

Technology when suitably applied to innovate for business purposes and customer needs always creates something unique. Technology in itself is not enough unless this application is done for meeting customer needs and solving business problems. A recent example of innovation done by Domino's Pizza using technology can be sought here to explain the relationship. When the company started getting criticism in the social media and online forums, they decided to use online tools to listen to their customers, understand them, seek feedback and in this process create a better pizza and a better experience. This included online ordering tool for pizza, allowing customers to pick and choose the combinations, tracking its progress and finally giving their feedback. The innovation in this case was in the area of better communication that gave them phenomenal results. In fact, they hold 53% online-ordering market share for the pizza category in several countries including Australia, India, etc. All this is due to their innovative use of IT capabilities.

When we use technology for innovation, it leads to business expansion by finding new opportunities for growth, creating products for new customer segments and markets. Selling shampoo in ₹ 2 plastic film sachets instead of a bottle was huge market expansion talked about in business circles. High quality branded shampoo is now affordable by masses who can spend ₹ 2 but not ₹ 200 to buy a bottle. Unless the sachet producing technology was applied to a customer need for new market, this revolution would not have come. Sachets were available for ages but were used for premium herbs, perfume, potpourri, etc. but their application for such need was nothing but a great innovation. Successful companies relentlessly use technology to support and enhance their market differentiators. ICICI bank, Kotak Mahindra bank and a few others always surprise their customers and competitions by launching new services using new technology ahead of others. To summarise, the driver of technology-led innovation comes from deeper knowledge of the business problem, customer needs and of course knowledge of technology to address them. When all three are put together, a new innovation comes to light.

Technology also gives opportunities to identify new or hidden needs. Adding a camera in cell phone was a great idea for people to click photographs as and when they needed to capture precious moments. Now mobile phones have become the centre of an individual activity; a mobile phone carries address book, helps in accessing mails, social networking, finding driving directions, acts as reminder and host of other features which are still evolving.

One of the welcome features of technology-led innovation is that it makes the product and services more affordable and widely deployable. Mass production has made possible for millions of users to use a product at an affordable price. Technology-led innovation also helps in greater efficiency, lower costs, lower emissions, less noise and requires less space. All this leads to saving precious environment resources as well.

Take the case of health care that has innovated itself using technology in a variety of ways, right from disease prevention, diagnosis to treatment. Technology-led innovation in health care has significantly lowered the affordability to access world class health care. Citizens of many countries manage their vital health parameters such as diabetes using application in the cloud or track heart rate with a wearable sensor, or even perform an EKG using a smartphone app. The use of sequencing a human genome, which takes just a couple of days and offers incredible insight into disease prevention and targeted therapies, costs less than $5,000.[8] It is not very far when mind-controlled artificial limbs will be a reality and one can do 3-D printing of human organs.

2.10 FIVE FORCES CHANGING THE WORLD

If we take a look at the current environment, we will notice that the five major forces are changing the way businesses are being conducted in almost all industries. These are:

- mobility of the workforce
- use of powerful analytics tools
- use of social media
- rapid progress of cloud computing and
- cyber intelligence.

All of these forces are unleashing the power of sustained innovations in business processes, products, customer service and expanding to new markets. All such innovations are leading to improved productivity and increased efficiency to reduce costs.

2.11 INNOVATION AND TECHNOLOGY ARE INTERDEPENDENT

In majority of the cases, innovation and technology are interdependent. Technology ushers newer innovation and the desire to innovate leads to new technology discovery. Innovations can be both sustained and disruptive, the later is an example of something new coming up in the market that changes the existing models. The use of digital cameras, eliminating the use of photo film camera, wiped some of the leading film camera producers is an example of disruptive innovation. E-book readers are going to revolutionise book publishing and there are many other

[8] http://nextrends.swissnexsanfrancisco.org/innovationinglobalhealth/accessed 14012014

such examples. All these disruptive technologies have imprint in bringing in newer innovations. These are new ways of generating value. It is recommended that managers should focus their energy in exploring, anticipating and conducting repeated proof of concept in adopting new technology to bring innovation in their businesses.

The role of technology in innovation can be summarised as:

(a) Technology helps in bringing in efficiency and driving down cost.
(b) Technology helps to make the product or services more affordable.
(c) Innovations such as social media, 3-D printing, etc., also create new opportunities and enhanced value for the consumers using technology.
(d) While technology can enable innovations, it is finally the business and customer needs that drive it.
(e) People factor cannot be ignored in managing such technology-led innovations as ultimately the people are the ones who use, implement and maintain technology.
(f) Technology also leads to business model innovations. A good example is the massive proliferation of outsourcing of services to low cost country due to information and communication technology innovations.

Technology development and adoption in the market follows a cycle of initial accelerated development followed by slow down. Technology manager must take a timely decision to invest, adopt or discard the technology based on the market adoption cycle.

2.12 TECHNOLOGY IMPACT IN DEFINING ORGANISATIONS STRATEGIES

Most firms are now competing at the global scale. At the global scale, just competing on cost or availability is not enough. These global firms need to continuously innovate in every area of their operations, product features, and its quality and customer services. While for many industries, technology innovation forms the basis of strategy, for the rest, it remains the most important enabler for the firm's competition. For example, a fast changing technology product like mobile handset, the competition is on the basis of newer technology introduction and adoption. But for matured industry like transportation, automobile and airlines, etc., technology can enable them to be more efficient, provide better customer service and other value added features at an affordable cost. Even low technology industry such as steel, the role of technology is well established in squeezing waste out of its production process. Technology is helping in all industries to remain agile and flexible in making suitable changes.

It may appear that technology is always changing and changing fast, hence its adoption cannot be planned or predicted, but this is not true. Since technology is changing fast and is unpredictable, firms must anticipate a course of action and quickly adopt the change. We will see this happening for many industries and leading firms, which did not respond to the new technology changes fast enough, faced almost near decimation in the marketplace. Nokia, for example, did not welcome the use of touch screen technology and surrendered its market dominance to Samsung and several other new players.

Technology giant Microsoft adopts a combination of strategy process that is both formal and flexible[9]. This has given rise to faster reaction to embrace new technology at a faster rate. Many of its successful products such as Internet Explorer or the Xbox became successful because the middle managers were empowered to work on these products and take them to stage of commercial success. Technology gives strategic flexibility to firm which is important these days for global competition. Rothaermel[10] opines that technology planning has now become like the planning done by the fire department of a city. The city fireman who saves our life, do resort to meticulous planning without knowing where the fire would take place. They visualise various scenarios and accordingly prepare themselves. Similarly, in the case of technology planning for strategic nature, a firm must visualise several opportunities (or threat) which may come from unforeseen sources of technology and be ready to deploy (or counter) them to their advantage. This will demand continuous innovation using technology and hence continuous change in the product and processes will be needed.

New product introduction in the marketplace has become a significant parameter to measure the vitality of a firm. Leading companies like Apple, Samsung, 3M and P&G, etc., relentlessly measure the percentage of their revenue coming from new products as a measure of their success. Innovation using technology in manufacturing, distribution, logistics and services process allows companies to maintain lower cost, better responses and improved services. Competition will surely imitate some of these, but by the time competitors copy these new introductions these leading firms in most cases come out with newer initiatives. Such response by the firm is possible only when they put a lot of emphasis on considering technology as a strategic differentiator and invest on their R&D efforts.

Technology is after all the new sources of strategic differentiator, or at least helps in creating one! No one should have any doubt.

2.13 ROLE OF GOVERNMENT IN TECHNOLOGY DEVELOPMENT

The role of government in technology development is manifold. At apex level, it is expected to formulate policies, rules and regulations to promote technology and innovations within the country. The government also undertakes funding for new projects or those where the initial cost is prohibitive for any private players.

We will take an example of how the government has in the past participated in technology development. Indian government invested in setting up research labs and new technology companies (popularly known as PSUs) in 50s and 60s of the last century. Successive Indian Governments have started several technology development missions since Indian's independence. Ushering steel making by SAIL and power equipment manufacturing by BHEL is one such example. Telecommission was established in mid-805 to extend digital telecommunications to every corner of the country, including remote villages. These efforts led to the establishment of institutions like Centre for the Development of Telematics (C-DOT), an autonomous telecom R&D organisation. Products like Rural Automatic Exchange (RAX) are well-known developments

[9] Hill, C.W. L., and Jones, G.R. (2007). *Strategic Management Theory. An Integrated Approach* 7th ed. Boston: Houghton Mifflin.

[10] Frank, T., Rothaermel., COMPETITIVE ADVANTAGE IN TECHNOLOGY INTENSIVE INDUSTRIES. Technological Innovation: Generating Economic Results, Advances in the Study of Entrepreneurship, Innovation and Economic Growth, Volume 18, 201–225, Chapter 7.

by C-DOT, done more than 25 years ago. (See more in the SALT 2.2 Story of RAX.) One of the key lessons for such technology development was its appropriateness for the Indian markets. Western telecom manufacturers were capable of supplying large capacity sophisticated switches but they would have needed much better environment like clean atmosphere, uninterrupted power, air-conditioning, etc., to run them. Technology should always match the need of the mosses never more, never less.

The Government of United States of America also funded a supercar project in late 90s to enable the U.S. car makers compete with their Japanese counterparts. (see SALT 2.3). But this was not successful.

SALT 2.2 Story of Rural Automatic Exchange (RAX) 1986

RAX was a welcome initiative for communication starved India in mid 1980s. Designed for Indian conditions of high ambient temperatures, dust and unreliable power, it needed no air-conditioning. Its latest digital switching technology with microprocessor-based controllers without any moving parts not only gave protection from dust which was causing failure to the older electromechanical Strowger and Crossbar exchanges in India. When first launched it was named 128 P RAX, a low capacity 128-ports switch. Located in remote areas and with its 24 analogue trunks connected it to a larger exchange in a nearby city, these exchanges could cater to a total of 80 subscribers. Yes just 80 subscribers, this too was a big relief where there were no connection. Millions of villagers in rural India used their first ever call through C-DOT RAX which acquired a legendary status in no time. This technology from C-DOT was extended to several manufacturers who went into RAX production and March 1993 over 10000 RAXes were produced. RAX was exported to other developing countries like Vietnam, Nepal and Bangladesh and upgraded to 256P, doubling its capacity.

Discussion Questions

1. When and why the government should intervene in technology development?
2. Do you agree in these words "technology has to be appropriate for use"? Why and why not?
3. What are the lessons learnt from the above story?

SALT 2.3 Failure of Super Car and Success of Toyota Prius

The oil crisis of 1070s shook governments around the world. The impact on economy was much serious especially for automobile companies. Many governments wanted to invest in the alternative fuels for propelling automobiles or develop fuel efficient engines. Millions of dollars were granted by the governments around the world to car makers.

In 1993 the US Government established a Partnership for a New Generation of Vehicles (PNGV) nicknamed Supercar projects after the President of America met the CEOs of Chrysler, GM and Ford and gave $1.5 billion in federal grants[11]. The idea of the government was to develop a clean car giving 80 miles per gallon of efficiency. PNGV or Supercar project was very ambitious with high expectations. It was expected that by 1998 the most promising technology will be selected, by 2000 each of the manufacturer would present a concept car followed with production prototype by 2004. While GM, Ford and Chrysler focused on diesel hybrid and

[11] http://www.hybridcars.com/history-of-hybrid-vehicles/, accessed 20 March 2016.

diesel became the fuel of choice. Best brains in the automobile world were drafted in the project and U.S. department of energy announced in 2000 that these three manufacturers have reached the first milestone of producing concept car which can give 72 to 80 miles per gallon. However, the industry leaders were privately sharing that the cost of the car would be nearly $7500 more as compared with the standard gasoline engine car. In January 2001, after George Bush's administration came to power, it discontinued the ambitious Supercar project by stating that it is not in line with the current market realities.

Toyota, was excluded from the PNGV project despite its representation to the US government to include it. Consequently, it created its own hybrid vehicle under a secret project called G21, (Global Car for the 21st Century) and produced Prius, a hybrid vehicle. Toyota projected the green credential of Prius rather than its fuel efficiency and kept its price $2000. Prius was a huge success in the marketplace after its launch in 2000. It also surpassed a million vehicles sale world wide by 2007.

Discussion Questions

1. Does co-optition (where competitors cooperate as well as compete) proved to be a bad idea for the Supercar project?
2. Why Toyota succeeded where Supercar project failed?

These two stories bring two different perspectives of government role in technology development and innovation. Failure and success apart, both these were great initiative for a noble cause to eliminate problems for the citizens of the country. But the first one was to meet the basic necessity and the second to serve the growing needs of higher sections of the society. More discussions on these two cases are beyond the scope of the book but are worth doing in the class room especially why the second one failed?

In the recent years, solar power R&D of other renewable energy sources are encouraged by many governments. The role of government is for both creating supply-push policies to increase R&D activities and demand-pull policies that support the development of markets for emerging technologies.

Government technology policy-making process takes into account the private sector and develops processes that intertwined in complex ways. A case in point is the Ministry for International Trade and Industry (MITI), a Ministry of the Government of Malaysia that has developed a wide range of long-term strategic plans, in association with the private sector.

Invariably, national level technology policy are formulated by the governments, especially, for sectors such as defence, space research, nuclear energy, environmental protection and now cyber security. The government provides funding for R&D and supports scientific and technological innovations in such cases.

In civil usage of technology, the role of government is to provide policy guidelines to protect interest of environment, countries security, etc., while promoting the development and use of new technologies. Liberalisation and divestment has led to many technology-based utilities (e.g., telecommunications, energy and water supply) which have been privatised. In such cases, the role of government has reduced in R&D and innovation for such sectors. Yet government technology policy helps to influence and steer private company policies and investments. The government takes the cause of technology development at national or international level to address issues of environmental sustainability, countries defiance/security requirements or to increase national industrial competitiveness.

The government also makes an impact in creating human capital to promote technology-led innovations. This includes running programmes and education initiatives to skill people in the areas of technology innovation. Physical facilities like setting up innovation incubation labs have been done by the Government of India in several IITs/NITs/IIITs and other institutions. In addition, government-run research institutions continuously work with industry to innovate their products or services. Setting up software technology parks, MSME institutes and setting up SEZs are few such initiatives that help innovation of business and industry. Government provides liberals grants, soft loans and technical as well as marketing and business development support. Government agencies organise trade fairs, promote competition and award innovative products and services to recognise the good work done by the industry which acts as source of encouragement for the innovators. The recent make in India initiative is a case in point where Indian governments along with its state counterparts are promoting entrepreneurs with loans, grants, trade fairs, technology exchange programmes, etc. In order to meet the industry needs of skills, the Indian government has launched skilling India programme. Students are advised to visit sites such as http://www.makeinindia.com/home and http://www.skillingindia.com/ to know more about these initiatives.

However, the latest trend is towards less direct involvement by the government and its role is limited to act as a facilitator rather than direct actor. Most technology projects are led by private sector players or in partnership with government. Policy making bodies have larger participation from the industry representatives. The role of government is now getting limited to give broad direction to a restricted range of technological issues.

In short, the role of government in technology innovation should cover the following:

- Encourage public-private partnerships to help successful technological innovation.
- Grants for R&D in universities and research institution act as laboratory for more risky research and incubating innovative high-tech companies.
- Portfolios and performance measurement of government R&D which should always be biased towards long term and riskier investments which are too risky for firms to undertake alone.
- Demand-pull policies which should help creating market for technological innovations.
- Niche market creation, initial market where the pilot projects and new developments can be tested.
- Complementary and enabling infrastructure for making attractive to the private sector. This may include physical as well as telecommunication infrastructure.
- Evaluating risk of technology on country's security or environment and forming appropriate policies.
- Creating a competitive environment to breed further R&D and innovation, not monopolising technology and restricting its adoption.
- Protecting for intellectual property rights by framing appropriate laws and grievance redressal mechanism.

SALT 2.4 Role of US Government in the success of iPhone

If you are asked a question as to who is responsible for the innovative and iconic success of iPhone, the answer may be to attribute to the company Apple or its promoter late Steve Jobs. But analysed deeper, one would notice that there is an invisible hand[12] of the US government, its policy makers and the infrastructure that it created such innovations to proliferate. Let us see how.

iPhone launched in 2007 was culmination of several features of communications and information technologies that were initiated and nurtured by the state. Its microchips are a net result of the US military and space programmes which built breakthrough technology in the 1960s. The sheer volume of production brought down the cost 50 times lower.

Mobile communication was supported and sustained by the US military and many of the developments are due to research happening in Department of Defence labs. Internet itself was developed and funded by the Defence Department's Advanced Research Projects Agency in the 1960s and 1970s.

GPS was originally created and deployed by the military's NAVSTAR satellite programme in the 1980s and 1990s.

Much liked multi-touch screen of iPhone's was first developed by University of Delaware researchers supported by the US government.

Yet most of us feel that iPhone is entirely produced by Apple!

2.14 LINKAGE BETWEEN TECHNOLOGY DEVELOPMENT AND COMPETITION

Technology development and competition have interdependent relationship. Competition is a cause and effect of technology development. Firms invest in developing technology to outsmart competition. Role of technology in economic growth and competitiveness is well-known. Some of the fastest growing economies in the last 50 years undoubtedly were successful due to massive dosage of technology, be it their infrastructure, defence preparedness, manufacturing including electronics goods, information and communication technology, space research or scientific research. Their achievement has been a mix of following a well-defined technology strategy and encouraging healthy open competition to benefit the first movers and also support the overall growth of technology development.

Recently Honda launched a new car named Amaze which has superior technology at a competitive price and it resulted into this product being the most sought after in its segment. Followed by this launch, they made significant changes in the fuel economy of its bestselling car Honda City as well. This change has further helped the best selling Honda City gain a pole position in its segment.

Please note that technology has become a prime driver of globalisation. A firm's competitiveness can be seriously compromised if it is not keeping pace with the rate of technological

[12]http://thebreakthrough.org/archive/american_innovation, accessed 14 Jan. 2014.

change. Technology-led innovation of products of services of any firm is a pre-requisite to participate effectively in globalisation. Those firms or countries that ignore this aspect of conducting their business will seriously be impacted.

Take the case of the telecom industry of India which every one is a customer and has seen its development for the past two decades. The growth of the telecom industry in India has led to several foreign players who manufacture state-of-art switching equipment as well as service providers to find business. The same cannot be said about domestic manufacturers or state-owned service providers who did not keep pace with technology-led innovation and development and, therefore, are not able to sell their products in telecom segment. This is also true for manufacturing industry, e.g., automobile, light engineering, etc., of many countries which has to surrender its advantage to other countries as they could not keep pace with technologically advanced products or services developed abroad.

In nineteenth century, Industrial Revolution caused increase in productivity; per capita income of countries went through the changes. Large growth due to development of the steam engine to harness fossil fuel energy to productive tasks enabled the Industrial Revolution to accelerate in Europe and America—enhanced production technology, building of infrastructure of railroads removed transportation bottlenecks and supported economies of scale. These countries became far more competitive than those who did not adopt the new technology fast enough. Indian cotton industries' sudden loss of eminence in world market and competitiveness in early 20th century is a case in point. Further transformations through repeated radical inventions, electricity, electronics, etc., further led to the development of industry and the business in western economies.

In the recent times, the development of information and communication technology, social media, cloud computing, etc., has given new impetus of technology-led competiveness. Those countries who have not embraced them quickly and effectively have found advantages slipping from them. Many researchers[13] have pointed that the phenomenon rise of the U.S. economy is attributed to proper management of technology research, devotement and adoption by promoting open competitions. America is the place where the first R&D lab created by Thomas Alva Edison was hailed as the first industrial research centre followed by a number of high profile research laboratories by private, government and defence establishments. All these efforts have taken the U.S. economy to the forefront of technology leadership of the world undoubtedly.

On the other hand, all opportunities are not lost for the developing countries. These developing countries have an advantage that they need not start from the basic research and reach to the stage developed countries have. They can join adopting the technology development and join the development curve at a later stage. They can quickly adopt and scale, innovate and create new value proposition. Indian IT Services companies are a precise example where these companies joined the new technology curve at a later stage and by sheer dedication to create better value proposition have become the world leaders in this segment. TCS, Infosys and many other Indian companies have left behind their global peers in this segment, at least up till now. So is the case with Chinese and Taiwanese electronics firms who have not done too much of basic research initially but were fast enough in adoption, scaling and innovating technologies coming out of western research labs. The results of these sectors of these countries are well-known.

---

[13] Technology, globalisation, and international competitiveness: Challenges for developing countries By Carl Dahlman http://www.un.org/esa/sustdev/publications/industrial_development/1_2.pdf, accessed 16 Jan. 2014.

Do not think that a developing country can achieve major success in technology R&D by just setting up few laboratories of technology research or just copying technology developed by their western peers. They would need to build technology development and adoption ecosystem. This would include several supporting activities such as encouraging the use of new technology in the domestic market, continuous improvement of products, processes and innovating business models. They have to focus on new technology acquisition, its adaptation, further dissemination and usage for local situations. Interestingly, fast growing Asian countries like Hong Kong, Singapore, Indonesia, Malaysia, Thailand and Taiwan as well as BRICM countries (Brazil, Russia, India, China and Maxico) grew their competitiveness through a two-pronged approach, using technology acquisition from the developed world as well as internal development of technology.

In case of India, its policy of liberalisation of economy, FDI investment in science and technology has helped improve its competitiveness and led to higher GDP growth rate from 6% in 2001 to 10% in 2010[14]. Any firm that wants to remain competitive has to initiate improvement of their products and services in the fast growing globally competitive and liberalised economy. A large number of Indian private industries have made significant investments in R&D that helped them produce world competitive products or services.

The challenge exists for both market leaders and market follower firms while choosing to invest in technology development to keep the competitive challenge at bay. The former may have money to deploy but no motivation to implement it. The market follower firm, which may include small and medium enterprises and start ups, may be motivated to deploy new technology to race ahead of competition but may not have adequate funds to deploy. This is the situation where the role of government and some "supra-state" (like European Unions, SARCC, ASEAN, etc.,) come in to support new technology development to increase the overall competitiveness of the industry.

2.15 MANAGING RESEARCH AND DEVELOPMENT (R&D)

Management of R&D is gaining importance in most organisations in the recent times. The purpose of this function is to build capabilities for coming out with new products, build a knowledge base for addressing competitive threat. This function has long-term orientation and lacks near-term results. The outcome of R&D efforts remain uncertain, difficult to measure its success, the rates of which are not very high. Yet this is an important function that top management has to endorse and support them as it impacts across the function.

The function of the R&D unit is to bring in new products and services or to bring in innovation to the existing ones. R&D function is also responsible for improving current technologies, discovering new technologies and identifying potentials of new technology. These could pose as a threat as well as opportunities for the firm. R&D units are also responsible for technology acquisition, technology transfer, collaboration and monetisation of technologies. R&D unit includes functions of technological planning for the firm. They undertake projects that help the firm to develop capabilities for the future which give new strategic direction. Their approach is to consider both technological development opportunities and their business values. The R&D activities should always be aligned with the corporate strategy and linked with overall business plan on which organisation is working.

---

[14] India's Growth rate has fallen to 5% in 2013 for host of factors such a global slow down, inflation, etc.

Most successful R&D units do not work in isolation but have closer interaction with the operating units. Since they have to conduct market feasibility and trial runs, they have established close linkages with the sales and marketing team. They have to work with the manufacturing unit to develop tools and technologies for manufacturing and finally with other support units like finance, HR and IT to garner financial, human and IT resources for successful implementation of new products or processes.

R&D is also industry specific and depends on the area. For example, developing a new aircraft may take 8-10 years or more and finding a new drug for life-threatening disease could be a decade long process but a new electronics product may be launched in the matter of 2–3 quarters. Accordingly, the money spent on R&D and resources required to conduct the R&D vary. Pharmaceutical companies aiming for new drug discovery are known to spend up to 15% of their turnover on R&D. Banks, on the other hand, could spend as low as 1% of their turnover. Software product companies spend 7–8% of their turnover for new product development and R&D. More about this topic will be covered in subsequent chapters.

2.16 MANAGING INTELLECTUAL PROPERTY

We have discussed the need for developing new technology and making continuous innovation as a corner stone for the success of a firm in the current times. However, the process of converting an idea to useful products, field trials and final launch is a time-consuming process. The question arises as to how the idea and all the intellectual work that has gone into can be protected so that the organisation is able to take advantage and it is not stolen by a competition. In this section, we will touch upon this very issue of managing intellectual work also called intellectual property or intellectual asset for the firm's advantage.

In brief, intellectual property is a term referred to as intangible products of the human brain that take the form of new inventions of products, components, devices, compositions, plants or designs for an equipment. This also refers to creative work like publication, computer software, video images or works of art such as paintings, murals, etc. For business purposes, the new design, new formulations/composition as well as software fall under the category of intellectual property.

While works of art, written documents and software get automatically copyrighted when created, they can also be registered with government authorities by paying fee before filing any infringement law suits. Such copyright lasts the life of the author plus 70 years or 95 years from publication or 120 years from creation.

New inventions, designs, methods, processes and product features, etc. are granted patents to the developers who can gain commercial advantage of its use and can prevent others from using it without permission.

A firm can also protect its symbol, monograms and words associated with the names of the product or company by taking a trademark license. Names like Apple, Motorola, Coca-Cola are all trademark protected and can be renewed indefinitely after 10 years of gaining of the rights by the competent authorities.

In addition, there could be trade secrets that a firm may not like to make it public and keep within itself under lock and key. Coke formula is one such trade secret.

These could be specialised knowledge about manufacturing using formulas, proportions, and can be maintained as secret where patents cannot ensure its protection and from being copied.

Loss of intellectual property to competition can compromise a firm's competitiveness besides losing enormous sum of money spent on its development. By jealously guarding intellectual property, a firm can not only hold monopoly of the products or design and, therefore, loosing competitive edge in the market place but earn substantial revenue by allowing its usage by other firms at a fee. The later is very common in the pharmaceutical industry where the leading firms do let other manufacturers to use their formulation at a fee or after accepting royalty.

Management of intellectual property is done at three levels:

(a) **Creating awareness:** Among employees, designers, managers and researchers about what constitutes an intellectual property and what precautions are needed to protect it from being known or copied by the outsiders.

(b) **Creating an IP management framework:** This refers to creating a process as to how various units of the firm will assess, document and disclose their intellectual work in the form it becomes an intellectual property. Typically, this task is driven by close knit group who work on behalf of the orientation and guide its team in filing patents, making IP/invention disclosures and obtaining licenses from the competent authorities.

(c) **Monetisation, legal protection for infringement:** This is the post-development activity wherein the IP is further shared at a fee with others or a legal recourse is taken in case someone else copies it or uses it.

The last one is more legal and commercial activity done by a team that has knowledge of law of IP protection. Every country has developed certain laws to protect the interest of the inventors and designers which can be applied if their rights are being infringed upon.

The challenge in the IP management is also because of the ability to copy, duplicate with minor modification or change the form of the object to circumvent the law. In the internet world, several cases keep coming up at regular intervals where in holders of intellectual property fight with those who have copied their patented design, product features, software codes, etc.

2.17 COMPETITIVE ADVANTAGE IN THE AI/GEN AI LANDSCAPE: REDEFINING VALUE CREATION, DELIVERY, AND CAPTURE

Competitive advantage, traditionally defined by a firm's ability to offer greater perceived value than rivals through superior products, lower costs, or unique market positions, is being fundamentally redefined by AI and Generative AI. Michael Porter's generic strategies—cost leadership, differentiation, and focus—remain relevant, but AI provides unprecedented means to achieve and sustain them.

AI and Gen AI enable hyper-personalization, a powerful new dimension of differentiation. Instead of merely offering a unique product, businesses can now leverage AI to craft unique *experiences* tailored to individual customer needs and preferences in real-time. This moves differentiation from broad market segments to individual consumers, potentially making mass customization the new competitive battleground. For instance, AI algorithms can analyze a customer's browsing behavior, purchase history, and even intent to deliver highly targeted product recommendations, leading to higher conversion rates and increased customer satisfaction. This level of personalization is difficult for competitors to imitate without similar AI capabilities and data insights.

Simultaneously, AI drives significant operational efficiencies, supporting cost leadership strategies. By automating repetitive, mundane tasks, AI frees up employees for more complex work, boosting productivity and reducing errors. This allows firms to produce goods or services at lower costs while maintaining or even improving quality. AI also facilitates the identification and targeting of new niche markets through tailored solutions, reinforcing the focus strategy. The ability of AI to impact both differentiation (through novel products and personalization) and cost leadership (through process optimization and automation) suggests that leading firms may leverage AI to achieve a "best of both worlds" scenario, effectively redefining the traditional trade-offs inherent in generic strategies.

2.18 AI/GEN AI'S ROLE IN PRODUCT AND PROCESS DIFFERENTIATION AND COST LEADERSHIP

Generative AI plays a pivotal role in both differentiating products and processes and driving down costs. In product development, Gen AI accelerates the creation of new products and services. It can optimize product designs, making them lighter, more efficient, or more aesthetically pleasing. For example, Siemens engineers use AI to generate dozens of design options overnight, resulting in redesigned parts that are 75% lighter and projects completed 30% faster. This capability allows for rapid iteration and exploration of design possibilities that human teams might miss.

In terms of process improvement, AI streamlines manufacturing operations and supply chains. AI-powered robotics enhances warehouse operations and logistics, minimizing errors and reducing processing times. Predictive analytics, driven by AI, enables companies to anticipate demand, optimize inventory levels, and identify potential disruptions before they occur, leading to significant reductions in logistics costs (up to 15%) and improvements in inventory accuracy (up to 35%). These efficiencies directly contribute to cost leadership. The dual impact of Gen AI on both differentiation (through novel designs and personalization) and cost leadership (through process optimization and automation) creates a strategic opportunity for firms. It allows them to pursue a hybrid strategy more effectively than before, transcending the traditional "either/or" choice and gaining a multifaceted competitive advantage.

2.19 STRATEGIC ACTIONS ENABLED BY AI/GEN AI (E.G., HYPER-PERSONALIZATION, PREDICTIVE OPERATIONS)

AI and Generative AI enable a new class of strategic actions that transform business operations and customer engagement. These actions move beyond mere efficiency gains to create fundamental shifts in how value is created and delivered.

One prominent strategic action is **AI-powered customer service**. Companies like Klarna have deployed AI assistants that handle a significant portion of customer chats (2.3 million conversations in one month, equivalent to 700 human agents), drastically reducing wait times and improving customer satisfaction. This allows human agents to focus on more complex, empathetic interactions.

In marketing and sales, AI enables hyper-personalization at scale. Marketing teams use AI to write a significant portion of marketing materials (30% at many companies), finishing work almost twice as fast and cutting content costs by 30-50%. Examples like Bayer's use of AI for marketing resulted in an 85% jump in clicks and 33% less cost per click. AI also transforms lead generation and sales workflows, with AI agents handling tasks from identifying prospects to personalizing outreach, leading to a leaner and more efficient sales process.

AI-assisted design is another critical strategic action, as seen with Siemens engineers using AI to generate design options and optimize parts for lighter weight and faster project completion. This accelerates product development cycles and fosters innovation.

Finally, **predictive operations** represent a significant strategic shift. AI-powered predictive analytics in supply chain management allows companies to anticipate disruptions and optimize performance with unprecedented precision. This moves operational strategy from reactive problem-solving to proactive, data-driven foresight, minimizing disruptions and optimizing resource allocation before problems arise. For instance, General Electric uses AI to predict equipment failures, enabling proactive maintenance and reducing machine downtime by 50%. This anticipatory management fundamentally alters how firms manage their operations, leading to enhanced resilience and competitive advantage.

2.20 SUMMARY

In this chapter, the role of technology as the source of competitive advantage was discussed. We started our discussion with defining competitive advantage which is a greater perceived value for a firm's products or services than its rivals. Then we described the sources of competitive advantage and where all it can come from where the technology can play its role. We also explained that technology remains a competitive necessity for any firm to remain efficient and effective besides being a source of competitive advantage. The key is in the innovative use of the technology by the firm to gain competitive advantage. Then we picked up the theme of technology as value creator and how technology plays an important role at every step of value creating process. The next inquiry was whether we can get competitive advantages through technology and how. We discussed the technology impact on management layers in any firm at all of its three distinctive layers such as strategic, tactical and operational level. We explained the role of technology at all these levels as that of strategy implementation, bringing in effectiveness and efficiency, respectively.We further linked the role of technology in product and process development. An important role of technology is to bring in innovation both sustained and disruptive for the firm and it was explained to our readers. This topic was summed up with describing technology impact in defining organisations strategies.

An important topic is to understand what role a government plays in technology development. The government provides funding for R&D and support scientific and technological innovations besides providing policy guidelines to protect interest of environment, countries security, etc. After this we established the linkage between technology development and competition.

Managing R&D is a key function a firm has to undertake in building capabilities for addressing competitive threat. Key concepts around this topic were discussed. A related topic managing intellectual property followed this discussion at the end.

Key Terms: Competitive advantage, Value creation, Value capturing, Technology strategy, Technology innovation, Technology development.

REVIEW QUESTIONS

1. Describe the role of technology as the source of competitive advantage. Why do we say that technology is also a competitive necessity for any firm?
   Answer: Sections 2.0 and 2.1
2. Establish that technology is a value creator and which plays an important role at every step of value creating process. You can draw the value chain of product or services firm and describe the impact at every stages of the value chain.
   Answer: Section 2.2
3. Can we get competitive advantages through technology? If yes, describe how.
   Answer: Section 2.3
4. Describe technology impact on various management layers in a firm.
   Answer: Section 2.4
5. Explain the role of technology in product and process development. What role does technology play in innovation as both sustained and disruptive for a firm?
   Answer: Sections 2.5 and 2.6
6. Describe technology impact in defining organisations strategies. Select any technology-led firm's successes to give your answer. **Answer:** Section 2.7
7. What are the roles a government plays in technology development? Establish the linkage between technology development and competition. **Answer:** Sections 2.8 and 2.9
8. How can a firm successfully manage R&D? How can a firm ensure that its intellectual property remains protected? **Answer:** Sections 2.10 and 2.11
9. What is the role of government in the growth of Indian IT industry? Trace these efforts since India's independence. **Answer:** Research the web
10. What are the initiatives needed by the government in the present times to promote technology-led innovations? Which sectors require government support for technology-led innovations? **Answer:** Research the web

ADDITIONAL READINGS

1. Value Chain for Services A new dimension of "Porter's Value Chain" (Published in the *IMS International Journal* – 2006), By Prof. Elisante ole Gabriel (PhD, Marketing) Lecturer–Mzumbe University, Faculty of Commerce, PO Box 6, Mzumbe, Morogoro, Tanzania, Visiting Professor of Strategic Marketing & Management – Finland, India, Australia & Kenya, E-mail: elisante_gabriel@yahoo.com http://www.olegabriel.com/publication-web-Gab/Value_Chain_for_Services.pdf, accessed 07 Jan. 2014.
2. Drucker, P. (1994), The theory of business, *Harvard Business Review*, 75 (September–October), pp. 95–105.

3. Hill, C.W.L., and Rothaermel, F.T. (2003). The performance of incumbent firms in the face of radical technological innovation, *Academy of Management Review*, 28(2), pp. 257–274.

4. Porter, M.E. (1985), Competitive advantage: Creating and sustaining superior performance New York: Free Press.

5. Porter, M.E. (1996), What is strategy? *Harvard Business Review*, 77 (November–December), pp. 61–78.

6. Grove, A.S. (1996), Only the paranoid survive: How to exploit the crisis points that challenge every company and career, New York: Currency Doubleday.

Chapter 3

Technology Management

Any sufficiently advanced technology is indistinguishable from magic…. Arthur C. Clarke Profiles of the Future: An Inquiry Into the Limits of the Possible.

At the end of this chapter, we will learn:

- What is technology management?
- What are the components of technology management?
- How to choose the right management strategies for technology?
- Technology management guiding principles
- Major components of technology management
- Technology management lifecycle
- Different perspectives of technology management

3.1 INTRODUCTION

Technology management is an evolving subject. While choosing a strategy defines our intent but the major task of implementation remains where the role of management comes in. One of the foremost questions now is to answer how we will implement technology strategy keeping the larger strategy of the business in mind. While business strategy does not change every day, the same is not true with technology. This chapter is focused to bring in the actionable aspects covered under technology management. We will precisely answer what technology management is and how a firm decides to adopt a particular technology strategy to gain and maintain competitive advantage. For this we will define the process of technology management and help our readers get familiar with the dos and don'ts of this important topic. We will also discuss the advantages and disadvantages of various technology management approach adopted by leaders as well as successful followers of any industry.

We will first define the components of technology management. Once we understand this, then we will discuss as to how we can chose the right approach. We will then identify technology management lifecycle stages. The chapter will also cover different perspectives of technology management.

3.2 WHAT IS TECHNOLOGY MANAGEMENT?

While technology strategy is a long-term plan and policies that a firm adopts with respect to technology decisions in line with its business strategy, its execution is covered by technology management. For example, if the firm's strategy is to produce low cost products for the mass consumer market, it would adopt technology strategy that lowers the cost of products and processes. While the business of the firm and at times products or services do not change over time, the underlying technology changes continuously. Technology may have to be upgraded or replaced following the larger technology strategy guidelines. Alternatively, if the firm wants to produce niche and differentiated products, then it needs to adopt cutting edge technology to make differentiated or unique products for which customers are willing to pay premium prices. Technology management principles will come into play here too to keep upgrading technology that enables making superior products.

Since technology strategy covers the entire value creation chain covering all processes along them, its management has to be done carefully. For example, if a firm wants to reach out to new markets and new customers, it would need to plan technology for processes that are required for supply chain, on-line selling, shipment management, etc. Technology management would play its role in scaling up the existing technology to new deployments at a faster pace.

Figure 3.1 shows the relationship of technology management with other interrelated areas such as business strategy, business processes, technology strategy and technology management processes.

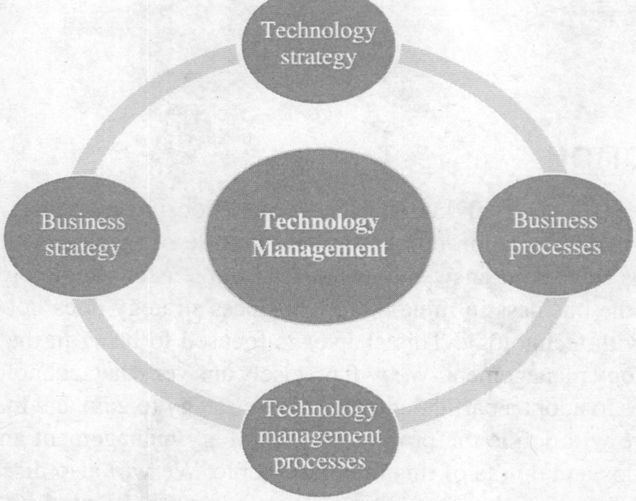

FIGURE 3.1 Technology Management is Interdisciplinary.

The technology management processes (as shown in Figure 3.2) are

- **Technology foresight:** Refers to crystal grazing new technologies that are initial stages of research
- **Technology identification:** Refers to identifying technology that can be adopted for product or processes of the firm
- **Technology evaluation:** There may be several contending technology for meeting the same objective with various advantages and disadvantages, this process does their evaluation
- **Technology selection:** Based on the evaluation report, business needs and strategy, the technology is selected
- **Technology adoption:** Refers to implementing technology in actual processes or in the products
- **Technology audit:** Existing technology in use are required to be evaluated for their efficacy and, if needed, are either discarded or deployed elsewhere as per the next process called reuse/discard
- **Reuse/discard:** Replacing the existing technology with something else and redeploying the technology at some other place is done using this process
- **External collaboration:** Technology development may take place outside so the firm has to keep its relationship open for external collaboration
- **Internal R&D and development:** Refers to research and development being carried out internally on select technologies, especially, those which are core for the firm product or processes.

The last two run in parallel with the first seven processes which run sequentially.

The interrelationship of various technology management processes are shown in Figure 3.2.

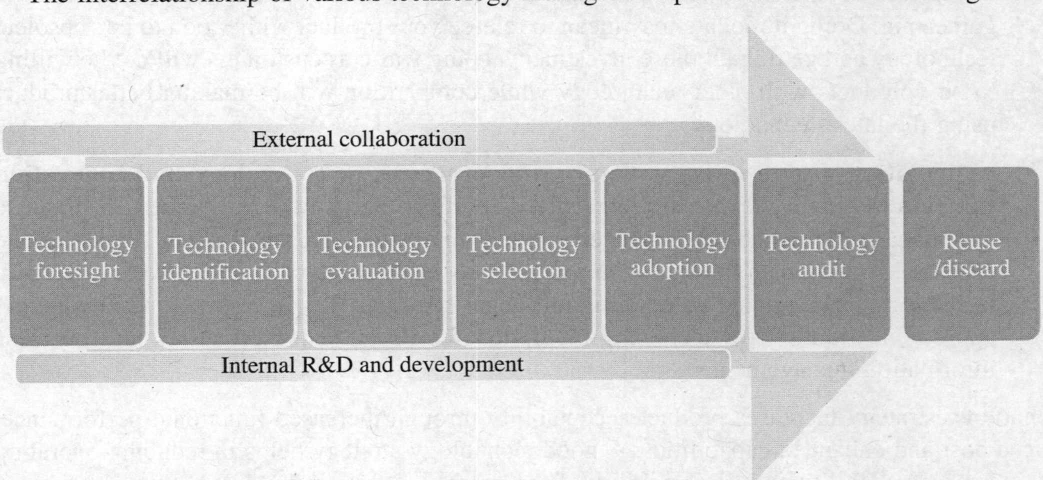

FIGURE 3.2 Technology Management Stages.

3.3 NEED FOR TECHNOLOGY MANAGEMENT

Technology has become a means to achieve business competitiveness for most of the firms today. All areas of operations of any firm have some impact of technology which is increasing day by day. Whether it is the need to reduce cost, bring efficiency or reach out to new markets or customers, technology plays its own role. Successful and market leader companies constantly evaluate new technological options and imbibe them to remain competitive in the market place.

In short, technology management for a firm will address the following needs:

- **Identify technology to gain superior capabilities:** This means identifying technology that will enhance abilities of the firm and make it unique. Leading retailer Wallmart who professes to "Save money Live better" uses Retail Link decision support system which acts as a bridge between Wallmart and its suppliers who can manage their production schedule matched with the Wallmart requirement. All low cost manufacturers dealing with mass consumption items typically invest in technologies and machines that produce large number of products at cost-effective rates.
- **Identify technologies as a part of core products:** For example, manufacturers of car choose between petrol or diesel, electric or hybrid. Telecom operators choose between GSM/CDMA and smartphone handset manufacturers choose between various operating systems.
- **Decide to develop or buy the technology:** Technology strategy is also to decide between developing technology in-house and acquiring it through collaboration, payment of license fee, etc. Both these choices have their own advantages and disadvantages.
- **Timing of technology adoption or launch:** This is to answer the question when? This requires timing decision that a firm must take to use the new technology in its products or services. Doing it too early will have a risk of uncertainty and a probability of being guinea pig. Doing it too late may mean to release your product with "soon to be" obsolete technology and getting all these investments going waste as customers will not be willing to buy products with older technology while competition will be making better product using the latest technology.
- **Articulating organisation structure and processes of technology and innovation function:** Finally, technology strategy determines the way a firm wants to organise and manage its technology management and innovation. This will mean setting up the processes, function and investing in resources to either conduct in-house R&D or acquire technology from outside by entering into legal contracts. It will also require conducting appropriate training for technology adoption for its products, processes and business information management.

Technology strategy increases product acceptability through increased functional performance, reduced cost and enhanced capabilities. A good technology strategy helps in reducing operating cost, increased reliability and serviceability of the product. While in the initial phases of a new technology, customers desire just the minimum functionalities but as the usage grows they demand more features. If we compare the passenger car when it was first launched with the high end variety that are available in the market now, the difference and increased injection of technology in its making as well as in its operation can be easily seen.

3.4 TECHNOLOGY MANAGEMENT BRIDGES THE GAP BETWEEN PRODUCT AND PRODUCTION REQUIREMENTS

Most often we consider a product as technology; for instance, the newly launched smartphone is considered a technology marvel. But the product is not technology! What has gone in the making of the product is technology. Similarly, if a company has come out with superior service by using technology, it is the process that has been improved using technology. Take the case of DELL computers who pioneer the on-demand manufacturing concept and ushered supply chain revolution to become the leading player in PC business. It used information technology extensively to optimise their online order booking systems as well as the back-end ERP system for their personal computer assembly. Their fresh approach of simplified product design and short assembly cycle allowed a "make to order" strategy work which helped them to lower costs, increase inventory turns and optimise supply chain function. The later included establishing closer linkages with fewer suppliers of components to ship components to a warehouse within 15 minutes of order issued from the assembly plant, using principles of Vendor Managed Inventory (VMI). In order to take care of logistics, Dell sets up a shipping arrangement with UPS.

Similarly, we hear of mobile phones being increasingly used for mobile payments and for online shopping. The technology behind these features are many, including internet, mobile manufacturing, payment gateways for bank and host of other technologies that enable the seamless payments to go through from one person's mobile phone to other's through their respective banks.

It is clear from such examples that technology management helps in bridging the gap between the product and what is needed to produce it.

3.5 STRATEGIC ROLE OF TECHNOLOGY

One question which must be considered while understanding technology strategy is its role in the overall business. Technology should always support competitive priorities for the business. In this process, technology impacts several areas of the business. Broadly, the impact and areas of influence of technology can be summarised under the following heads:

- In the making of product or delivering the services
- In executing processes of manufacturing or services
- Supporting business function using information technology
- Developing and managing the ecosystem

We will discuss the role played by technology strategy in each one of these areas.

(a) **In the making of product:** Technology role in functioning and design of a new product is well understood. We see more efficient, usable and feature rich products every day. The role of technology is to make components and make sure they work properly. Take the case of music instruments or cameras which have gone a total transformation in the features and capabilities over the last 10–15 years. The products have all become digital technology and hence have eliminated some of older types of products such as film camera or cassette player or CD player.

(b) **In executing processes:** This refers to the role technology plays in the production or service process. If we have to make better steel, then the production process has to adhere to the quality standards. A better car can only be made by superior manufacturing process. Technology is used at every stage of these processes. All these processes will also undergo change when the product features undergo a change.

(c) **Supporting business function using information technology:** Information technology impact is visible across business functions, especially in the back office operations. The business management functions like sales, marketing, finance, operations management cannot function without information technology. With the use of internet, cloud computing and mobile computing, ERP, E-business, SCM, Business Data Analytics, etc., are giving a superior edge to the business decision makers.

(d) **Developing and managing the industry ecosystem:** While smaller firms would have no major influence on the ecosystem, the industry leaders and government agencies do impact the industry ecosystem. Microsoft has thousands of developers who develop software code around Microsoft technologies. So are the instances of ecosystems for IOS or Android platform. IBM PC was one example that created a large ecosystem of manufacturers, component suppliers, software developers to meet the desktop computing requirement in 1980. Taking non-IT example, we can see that automobile companies are well-known for establishing an ecosystem of tier 2 and tier 3 suppliers of components and assembly around their factory units. Any change in the technology by the market leader impacts the downstream manufacturers and suppliers. Such leading companies have unstated responsibilities of leading technology strategy for the ecosystem. Governments and many independent industry bodies are also known to have developed technology strategies examples of which could be found in telecom space (CDMA vs GSM technologies), electrical appliances (110 V vs 220 V), automobiles emission standards, nuclear technologies, etc.

3.6 CHARACTERISTICS OF TECHNOLOGY MANAGEMENT

We know that competitive advantage of a firm is achieved when it matches its core capabilities with the opportunities and provides superior value to the customer. Therefore, technology management has to relentlessly look for opportunities to improve the firm's cost and efficiency and find opportunities to add features to delight the customers. The role of technology is to continuously improve processes of manufacturing or servicing the customer that leads to lower cost and efficient operations. Use of technology in delighting the customer with innovative features that make customer's life easier is yet another value creating activity by the technology. A pertinent example is the use of GPS and driver navigational system in passenger cars. This innovation has made driving easy on the road and also helps in saving the fuel by finding out the less busy or shorter route. All these are examples of good technology management.

However, when technology management is not able to meet the stakeholders' expectations and starts making negative impact on the ecology and environment, it creates negative consequences. For example, good packaging material helps delivery of a product in good condition without damage. However, unrestricted use of plastic waste clogs drains and impacts environment. Electronics wastes, used batteries and CFL lamps are creating environmental hazards that are among the negative side of the technology. Nuclear technology, once considered an answer to the increasing energy requirement, also has the danger of radio activity, especially, if the nuclear reactors are damaged due to earthquake or tsunami.

Technology management must follow and adopt the prevailing standards. Those firms which do not keep pace with evolving standards find it hard to survive in the marketplace. A good example would be the emission standards such as Bharat Stage IV or Euro 4 which mandate certain class of vehicles to adhere to these standards, otherwise the registration would not be granted. Those manufacturers who do not comply with these standards would find their customer base shrinking.

A good technology management enhances the predictability of products or services delivery as warranted by the customer. This way it ensures that technology is able to add to customer's value proposition either perceived or real which would be difficult to copy by competitors. The later is due to knowledge, expertise and experience a firm develops with the technology and its usages.

Use of technology also causes dependency on the intellectual assets and would add to the cost. Not all technologies deliver the stated benefits, hence they need to be carefully selected, used and, if necessary, discarded. Using a particular technology strategy would demand changes and correction in the overall strategic plan and operational strategy. The choice of technology is an important strategic decision as it would cost money and reverting this would be very difficult if the choice goes wrong.

3.7 COMPONENTS OF TECHNOLOGY MANAGEMENT

Technology management has to answer question such as why, what and how a particular technology choice should be adopted by the firm for its products, services, processes and managing business functions.

Depending upon the overall business strategy, the firm should decide which technology will help to achieve a lower cost position or produce niche products. Technology management helps in making a choice that a firm exercises to be either a leader or a follower during its adoption. By being a leader, it gets the first mover advantage but with it is also associated risk and cost that goes through the initial testing and adoption phase. Technology management also encompasses the timing of commercialisation and whether the technology choice would be to make, borrow, buy or share with other similar manufacturers. Most follower companies either use common technology or at times share the same production facility and just do their respective branding. This explains the fact that fridges and air-conditioners of several brands are manufactured by a few manufacturer following similar standards. Technology management also examines stages of value chain where it can impact and improve the product. It determines a comprehensive approach that covers value chain, resource commitment, organisation, competitive positioning with respect to other firms. It also borrows from experience of the firm and that of its peer to adopt a particular strategy. The degree to which a firm can claim to be technology savvy by adopting a cutting edge technology is deeply determined by its capabilities and past experiences. It is also a factor of stage at which the technology evolution is currently happening and how much of it is being adopted by the peer group companies.

3.8 CHOICES FOR TECHNOLOGY DEVELOPMENT AND ADOPTION

Technology development and adoption is an important activity within technology management by the firm to decide how it will deploy technology.

Amongst the various choices, what a firm has are as follows:

- Develop technology through internal R&D: This may seem costly and time-taking in the beginning, but it will also pay handsomely in the long run. This route is adopted by leading pharmaceutical companies which yield them high profit from patented formulations for a long time.
- Buy technological knowhow or product components by paying necessary fee: Computer chips are brought by all laptop manufacturers as it is too specialised a component to be developed and manufactured through their own R&D efforts. A company can produce a product with brought out knowhow and market under their brand name. A large portion of profit would have to be shared with the technology provider.
- Collaborate and jointly develop a technology that can be used by all collaborating parties: Sometimes industry consortiums or government-to-government funded projects are created for complex technology development. Breakthrough products can come out of these efforts but they find difficult to sustain their continued efforts. (Refer Supercar project in Chapter 2.)

In addition, technology adoption also covers its usage in product and process of the firm. Decisions like putting a technology in service, its support, setting up an organisation to build knowledge are all part of technology management decision.

Finally, implementation of technology strategy must take into account the feedback from customers, process users and field staff to make it robust and in line with the market needs. All these feedback will help the firm to fine tune its technology strategy and build necessary capabilities to support and maintain the technology strategy.

Technology strategy is a manifestation of technical capabilities or competencies developed by the firm which is enhanced through experience and feedback from the customer and the firm's own field staff.

3.9 CHOOSING STRATEGIC ALTERNATIVES

A firm can choose between strategic alternatives such as to be a technology leader or a technology follower.

A technology leader gains the first mover advantage and builds a brand loyalty with its users. A good technology product creates a benchmark so that customer does not switch the brand easily. A leader also gets better control on the marketing and distribution network and, in most cases, sets up a standard for the industry. Technology leaders can command higher price for their product, be it Apple iPhones or Mercedes cars. But it also requires a lot of upfront investments in developing technology, guarding its secret, deciding the timings to test the market and customer education cost.

A technology follower understandably has lower cost of launch since much of the ground work has been done by the leader; however, a follower can never command premium or brand loyalty that a technology leader enjoys. Follower strategy is safe and less costly but it does not allow a firm to differentiate itself unless they make efforts to give superior after-sales service or other bundled products that make their value proposition more attractive.

3.10 LIFECYCLE OF TECHNOLOGY AND ITS IMPACT ON TECHNOLOGY MANAGEMENT

Any Technology development has become fast paced and it is soon hits the stage of obsolescence where new technology takes over. The lifecycle of a technology is very short—almost less than 3 years—as seen in the case of mobile communication where new models are launched every other quarter. The good news is that the prices are more competitive with more features than the earlier one. But the same may not be true in certain other industries such an automobile, petroleum, engineering products or capital goods, but the technology advancement of the peripheral or associated product does make significant impact on the cost of the product. For example, steel sheets were common items used in the car body but with advancement of plastic technology, strong and resilient components are being built out of plastics. Examples of such replacements are car bumper and fender which protect the front, back and side of the car frame from shocks or impacts.

Another prominent characteristic is that technology is becoming efficient and ecofriendly. A lot of efforts are being made to make the products consume less energy, e.g., electrical items and are ecofriendly. Use of solar lamps, LED bulbs, etc. are one such example.

Also the speed of technology development ecosystem is important and a slower development may lead to lower adoption. For example, electrical vehicles which are still struggling for large scale adoption due to practically absent infrastructure for recharging on roads or getting a replacement battery at short notice. Figure 3.3 gives some of the characteristics of technology developments.

3.11 TECHNOLOGY STRATEGY MANAGEMENT GUIDING PRINCIPLES

As we have seen in the earlier section, any industry based on technology depends on other technologies for its survival and growth. Railroads have improved because electrical engines could be made which can run on long haul. Aircrafts have been able to fly due to large amount of automatic control and computer-based assistance to pilot in navigation. So it is not just one product or manufacturing technology but the entire ecosystem that has to be considered for studying the process of technology development and its management. We outline here some of the guiding principles while formulating technology management steps.

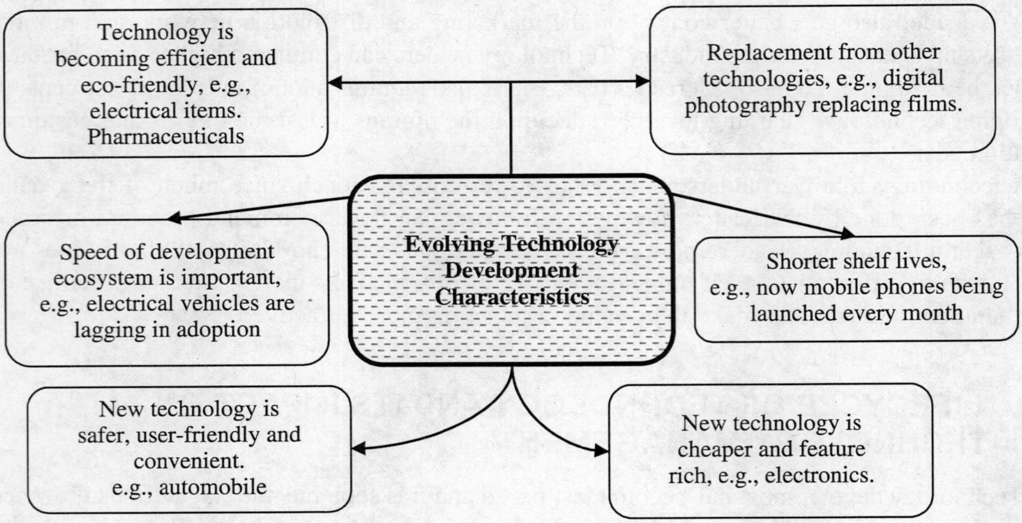

FIGURE 3.3 Characteristics of Technology Developments.

- **Technology must have a purpose:** Gone are the days when technology was being considered something exotic, and only relevant to luxury and high profile users. Now the technology is enabling the common man and being developed with a larger purpose.
- **Partner and differentiator:** Technology is no longer an essential behind-the-scenes supporting partner but is a key differentiator.
- **It must conform to regulation:** Technology is being developed to meet uncertain landscape marked by evolving regulatory issues. Most automobile technology improvement has happened due to strict emission laws enacted by many countries.
- **Must have better returns:** Technology is only be accepted when it gives better investment returns.
- **Meet customer changing preferences:** New client service demands fuels new technology development which is asking more flexibility, responsiveness and WOW factor.
- **Enable partnership with others:** Technology management is no longer isolated but is witnessing unprecedented partnership between industry, academia and government. In some cases, string industry-wise associations also participate.
- **Consider new opportunities from across the ecosystem:** Emerging technologies, internet lifestyles are presenting a new set of opportunities as the mobile consumer armed with multiple devices and engaged in multiple tasks takes to the road, while connected to multiple environments. This will need a variety of the industries, almost all, to embrace mobile delivery of services and products that can fit and support these customer preferences. Books publication, for example, have to increasingly adopt e-books, selective

choice of reading and multiple formats across various mobile devices. So will be the education industry that needs to be available across all the three platforms, viz., internet, mobile phone as well as face to face publication.

3.12 THREE PERSPECTIVES OF TECHNOLOGY MANAGEMENT

The interconnected and globalised world has given rise to newer thinking for technology management. We must, therefore, identify three perspectives of technology management that businesses must consider as part of technology management initiative.

We classify enterprise technology management in three perspectives:

(a) Value creating perspective
(b) Value enabling perspective
(c) Ecosystem perspective

We will describe each one of them in detail in the subsequent section.

Figure 3.4 shows them in a pictorial form.

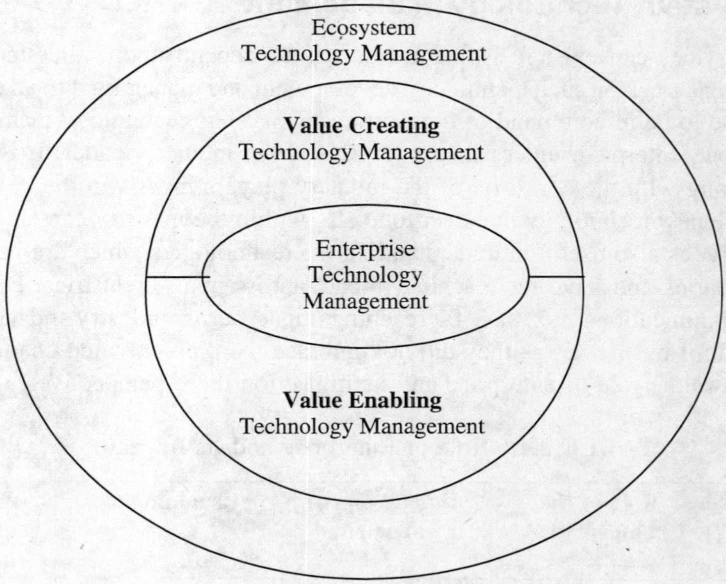

FIGURE 3.4 Enterprise Technology Management Components.

3.12.1 Value Creating Technology Management

All organisations exist to create value for its customers. It may be in the form of producing certain products from raw materials or half-finished inputs into a useful product. This technology also refers to those which are used by the services company to manage their services operations. Value creating technology management refers to the management of these technologies that an enterprise uses for its production environment for operational purposes. For example, steel making will be a value creating technology for the steel plant or machining, foundry and several others for an automobile unit. Similarly, aircraft technology will be value creating technology for an airline which forms the basis of how their operations can be run. Please note that these technologies would invariably be specific to the particular industry and keeping a track of this makes sense for the enterprise to remain at the cutting edge of their operations.

3.12.2 Value Enabling Technology Management

While the core value creating technology would differ from industry to industry, all firms have to use technology to support their businesses. These are called value enabling technologies that do not become part of the core value production chain of the enterprise but those functions that support value creation. This will include technologies for supporting business operations like information technology or technologies to support logistics, material handling, energy generation transmission, packaging, etc.

3.12.3 Ecosystem Technology Management

No product or services can exist in isolation and has to depend upon other industries in the ecosystem. Keeping a track on such technology development and managing it to an extent possible will help enterprise to be in command of their future. Ecosystem technology management is not done usually by one enterprise unless that enterprise is the industry leader. In such cases, the industry leader along with the consortia of the industry players invests in the development and management of the new technology that everyone else within the industry can take benefit from.

This perspective is also useful in understanding the technologies which are being developed on industry boundaries and have far reaching impact across many industries. Digital imaging, internet bases communications, etc., have far reaching impact across industry and have made many leading players out of businesses as they did not embrace them quickly and change themselves.

Table 3.1 shows the role of enterprise and its impact on these perspectives.

TABLE 3.1 Role of Enterprise and Its Impact

Technology management perspective	Role of the enterprise	Impact on the enterprise	Usual method	Investment required for new development
Value Creating Technology	Decisive/Driving	Major	In-house	High
Value Enabling Technology	Evaluative	Significant	Outsourced	Low
Ecosystem Technology	Observer	Disruptive	Industry body/ consortia	Minimal

3.14 AI/GEN AI IN TECHNOLOGY FORESIGHT, IDENTIFICATION, AND EVALUATION

Technology foresight, the process of anticipating future technological developments, has traditionally relied on expert opinions, trend extrapolation, and S-curve analysis. AI and Generative AI are now enhancing these methods by enabling the processing of vast amounts of unstructured data, such as research papers, patents, scientific literature, and market trends, to identify emerging technologies and predict their trajectories with greater accuracy.

AI agents can automate literature reviews, synthesize complex information, and even generate hypotheses for future research directions. This capability democratizes and de-risks technology identification, moving foresight from an expert-driven, often intuitive process to a more data-driven, systematic one. The ability of AI to scan and analyze global scientific output can significantly reduce the "blind spots" that have historically led to industry disruptions, allowing firms to identify potential opportunities and threats earlier. This means technology foresight can become a more continuous, real-time activity, relying heavily on AI-powered intelligence gathering rather than periodic, manual expert panels.

3.15 MANAGING AI-NATIVE SYSTEMS AND ARCHITECTURES

The concept of "AI-native" organizations and systems represents a profound shift in enterprise architecture. Unlike traditional businesses that integrate AI functionalities into pre-existing systems, AI-native companies are fundamentally designed with AI at their core. This means AI is engineered intrinsically from the ground up, becoming a pervasive component of operations and services. This foundational AI integration allows for rapid adaptation to new technological advancements, positioning these organizations as leaders in innovation and adaptability.

AI-native systems leverage a data-driven, knowledge-based ecosystem, replacing static, rule-based systems with the ability to learn and adapt continuously. This approach drives transformational changes across industries, enhancing efficiency and enabling new business models that were previously unfeasible. However, managing AI-native systems introduces unique challenges, particularly in areas like data governance, ensuring the ethical integration of AI, and managing the lifecycle of AI-based functionalities to ensure trust and fairness. The shift towards AI-native architectures implies a fundamental re-architecting of enterprise IT and operational systems. This is not merely an IT upgrade but a strategic transformation that permeates organizational structure, talent acquisition, and corporate culture. It challenges legacy firms to consider radical redesigns to remain competitive against agile, AI-first entrants.

3.16 STRATEGIC CHOICES: LEADING VS. FOLLOWING IN AI/GEN AI ADOPTION

The decision to be a technology leader or follower has always involved a complex trade-off between the advantages of early market entry and the risks of unproven technology. In the context of AI and Generative AI, this dynamic is intensified by the unprecedented speed of adoption. Generative AI adoption has been notably faster than both personal computers and the internet.

This rapid diffusion rate makes a purely "late-mover" strategy considerably riskier, as the window for catching up and gaining significant market share shrinks dramatically. Early adopters, such as ChatGPT, reached 100 million monthly active users within two months of launch, demonstrating explosive adoption.

While first-movers incur higher costs of research and development and face market uncertainties, they also gain significant advantages in establishing brand loyalty and setting industry standards. However, for complex technologies, late-movers can sometimes benefit from observing the first-mover's challenges, refining product designs based on known functionalities, and avoiding the costs of experimentation. The accelerated adoption of Gen AI means that while a "late-mover advantage" might still exist for complex AI applications (where waiting for more functionalities to be known allows for superior product designs), the timeline for this advantage is severely compressed. This creates a high-stakes environment where the speed of organizational learning and iteration becomes paramount for both leaders and followers. Firms must cultivate extreme agility and a culture of continuous experimentation to either lead or quickly refine and optimize based on early market feedback, avoiding the perilous position of being a "laggard."

3.13 SUMMARY

We started this chapter to understand what technology management is and how a firm decides to adopt a particular technology strategy to gain and maintain competitive advantage. Technology strategy is what a long-term plan and policies that a firm adopts with respect to technology decisions in line with its business strategy and the management ensures its continuous implementation. We discussed the need for technology management, becoming a means to achieve business competitiveness for most of the firms today. We established that technology management bridges the gap between product and production requirements.

Our next concept building was around strategic role of technology and how it impacts several areas of the businesses such as making products, in executing processes, supporting business function and developing and managing the ecosystem. We also examined if technology can give technology a competitive advantage and considered the negative impacts of the technology, especially on the ecology and environment.

We then defined the components of technology management and methods to implement it. At this point, it was necessary to dwell on aspects of choosing strategic alternatives to be a technology leader or technology follower. We then defined the lifecycle of technology management.

Our next significant discussion was on the evolving landscape of technology management. We advocated that firms should consider the entire ecosystem for studying the process of technology development and its management rather than just one product or manufacturing technology. Technology must have a purpose, a key differentiator and must conform to regulation. We discussed other characteristics as well by linking it with three perspectives of technology management as that of being a value creator, value enabler and ecosystem technology management. We finally discussed the role of enterprise and its impact along with these three perspectives.

Key Terms: Technology Management, Technology foresight, Technology evaluations, Technology audit, Vender managed inventory ecosystem.

REVIEW QUESTIONS

1. What is technology management and how a firm decides to adopt a particular technology strategy to gain and maintain competitive advantage?

   Answer: Sections 3.1, 3.2
2. What is the need for technology management? Establish that technology management bridges the gap between product and production requirements.

   Answer: Sections 3.3, 3.4
3. What is the strategic role of technology and how it impacts several areas of the business?

   Answer: Section 3.5
4. What are the characteristics of a good technology management? What may lead to negative impact of the technology especially on the ecology and environment?

   Answer: Section 3.6
5. What are the main components of technology management and what are the methods to implement it?

   Answer: Section 3.7
6. What are the choices for technology development and adoption?

   Answer: Section 3.8
7. How does a firm choose between the strategic alternatives to be a technology leader or technology follower?

   Answer: Section 3.9
8. Define the lifecycle of technology and its impact on technology management.

   Answer: Section 3.10
9. Describe the technology management guiding principles.

   Answer: Section 3.11
10. How will you define the three perspectives of technology management? What is the role an enterprise plays for each one of them?

    Answer: Section 3.12

Chapter 4 Innovation Management

Business has only two functions, innovation and marketing.

— Peter F. Drucker

At the end of this chapter, we will learn:

- Meaning of innovation and creativity
- Goals of innovation
- Sources of innovation
- Innovation dimensions
- Types and patterns of technological innovation
- Process of innovation
- What is innovation life cycle
- Disruptive, continuous, open or closed innovation
- Impediments and success factors in promoting innovation.

4.1 INTRODUCTION

The legendary innovator and Apple founder, Steve Jobs is said to have commented that innovation distinguishes between a leader and a follower. In the current world of business, if you want to be the leader in your line of business, you will have to lead by innovation. So indisputably innovation is going to be the major differentiator for any business in the present times. As most businesses are getting matured, the earlier model of competing on parameters such as cost, better quality, niche marketing, etc. may not sustain for long. In this chapter, we will understand the conceptual foundation of innovation and how technology plays a role in driving innovation.

Economic growth and globalisation has given rise to new opportunities as well as new challenges to most firms. Firms need quick adoption of technology to innovate products, processes, business models and services. It is therefore important that the role of technology is properly understood in ushering innovation in not only the end product but also value chain processes. We will underline how innovation efforts in a firm increasingly require technology to maintain and sustain. Given the wider impact on innovation across various parts of the businesses, the need of the hour is to install a robust innovation process. The absence of a robust innovation management process within a firm leads to slow response of the firm to meet new market demand and the changing customer's needs. However, if the firm has established a sound innovation process and meticulously practising it, then it would respond faster to newer market as well as customer needs. This chapter will cover this interplay of innovation using technology for the benefit of our readers.

4.2 INNOVATION DEFINED

There is much confusion about what innovation is and how it is different from invention. Contrary to the popular belief, innovation is not always developing something totally new. The later is called invention. Innovation is basically to find some added value for the firm by introducing new ideas. These ideas could be either a new product based on the existing technology or adding new features to exiting products to make them more attractive to its users. The most talked about products such as iPod, iPhone and iPad marketed by Apple are not new inventions but examples of innovation. The technology components used in these products were either in use for some other purpose or already well-known. However, by combining various elements of the technology and creative business model, Apple has been able to create very successful products in a row which according to some estimates contributes to about 1% US GDP. Such examples will help us understand the relationship between technology and innovation which we will take up in the next few sections.

4.3 THE THEORIES OF TECHNOLOGICAL CHANGE

Technology is a means through which the human race improves its life. Technological change brings in improvements in the products, manufacturing processes and other support processes. If we understand how a technology evolves and can predict its future potential, then we can use this technology as a source of next wave of innovation in the firm. For doing this, we need to identify and select a few significant technologies for our business among those available or likely. Then we should assess the impact of these potential technology in changing the firms' ways of doing business. Finally, we need to implement these technology in the best efficient manner.

Noted researcher Joseph Schumpeter[1] proposed that technological change follows a process described as invention-innovation-diffusion trilogy. He espoused that these three happen one after the other and followed by any new technology that comes to reality.

As outlined by Schumpeter, the first stage of any technology development is invention. At this stage, the new ideas are generated. This stage is the stage of basic research. Usually at this stage, the scientific principles are converted into some useful output that can be of some use to mankind. Inventions of steam engine, electricity, nuclear energy, etc., are many such things where the scientific principles and discoveries were converted into some useful products or services for the human race.

[1]Joseph Alois Schumpeter (1883–1950) at a young age of 23 received his Ph.D 1906. Among his noted books are *The Nature and Essence of Theoretical Economics* (1908); *The Theory of Economic Development* (1911), and *Economic Doctrine and Method.* (1914).

At the second stage called innovation, these new ideas start getting converted into marketable products and processes. The steam engine was the invention but using it for locomotive or running ships were making them marketable products. The power of steam was innovated into multiple use as described above. These are called innovations of the steam engine.

The third and last stage is the diffusion stage when the new products and processes spread all across the potential market. Finally, the invention becomes acceptable and adopted by a large number of people. When technology reaches this stage, it is called a stage of diffusion. This is the stage the technology starts creating market impact. For example, mobile phone technology is at the stage of diffusion in the present context.

However, this trilogy process is not linear in nature and every stage provides feedback to the earlier stage. At every stage, there is process of selection and at every stage few inventions and innovations are dropped and not carried to the next stage. At the stage of diffusion, market forces propel more innovations and inventions. This is the stage when technology starts yielding business profits and provides incentives for more research leading to inventions and innovations.

Finally, the stage of diffusion leads to commoditisation of the technology when further development slows down and the industry waits for new breakthrough technology, as shown in Figure 4.1.

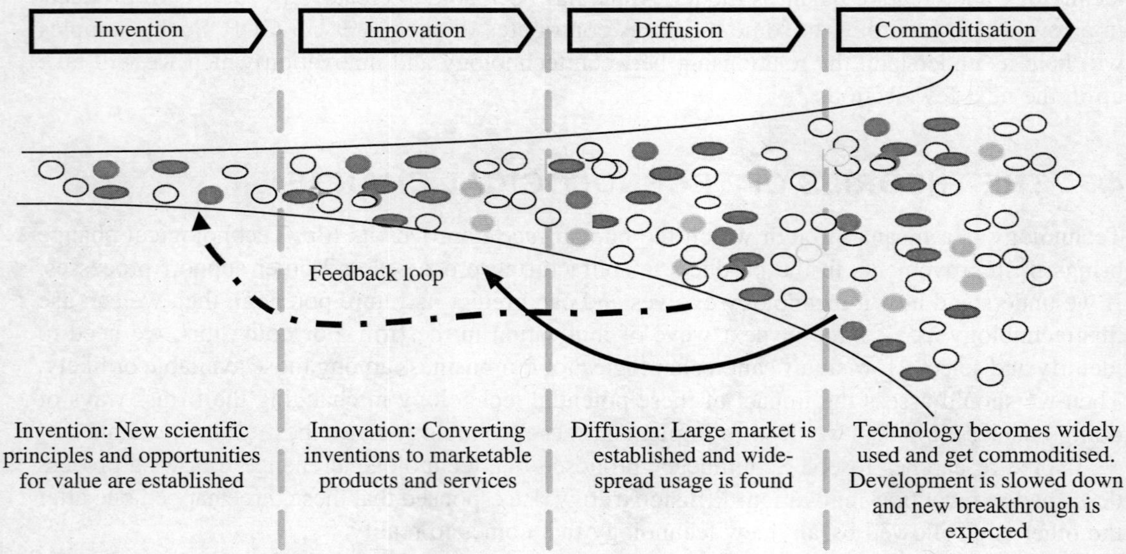

FIGURE 4.1 Technology Development Trilogy Stages.

It may be noted that at the early stages of this trilogy it is largely the application of scientific principles which drives the development. This stage is led by deep academics, researchers and creative thinkers. Technology which is nothing but the application of science takes centre stage at the later stages after invention. Technology helps in development of new products and processes which facilitates better use.

4.4 DIFFERENCE BETWEEN INNOVATION AND CREATIVITY

The words creativity and innovation are interchangeably used, and at times, it is confusing to many. Franken[2] defines creativity as the ability to generate or recognise new ideas, alternatives, or possibilities that may be useful in solving problems, communicating with others and entertaining ourselves and others. He outlines three reasons why people are motivated to be creative. Creative people inherently desire to solve a problem, communicate ideas and derive stimulus while addressing novel, varied and complex situations. Creativity is ultimately the act of converting new and imaginative ideas into reality and requires a person to view things in new ways. A creative person is able to generate new possibilities or new alternatives which would be unique and useful. All this requires deep knowledge about the subject and several other subjects directly or indirectly. Such persons have unique capabilities such as flexibility to adopt new ideas, tolerance of ambiguity, unpredictability of response and an ability to create something that has never been known earlier.

While creativity is applying mind to unleash new ideas, innovation is how this idea can produce business benefit. The former is not measurable but the later is. Innovation is about making changes in the existing systems using new ideas to make it more viable. Innovation is always focused to meet unrecognised and unmet needs so that the company can deploy its creative resources to convert the creative ideas into business outcome and obtain a return on its investment. Business world seldom appreciates good and novel ideas but values it only when it is properly implemented. To quote Theodore Levitt[3], noted Harvard Professor who said that organisations do not lack creativity in the idea-creating sense but often lack in innovation which is action-producing, i.e., putting ideas to work.

4.5 INNOVATION AND CREATIVITY IN BUSINESS CONTEXT

Unlike creativity in the field of art, craft of literature, business creativity is more focussed to solve business problems. Creative people in the field of art or literature are motivated to act to give expression to their inner desires, thoughts or providing entertainment to its audience. However, business creativity directly impacts business outcome by addressing customer needs and generating business revenue (or profit) for the firm. If the creativity in the business is not impacting the business results, then it is neither appreciated nor valued.

According to James March[4], the need of business creativity is simply because there are so many problems businesses face every day which have few standard solutions. The chance of finding a solution to a particular problem is low using the existing methods, therefore, the need of creativity in problem solving. A person with a capability of business creativity challenges the problem at hand through the creative process to produce new ideas and perspectives to solve it.

Another confusion with regards to creativity and innovation persists that one cannot force creativity or innovation to happen within the organisation even if we apply concerted efforts.

---

[2]Robert E. Franken. *Human Motivation*. 3rd ed. (page 396)

[3]Theodore Levitt, Creativity Is Not Enough. http://hbr.org/2002/08/creativity-is-not-enough/ar/1 accessed 13 May 2014. ,

[4]Barbara Levitt; James G. March, Organizational Learning, *Annual Review of Sociology*, Vol. 14, (1988), 319-340.

People think that creativity is like a trigger of new idea that cannot be forced to happen as and when we desire. Such creative ideas come to people only in bath tub or while walking on a deserted beach during a full moon night! After all, these are all related to thinking, how can one force one to think while sitting in the office! Fortunately, this line of thinking have dwindling supporters and it is now challenged by many thinkers and researchers. It has been proved in many business situations and by many firms that by adopting certain scientific processes, such as design thinking, Edward de Bono's Six Thinking Hat and many others, any organisation can create an environment of creativity and innovation. These scientific processes help in generating new ideas, cross-fertilisation of existing ones and finally controlling and managing creativity. These principles also enable better measure of the organisation efforts in this direction.

At the risk of repeating, we would once again say that any creative idea has no value unless it is successfully implemented in the organisation and converted into business value. When we implement a creative ideas and reap business benefits, then only that great idea becomes a brilliant idea! Creativity may come from an individual thinking but has to be implemented by the organisation. Hence individual idea has to garner support from the organisation team and resources while taking it through the implementation process. This is precisely the process of innovation which converts a good idea into brilliantly implemented idea.

From idea to implementation, they go through stages in an organisation set up. Once the idea is put forward in documented form and accepted by the initial screening committee, it goes to the stage of proof of concept where the idea is implemented at small scale preferably in a controlled (laboratory) environment. If this stage is passed successfully, then the next stage of prototype development is done. At this stage, a workable model is created and field trials are conducted. If the product comes out successful after the field trail where the prototype is successful or near successful, then management and stakeholder's approvals are sought for commercialisation. The feedback received during prototype test is incorporated and processes for commercial manufacturing, marketing, support, after-sales service, etc., are developed. This requires a massive investment and is done after serious evaluation. However, all these stages have to be crossed within a reasonable time frame, otherwise the idea may become obsolete, competitors may launch similar product early and the firm may lose its first mover advantage.

A creative idea converted into reality will require a combination of right skills, continued momentum to pursue it till completion and requisite management support. Frequently, the team is required to be motivated, at times coaxed and assured by the senior leadership. While creativity is the starting point of the improvement journey, it is the innovation process that leads to business results by producing better products or services. This is called innovation management.

Many firms are not able to take the path of innovation and launch new products or services after dumping the existing one which is already in the market. They find it hard to change something which is very successful in the present times and have huge established market share. Such management finds it difficult to stop making the current successful product and replacing it with something whose worth has not been proved so far. No wonder so many established firms remain producing products with old technology and resist imbibing newer technology. Consequently, newer technology innovations come from unknown new company which takes the market by storm. The entrenched players finally become a mute spectator when their market share erodes. By the time they get their acts together, the new player establishes itself firmly. For example, during the initial years of this century, Nokia, the world leader in mobile phone industry, resisted launching mobile handsets with touch phone technology till they were surprised by newer manufacturers like Apple and fast followers like Samsung. The new space was created by these manufacturers and Nokia faced major setback.

The reason for such resistance to adopt new technology in large firms is due to their own background. Most established firms have rigorous process of review for any new projects (including ideas for innovation) which usually reject more ideas than adopting them. These firms want to take low risk and seek higher returns from all such new ideas. Since the idea and resulting product or services is new, the final outcome is very hard to predict, hence invariably rejected. Newer firms have no past baggage of investment in older technology, nor do they have an established market share which they fear being cannibalised. Hence they are able to explore new technology fairly quickly and take risk frequently despite the fact that they do not much fund to invest as compared to their established peers. Yet these new firms succeed with new technology whereas the established ones fail.

All innovation involves risk, and all risks include the possibility of failure. If the firm has low tolerance of failure for innovative ideas, then it is unlikely to bring out newer innovation on a regular basis. In order to be innovative, one also needs to be prepared for failure and it should not be treated as black mark on the team or the individual. The leadership of the firm must encourage failure in order to be innovative, otherwise the firm will never be able to imbibe innovation as a culture to serve their customers with better products and services.

4.6 GOALS OF INNOVATION

Most firms adopt innovations for a wide variety of reasons. Several researches have been conducted across geography and wide ranging industry to identify why a firm undertakes innovation. We summarise some of the key goals that organisations typically adopt for their innovation process from these studies for our readers. These goals will be of all types of innovation such as those related to product, process, services, business model, etc.

In short, they can be summarised as 5C's of innovation goals. These 5C's are as follows:

(a) **Cost reduction**: By innovation, a firm can bring in more efficiency and reduce cost. A better product that is efficient to operate can help the customer save cost of operations and hence sell product at lower cost, thus making it more attractive to buy.

(b) **Customer satisfaction:** Customer satisfaction can be achieved through improved quality of products and services. This is by far the most widely sought after goal to innovate process of making product, maintaining its quality and its services. In addition, the product can be tailored to serving new markets meeting its unique requirements. McDonald's Mc Aloo Tikki is one such example of product innovation for Indian markets. Similarly, most American cars which are left-hand drive are converted into right-hand drive to suit Indian markets. Banks and insurance firm offer customer services using mobile apps, online chats and through 24×7 call centres across the globe. Customer satisfaction goal can also be met when the firm expands its product range by launching several variants to suit the specific needs of a customer segment by innovating products. Banks routinely launch investment plans for children education, marriage or retirement, which are innovation to suit specific customer segment. This is the precise reason for many variants of automobile, mobile phones and electronics goods to suit pockets and requirements of a wide variety of customers through innovation of the product range.

(c) **Compliance and regulation**: Innovation goals are also to meet compliance and regulatory requirements such as cyber security laws.

(d) **Competitive pressure:** Another innovation goal is to keep improving the firm's processes and products so that they are always better than the comparable ones in the market.

(e) **Climate protection:** This refers to innovation made for preserving environment, reducing pollution and making the world safer.

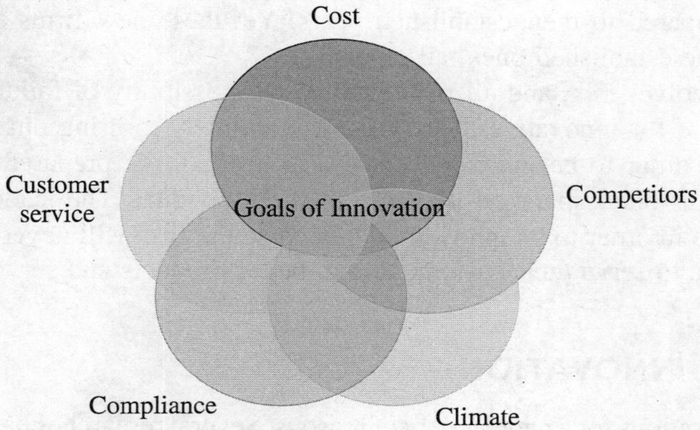

FIGURE 4.2 Goals of Innovation.

4.7 DESIGN THINKING PROCESS FOR INNOVATION

Stanford Professor McKim's[5] was the first one to popularise the idea of design thinking as a method of creative action. This idea was further picked up in business context by IDEO by David M. Kelley. Peter Rowe's, in his book Design Thinking[6], described methods and approaches used by architects and urban planners and more work has been done in the business context using this principles by many companies (see Box 4.1 for profile of a design thinker by Tim Brown).

In short, design thinking breaks the myth that creativity and innovation is just a flash in the mind of a creative individual. It is no such activity upon which there is no control, as to when and how it will come. We are frequently told the story of a falling apple that gave the great scientist Issac Newton the idea of gravitation principles or Archimedes floating in the bath tub to get to the principles of buoyancy.

[5]Robert H. McKim, *Thinking Visually: A Strategy Manual for Problem Solving*, Lifetime Learning Publications (1980). ISBN-10: 0534979785.

[6]Peter G. Rowe, *Design Thinking*. The MIT Press (1991). ISBN-10: 026268067X.

In the modern world, researchers have come up with methods that help arriving at new ideas through disciplined thinking and their further evaluation lead them to the business viability and ultimate success. Design Thinking Principle is one of these techniques. We will briefly summarise this in the following few paragraphs.

(a) **What is design thinking?** Basically, design principle is a method to facilitate innovation by focusing on what people need and their wants are, what their likes or dislikes are, which can be used in various aspects of product and package design, marketing and supporting them. It helps a designer come out with a product or services that is valuable for the customer and has market potential because it is focused on people wants and needs.

(b) **How does it work?** The overall process of design thinking comprises three stages: inspiration, ideation and implementation. These stages have distinct activities to be performed by the team who have gathered to work on arriving at innovation ideas around a problem or opportunities. In the first stage, i.e., inspiration, it is largely addressed to identify a problem or opportunity. Many situations may seem to work perfectly yet there are chances of improvement. Once the problem is clearly identified, in the second stage, i.e., ideation, a simple prototype is developed. Once the prototype is perfected after several iterations, the last phase, implementation, follows.

(c) **What are some of the success examples?** For example, IDEO a well-known design firm, among the top 25 innovative companies and Winner of 38 Red Dot awards and have been credited for designing Apple's first mouse, Palm V and many other products uses design thinking. There are several other companies that follow design principles.

Box 4.1 Profile of a design thinker by Tim Brown

In an HBR Article[7] Tim Brown CEO and president of the innovation and design firm IDEO claims that Design Thinkers possess certain inherent traits which can be further shaped through training and mentoring. He opines that possession of certain skill sets that can help them to connect with their customers. These skills would help the design thinkers to understand their customers better. In short we will use the acronym CREATIVE to remember these skills of a design thinker.

- **Collaborator:** A design thinker is a team player who knows how to collaborate well and draw creative power of the team to come out with the best possible solution.
- **Realist:** While coming out with new and path breaking ideas he or she is always grounded and weighs business advantages, disadvantages and associated risk.
- **Empathy:** Instead of clinging to his or her own ideas the design thinker is willing to empathies with others.
- **Aware:** Such a person is always close to what is happening around so that the new development can be incorporated in his thinking process.
- **Thinker:** The person must develop the ability of thinking deep to arrive at conclusions after considering various permutations and combinations.

[7]https://hbr.org/2008/06/design-thinking Design Thinking by Tim Brown FROM THE JUNE 2008 ISSUE accessed 24122016

- **Intuitive:** they possess ability to visualize things that are not yet enunciated. As rightly said by legendary Steve jobs who advocated that people should develop a skill to read from the blank page!
- **Visualizer:** they possess the ability to visualize all aspects of a confounding problem
- **Experimentalist:** Ability to Experiment with multiple options and possibilities.

4.8 SOURCES OF INNOVATION

Peter Drucker, one of the noted Gurus of the management thinking identified seven sources of innovative opportunity in his book *Innovation and Entrepreneurship*[8]. The following were identified as sources of the information:

(a) **The unexpected:** Opportunities can come from unexpected sources by studying the market that every managers must do. Areas of inquiry may be around changes in demand and convert unexpected changes into opportunities. Examples like Walkman, Post–it and NutraSweet fall under this category.

(b) **The incongruity:** This refers to conflicts between opposing functions, requirements, or values which may trigger an innovation. A small car with enough space inside is solved by redesigning the car.

(c) **Process need:** Innovation can also be due to the process need by identifying non-performing areas and redesigning the process. Techniques like BPR and process innovations fall under this category where technology helps to innovate the process and remove inefficiencies.

(d) **Industry and market structure change:** They are the source of innovation. The mobile phones have now become smart phones doing a variety of functions and the telecom companies are not just selling minutes of usage but several value added services and ending up with huge revenue. Apples iTune is one example that revolutionised the industry. Other examples are globalisation, deregulations, etc., which give opportunities for companies to get first mover advantage.

(e) **Demographics:** Changes in populations, income levels, human capital (education) and age ranges gives opportunities for the new products and services. As the population is aging in many countries several products that cater to old age have come up. Life style drugs, anti aging creams are just examples of innovation.

(f) **Changes in perception, meaning and mood:** It has been proved that people perception and mood changes and with that changes the needs of the people. A phenomena called "down aging" in which older people want to look younger and cosmetic and personal care industry has come up with products and services.

(g) **New knowledge:** New knowledge gives more opportunities for innovation. Use of internet for retail marketing, education for e-learning and several improvements in the government have been seen due to technological revolution.

[8]Peter F. Drucker, Harper Business. *Innovation and Entrepreneurship.* Reprint edition, (9 May 2006).

4.9 INNOVATION DIMENSIONS

Kamm[9] defines the following dimensions of innovation:

(a) **Form:** It refers to where the innovation is being attempted at. It will cover generation or adoption of technology (product, process service), market (users, buyers, clients) and organisation (structure, function).

(b) **Function:** Most innovation happens on the functional area. This covers innovations to improve quality, reduce cost and add new functions. It also refers to innovation for improving current market attractiveness of the product, enhancing market reach. Functional innovation also leads to increased learning curve within the organisation and attempt production at larger scale, better quality and enhanced skills.

(c) **Extent:** It refers to the scale and coverage of innovation whether it is incremental, revolutionary and existing vs new product or services. In Figure 4.3, various extent of innovations can be seen.

(d) **Timings:** This refers to the aspect of when the innovation is being attempted as compared to competition. This could be first-to-market, quick second, quick third or late follower.

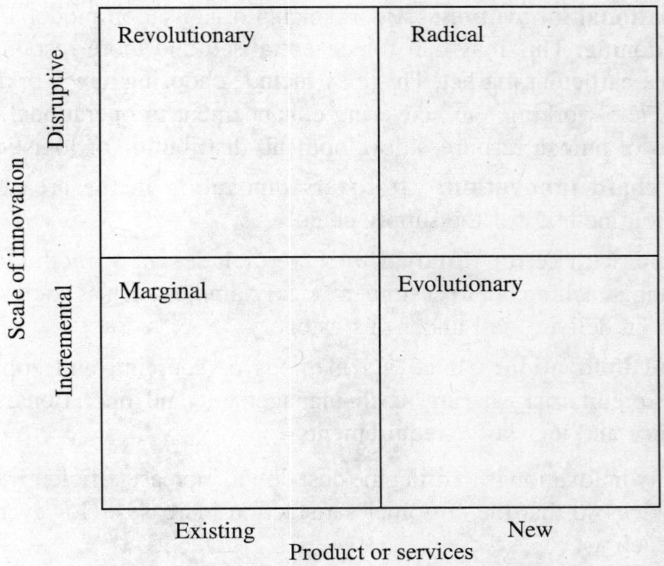

FIGURE 4.3 Extent of Innovation.

[9]Kamm, J.D. (1996), The Portfolio Approach to Divisional Innovation Strategy, *The Journal of Business Strategy*, 7(1), 25–36.

4.10 TYPES OF INNOVATION

- Innovation management is defined as a discipline of managing the process of carrying out innovation in the organisation. This process can be applied for any kind of innovation such as product, process or services innovation. However, variation of the innovation process is expected depending upon the type or the organisation size. Innovation can be done on a variety of areas of a business that may include innovation which is relevant in any organisation and can be applied in a number of different ways.
  (a) **Product innovation:** It refers to developing new or significantly improved products that have better features, functionality and technical capability of convenience.
  (b) **Service innovation:** It refers to improved service that is easy, less costly and cumbersome to use.
  (c) **Business model innovation:** New methods for conducting business by reaching out to customer in new ways with combined offerings. Low cost airlines, Dell make-to-order, etc., most e-commerce sites who use advertising as their source of revenue and give free service to its user fall under this category.
  (d) **Process innovation:** It covers more efficient and improved production, service or delivery process.
  (e) **Organisational innovation:** Reorganising organisation model and structure to do the functioning. This may call for decentralised and more responsive organisation suited to a particular market. This may include choosing new working hours, remote working, tele-working, etc., covering enhancement in operational efficiency, better processes of human resources development, distribution or logistics.
  (f) **Supply chain innovation:** It covers innovation in the areas of sourcing and distribution methods of the supply chain.
  (g) **Sales and Marketing innovation:** It includes new methods for marketing, advertising, reaching out to customers, etc. Examples such as social media promotion and cash on delivery fall under this category.
  (h) **Financial innovation:** It covers methods of sourcing and application of funds covering credit, risk-sharing, cash management and operational process to meet compliance and legislative requirements.

The purpose of any innovation is to bring the cost down, increase efficiency, add new features to the product or services so that the customer satisfaction increases. However, innovation also carries certain risks such as:

- Failure to meet the anticipated benefits such as cost saving or improved customers response
- Investment in innovation may go waste if the innovation is not successful
- Loss of face and reputation in the marketplace for failed innovation

The failure rate of research based innovation is quite high and some figures quote it as high as 60% where the innovation has not been able to achieve the desired results. Yet innovation cannot be avoided as the risk of not innovating is losing the competitive edge and market share.

4.11 THE PROCESS OF INNOVATION

A firm is required to implement process of innovation to channelise creative energy from within the organisation. Innovations do not happen unless the organisation drives its people and team towards it. Even though the ideas may strike to someone within the enterprise but the enterprise must have a well-articulated, simple and fair process to pick up innovation ideas further. Organisations have to take these ideas to a logical conclusion of reaping results for the benefits of the enterprise. The process of innovation is not a complicated process which should be intimidating to an ordinary employee to participate and put forward his/her ideas. Many Indian companies run suggestion box scheme where ideas are submitted for evaluation by a committee. In every case, the person giving suggestion is appreciated and acknowledged for his ideas even though the ideas are not taken for implementation for some reason. The commensurate benefit arising out of the innovation idea is also shared with the employee at a proportion of the benefit in a transparent manner. The difference in the digital world has been that instead of a physical drop box for submitting ideas, a mail id is used to send the idea. Instead of roll of honour displaying the most useful ideas at the entrance of the suggestion management department, these names are displayed on the landing page of the company's website. But the underlying features of simplicity, transparency of evaluation as well as implementation remain as much important as they were before. One more change in the recent times is to include people from outside the firm for idea solicitation process. These people could be customers, suppliers, partners and other stakeholders who may like to propose innovative ideas. Companies engaged in customer service business like hotels and airlines do seek feedback from customers on routine basis. These feedbacks may trigger newer innovation to address these complaints or suggestions. We present here a generic framework of innovation management process which can be used in all situations. Please note that these steps may require IT systems support to lodge all ideas in database and workflow tool to take each idea through the evaluation process. This is presented in Figure 4.4

4.12 INNOVATION LIFE CYCLE

Managing innovation requires a concerted effort on the part of the organisation to take any innovation idea through a series of steps from conceptualisation to realisation. Innovation is no longer a preserve of the R&D department or those involved in marketing or sales alone However, R&D and engineering departments are involved to take innovative ideas to implementation. Innovation ideas can come from anywhere and anyone within or outside the organisation and such ideas are required to be tapped, nurtured and commercialised.

This process is known as innovation cycle that goes through the following steps:

(a) **Develop innovation strategy:** This is a broad activity for the senior management of the firm to decide long-term plan for imbibing innovation at various areas of the business.

(b) **Gather innovation ideas:** At this stage, idea of innovation is gathered. Ideas may be internally generated, externally sourced or adopted from the competition. These ideas may come from structured set ups within the organisation such as R&D units or external sources such as universities and other similar organisations. Sometimes firms solicit ideas through periodical campaigns, running innovation contests or resorting to online social media such as Jamming.

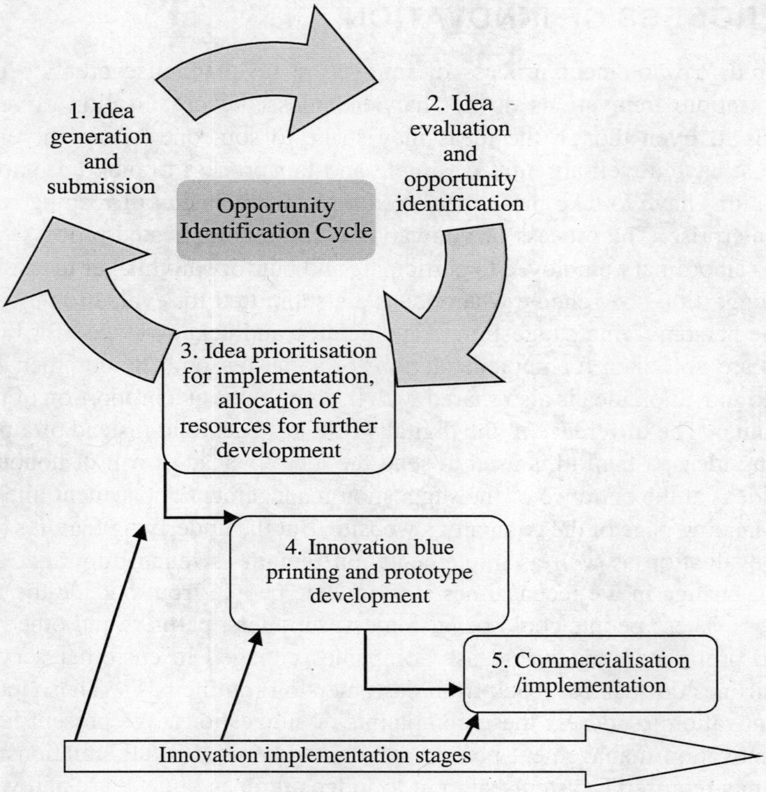

FIGURE 4.4 Innovation Process at Broad Level.

(c) **Evaluate ideas:** Ideas are evaluated based on cost and benefits potential and its likely response from the customer. Those innovations that lead to internal process or efficiency improvement is usually passed through a committee that evaluates and does prioritisation of these ideas based on which resources are allocated.

(d) **Deploy resources:** At this stage, resources such as money, manpower and technical expertise are allocated to work on these innovation ideas to generate prototype, conduct market feasibly, research, etc.

(e) **Design and develop:** At this stage, innovation ideas are taken up for further development where it is translated into new product or product features. Further investigations for adding new features, protecting or generating the intellectual property are carried out

(f) **Produce/implement:** At this stage, the innovated product or process is implemented or taken through the production process.

(g) **Commercialise:** At this stage, the innovation is brought in the market and sold after doing proper marketing campaign, advertising and popularising with the customer. With this the innovation passes to the hands of actual users who may like or dislike the innovations. It is the responsibility of the firm to take feedback of the new changes and quickly correct the shortcomings before the actual customer rejects the innovation. It may be noted that new innovations may replace the old products or services but they still may be used or liked by the customer. Support for older products that are still with the organisation remains a crucial activity. These stages are also depicted as innovation funnel showing various stages of innovation lifecycle as shown in Figure 4.5.

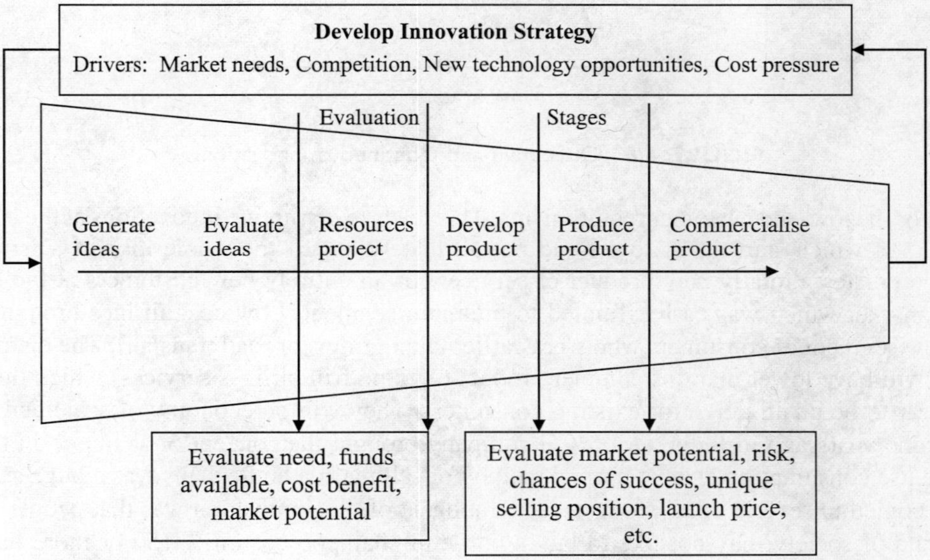

FIGURE 4.5 Innovation Lifecycle.

4.13 DISRUPTIVE AND CONTINUOUS INNOVATION

A well-renowned Professor of Harvard Business School Professor Clayton M. Christensen coined the word "disruptive innovation" in his seminal book Innovators Dilemma. Professor Christensen attributed disruptive innovation to those innovation that creates a new market and new value network and eventually disrupts an existing market and value creating ecosystem that makes the existing markets and its leaders severely impacted. The innovation of digital imaging technology was one such that made photo film technology obsolete. Touch screen technologies were disruptive in nature as compared to old push button technology used in the mobile phones. Figure 4.6 shows how a disruptive innovation quickly takes over the existing firms.

The argument[10] given by Professor Christensen is that while companies continuously innovate to meet higher-end of the customer requirement by bringing out too sophisticated, too expensive and too complicated products that may not be needed by the mass market category of consumers. Since large company focus is towards premium customers who give higher margin tend to ignore

[10]http://www.claytonchristensen.com/key-concepts/ accessed 21 Feb. 2016.

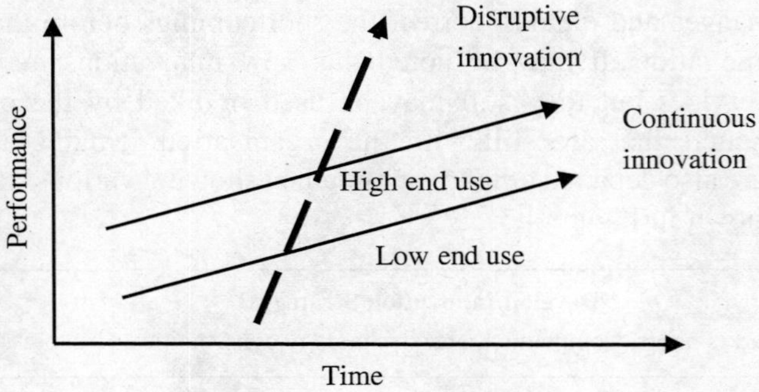

FIGURE 4.6 Disruptive and Continuous Innovation.

the needs of the low-end customer requirements. This leads to disruptive innovations at the bottom of the market which start at the lower-end but ultimately engulf the whole market. Disruptive innovation creates a totally new product or services for an entirely new customers at the lower end of a market which was earlier limited to premium segment. Low cost airlines brought in a totally new segment of consumers who were earlier taking trains or road transport. The disruptive products will have lower margins, simpler product (e.g., no frill airlines services) which initially may appear to be unattractive for existing consumers. They win on economy of scale and mass usage. Some years ago in India, an FMCG company brought the concept of shampoo in sachet for single use consumption against normal method of selling in a bottle. This was a huge success and then copied in several other products. The rationale of this innovation was that people at the lower strata of society may not like to buy a bottle of shampoo costing ₹ 150 or more but can buy at ₹ 2 a sachet for single use. However, this innovation was copied for higher-end markets as well as for hotels who started keeping these sachets in the hotels rooms and business travellers who also kept a pouch or two in their travel kit as well.

It is not unusual to note that established players resist or ignore such disruptive innovation as they are already ensconced in their markets. But as the disruptive innovation starts taking shape, the established players are also forced to take actions to either copy or follow the disruptive innovations but at times they lose the first mover advantage and take efforts to recover due to their marketing might and presence. When Nirma launched a low-cost washing powder in India in 1969, it created a history of sorts and gave tough competition to established players like Hindustan Lever and Tata Chemicals. Starting as a one-man show of the legendary entrepreneur Karsanbhai Patel, today Nirma has over 15000 employees and a turnover of over ₹ 3550 crore and is one of the largest volumes sold in the world using a single brand 'NIRMA'[11]. Some of the innovations done by Nirma was low-cost manufacturing process, special packaging for daily purchasing and value pricing. Hindustan Levers were forced to launch a lower end product called Wheel to counter Nirma's challenge. The story of disruptive innovation does not end with Nirma as in 2011 another upstart brand Ghari has emerged as today's Nirma. Ghari is now market leader in single product category followed by HUL and Nirma. Today, as per a report[12], Ghari is the

[11] https://en.wikipedia.org/wiki/Nirma accessed 22 Feb. 2016.

[12] http://timesofindia.indiatimes.com/business/india-business/Ghari-detergent-all-set-to-enter-Nirmas-home-turf/articleshow/47938452.cms accessed 22 Feb. 2016.

second largest detergent player in India with a market share of 22.8% in 2014-15, while HUL is leader with 34% share with its three brands—Surf, Wheel and Rin. Procter & Gamble (P&G) has 18% share for its brand Tide and Ariel, and Nirma holds less than 12%, as per the industry estimates.

It may be pertinent to note that large firms will have to depend on continuous innovation as a mainstay of their innovation approach since the disruptive innovation typically happens outside and is largely entrepreneur-led. Continued innovation requires several initiatives by the enterprise to make it sustainable as well as enhance the bar of new product or services and keep delighting the customer. The continuous innovation initiatives require a holistic approach to leadership and organisations to create an innovation climate and seamless interaction. It also needs better coordination of innovation process because without continued innovations the organisation will find it difficult to sustain. Continuous innovation is needed for all types of firm, be it a start-up or large firm. While new technologies are not invented every day, innovations can happen at much more rapid pace provided the firm follows some key principles and best practices.

4.14 OPEN AND CLOSED INNOVATION

This is yet another concept that is very relevant while managing the innovation process in the organisation. While closed innovation refers to managing innovation process within the closed boundaries of the firms, the term open innovation refers to partnership and collaboration at different stages of innovation. The advantage of open innovation is the wider base from which the ideas can be sourced, implemented as well as quickly diffused to create an innovation ecosystem. But it also leads to intellectual rights dilution and to some extent loss of control on the entire management process of innovation. Closed innovation is finding less favour in the recent times from among the practitioners and researchers due to several reasons. Primarily among them are the pace of change and interdependence of one industry over others due to rapid advancement of information and communication technologies.

Professor Henry Chesbrough of Haas School of Business in his seminal book Open Innovation[13] and his first article[14] advocated the open innovation principle with an assumption that no firm can ever get all the good people and all the bright ideas from within the enterprise. Not only external R&D has value, should be acquired, but the internal R&D which is not in line with the appetite of the firm's long-term vision can be licensed, or made to spin-off to explore new markets and new products as well. So making best use of internal and external ideas was proposed to be a recipe of success. Professor Chesbrough gives more importance on creating the business model than just the product and owning the IP.

Figure 4.7 shows the difference between closed innovation and open innovation model proposed by Professor Chesbrough.

[13] Henry W. Chesbrough. OPEN INNOVATION. HBS Press, 2006.

[14] Henry W. Chesbrough, The Era of Open Innovation SPRING 2003. *MIT Sloan Management Review*. Vol. 44 No. 3, Reprint Number 4435.

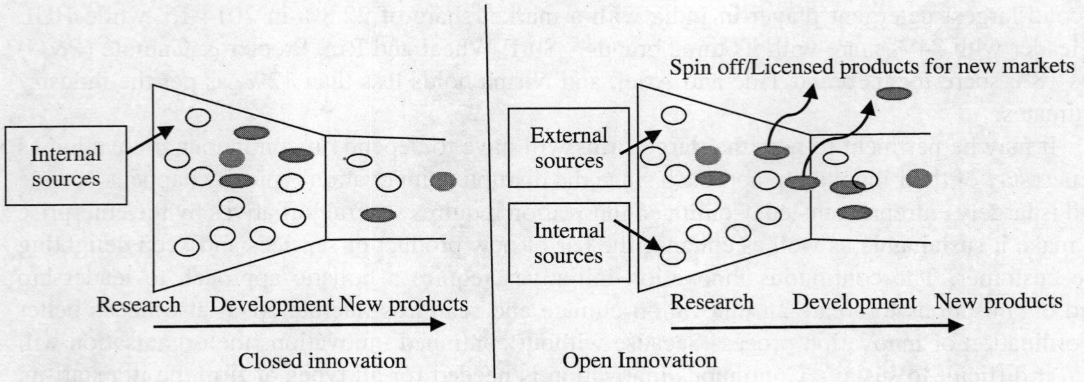

FIGURE 4.7 Chesbrough's Open Innovation Model.

By keeping the open innovation model, a firm can license out technology researched within the firms, license in technology that is researched from outside and spin off or spin in.

4.15 IMPEDIMENTS IN THE INNOVATION PROCESS

Despite the fact that most companies want to be innovative and even spend a lot of time and money in propagating the cause of innovation, a few present a good track record of innovation. Many research studies have concluded the following impediments towards successful innovation:

(a) **Lack of goal clarity:** Many companies are not clear of the goals of innovation and worst still the goal is not clearly articulated to the employees and the stakeholders. It would be next to impossible to gather thousands of unconnected ideas and put them through the evaluation process and provide resources for the implementation. Innovative organisations clearly define short-term and long-term goals of the innovations and even solicit ideas at regular intervals aligned to the goals.

(b) **Lack of role clarity:** Unless a clear role and responsibility is assigned to take the innovation ideas forward, no idea will be implemented. People resist implementing ideas that have not come up from within and try to sabotage any new idea that may be impacting their performance or undermining their authority.

(c) **Action paralysis:** The biggest impediments is the lack of follow up actions within the organisation. Organisation has smart people with hundreds of good ideas but not many is acted upon and therefore ideas remain on paper.

(d) **Resource constraints:** This happens in most struggling organisations who despite knowing fully well that innovation is the only way to survive and grow fail to allocate adequate resources for trying out innovation.

(e) **Communication chaos:** If the communication is not proper and regular, then the purpose and benefits of the innovation will never be understood or realised.

(f) **Absence of teaming:** Innovation usually requires a multidisciplinary team to work on new ideas and this requires good team synergy, the absence of which impacts innovation process.

(g) **No mechanism to welcome ideas from outside world:** As seen in several cases, the innovative ideas need not come from within the employees but also from other people who are part of the larger community. If an organisation has not implemented a mechanism to solicit ideas from the community of its stakeholders, it will find its innovation efforts limited in scale as well as quality.

(h) **Skewed measurement of results:** Some organisations do not measure the progress and results of the innovation project which make it impossible to ascertain the benefits of the innovation. In some organisations, the measurement is so rigorous that all futuristic ideas are killed before they take off. A balanced approach is required.

4.16 KEY FACTORS THAT WILL PROMOTE INNOVATION

Every organisation must focus on certain key factors to build an innovation climate and lead the path of successful innovation.

(a) **Articulate innovation goals:** This refers to not only defining the goals but also making it known to contributors of innovation ideas as well as its implementers.

(b) **Develop an inspiring leadership:** Success of Apple as a leading innovative company is attributed largely to the vision of the legendary Steve Jobs. Many start-ups have passionate and inspiring leaders who have kept the pace of innovation at their forms. Even the much talked about innovation of low cost car by the house of Tata's was due to personal involvement of Ratan Tata, its Chairman emeritus.

(c) **Take risk without which no innovation can take place:** Many established organisations do not want to deviate from the well laid out path and take failures very negatively. They will have issues in promoting innovation culture if they do not promote risk taking culture.

(d) **Formalise a new product development process:** So that the efforts towards new products are properly aligned.

(e) **Entrust innovation ownership to some who can champion the cause:** Every innovation effort has to entrust to a champion who is passionate and has authority and resources to execute it. This person need not be CEO but another leader with maturity and dedication.

(f) **Develop sound hot bed of idea management inviting ideas for exploration and evaluation:** Be transparent in idea selection. This is to make people comfortable to propose newer ideas.

(g) **Provide resources for innovation projects as required:** Once an idea has been accepted, necessary resources should be provided to get the idea converted into reality.

(h) **Take concerted actions to achieve goals:** Many ideas do not get to see the reality because concerted actions are not taken to achieve the goals despite providing necessary resources. A sense of urgency to take action is an important factor for creating an innovation climate.

(i) **Ensure more participation of individuals and working in teams:** People factor which includes participation and working in a team to achieve the end results is also very important. Increase involvement of people by creating cross-functional teams without boundaries between disciplines focusing in products or services.

(j) **Greater communications and building of communities:** Many innovative ideas do not take off if the entire community does not participate in making it a success. This can be ensured through better communication using several IT tools such as creating innovation community, running innovation jam sessions, writing blogs on successes, etc. These are cost-effective and easy to use tool to promote better communication among the innovation community.

(k) **Innovation must add profits, save cost or customer satisfaction:** Innovation for just ornamental change is no good.

(l) **Create capabilities** that is elastic in nature by borrowing resources and partnering with likeminded firms, universities and individuals.

(m) **Multi-skilling across the value chain of people.** It is found that the job rotation and multi-skilling helps in the germination of new ideas.

(n) **Instill a sense of urgency with assigning accountability.** Innovation must be a dream, but with deadline and should not go on forever without a concrete output.

(o) **Train people in best practices.** Innovation requires tools and knowledge of technology. People have to be trained in innovation methods, processes, new technologies and implementation and then only innovation will find its root in the company. Resort to training and coaching.

(p) **Track progress and measure results of every task and innovation.** Better monitoring of results will help in prioritisation of resources and taking mid-course correction.

(q) **Recognise success and reward the team:** Provide timely rewards and recognition to team for their success.

As the pace of external change accelerates, the need for continuous innovation grows.

SALT 4.1 (Stories and Learning Task) How Google Manages Innovation

Google is, by far, one of the most innovative organisations of the recent times. Not only it has invited attention from stick markets but the researchers and academic community is equally interested to know how Google has been able to remain so innovative in the last decades of its existence. In a research conducted by Annika Steiber titled How Google Manages Continuous Innovation in a Rapidly Changing World[15], several key points are brought out.

One of the key points is the realisation of the fact that inability of large corporation to keep pace with the change makes large and previously enviable companies lose market share. So the only way to keep pace with change is to increase dependence on employees' creative abilities and keep changing traditional management methods. By 2012 within fourteen years of its birth, Google become the most valuable brand, clocked sales of 50 billion dollars and nearly 11 billion dollars in gross profits. Google been able to combine deep engineering skill in computer science and expertise on managing human resources based on six management principles.

- Dynamic capabilities. By ingenerating external and external capabilities quickly.
- A continuously changing organisation proactively.

[15] http://www.strategos.com/google-model-managing-continuous-innovation-rapidly-changing-world/ accessed 23 Feb. 2016.

- A people-centric approach based on the belief that people are and want to be creative and as a company Google must give them the opportunity.
- An ambidextrous organisation, which is conventional and planned for routine tasks by being flexible and open for innovation and experiments.
- An open organisation which exchanges information with their community quickly andeasily.
- 70-20-10 rule. Doing 70% of the efforts on core product, 20% on supporting and the remaining 10% for innovation of each employee's choice.

Discussion Questions

1. Trace various types of innovations done by Google in recent times.
2. What challenges you visualize if these principles are to be implemented in traditional organisations?

4.17 AI/GEN AI AS A CATALYST FOR CONTINUOUS AND DISRUPTIVE INNOVATION

Innovation, the process of introducing new ideas to create added value, is a critical differentiator for businesses. Generative AI acts as a powerful catalyst for both continuous (incremental improvements) and disruptive innovation (creating new markets or value networks). Gen AI models can rapidly generate novel concepts, solutions, and prototypes across various domains, significantly accelerating the initial stages of the innovation funnel. This enables organizations to explore a much wider range of possibilities than previously feasible, driving continuous product and process enhancements.

Beyond incremental improvements, Gen AI fosters disruptive innovation by enabling "mass personalization" and "customization at scale". This capability allows businesses to create highly personalized products, services, and experiences tailored to individual user needs, fostering deeper customer engagement and loyalty. This is a new dimension of disruption, as it fundamentally changes the relationship between producers and consumers, moving beyond mass-market models to hyper-tailored experiences. For instance, AI-powered marketing can generate personalized content at a fraction of the time and cost, leading to higher conversion rates. This capability can also help overcome the "innovator's dilemma" by enabling firms to explore and serve new, potentially lower-margin, customer segments with tailored solutions that might have been uneconomical with traditional methods.

4.18 AI-DRIVEN IDEATION, CREATIVITY, AND DESIGN THINKING

Generative AI is profoundly reshaping the processes of ideation, creativity, and design thinking. It moves beyond simply assisting human thought to actively participating in the generation of novel ideas. Gen AI models can rapidly generate hundreds of potential solutions by mixing existing knowledge in surprising ways. This significantly accelerates the front-end of the innovation funnel, allowing organizations to explore a much wider range of possibilities than previously feasible.

AI functions as a powerful augmentation tool for human creatives, generating content, visuals, and ideas that complement and inspire their work. This human-AI symbiosis can lead to more original, impactful, and differentiated innovations. When human innovators collaborate with AI systems, ideas can be processed in parallel, teams can avoid groupthink and status-based filtering, and connections between different knowledge areas can be identified in ways humans might miss.

The integration of AI into the design thinking process transforms it from a purely human-centric endeavor to a human-AI collaborative one. In an AI-Centered Design Thinking framework, AI tools are embedded at each stage:

- **Empathize:** AI analyzes vast customer data to identify unstated needs and pain points.
- **Define:** AI clusters problems to reveal core challenges and opportunities.
- **Ideate:** Generative AI produces diverse solution concepts and preliminary designs.
- **Prototype:** AI tools rapidly visualize ideas and create virtual prototypes, enabling quick testing without building physical models.
- **Test:** Machine learning algorithms identify patterns in user feedback, providing insights for refinement.

This integration implies a shift in the skills required for innovation teams, emphasizing prompt engineering, critical evaluation of AI outputs, and the ability to effectively orchestrate AI tools to drive the innovation process.

4.19 OPEN INNOVATION IN THE AI ERA: LEVERAGING EXTERNAL AI CAPABILITIES

The concept of open innovation, where firms leverage external ideas and pathways to market in addition to internal ones, is becoming even more critical and expansive in the AI era. Generative AI's capabilities facilitate broader external collaboration and ecosystem-driven innovation models.

The proliferation of open-source AI models, such as Llama by Meta , and the increasing accessibility of powerful AI platforms offered by cloud providers like Amazon Bedrock and Azure OpenAI Service, significantly lower the barrier to entry for AI innovation. These platforms and models allow firms to consume sophisticated AI capabilities via APIs or fine-tune existing models without the prohibitive cost and time of building AI from scratch. This democratizes AI capabilities, making "open innovation" a competitive necessity rather than merely an option.

Firms can now license in advanced AI models , partner with specialized AI startups, or leverage open-source AI models to accelerate their innovation efforts. This approach facilitates frictionless partner integration, data and intellectual property sharing (within defined governance frameworks), and co-innovation workflows, maximizing collective innovation potential. AI can even be used to scan external sources like patents, research papers, and social media to identify complementary technologies and potential partners more efficiently. The accessibility of powerful AI models means that organizations can no longer rely solely on internal R&D; they must constantly scan, integrate, and leverage external AI advancements to remain competitive, pushing open innovation from a strategic choice to a fundamental operating model.

4.20 MEASURING CREATIVITY AND INNOVATION IN AI-DRIVEN ENVIRONMENTS (BEYOND TRADITIONAL ROI)

Measuring the success of innovation has always been complex, often relying on traditional financial metrics like Return on Investment (ROI). However, for AI and Generative AI initiatives, traditional ROI metrics often fall short and can even be misleading. AI's impact compounds over time, and its most significant value often stems from operational efficiencies, enhanced innovation capabilities, and risk reduction, which are inherently difficult to quantify in immediate dollar terms. A singular focus on ROI can lead to short-term thinking, causing organizations to prematurely abandon AI projects before their full strategic value is realized.

The inadequacy of traditional ROI for AI highlights a deeper challenge in organizational performance measurement: how to quantify the value of strategic, long-term, and transformative initiatives that do not fit neatly into existing financial models. This necessitates a shift towards a more adaptive and multifaceted measurement framework, moving beyond direct cost savings to encompass innovation, risk mitigation, and the unlocking of human potential.

Instead of solely chasing a single ROI number, organizations should track a broader set of metrics across four key areas to truly capture AI's value:

4.21 AI-DRIVEN INNOVATION METRICS

Metric Category	Specific Key Performance Indicators (KPIs)	Value and Significance
Operational Efficiency Gains	Time and effort saved by the team, reduction in manual tasks, faster decision-making (real-time insights), employee productivity (AI-assisted workflows reducing workload).	Directly quantifies the immediate benefits of AI in streamlining operations and freeing up human capital for higher-value work.
Adoption and Usage Metrics	Adoption rate (employees actively engaging with AI tools), usage patterns (strategic vs. basic tasks), employee AI fluency (skills improving over time).	Crucial for ensuring AI tools are actually being utilized effectively. Poor adoption can negate any potential ROI, as AI's value is realized through its application.
Business Impact and Innovation	Revenue growth from AI-driven insights, customer experience improvements (e.g., faster response times, personalization), new business models or product innovations.	Measures AI's contribution to top-line growth and strategic differentiation, indicating its role in creating new value and competitive advantages.
Risk Reduction and Compliance	Fewer compliance violations (automated monitoring), better decision-making reducing costly errors, cybersecurity improvements (AI-driven threat detection).	Quantifies AI's role in safeguarding the business from avoidable risks and ensuring adherence to regulatory standards, contributing to long-term stability and trust.

This comprehensive approach to metrics helps organizations understand the multifaceted impact of AI, moving beyond a narrow financial view to a holistic strategic one. It forces finance departments to evolve their analytical capabilities and embrace a more sophisticated understanding of value creation that integrates strategic and operational KPIs with traditional financial ones. Furthermore, frameworks for measuring creativity in AI-driven innovation are emerging, focusing on criteria such as relevance, effectiveness, problematization, propulsion, elegance, and genesis of the generated solutions. This allows for a more differentiated assessment of product creativity within the broader innovation process.

4.22 SUMMARY

This chapter was focussed on innovation management. It started with outlining conceptual foundation of innovation and how technology plays a role in driving innovation. We first defined what innovation is and how it is different from invention. As stated innovation is not always developing something totally new which is called invention. Innovation is basically finding some added value for the firm by introduction of new ideas. We then discussed the theories of technological change as invention-innovation-diffusion trilogy. The next topic discussed was the relationship of innovation and creativity in the context of business. Business creativity directly impacts business outcome by addressing customer needs and generating business value for the firm and, therefore, there is a difference between innovation and just plain creativity. We postulated that companies must not only have creative ideas but should also run the execution process of converting these ideas into business result through the process of innovation management. Having established these fundaments, we defined the goals of innovation, which were summarised as 5 Cs covering Cost reduction, Customer satisfaction, Compliance and regulation and meeting Competitive pressure and climate protection. The next discussion in this chapter was on design thinking as a way for innovation, a topic which is drawing a lot of contemporary attention as well as curiosity. The next topic was to outline the sources of innovation and various innovation dimensions such as form, function, extent and timings.

The next major discussion was on innovation management process and its various impacts and outcome. The innovation life cycle was discussed to explain various stages of carrying out innovation.

This chapter also covered some of the latest researches on newer topics of innovation such as disruptive and continuous innovation as well as open and closed innovation.

We then discussed the likely impediments in the innovation process and key factors that will promote innovation for any firm. We ended the chapter with SALT (Stories and Learning Task) on How Google Manages Innovation. A case of Tata Nano, a case study of innovation, was also discussed.

Key Terms: Disruptive Innovation, Continuous Innovation, Open Innovation, Closed Innovation.

REVIEW QUESTIONS

1. What is the difference between continuous and disruptive innovation?
   Answer: Section 4.13
2. What is the difference between open and closed innovation? **Answer:** Section 4.14

3. Why established companies fail to bring disruptive innovations?
4. What are impediments in conducting successful innovations within a large enterprise?
5. Suggest at least ten best practices that can promote health innovation climate within a company.
6. Outline a typical innovation processes and define its various stages with inputs and outputs. **Answer:** Sections 4.11, 4.12

APPLICATIVE QUESTIONS/PROJECT/TEAM ASSIGNMENT

Examine the disruptive innovations in ICT space in Indian Context. Do you think the popular Indian railways site IRCTC.com is an example of continuous or disruptive innovation? Trace its development over last five years to give your answer.

REFERENCES

"Too Much Ventured Nothing Gained: VCs Are a Hurting Bunch, New Companies Feel Their Pain," Fortune, 25 November 2002.

For an account of Nokia's R&D approach to GSM, see M. Häikiö, "Nokia: The Inside Story" (*London, Financial Times*, Prentice Hall, 2002), 120–121 (in particular).

M. Sawhney, E. Prandelli and G. Verona, "The Power of Innomediation," *MIT Sloan Management Review 44* (winter 2003): 77–82; and J.D. Wolpert,"Breaking Out of the Innovation Box," *Harvard Business Review* 80 (August 2002): 76–83.

CASE STUDY

Tata Nano, a Case Study of Innovation

Tata Nano is considered as one of the cheapest cars in the world. Produced by Tata Motor Limited, the most respected names in Indian automobile industry who are well-known for their commercial vehicles over the last 50 years. This car was a dream project of its Chairman Mr. Ratan Tata who envisioned an affordable car for people who is buying a car for the first time. Some reports have quoted in the press that Mr. Tata saw an Indian family of four, two adults and two children in a scooter while in a heavy rain that moved him to take the lead. Such sight is very common in Indian cities, especially, smaller ones where middle class depends on two wheelers like scooters or motor cycle for local commuting and the entire family rides on it. For Mr. Tata the common sight was moving from the point of view of the safety as well as unfulfilled need that the ace car maker visualised. Mr. Ratan Tata, Chairman of Tata Group pioneered an innovation, like Nano for the people of India and transportation. Such innovation was much needed in India where poor mass transportation system forces people to depend on their own transport but they cannot afford expensive cars which could be safer and instead they use two wheelers. While the father drives the scooter, the elder child stands in the front and the younger one sits on the lap of the pillion rider mother. Tata Nano was visualised to give a safer mode of transport in an affordable basis to such millions of middle class families in India. That is how Tata Nano as a "People's car" was borne which would be affordable for almost everybody.

Tata Motors is a well-established name in India which was established in 1945 as manufacturer of diesel locomotives for Indian Railways. Its first commercial vehicle, a truck, was made in 1954 by seeking technology transfer from Daimler-Benz AG of Germany. Though this collaboration ended in 1969, Tata Motors continued its growth in this segment and expanded into a variety of large and small trucks and buses for the commercial segment. During March 2008, Tata Motors acquired British Jaguar Land Rover (JLR) which has famous luxury branded cars, such as Rover, Daimler and Lanchester.

When Tata Nano was unveiled, it created a market storm of sorts. During the first two days of opening, it received 5000+ booking which kept on increasing every day since the launch. It had stylish and comfortable design and was using a fuel-efficient engine. The car was designed to meet all safety requirements. Its promotional tag line said, "Have Fun, Pay Less, get more with Tata Nano" and created huge customer expectations. Eager customers touted this as "One lakh car" and Tata Motors resorted to innovative methods to meet that expectation. It used target costing method, used penetration pricing and kept low pricing policy with minimum profit margin.

A revolution was in the sight. But soon after the launch, Nano started getting adverse customer feedback while in use. Its plastic body was prone to breakage on minor impact on crowded Indian roads. The small fuel tank capacity of 30 ltr was not suitable for people to take it on long route. In addition, lack of all safety features, such as no disc brakes created apprehensions in the minds of the customer. Its rear-mounted engine was found to be heating fast and on some occasion caught fire which was widely reported in media. In the absence of front engine, the impact on passengers in the event of a head on collision was great. Their manufacturing facility in West Bengal ran into difficulties due to protest from locals who wanted their land back and the new government ordered the closure of the plant. Its lower manufacturing output, heavy cost due to relocation of the plant from Singur West Bengal to Gujarat and Uttarakhand created heavy cash out flow. In addition, its low sales resulted in less than projected income. This problem was further increased due to significant economic downturns leading to lower demand in the market. Since its launch in 2009, it never witnessed sales growth and lunged to 74% by the quarter ending September, 2013 and just 948 units were sold in the month of April, 2013 and not a single car was exported. Mr. Tata, in an interview to CNBC[16] said, "It (Nano) became termed as the cheapest car by the public and, I am sorry to say, by ourselves, not by me, but the company when it was marketing it. I think that is unfortunate." His words sum up the reason of Nano's poor showing is due to stigma of being cheap car. In India car is a symbol of prosperity and no one wants to own a cheap car!

The revival of Nano is going on under the new chairman according to the press reports.

Questions

1. Do you think Tata Nano is a disruptive innovation?
2. What are its future potential?
3. What went wrong here, technology, innovation, branding, positioning or something else?

[16] http://trak.in/tags/business/2013/11/30/ratan-tata-nano-failed/accessed 31 May 2016.

DISCUSSION QUESTION

1. Suppose a new solar vehicle is to be launched by an established auto manufacturer like Tata Motor. What innovations would you suggest in product, process, busines model, marketing and organizations?

ADDITIONAL READINGS

1. Anderson cyclical model of technological change, *Administrative Science Quarterly* 35: 604-633, Press: Cambridge, UK.
2. Suarez, F. and J. Utterback, 1995, Dominant designs and the survival of firms. Strategic, 15:285–305.
3. Tim Brown, Design Thinking, *Harvard Business Review*, June 2008.
4. Tom Kelley, *The Art of Innovation*.
5. IDEO's Design Thinking for Educators website.
6. Susan Weinschenk, 100 Things Every Designer Should Know About People.
7. Teacher Resources on Design Thinking at Henry Ford Learning Institute.

Chapter 5

Technology Forecasting, Assessment and Acquisition

Business has only two functions, innovation and marketing.

— Peter F. Drucker

At the end of this chapter, we will learn:

- Understanding Technology Trends
- Technological forecasting and assessment
- Forecasting methods: Intuitive, extrapolation and growth curves
- Tracing technological evolution in various contexts: Industry, organisational and strategic
- Technology monitoring process, explorative and normative
- Technology morphological analysis, mission flow diagram
- Technology choice, technological leadership and followership
- Technology planning, tools
- Technology acquisition methods
- Timings of entry of technology

5.1 INTRODUCTION

Forecasting anything is tough especially about technology which is ever changing and its outcome unpredictable. Yet in a fiercely competitive world, firms will have to do continuous crystal grazing to keep a watch on upcoming technologies that can be a source of advantage, or which can challenge or disrupt their existing game plan. By keeping a tab on what is likely to happen that can be of interest, a firm can also invest in developing them to get better returns early on for their business. This chapter will focus on the processes and methods adopting which a firm can conduct technology forecasting function, prepare itself for adopting it and take calculated risk of delaying its adoption. Many leading companies have faced serious consequences for ignoring the adoption of the upcoming technologies that were quickly marketed by the competition leading to loss to their business.

In this chapter after introducing the concepts of technological forecasting and assessment, we will discuss the popular methods for technology forecasting. We will trace technological evolution in various contexts such as industry, organisational and strategic and explain its monitoring methods. We will undertake technology planning process and tools used to trace trajectories of technology. Finally, we would discuss technology acquisition management and technology timing for adoption.

5.2 UNDERSTANDING AND MONITORING TRENDS

According to business dictionary[1], a trend is a pattern of gradual change in a condition, output, or process, or an average or general tendency of a series of data points to move in a certain direction over time, represented by a line or curve on a graph. In case of technology, this represents the evolution of the technology and its likely maturity over time. By understanding trends a manager can take appropriate decision about when and how to invest in the new technology and reap reward by staying ahead of its competition.

Understanding and observing trend of business is equally important to understand which direction businesses are going. All businesses evolve over time and newer ways of doing things emerge to support the evolving needs of the customer. By understating and monitoring the trends on the business and customer side, a technology manager can choose appropriate technologies that can help support meeting the new requirements.

Understanding trends involves various activities that a firm may perform to get deeper insight of the emerging trend. This has the following steps:

- Analysing the trend involves studying why such developments are happening, what its sources are and its speed of development and potential impact on the current scenario. Using some of the mathematical techniques, historical results can be used to predict future outcome.
- Monitoring trend involves observing key changes and reporting the same to the decision makers.
- Trend projecting involves using the past data and present observation and applying them to project the future course. Trend projection could be as simple as extrapolating a curve and could be as complex as using expert opinion to see cyclical fluctuations or changes due to environmental triggers.
- Simulating trend: In many cases, the future prediction of the trend may not be done using a mathematical formula. This could be due to multiple variables which may be moving in different directions. Hence the method of simulation is used to predict the future. Simulation also includes dealing with uncertainties by applying probability of few variables while predicting the future of any trend.

There are various reasons why a manager should study trends. Some of them are as follows:

(a) It will help in generating new ideas and opportunities.
(b) It will give early warning signals when things start going wrong and suitable course corrections may be applied.
(c) By keeping a close watch of the trends in the business and the related technology will give immense confidence to the business managers. They will know what they are doing or not doing and why so.

[1] http://www.businessdictionary.com/definition/trend.html#ixzz3yERvp69a accessed 250116

(d) By taking proactive action to position the firm with latest technology and customer offerings of products or services, the firm can do better than the competition.

(e) Understanding, monitoring and taking appropriate actions based on the business and technology trends will help the manager to chart out a well-balanced strategies.

(f) Having a good grasp on the trends, the firm will be better prepared for the future.

5.3 METHODOLOGIES FOR STUDYING TECHNOLOGY TRENDS

One of the popular methodologies proposed by globally renowned research firm Gartner is called Gartner Hype Cycle Methodology. This is a curve which plots emerging technologies at various stages from their inception to maturity and predicts the time it will take to reach the maturity stage. Every technology according to Gartner goes through the five stages lifecycle. The present placement of the technology along the Gartner hype cycle curve denotes the stage along its lifecycle. The legend of the technology shows the time it is expected to reach the maturity stage. The five stages of the Gartner hype cycle methodology are as follows:

- Innovation Trigger
- Peak of Inflated Expectations
- Trough of Disillusionment
- Scope of Enlightenment
- Plateau of Productivity

The two factors that the graph considers are time to maturity and the present state of the technology. Figure 5.1[2] gives trends of various emerging technologies in IT sector. Similar trends are projected by Gartner and other research firms in other sectors as well.

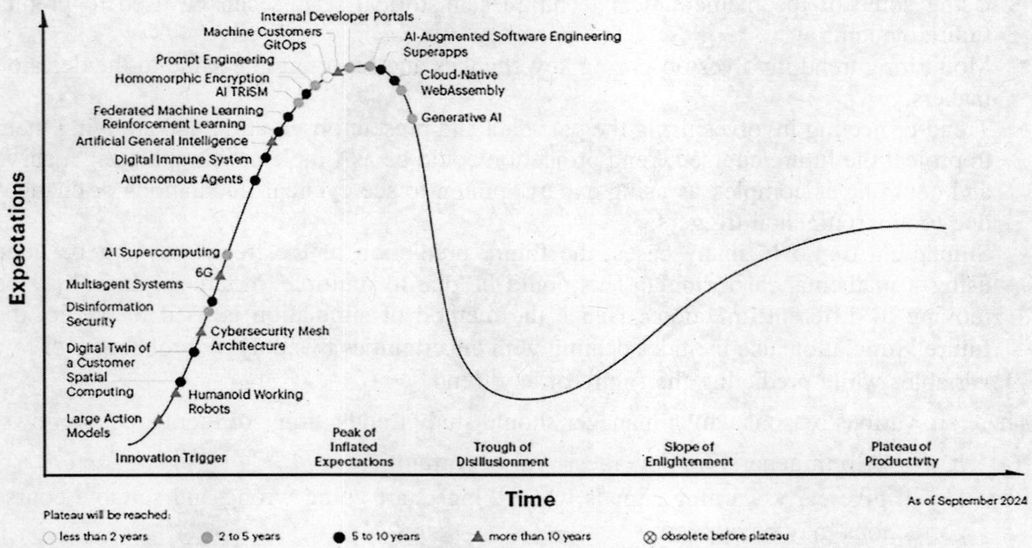

Source: Gartner

FIGURE 5.1 Hype Cycle for Emerging Technologies, 2024.

[2] https://www.gartner.com/en/articles/hype-cycle-for-emerging-technologies accessed 23082025

5.4 WHY FORECAST TECHNOLOGY DEVELOPMENT?

One of the prime reasons for technology forecasting is to prepare the organisation to grab new opportunities as well as fight from obsolescence arising due to new technology. Technology forecasting entails visualising the improved performance characteristics of technology on products and services. These performance factors could be lower power consumption, optimum use of raw material, increased capacity, better speed, etc. For example, a number of transistors in a chip has been used to forecast the miniaturisation of electronics components for several decades. Haulage capacity of aircraft, speed of the trains or cars are similar such examples of forecasting technology performance characteristics. In the consumer world, the processor of the mobile phones, pixel density of the camera, etc. are yet another way by which the advancement of technology can be predicted even though one may not know how and when it will be achieved. Forecasting is always done for useful machines, services or commodities that have large number of users and is usually not done for experimental or luxury items.

Technology forecasting is necessary for planning and making investments in either developing or acquiring technology. This exercise is not only required at the company level but also for the country or region so as to give incentives around adoption and development of new technologies. Companies can prioritise research and development expenditure; plan new products as well as make improvements in the existing one and also take strategic decision for technology licensing, joint ventures or creating alliance or consortium to develop them. Small companies need Technology Forecasting (TF short form for the discussion in this chapter) to innovate quickly and compete with large and established players who may be reluctant to adopt new technology as they may have made investment in the older one already.

Competing companies adapt to technology forecasting to gather Competitive Technological Intelligence (CTI or TI in short) so that they can prepare themselves. They may have to adequately plan marketing campaign to educate the users in case their technology roadmap is competing with others. In the mobile world, CDMA vs GSM technology used to be a hot topic for discussion. Touch phones have revolutionised the mobile handset industry which several players have gained due to good investment, planning and acquisition of technology ahead of their competition.

TF is not just done to predict when the technology will mature and become viable for the commercial use but also to predict its wide spread adoption for the masses. Similarly, Technology Forecasting and Assessment for those technologies impacting society are done to predict long-term impact on the society. Those emerging technologies that improve health, sanitation, safety and similar usage would require governments to fund their development and formulate public policies. Solar electricity or solar powered vehicles is such technology that requires more efforts to make it wide spread adoption through incentives from government as they impact the larger social impact on energy conservation, pollution free environment.

5.5 TECHNOLOGY FORECASTING ANALYTICAL FRAMEWORK

Technology forecasting and assessment can serve various purposes which can be grouped under the following approaches[3] as shown in Figure 5.2.

[3] A MIT Study titled Technological Forecasting—A Review, by Ayse Kaya Firat, Wei Lee Woon, Stuart Madnick, Working Paper CISL# 2008-15, September 2008, gives a good insight. http://web.mit.edu/smadnick/www/wp/2008-15.pdf accessed 29 Dec. 2014.

- Technology monitoring
- Technical or competitive intelligence
- Technology prediction
- Technology roadmapping
- Technology assessment
- Technology foresight

All these TF approaches though somewhat overlapping has different purpose to serve. While these TF approaches may use similar tools or accomplish similar end results their end result is different. Some of these approaches are for the purpose to serve as a thought paper for policy formulation and initiating discussion but some others are to prompt actions or link the former with the later.

Although TF is usually done for a specific technology, yet sometimes its scope can be broad and wide covering a set of related technologies. For example, semiconductor technology impacts electronics industry, fuel research impact automobile and aviation, and IT impacts practically all other industries. So TF in one technology may have impact on the other and this needs to be taken into account.

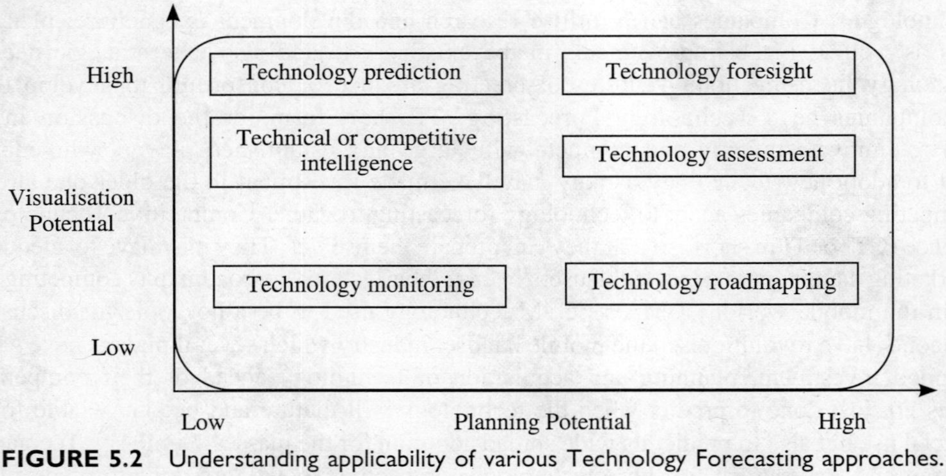

FIGURE 5.2 Understanding applicability of various Technology Forecasting approaches.

5.6 TECHNOLOGY FORECASTING TOOLS AND METHODS

As discussed earlier, TF uses various tools and methods, the most commonly used ones are Delphi method, growth curve and its extrapolation, scenario development, relevance trees, morphological models, mission flow, diagrams, etc. All these techniques can be further classified into ***exploratory*** and ***normative*** methods. These terminologies are well-established but sometimes it may confuse us. Let us define them in detail to gain more clarity.

- **Exploratory methods** start from present and extrapolate all the past trend to define a point in the future. This technique is also termed as "outward focused". These methods include tools such as trend analysis, cross impact analysis and Delphi techniques. Figure 5.3 represents it diagrammatically.

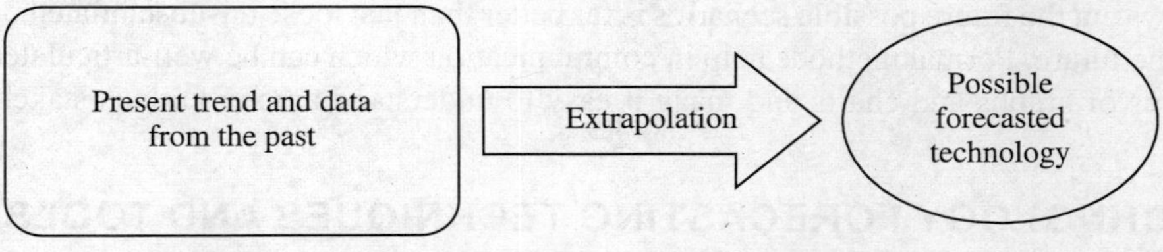

FIGURE 5.3 Explorative Methods.

- **Normative methods (as shown in Figure 5.4),** on the other hand, visualise a tentative view of a possible or desirable future and they try to work backwards to see if the current situation, achievement, constraints and past trends support it or not. These methods also bring out how the foreseen future can be achieved or cannot be achieved with the given limitations. A good example is of the visualising speed of the railway trains or automobiles and then working backwards if it can be achieved. IT has several examples where the future is visualised either by researchers or science fiction writers and the rest of the people work backwards to arrive at means to achieve them. These normative methods are more suitable for technology planning and include various techniques such as morphological analyses and relevance trees, Goals Delphi, Success scenarios, Aspirational scenario workshops, etc. We will discuss each one of them in detail later in the chapter.

  However, in each of these techniques broadly a shared vision of expected as well as desired future is drawn. The team then carves out the most plausible one and then participants are asked to work backwards to check how with present capabilities and constraints can make it possible.

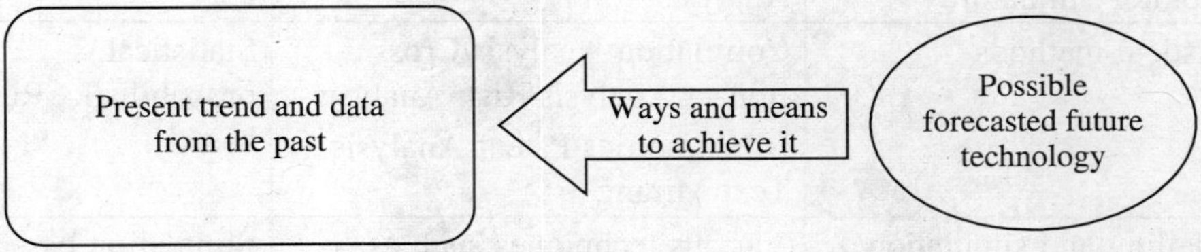

FIGURE 5.4 Normative Methods.

- **Which is the best approach amongst the two?** In fact, none of these approaches can be hundred per cent accurate or can stand of its own to guarantee a fair degree of certainty. In practice, a combination of the two methods with several supporting tools and techniques are used. While in goal-oriented situation where the new technology goals is already been established, the normative approaches are most useful. However, defining a shared goal and bringing consensuses is a tough call for any technology forecaster. In such a situation, exploratory methods can be used to project the future.
- **Why use formal approaches?** One question can be asked that if future is so hazy and unpredictable why use any formal method at all and instead base our judgement on experience inputs. But this is not a correct way to address this problem. Use of formal methods and tools enhances the value of the forecasting exercise and provide legitimacy. Any exercise that has structured collection of anticipatory intelligence, data and then

draws out the future possible scenarios is far better than just loose unsubstantiated opinions of the future. Formal methods help in communication which can be well-articulated in the forms of graphs and charts and make it easy to understand among various stakeholders.

5.7 TECHNOLOGY FORECASTING TECHNIQUES AND TOOLS

In this section, we would briefly present the forecasting techniques and tools which can be used at different stages of the technology forecasting and assessment process.

It may be useful to start with a brief categorisation of these techniques in terms of their characteristics, applicabilities and key advantages as well as limitations as per Table 5.1.

TABLE 5.1 Classification of Various Techniques for Technology Forecasting[4]

	Broad category	Techniques or method	Key characteristics
1	Experience and expertise based	Delphi	Polled expert judgement
2	Experience and expertise based	Participative workshops/ interviews	Consensus judgement
3	Based on past trend, Exploratory in nature	Trend Extrapolation using Growth Curve including Trend Impact Analysis	Data based
4	Based on past trend, exploratory in nature	Precursor Analysis/Long Wave Analysis	Analytical fact based
5	Statistical methods	Correlation Analysis/Cross Impact Analysis/Risk Analysis Bibliometrics/Patent Analysis, Text Mining	Statistical, probabilistic, Research based
6	Modelling and simulation	Various techniques such as: Agent Modelling • Cross Impact Analysis • Sustainability Analysis • Causal Models • Diffusion Modelling • Complex Adaptive System Modelling	Simulation based, probabilistic
7	Systems simulation, System dynamics, KSIM (Kane simulation)	• Technological substitution • Scenario-simulation • Economic base modelling • Technology assessment	As above

(contd.)

[4] Classification Source : Technological Forecasting – A Review, by Ayse Kaya Firat, Wei Lee Woon, Stuart Madnick, Working Paper CISL# 2008-15, September 2008, gives a good insight. http://web.mit.edu/smadnick/www/wp/2008-15.pdf accessed 29, Dec. 2014.

TABLE 5.1 Classification of Various Techniques for Technology Forecasting (*Contd.*)

	Broad category	Techniques or method	Key characteristics
8	Scenarios building methods	Scenarios management • Scenario-simulation • Field Anomaly Relaxation Method [FAR]	Explorative, visualisation based
9	Valuing/Decision/ Economics methods	Relevance Trees • Action Analysis • Cost-benefit Analysis • Decision Analysis • Economic Base Modelling	Financial justification based
10	Descriptive and matrices methods	Analogies • Back Casting • Checklist for Impact Identification • Innovation System Modelling • Institutional Analysis • Mitigation Analysis • Morphological Analysis • Road Mapping • Social Impact Assessment • Multiple Perspectives Assessment • Organisational Analysis • Requirements Analysis	Analysis based
11	Creativity oriented methods	• Brainstorming or Brain Writing; Nominal Group Process (NGP)] • Creativity Workshops • TRIZ • Vision Generation • Science Fiction Analysis	Futuristic idea generation based

5.8 TECHNOLOGY FORESIGHTING METHODOLOGY

Any methodology is broadly the sequence of steps to accomplish certain objectives. In the case of technology foresighting, we will need a sequence of methods to achieve our objectives to arrive at possible technology scenario of the future and steps to plan actions for our company. This framework can be simply captured in three-step process as shown in Figure 5.5.

5.8.1 Technology Assessment

This refers to understanding the current state of the relevant technology, current research work, patents being filed, field trails being conducted or technology grazers hypothesising of the future.

This also entails assessing what is the state of the current technology being used in the firm and its own state of affairs as far as the technology research, development and skill building is concerned. In short, this stage covers to understand where we (the firm as well as the world) stand.

5.8.2 Technology Predicting

This is the phase to define or visualise the future of technology. This is the phase where one needs to explore what can happen (Prognosis). This is a core and creative phase of the foresighting methodology and future studies. This phase is not to predict but to visualise various possibilities of a possible future and the challenges that it may impose. It helps to prepare the decision makers for anticipated future.

Scenario planning method is useful at this stage to visualize various alternatives of the future. Initially adopted from classic methods used in military, this method visualizes various impacts such as demography, technology, mineral reserve, economic, environmental, and political trends. Simulation and statistical techniques make the futuristic visualisation more robust as they bring data to support the likely scenario based on the past trends and present situations. Such data collected through earlier phases or data-oriented methods make the discussion useful between the stakeholders to gain their acceptance. Sometimes survey using Delphi method would be appropriate.

5.8.3 Technology Planning

This is the phase where the firm does the action to prepare itself towards the futuristic technology. This phase is similar to the exercise done in strategic planning exercise where you define a road map meet the strategic goal. The only difference here is that this is a technology future that the organisation is visualising and accordingly it is taking steps to go step by step to reach there. Prescription methods originate in strategic planning. Tools such as road mapping, back casting, cross impact analysis, scenario building and modelling and simulation are used depending upon

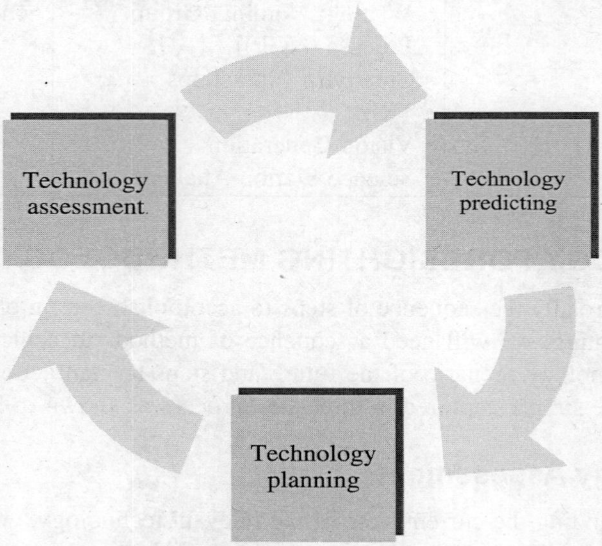

FIGURE 5.5 Technology Foresighting Stages.

how certain or hazy the technology future appears. For example, if the technology forecast is very definite, then road mapping is the best tool. If the firm wants to establish, then when and which are the stages of decision points the back casting tool should be used. In the situation where a number of alternatives exist for the future, modelling and simulation will be more useful at this phase. In certain cases, scenario building can also be used to establish the outcome of the actions today on the future canvas. Suppose the future of technology has multifaceted interaction and impact on each other, tools like cross-impact analysis will help in arriving at the structured analysis of their interaction.

5.9 THE CONCEPT OF S-CURVE

S-curve is a widely used model to explain the development of any technology across its lifecycle. It is also used to explain adoption or diffusion in widespread use. Though both S-curves look the same but the stages of its various portions convey different meaning.

5.9.1 S-curve for Technology Development

Most technologies follow a predictable pattern of development following that corresponds to the slanted capital letter S. Plotted against two ordinates of performance and time, any technology takes a slow start of development at the beginning. After some time, the initial breakthrough is achieved and technology gets rapid expansion and commensurate enhancement of its performce over shorter period of time which is shown by the rapid rise of the S-curve indicating the rapid growth. After some time, the technology improvement starts to reach its limit and performce improvement does not take place as fast as it used to be at the initial stages. As shown in Figure 5.6, the various stages are shown as Stage I, II and III. The initial slow growth of technology is because of many reasons. Primarily among them are low level of interest amongst

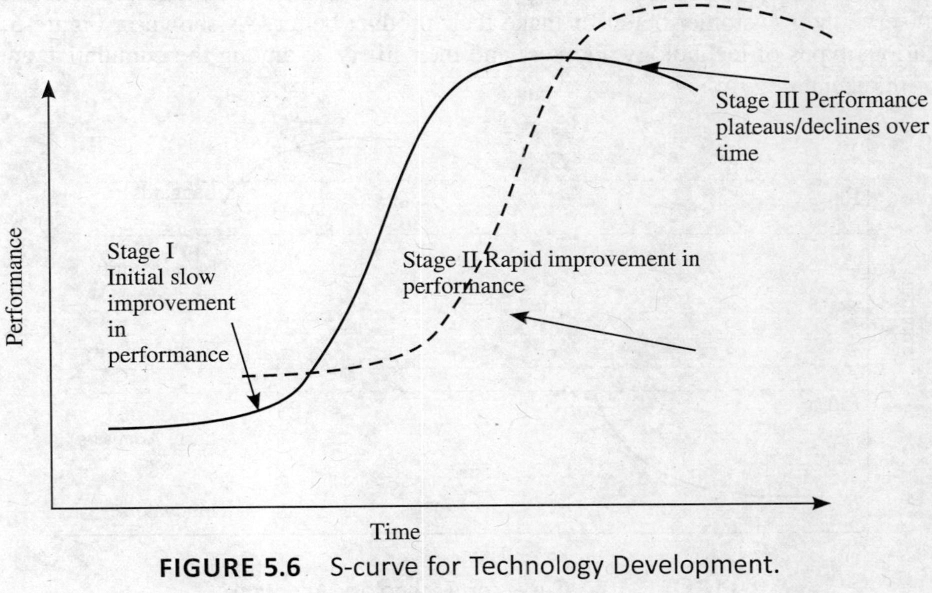

FIGURE 5.6 S-curve for Technology Development.

the researchers who may consider limited potential for such technology and do not commit resources such as efforts or time. When few initial successes are seen more and more researchers of companies join the bandwagon and hence the development takes at a faster pace. While more and more development takes place, the technology soon hits the limit and plateaus unless a breakthrough is hit and another S-curve starts from thereafter.

Technology plateaus are often overcome by a disruptive technology. In the computer storage area, newer technologies take a leap of storage density giving rise to floppy disk, CD, memory stick, etc., each able to compress and store larger amount of data than its predecessors. In other times, a competing technology is following a similar pattern but takes higher level of performance as shown by the dotted line.

- **S-curve for technology adoption:** While the technology development is taking place, its adoption by the users also follows a similar S-curve, the stages of which are quite different from that of the earlier one. Figure 5.7 S-curve of technology adoption shows the type of users or firms who adopt the new technology at different stages of the technology development. The widespread adoption of technology in the real world also called technology diffusion is plotted against ordinates of cumulative adoption percentage and time. Rogers is credited to create a set of nomenclature for user population that adopt new technology who wrote a seminal book on diffusion of innovation. At the initial stages, those people who adopt the technology are called innovators who are miniscule percentage of the total adopters of the technology over its lifecycle. This is usually 2–5 % of the adoption volume. The next set of adopters are labelled as early adopters who see potential in the technology and are willing to take risk and use/adopt the technology in their place of work. Once the technology proves its mettle, a large number of people adopt the technology form the early majority followed by the next section called late majority. There are still a small percentage of users who take time to adopt the technology and are called laggards who fail to see the potential of the new technology and adopt it much late when the technology is either declining or has reached its potential limits as well as navelless. In the process, they also lose out to take advantage of the technology to serve their customer better or make their product better. As shown in Figure 5.7, the various types of technology adopters and their likely % among the cumulative adopters of the technology.

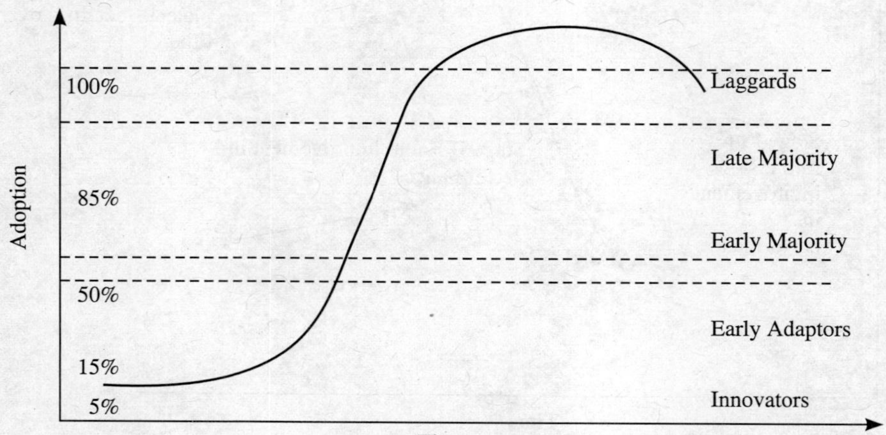

FIGURE 5.7 Curve for Technology Adoption.

What is the use of S-curve? S-curve is a useful tool for users to keep an eye on the technology development and weigh the advantages and disadvantages of adopting it too early or too late. In the case of the former, the early adopters may have to undergo the pains of trails and shortcomings of the new technology but have the advantage to start their learning curve too early. In the case when the technology succeeds, the early adopters have the advantage over their peers. However, they also have the risk of technology failure and making investment in maturing the technology. Late adopters have limited windows to reap benefits of adopting the technology in their process or products as by the time they will be ready with the improved products or processes, the new technology might already be in use or in early stages of development. The market share of various types of adopters are shown in the form of bell curve as in Figure 5.8.

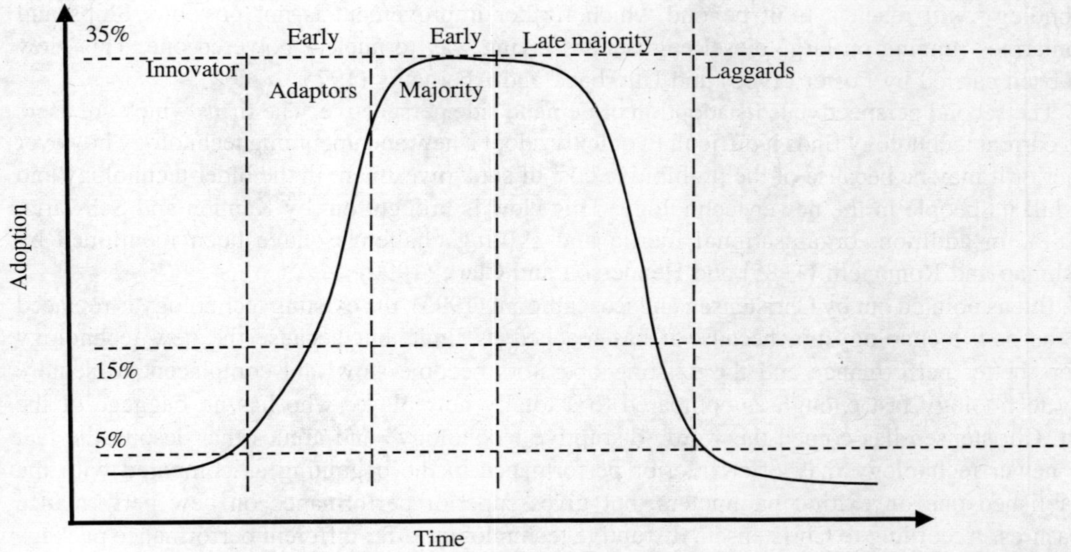

FIGURE 5.8 S-curve for Technology Adoption or Diffusion.

5.10 SEGMENT ZERO PRINCIPLE

This principle was first enunciated by Andy Grove, former CEO of Intel, who opined that as technology advances take place, the lower end of the technology is good enough to the mass market needs. Companies sometimes keep on releasing higher end products using improved technology but neglect the lower end augment which can be captured by the completion. This was the case of launching Celeron processor by Intel as their PCs and laptops and the same was the philosophy behind Nokia's launching ASHA series of smart phone for the mass market. The customer needs develop slower than the pace of technology and hence the lower end technology could suffice the needs of the mass market. Tata Ace a 4-wheeler small foot print goods career is a case in point for servicing the segment zero of the transportation business. They do not need very high speed or large capacity carrier to server the small by-lanes of the cities and small towns.

5.11 TECHNOLOGY DEVELOPMENT: SUPPLY AND DEMAND SIDE PERSPECTIVE

It has been discussed that every technology will go through phases of development and finally hit the plateau when it will be replaced by a new improved technology. Propeller-based airplanes were replaced by jet engines as the latter produced more thrust, speed and carrying capacity. Photo film cameras were quickly replaced by digital cameras which have now become a permanent and most sought after feature in any mobile hand set. The researchers view the technology development from two different perspectives. The first perspective is to see the technology growth and development for those who are engaged in research and development of the technology also called supply side perspective. This perspective enunciates that improvement of an existing technology will reach a limit beyond which further improvement is not possible. Ships and submarines running on large diesel engines are giving way to nuclear powered one. This view has been carried by Foster (1986) and Utterback and Abernathy (1975) .

The second perspective is its adoption or demand side perspective. The firms which are users of a current technology finds it difficult to quickly adopt a new and upcoming technology however superior it may be because of the prohibitive cost of sunk investment in the older technology and re-skill its people in the newer technology. This view is brought out by Kamien and Schwartz, (1982). In addition, organisational inertia and skilling challenges have been mentioned by Tushman and Romanelli (1985) and Henderson and Clark (1990).

But as pointed out by Christensen and Rosenbloom (1995), the existing technology is replaced by the new technology not because it has reached its limit, but because the new technology offers better performance and the existing operators become slow and complacent to acquire new technology fast enough as compared to a totally new player who has no baggage of the past. Christensen has coined the word "disruptive technology" and argues that despite the fact the newer technology may offer inferior performance in the beginning as compared with the established one on exiting parameters, but gives superior performance on new performance measures. According to Christensen, disruptive technologies offer different performance package and satisfy the mainstream customers. Take the case of watching movie on mobile phone using live streaming. In current times, when this technology is at the initial stage, the performance on the scale of picture quality, screen size and related interruption due to bandwidth constraints may categorise it as inferior to cable TV technology but it scores over cable TV in terms of mobility, any time, any place as well as the flexibility to watch replays.

It may be noted that once the disruptive technology reaches a critical scale of adoption, it proliferates very fast and newer applications or usage of the new technology come into play.

5.12 TECHNOLOGY ACQUISITION

Technology acquisition is a critical activity in the overall gambit of technology and innovation management. It is unfortunately not an easy task and have several challenges. The current processes followed by most organisations of first coming out with a detailed requirement document before embarking upon the technology identification and evaluation process leading to final acquisition is painfully slow. In most cases, when the new technology solution is finally commissioned, this delay would have already cost too much and major part of the requirements would have changed. In many cases, the new technology might have been obsolete or reached the last stage of its development lifecycle being threatened by another upcoming technology. Not only this delay leads to loss of opportunity for technology innovation but also fails to address urgent requirements.

In such cases, the agile approaches for acquisition and operational deployment of Technology are recommended and we will discuss about it in this section. This approach is much different than the old age ponderous and detailed process-bound methodology of technology acquisition. The method called evolutionary acquisition (EA) method, is iterative in nature and is designed to adopt technologies that are in the maturation process. In the early increment stages, basics of capabilities are provided to the end users and more complex needs are met through later increments.

As against this interactive incremental development (IID) approach, a matured technology is used in iterative fashion to address increasingly complex requirement. This approach also facilitates capturing more detailed requirements by letting the user interact with the first cut system and based on that feedback more functionalities are built in the system using the same technology.

5.13 TECHNOLOGY ACQUISITION PROCESS

Irrespective of the technology acquisition method used whether it is traditional or agile, some common steps have to be adopted to get ahead with the process. These steps are detailed out as follows:

Understanding requirements: At this stage, the requirement at high level is gathered and documented for which the technology is needed to be acquired. Many a times, these requirements may come from the end users who are facing difficulties while using the existing system or it may have been promoted by the competition launching a newer products or services. Sometimes the need is expressed also by the customer which is also taken in account.

Linking requirement to mission and objectives: Once the requirements are gathered, they are further linked or vetted with the mission or objectives of the firm. Some of the requirements may be dropped if it is not in line with the defined mission or objectives of the firm.

Forming the acquisition team: The acquisition team comprises people drawn from business users, technology management, procurement, quality and finance. Legal and compliance inputs are sought from time to time.

Defining the functional/performance need: The team further details out the functional and performce needs for acquiring the technology.

Researching technology marketplace for possible candidates: This is the task done by the technology management team.

Evaluating various alternatives: The advantages and disadvantages of each technology and its supplier is done at this stage.

Cost-benefit assessment, investment planning and outflow: This is an important activity of the technology acquisition process that covers all types of cost such as one-time investments on software or technology patent licenses, hardware, services for installation and commissioning, training and ongoing post implementation/acquisition cost of maintenance support, payment of lease.

For calculating benefits, calculation such as saving of material and/or people costs, growth in sales, better service/features as against competition are used. All benefits must get converted into monetary value. If the cost benefit analysis is not favourable, the current situation may be continued.

Risk and mitigation strategy: Most new technologies come with inherent associated risk and that need to be considered while acquiring any technology. The purpose of risk and mitigation strategy is to help achieve the overall objective of the firm. So possible risks and its mitigation strategies are worked out several times during the technology acquisition process. Some of the typical risks to be considered are:

(a) Technology risk covering it being new, untested or not proven for scalability
(b) Vendor risk covering capabilities, financial strength of the vendor may be unproven
(c) Project management risk where commitment and capabilities of the stakeholders are suspected
(d) Environmental risk covering changes in the regulatory policies, environmental laws, international issues

5.14 TECHNOLOGY ACQUISITION STRATEGY

Technology acquisition is a long term action for any organisation and hence it has to be done from a strategic perspective. This step decides the overall approach as to how the firm will acquire the technology. This will answer questions such as own development, technology transfer or buy out, leasing, etc. The firm must decide a long-term game plan on the method receiving and using new technologies based on the technology capabilities the firm needs to conduct its business. Technology acquisition strategy will be based on the strategic position the firm wants to aim for such as innovator, early adopter or late adopter, etc. It also has consider the lifecycle position of the technology and take appropriate choice. For example, at a late adopter stage when the technology has become commonplace, it may be a good idea to outsource the technology rather than maintaining and developing it in-house. In short, the choices of technology acquisition strategy could be—

(a) In-house R&D
(b) Buying the firm possessing technology
(c) Joint development or joint venture
(d) Contract R&D
(e) Obtaining licensing to use
(f) Purchasing final product and doing the branding and marketing
(g) Making equity investment in the technology firm

All these choices are presented on technology acquisition strategy cube that has three ordinates: time, cost and risk. We will discuss about the collaboration in some more detail later in the chapter.

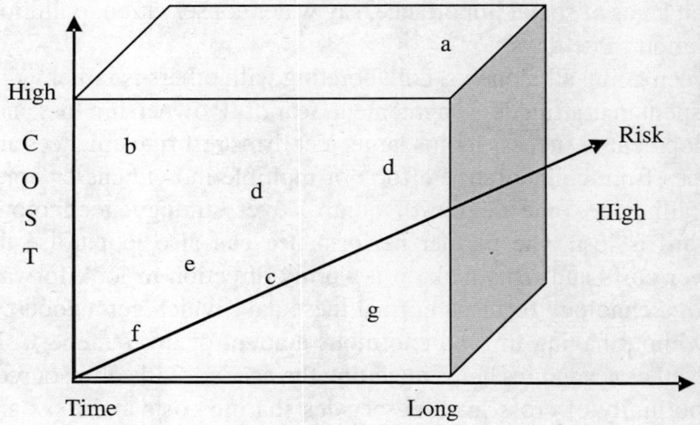

FIGURE 5.9 Technology Acquisition Strategy Cube.

5.15 TECHNOLOGY ACQUISITION PLANNING

Technology acquisition planning is a process to ascertain where, when and how the capital will be required and how the new technology competes with competitions technology and how customers will react or accept the new technology. Technology acquisition planning become more significant as based on the acquired technology the firm is likely to chart ahead its future course. Technology Acquisition Plan is a formal document that covers potential risk and its mitigation plan with timetable and specific milestones.

5.16 TECHNOLOGY ALLIANCES AND COLLABORATION

As discussed earlier, one of the approaches companies may adopt to acquire or develop technology is to enter into alliance with similar/likeminded companies to reap the huge market potential. Strategic alliances for R&D are usually a joint venture or consortium, where two or more companies together embark on a research for particular technology. There are several instances of the successful alliances such as Nokia and Microsoft in alliance to make Zune phone and Philips and Sony jointly launched the mini-CD. In the recent times, Alcatel–Fujitsu through a joint venture developed the third generation of cellular telephone equipment and likewise Samsung and Sun Microsystems created alliance to provide solution for innovative business computing system.

Typically, technology alliance is created to do deep research on technology that requires a high investment and can benefit all participants in more or less equal proportion. For example, research for fuel efficient cars was sponsored in the U.S. called "Super Car" project[5]. Sometimes such joint R&D is funded and approved by the government or multi-government agencies such as European Commission or the World Bank. Multi-company research and partnering with

[5] "Supercar" was nickname of the United States Department of Commerce R&D program called New Generation of Vehicles (PNGV). The program aimed to support the domestic U.S. automakers (GM, Ford, and Chrysler) develop prototypes of a safe, clean, affordable car the size of the Ford Taurus, but delivering three times the fuel efficiency. Source : https://en.wikipedia.org/wiki/Supercar accessed 29 May 2016.

universities on several areas of social importance, say water conservation, pollution control, cyber security, etc., is common these days.

The choice between going all alone vs. collaborating with others is rather a difficult decision. The amount of time spent in drafting legal agreement, fear of IP ownership loss and who will drive the technology development to success looms large. Yet firms resort to alliances and collaboration because success comes from collaborative efforts of multiple individuals or organisations.

While forming alliance, some degree of control over strategy, technology development and getting the reward is lost. The partner performance can also jeopardise the success. But the benefits like lower costs and risks make it a worthy direction to look forward to. Alliances with universities with technology forms is normal these days which get a good pool of energetic research resources without having to fund enormous amount of investment. Collaborating with other companies as well as academics helps in getting the needed skills or resources more quickly, more flexibility, opportunity of cross-learning besides sharing costs and risks and developing a common standard.

Organisation decides not to pursue alliances or collaboration if they feel they have enough capabilities to successfully complete the R&D by their own means.

By developing everything in-house, the firm can develop new competencies and does not have the risk exposing their knowledge to a partner. Subsequent control technology development can be under their control. Companies like Monsanto develop on their own a genetically modified seed. They have made bio-technology as strategic focus and hence there is no need to partner. Similarly, Honda Motors never joined any alliance to ensure that it has control over the development process. Leading aircraft Boeing does it all alone to ensure that it retains capabilities to create a new airplane every 12 to 15 years.

5.17 TYPES OF ALLIANCES AND COLLABORATION

Technology companies can form different arrangements to collaborate with each other. The possible choices could be:

- **Joint ventures:** This is created as separate legal entity after all parties contribute in the form of equity and set up a new team. Tata-IBM, Wipro--GE Medical are few examples from Indian subcontinent.
- **Licensing:** In this arrangement, technology is granted to other company under a contract in exchange for royalties.
- **Outsourcing or contract manufacturing:** This is a clear model where some other company does the manufacturing for an organisation following their specification and process guidelines. Apple iPhone is one good example which is assembled mostly in its facilities in China. This gives advantage of flexibility without long-term capital investments and helps the firm achieve economies of scale and faster response time at a lower cost.
- **Consortium or collective research:** This is route when many firms come together to research a technology. Such initiatives are driven by industry bodies, intergovernmental agency, and group of universities or private research bodies.

5.18 TIMING OF ENTRY OF TECHNOLOGY

The timing of adopting a cutting edge technology and using it in the products or services is a key. Embracing something new gives the first mover advantage (FMA) which leads to delighting the customer with new features and surprising the competitors. First mover companies create awareness about the technology and pave way for fast followers to imitate. In addition, being the first they can also lead to set standards in the industry. It also gives other enduring advantage that a large number of complementary products can be created and ecosystem will be built. Sony Walkman was successful because of a large number of cost-effective recorded cassette were available in the market. Legendary Late Andrew Grove former chairman of Intel had famously said that in the technology market if you want to be the leader then you have to be the pioneer and first mover.

First movers have several advantages such as creating brand loyalty (e.g. Apple iPhone, Blackberry), capturing scares resources (mobile companies lock in Tower locations) and exploitation of buyer switching costs. But FMA also has associated risk such as market uncertainty, unpredictable customer acceptance of the new and massive investment in taking the lead. Firms sometimes have great expectations on the new technology and consequently high hope of market potential and in the process ignore other factors such as customer preferences, need for associated supporting ecosystems, etc. Solar powered vehicles are not selling in large numbers is also because there are not many publically available charging stations. A commuter is afraid of getting stranded on the street in the middle of the night in case the battery charge goes off. A high failure rate at around 47% for all new product launches is a discouraging factor.

Second mover firms typically imitate the market leaders through better design, improved service, market reach or just being cost effective. They have the advantage of lesser demand uncertainty and can focus on market research to identify features to satisfy other customer needs. They can also learn from the first mover's successes and shortcomings and can focus on product improvement R&D rather than basic research. They also have significant disadvantages such as loss of opportunity to establish brand loyalty. They always have to position as less premium than the first mover unless they are having superior brand positioning or added features.

Being the first, second or late is also a manifestation of a firm's management thinking and strategy. If they have not made good investment creating capability for innovation, they would never take the lead. In comparison, some firms always and relentlessly try new technology for innovation and learn from success as well as failure. Their few successes are so massive that the other failures are taken as few steps to remain ahead of their counterparts. Just making early market entry does not guarantee success and sustainable business but the novelty and the value proposition does. History is full of examples where a powerful established firm's delayed adoption of new technology has let an upstart rival eat into their market share. While Blockbuster waited, the rival Netflix pioneered and earned seven-fold profit. By the time Sotheby's ignored, eBay flourished. Even Barnes & Noble waited seventeen months to respond to Amazon.com and made it the leader of e-selling of books. Most ecommerce firms are following the principles of FMA and challenging the established old style technology challenged firms. In Indian context, while Flipkart, Amazon, Snapdeal and other e-commerce firms flourished, their powerful, cash rich, inventory surplus brick mortar retailers like Big Bazar and Reliance retail did not embrace e-commerce technology to reach out to their customer. When G-mail came with innovation for e-mail, the market leader quickly matched the challenge and retained its position. However, Yahoo also failed to recognise the growing influence of search engine and even outsources this feature to Google and funded the start up. Google's ability as second mover in search or e-mail business is not to conclude that it is good to be a second mover but to only highlight that when the first movers are not able to monitor and respond to the improvements made by the powerful followers the fast followers would succeed.

Deciding about the timings of technology entry will depend on parameters. The two important parameters to consider are:

(a) **Technological uncertainty:** This refers to uncertainty regarding the technological features of the product and the stage at which the technology maturity has reached. Firms may consider if the technology has evolved a standard and dominant design or not.

(b) **Market/demand uncertainty:** This factor prompts the firm to ascertain uncertainty regarding the size and growth rates of the markets for new products. It must ascertain the potential user base, likely growth in numbers, threat from substitute products and potential to create an ecosystem through complementary products.

All this will require a deep understanding of customer preferences by the firm. The firm must also evaluate the amount of improvement/newness over the existing products and whether the company is prepared to bear the losses if the game plan does not succeed. In case the technology is closed and propriety then the firm has an upper edge as it would not be replicable easily by the competing firms. In case of open technology, other factors such as brand, marketing reach, service qualities, etc., do come into play.

5.19 FORECASTING AI/GEN AI TRENDS: ADAPTING S-CURVES AND HYPE CYCLES

Technology forecasting is essential for anticipating future developments and preparing organizations for opportunities and obsolescence. While models like the Gartner Hype Cycle provide a useful framework for understanding the maturity and adoption of emerging technologies, their application to AI and Generative AI trends requires re-interpretation due to the unprecedented speed of their evolution. The adoption of Gen AI has been faster than both personal computers and the internet, implying that technologies may move through the hype cycle much more rapidly than historically observed.

This accelerated pace makes traditional, slower-moving hype cycles less predictive and more volatile. The "fluid stage" may be shorter, the "peak of inflated expectations" reached quickly, and the "trough of disillusionment" potentially very brief or even bypassed for highly impactful AI applications. This dynamism challenges the ability to accurately predict when a technology will reach its "plateau of productivity". Consequently, technology forecasting must evolve from periodic expert panels to a continuous, real-time activity, relying heavily on AI-powered intelligence gathering and analysis of vast datasets (research, patents, market trends) to identify emerging technologies and predict their trajectories with greater accuracy. This allows for a more robust and less subjective technology foresight, leading to better strategic decisions in a rapidly changing environment.

5.20 STRATEGIC AI/GEN AI ACQUISITION: BUILD, BUY, PARTNER FRAMEWORKS

The decision of whether to build, buy, or partner for technological capabilities is a cornerstone of technology strategy. For AI and Generative AI, this framework takes on new complexities and strategic implications. The increasing prevalence of "partnering" for Gen AI capabilities, particularly through cloud providers and specialized AI firms, suggests a fundamental shift in how organizations acquire core technological capabilities.

Many organizations are choosing to leverage managed AI services from major cloud providers like AWS (Amazon Bedrock) and Microsoft (Azure OpenAI Service, Microsoft 365 Copilot). This approach allows businesses to access powerful, pre-trained AI models and infrastructure without the massive upfront investment and specialized talent required to build AI capabilities from scratch. Specialized Gen AI development companies also offer tailored solutions, further expanding the "partner" option. This shift moves from traditional mergers and acquisitions or internal R&D to a more distributed, ecosystem-dependent acquisition model.

While partnering offers advantages like accelerated deployment and reduced initial costs, it also introduces considerations around vendor lock-in, data sovereignty, and the long-term strategic control over core AI capabilities. Organizations must carefully evaluate whether to build in-house AI-native capabilities for strategic differentiation or to rely on external partners for more commoditized AI services. This decision impacts vendor management, data governance, and the overall strategic direction of the firm, requiring a nuanced approach to technology acquisition.

5.21 TIMING OF AI/GEN AI ENTRY: FIRST-MOVER VS. LATE-MOVER DYNAMICS

The timing of entry into a new technology market, whether as a first-mover or a late-mover, has significant implications for competitive advantage. For AI and Generative AI, the dynamics of this timing decision are highly amplified due to the rapid pace of adoption. Generative AI has seen adoption rates faster than both personal computers and the internet, creating a high-stakes environment.

First-movers in AI can establish brand loyalty, capture scarce resources, and potentially set industry standards. However, they also bear the highest costs of research and development and face significant market uncertainty. For complex technologies, a "late-mover advantage" can exist, where firms can learn from the first-mover's mistakes, refine product designs based on known functionalities, and avoid the costs of early experimentation.

In the context of rapid AI adoption, the optimal strategy for many firms may not be to be the *very first* to launch a raw AI product, but rather to be a *fast follower*. This approach involves quickly refining and optimizing AI capabilities based on early market feedback and established functionalities, thereby benefiting from reduced R&D costs while still capturing significant market share due to speed and refinement. This strategy demands significant organizational agility, a strong capacity for continuous monitoring of technological advancements, and the ability to rapidly iterate on AI-driven products and services. Failing to adopt new AI technologies quickly, even as a fast follower, risks becoming a "laggard" and losing competitive edge as the market rapidly evolves.

5.22 SUMMARY

This chapter on technology forecasting and assessment began with defining forecasting and why it is tough to forecast technology, We focused on the processes and methods adopting which a firm can conduct technology forecasting function, prepare it for adopting and take calculated risk of delaying its adoption. We opened up the discussion with explaining why a firm should undertake to forecast technology development. It was explained that technology forecasting is necessary for planning and making investments in either developing or acquiring technology. We then presented the Technology Forecasting Analytical Framework covering technology monitoring, technical or competitive intelligence, technology forecasting, road mapping, assessment and finally technology foresight. Subsequently, various technology forecasting tools and methods were discussed. The chapter then presented to its readers technology foresighting methodology framework.

The next section was devoted on to present the concept of widely used model called S-curve and its relevance for technology development as well as adoption perspective. S-curve is a useful tool for users to keep an eye on the technology development and weigh the advantages and disadvantages of adopting it too early or too late.

The chapter then defined Segment Zero principle, first enunciated by Andy Grove, former CEO of Intel. The chapter then explained technology development from supply and demand side perspective. Further the concept of technology acquisition and its process was explained in detail. The chapter also explained technology acquisition strategy and technology acquisition planning in-depth. We discussed various collaboration methods for technology development, their advantages, disadvantages and applicability.

Finally, we explained the concepts involved in timing of adopting a cutting edge technology and advantages and disadvantages of being first or the follower in adopting the technology.

Key Terms: Technology Forecasting, Technology Assessment, Segment Zero principles, Technology acquisition, S-curve.

REVIEW QUESTIONS

1. Why do we understand and monitor trends in the context of technology development? What are the methodologies for studying technology trends?
Answer: Sections 5.2, 5.3
2. Why do we forecast technology development? What benefits a firm would get and what would be the loss if it does not do? **Answer:** Section 5.4
3. Describe the technology Forecasting Analytical Framework with suitable diagram.
Answer: Section 5.5
4. Describe some of the technology forecasting tools and methods using suitable examples. Where will they all be applicable? **Answer:** Sections 5.6 and 5.7
5. Describe the various stages of technology foresighting methodology with suitable examples. **Answer:** Section 5.8

6. Describe the concept of S-curve from the perspective of both technology development and its adoption. Use suitable examples to explain the curve. **Answer:** Section 5.9
7. What is Segment Zero principle as applicable to technology? Explain with examples. **Answer:** Section 5.10
8. Explain in the context of technology development the two important perspectives, namely supply and demand side perspective. **Answer:** Section 5.11
9. Why technology acquisition is critical activity in the overall gambit of technology and innovation management? What are the different strategies for technology acquisition? **Answer:** Section 5.12
10. Name the advantages and disadvantages of collaborating on a development project. How does various modes collaboration help the organisation? **Answer:** Sections 5.16 and 5.17

APPLICATIVE QUESTIONS/PROJECT/TEAM ASSIGNMENT

1. With reference to Indian scenario, identify an example of collaboration between two or more organisations. What were the advantages and disadvantages of collaboration versus independent development? What collaboration mode did the partners choose?

DISCUSSION QUESTIONS

1. Identify what precautions should be taken into account when developing a new technology?
2. What are the possible technologies that can help innovating India's service economy.

ADDITIONAL READINGS

1. Bower J.L. Christensen C. 1995, Disruptive technologies: catching the next wave. *Harvard Business Review* 73(1): 43–53.
2. Christensen, C.M., Rosenbloom R. 1995, Explaining the attacker's advantage: technological paradigms, organizational dynamics, and the value network, *Research Policy* 24(2): 233–257.
3. Dosi, G. 1982. Technological paradigms and technological trajectories, *Research Policy* 11: 147–162.
4. Foster, R., 1986, Innovation, the Attacker's Advantage, Simon and Schuster, New York.
5. Kamien, M.I., Schwartz, N.L., 1982, *Market Structure and Innovation.*, Cambridge University Press: New York.
6. Tushman, M. Romanelli, E., 1985, Organizational evolution: a metamorphosis model of convergence and reorientation, In, Research in Organizational Behavior, Vol. 7, Staw B., Cummings (L) (Eds). JAI Press: Greenwich, CN; 171–222.
7. Utterback, J., Abernathy, W., 1975, A dynamic model of process and product innovation, *Omega* 3(6): 639–356.

8. Anderson cyclical model of technological change, *Administrative Science Quarterly* 35: 604–633, Press: Cambridge, UK.
9. Suarez, F. and J. Utterback, 1995, Dominant designs and the survival of firms, Strategic, 15: 285–305.
10. Tim Brown, Design Thinking. *Harvard Business Review*. June 2008.
11. *The Art of Innovation*, by Tom Kelley.
12. IDEO's Design Thinking for Educators website.
13. 100 Things Every Designer Should Know About People, by Susan Weinschenk.
14. Teacher Resources on Design Thinking at Henry Ford Learning Institute.

Chapter 6

Product and Process Development and Role of Technology

From a product development perspective, choosing whether a technology is disruptive at a potential moment is key.

—Steven Sinofsky

At the end of this chapter, we will learn:

- the various stages of the product life cycle
- the process of developing new-product ideas
- how companies run new-product development process
- the role of technology in product development
- the concepts of how to manage new product development teams
- overview of managing research and development (R&D)
- how to manage intellectual property and protect innovation
- product deployment strategy

6.1 INTRODUCTION

Companies survive and grow because they come out with breakthrough innovations using efficient process. At the same time, many companies have failed in the market just because they could not keep pace with the product development and innovation. Of late while product design and development is being done by the owners of the product idea or brand, its manufacturing and distribution is outsourced to another company. Yet the entire combination of the brand owner, manufacturer and distributors has to continuously innovate the underlying process relentlessly to fight the regular pressure from competition.

In this chapter, we will examine the product lifecycle and product development process. We will cover various aspects of product development from idea generation to implementation by taking our readers through various stages of the product lifecycle. We will understand the process of developing new-product ideas and learn how companies run new-product development process. Technology has a significant role in product development to manage both the processes and teams.

We will put special emphasis on the role of technology in product as well as process development and how a firm can guard its intellectual property, inventions and patents. We will also discuss the management aspects related to R&D process and the role of team that is the cornerstone of the success of any innovative firm.

6.2 UNDERSTANDING PRODUCT LIFECYCLE MANAGEMENT (PLM)

Most products follow a lifecycle pattern that starts from conceiving a new product idea and ends with taking the product off from the market and replaced by some other product. A product lifecycle is a useful concept to chart out various stages of a product or product family. When we talk about product lifecycle management (PLM), we refer to the entire process from conceptualisation, through design, engineering, development, construction (or manufacture) and finally after-sales service and cessation of manufacturing of the product. In case of software the popular word for stopping production is called sun setting. This PLM is different than product lifecycle discussed in marketing (PLCM) which refers to commercial aspects of the product like market introduction, growth and finally plateauing of sales in the market.

The process of PLM (product lifecycle management) is partially physical as well as informational. In the case of physical, a product needs to be designed and made. The informational aspect is that the knowledge and information has to be acquired and disseminated among the team split across various functions. The time required from conceptualisation to realisation and marketing of the product is very significant to meet the competitive pressure. Knowledge about the product features, its finer nuances of servicing and enhancing for the field engineers is as much important as the performance feedback from the field to the designers. A PLM process ensures a seamless connectivity so that the company is able to design and launch products with good customer service to remain the market leader.

Product lifecycle management is an important function supported by IT in any manufacturing set up. There are tools available to support various phases of this activity. At various phases of PLM tools such as computer-aided design (CAD), computer-aided manufacturing (CAM) and product data management (PDM) are used which integrate knowledge and information management part of the product lifecycle management.

Various stages of PLM are as follows:

(a) **Conception stage:** In this stage, a product idea is conceptualised. Typically, the product idea is vetted with the marketing team which comments upon whether or not a need exists in the market for such a product. At this stage, the high level specification of the product features are also developed.

(b) **Design and prototype stage:** At this stage, detailed specification of the product is worked out. This may involve detailing out specification of the components and subcomponents, their functional arrangement as to how they will operate and what type of material is likely to be used for making those parts.

At this stage, validation of the design is done through using simulation tools or making lab based models or prototype. Earlier models were made using clay, now 3D printing is becoming popular to make small prototypes/models. These models may not be fully functional or workable but would give a fair idea of the product.

Design stage also covers the design of tools that will be used to make the product or its components. There may be a steel or plastic part that would require machining or die where the component will be cast. For metal product, the tools required may be press, machines like CNC lathe, planner, etc. Many a times, the product or its component manufacturing may be outsourced where the information sharing software becomes important.

(c) **Manufacturing stage:** The successful prototype is followed with mass manufacturing stage. At this stage the company may choose to make all its components and assamble into final product or outsource some of these activities. Manufacturing on a large scale would require setting up production units, production process and hiring skilled people who can convert the design specification into a workable product.

Tools and equipment will be required to check the quality of the products and its performance in the actual working conditions before releasing it to the customers.

(d) **Sell, serve and maintain:** Once the product is successfully manufactured, it is then sold to the customers. This will further require service and maintenance of the product. This phase will collect data about performance of the product in the actual used conditions. This data is used as an input for further improving the product. Information systems used to sell and serve the customer is called customer relationship management (CRM). This software captures field level complaints and defects which can be further analysed and incorporated in the next release of the product after suitable design change.

All products will require maintenance from time to time. This may call for replacement of worn out parts or those part that fail due to usage or manufacturing defects. Predicting the lifecycle of a component is an important exercise so that the part can be replaced much before the end of life is reached while the product is still in use. Replacing the parts at desired intervals, will enhance the life of the product and will eliminate trouble arising out of failure in the field at a critical hour.

(e) **Discard and dispose off:** Once the product fails beyond repair or reaches end of life, it has to be disposed off. The disposal process involves reclaiming useful material and properly disposing material that may be hazardous in nature. The latter activity is inviting a lot of attention from the environmental groups and is becoming an important activity to be undertaken as part of product lifecycle management. All then stages are shown in the Figure 6.1.

6.2.1 PLM is an Integrated Process

Despite the fact that all these stages are led by different functional groups within a firm, in reality all these groups should be interrelated and integrated. None of these tasks or activities is performed in isolation. At the same time, all these activities and phases have significant overlap over each other. Even design is an iterative process which modifies product features based on manufacturing constraints or customer preferences or based on conventions of particular region or country.

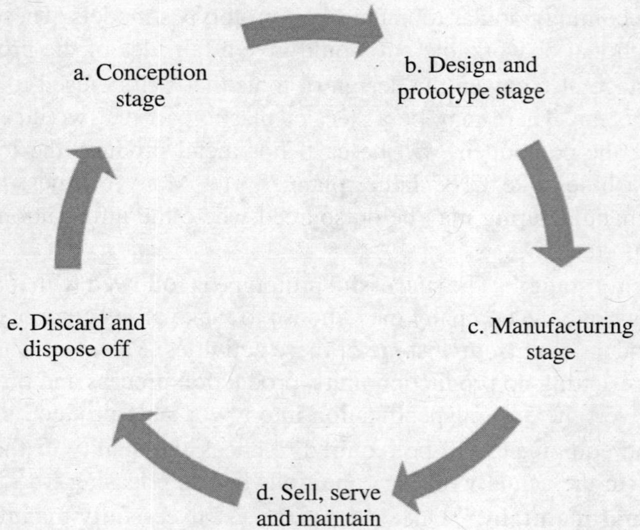

FIGURE 6.1 New Product Development Process.

6.2.2 Corresponding Technologies at Various Stages of PLM

There is no one technology that can serve all the stages of the product lifecycle. It is a collection of software tools which are integrated to meet requirements of various stages of the product lifecycle.

(a) **Tools used during conception stage:** At this stage, the idea is crystallised and feedback sought from marketing, legal, regulatory bodies and technology/material science specialists. Use of pencil, clay models and that of two dimensional CAD or 3D CAID (computer-aided industrial design software) is very popular at this stage.

(b) **Tools used during deign and prototype stage:** Apart from CAD or CAID tools, several other tools that can model and predict the performance of the product is used. Software such for simulation and hybrid modeling, reverse engineering, KBE (knowledge-based engineering), NDT (non-destructive testing) are used here. While CAE (computer-aided engineering) is used for simulation, other software used are for stress analysis, FEA (finite element analysis); kinematics; computational fluid dynamics (CFD); and mechanical event simulation (MES). Tools and software for product quality or dimensional tolerance analysis are also used.

(c) **Tools used during manufacturing or build stages:** Apart from all the tools mentioned so far that continue to give inputs to the manufacturing stage, CNC machines are used which directly translates CAD inputs to manufacture a component to the specification. Tools are also used for process simulation such as CAPE (computer-aided production engineering) or CAP/CAPP—(production planning) for layout and production simulation.

(d) **Tools used during sell, serve and maintain stage:** Most popular software is CRM and it is supplemented with maintenance, repair and operations management (MRO) software.

6.3 NEW PRODUCT DEVELOPMENT PROCESS

New product development (NPD) process is not a simple process and requires deep preparation and meticulous execution. Bringing anything new is not easy, especially, when it is related to meet customer expectations and has features that are ahead of competition to seize a market opportunity. A product can be tangible such as car, toy or apparel but it can also be intangible like a mobile app. Underlying all product development is the thorough understanding (or visualisation) of customer needs and wants that the product is likely to address. All this has to be done at a reasonable cost in comparison with the competition. The time to develop a new product and take it to market is also important as a late launch of product may jeopardise the chances of success. Finally, the NPD process must ensure that the product meets quality standards including build as well as use quality. All these three aims require companies to establish processes following certain strategies.

New product development is defined to include all activities beginning with the understanding of customer needs and market opportunities, visualising product that meets those needs and then planning and executing its production, distribution and sale of the product. It may be noted that the need of the customer is very vast and different products in different forms and fashion can meet it. While Airbus is focusing to make large 550 seated aircrafts, its rival Boeing specialises in smaller, faster 'sonic cruiser'. The need of size is being challenges by the need of speed in this case.

According to various published surveys, only 40% of the NPD initiatives reach marketable stage, out of which only 60% new products are able to bring profit for the company. This means only 24% of the initial idea ends up as successful profitable marketable products. A well-orchestrated and well thought NPD process ensures that the NPD initiative is successful. There are several challenges which the NPD process has to face, some notable ones are:

(a) Lack of good understanding of customer real needs
(b) Not able to follow a family of product or product portfolio approach and hence ending up with one off product which is launched or withdrawn without deep thinking
(c) Not quickly identifying and then resolving performance issues
(d) Outsourced partner's inefficiency or ineffectiveness
(e) Improper process for managing product change
(f) Inability to quickly prototype and convert prototype into mass-manufactured product
(g) Improper estimation of market size, too small or overestimation.
(h) Poor product quality
(i) Market is not ready for accepting the product
(j) Poor execution of NPD process

6.3.1 How Companies Run New-product Development Process

Product development process is a critical process for the success of the enterprise. It has also evolved in several ways in the last three or four decades. With more and more globalisation and competitive threats coming from all around the world, the speed and flexibility of the NPD Process is getting high in demand. The emphasis of NPD has also shifted from product quality to objectives such as time to market and release frequency of new products. Lewis and Wong[1] (2004) opine that the "time to market" is more important in today's context for a technological product than cost of development. No wonder products like mobile phones, televisions, air-conditioners are launched with new features at regular intervals by the market leaders. This is why the NPD process has also undergone a significant change from being a slow serial and controlled process to a new iterative, agile and fast paced process. Takeuchi and Nonaka[2] (1986), in a seminal article, defined the need of changing the NPD process from being a serial process as followed in the traditional method where the baton is passed to the next team managing the next phase at the completion of earlier phase to be more agile and fast paced.

Many researchers advocated that NPD should be more holistic in nature "as in rugby, where the ball gets passed within the team as it moves as a unit up the field". Instead of teams working in silos, the new approach is to have multidisciplinary team that works across various phases and learns from the feedback from the team who are managing those phases. These differences of approach between linear and overlapping (holistic) approach is illustrated in Figure 6.2.

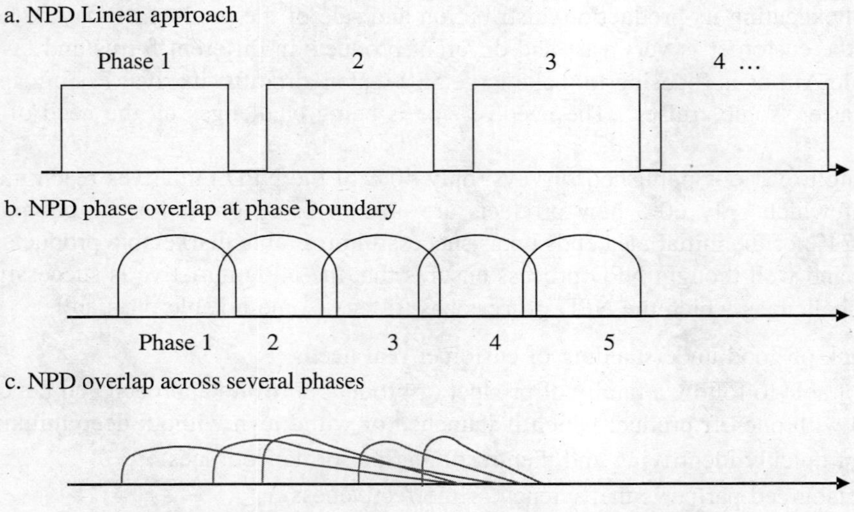

FIGURE 6.2 Various process approaches for NPD.

NPD process of traditional approach is followed at NASA or most government-based research programmes as shown in type a. Whereas type b NPD approach is followed at Fuji-Xerox and a type C NPD approach at Honda and Canon. It is evident here that the integrated overlapping approach encourages trial and error giving opportunities for learning across different levels and functions within the organisation. The last two approaches of NPD have several noticeable characteristics to facilitate them as a flexible team such as:

- Start with broad product goals than specific product idea, giving freedom to search for breakthrough ideas to meet market challenges.

[1]Lewis, J., & Wong, L. (2004). Accelerated Project Management. McGraw-Hill Companies.
[2]Hirotaka Takeuchi and Ikujiro Nonaka, HBR, January 1986. The New Product Development Game.

- Team is allowed to work like a start-up organisation without any prior information or structure. They gather ideas and resources to develop and execute. They evolve, plan and self-correct.
- Team seeks learning from a wide variety of sources as well as from each other. They work as autonomous unit with little supervision from corporate headquarters. When IBM developed the PC, this was done through an autonomous team situated far away from the corporate headquarters. The successful Honda City car project team was selected with an average age of 27 years to design a car that youth would like to possess.
- Stretch your boundary: Such autonomous teams go beyond what the conventional thinking dictates. In Honda city project, the challenge was to develop a car that has space and features yet it is fuel efficient and low cost.
- Cross fertilisation of learning is yet another distinctive feature where people from diverse functional groups learn with each other as they all work together. They may have people from R&D who have deep knowledge of the subject but they depend on manufacturing people to understand the difficulties that a particular design may put forth. If you notice the NPD process type c, the involvement of R&D may be longest and that of manufacturing shortest but they all work together.
- Multilayered learning is another feature found in the approach c and to some extent in approach b. Since the team of all discipline work together, they learn from not only people of the same discipline who may be senior or tech savvy but other disciplines as well.
- Absorb changes as they go. These teams with holistic approach are able to make suitable changes in the product to meet the changing market requirements.

6.3.2 Selecting a Right NPD Process

The choice of NPD process also depends upon the objective, the process and the end goal. In some situation, the linear method may be more suitable than the holistic approach as shown in approach b and c. Figure 6.3 shows various objectives based on which the choice of NPD method

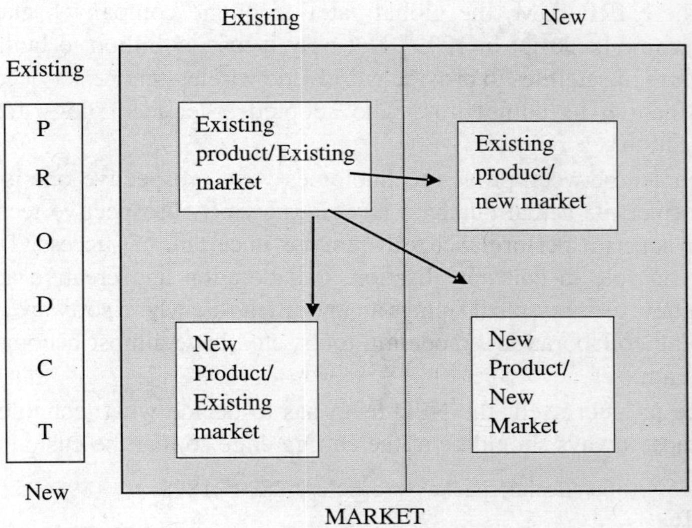

FIGURE 6.3 NPD objective.

can be exercised. Among the various objectives, it could be either the firm wants to introduce totally new product, extend the features of the existing one in an existing or new market. All these various types are given names such as product line extension, new market for existing products, etc. One can easily understand that when there is extension of the features of an existing product, then the traditional method is far more suitable than the holistic method that would be needed in conceptualising totally the new product for a new market.

Various researchers have pointed out that if the objective is to reduce cost of product or make improvement in the existing one, then the choice of NPD is much simpler. However, if the objective is to develop product for a new market or for a totally new requirement, then the NPD processes are difficult to establish.

6.3.3 Assimilate the Role of Technology in Product Development

Role of technology in the current technology intensive world can never be under estimated. Broadly the role of technology in product development can be assimilated at three levels:

(a) Role of technology in the product development process
(b) Role of technology which is embedded in the product itself
(c) Role of technology in the product manufacturing and marketing

We will briefly discuss each one of them.

(a) The role of technology in the product development process is critical yet it is largely supportive. Newer advanced technologies may give better performance but its incorporation may be difficult due to its uncertain future. It may be worthwhile mentioning a famous case of satellite phone technology propagated by Motorola in the project called IRIDIUM which is a case in point where the new technology proved too costly to develop and finally failed where a less optimum technology like GSM could succeed in the telecom space. It is also an example of biggest technology project failure where IRIDIUM, the global satellite phone company backed by Motorola (MOT) became bankrupt in 1999[3]. Not only it lost $5 billion to build and launch its infrastructure of satellites to provide worldwide wireless phone service, but also pushed Motorola behind its competitors who adopted other technology for mobile phone communications.

The choice between proven technologies vs. a prospective one is difficult. In the case of former, its actual outcome is well-known. A prospective technology while it may offer superior performance still remains uncertain of success. Technology plays an important role in conceptualisation, collaboration and creative activities such as designing new features, etc. IT plays an important role where software like CAD, Group ware, online collaborations, modeling tools, etc., have almost become a necessity for an NPD team.

(b) Within the product itself, the NPD team has to decide what technology will be used which almost always should be at the cutting edge so that the customer welcomes the

[3]http://content.time.com/time/specials/packages/article/0,28804,1898610_1898625_1898640,00.html accessed 09 Jun. 2016.

product. However, every new technology will have a price attached and may have certain amount of risk as it may be unproven. Other factors like the impact of technology in the environment, its maintainability in the field while in use become important. Selection of appropriate technology for the target customer segment or market becomes all the more important especially for a country like India which has wide variation in the local conditions such as weather, economic affluence and skill of its users.

6.4 NEW PRODUCT DEVELOPMENT TEAMS

NPD has become much more complex process due to global competition and geographical spread of the teams. While the fundamental challenge of quality, reliability and cost of the product remains at the top of the agenda, customer preferences and desire for enhanced features that provide more value to them have also become significant. Most global manufacturers have now realised that speed with which they are able to launch new products is not enough to meet customer expectations. In addition, customers are demanding more innovation and have no hesitation to switch to the competing brands or product.

NPD is no longer just development of the product but has become a holistic process which includes design and development of manufacturing and support processes. Some organisations rightly call this group (or team) as integrated product development (IPD) team. The advantage of IPD can be clearly seen as it will lead to accelerated implementation of new product through reduced cycle time, better quality, lower cost and innovation which will result into higher product value. In IPD approach, the manufacturing, supportability and serviceability are concurrently evaluated and the limitations are fed back to the product design team to think of alternatives.

Since the NPD teans are globally dispersed and manufacturing is sourced from around the world, NPD/IPD task be comes very complex. It may be noted that the complex products of our times require deeper and narrower expertise from individuals who may come from diverse background and locations. Making them work as a unified team and without any communication gap and with synergy is important. Team management has to organise the team to ensure that formal and informal communication is seamlessly established between multi location team so that sharing of requirements as well as limitations of manufacturing or serviceability is exchanged with the design team much earlier in the product development cycle. All this leads to concurrent design of product as well as process that considers all constraints and factors which can impact manufacturing of successful products.

NPD/IPD team can be very large depending upon the product being designed. When Airbus developed its new A380, several thousand worked on its design and development. Auto-makers like Tata and Mahindra have hundreds of people working on new auto design. So is the case of IT products, several dozen work on hardware design and several hundred in development. Considering the large number of people involved, having a suitable team structure is important. The structure will also depend upon the type of the product and customer segment. Researchers have proposed various structures for NPD/IPD team but none can be called to be the best as each one of them will have some advantages as well as disadvantages. On one end of the spectrum are the organisation structures that are formal with rigid definitions of roles and responsibilities and on the other end are the evolving informal structures. Keeping roles and responsibilities somewhat flexible does allow cross-fertilisation of ideas and support across functional specialist.

Some most popular NPD team structures are:

(a) **Specialisation-based structure:** Team is grouped under different specialised sub groups and they are allowed to participate in the process. Example of this structure is a formal R&D, marketing, manufacturing, etc., units who participate in new product development by running an NPD process. In this structure, there will be issues of coordination across each specialised functional area. This is a classical way of structuring NPD and can be used in stable product environment (Figure 6.4a).

(b) **External-internal:** In some companies, the NPD/IPD team is divided between those who deal on the customer (external) which work on the requirement side and R&D (Internal) which work on the development of product and process (Figure 6.4b).

(c) **Product area-wise:** Both internal and external members are further grouped under various product area. Automobile manufacturers' organise their teams under different product lines or models (Figure 6.4c).

(d) **Evolving:** No formal structure, a core team of 8–10 people is created who co-opt more part-time and support members from external or internal world. This structure facilitates better understanding of requirements from both customer point of view and manufacturing and service angle. This structure also facilities balanced discussion of issues and alternatives leading to consensus approach for both the new product and its manufacturing processes. This approach promotes innovative thinking leading to better products, processes and customer satisfaction (Figure 6.4d).

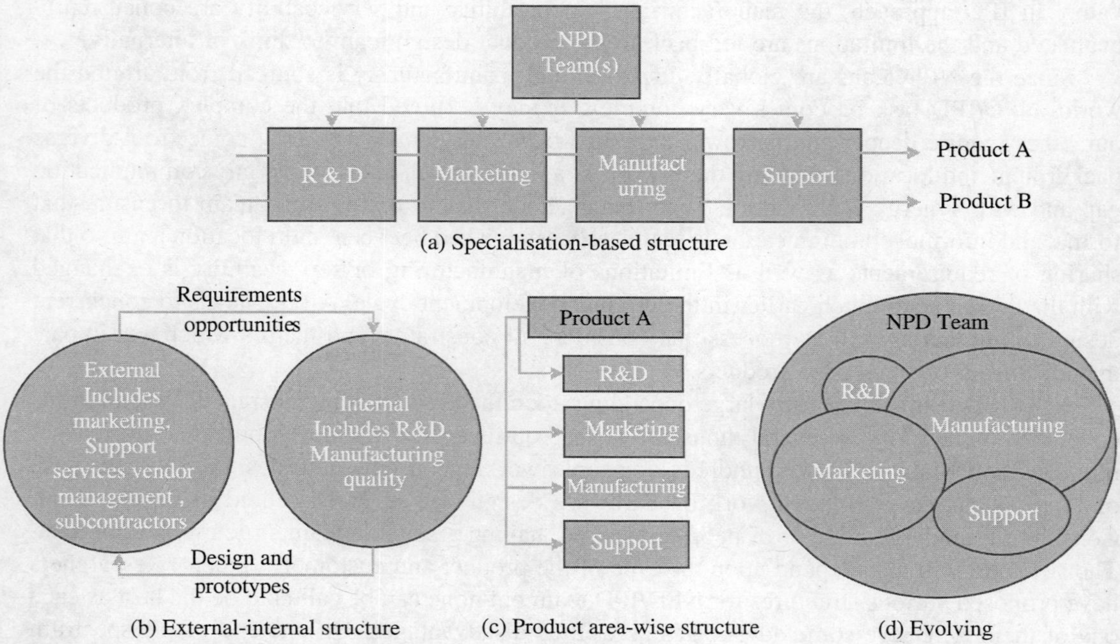

FIGURE 6.4

6.4.1 Characteristics of a Good NPD Team

A good NPD team is one that churns out successful products on schedule, within cost and which is liked by the customer. Some of the characteristics of a good NPD teams are described as follows:

Diversity: NPD/IPD is all about creativity and doing something new. You can summarise them in an acronym CUBE which symbolises creative, useful, balanced and efficient. While creative addresses aesthetic and performance aspects of the product, it must be useful to the user and to the society, environment. The team should take a balanced approach to optimise cost of the product as well as the cost of making it. Finally, the product should be efficient to manufacture and in actual performance. Given these requirements, a diverse team that comes from various functional disciplines, genders, age group, nationalities, expertise, etc., are most suitable for NPD/IPD.

Co-location: It is one of recommended practices to give physical proximity to each other with the team members. In a seamlessly connected world, this objective is achieved through electronic means such as video conferencing, giving camera feed of one location to other and communication tools such as chat. Sharing of information and document is achieved through team rooms and repositories which can be shared by the team across locations. A variant of this could be grouping sets of people at common locations who interact with each other in a seamless manner.

Display the progress: Commonly, the project team engaged in NPD/IPD activities would use a progress wall where the milestones and progress of the team is displayed. It could be as simple as white board with sticky notes and colourful markers or it could be sophisticated electronic board used in call centres and other production units, accessible on internet.

Consensus approach: NPD/IPD team always try to reach a consensus so that everyone's view is heard and taken into account. Disagreement if any is resolved through discussion and by seeking intervention of the steering committee in some cases.

Maturity of team leader: NPD/IPD teams require a team leader who is matured and acts more like a coach and facilitator than a manager. Most NPD/IPD team is self-managed and the team leader is one of the players who is also respected for his expertise, experience or team-building ability.

Meticulous planning: Don't get confused when we said that NPD team is self-managed and its leader is a mere facilitator. No NPD/IPD efforts will ever succeed without meticulous planning and flawless execution. The role of planning is assigned to a few selected members while other participate. NPD/IPD process is also about discovery of new problems and opportunities along the way which may, through the planning, off gear and execution off track. So re-planning and putting the deadlines back on track is essential.

Happy team: NPD/IPD teams have to be characteristically happy otherwise they would not be creative and problem solving. This leads to a need of proper selection of team members and having regular exercise of team building so that all members jell with each other better. If the team is not maintaining a healthy interpersonal dynamics, its outcome will be seriously impacted.

Self-driven and empowered: A good NPD/IPD team has nowhere else to go to solve their problems. Hence they have to be self-motivated, self-driven and empowered enough to take decisions. They are given financial and administrative freedom without which their work will get impacted.

Positive culture: A good NPD/IPD will build a culture of positivity, help each other, solve problems as they appear and blame no one. Such team is hard to build and harder to sustain but once this is achieved it is hardest to break as shown by several successful and legendary NPD/IPD teams, the recent example being APPLE. Most of the times, this responsibility lies on the management to guide the team towards such culture by defining roles and responsibilities, ironing out differences and bringing in necessary capabilities that has good soft skills capabilities as well.

6.5 MANAGING RESEARCH AND DEVELOPMENT (R&D)

In the current world, research and development (R&D) has become an important function to fight the competition. This function is more important for technology companies who make technology products. But almost all products use technology in some form or the other, hence the role of R&D becomes important for everyone. Pharmaceutical companies and those engaged in biotechnology research usually make significant investment in setting up in-house R&D facilities. This is considered to be a source of winning in the marketplace. Similarly technology-intensive product companies who make products like cell phone, electronics, computers, etc., are usually engaged in in-house R&D while others take final researched outcome by paying a fee to use them. R&D management includes the activities carried out for new product and process research leading to smooth transfer of new know-how and technology to other parts of the organisation such as manufacturing, marketing, support, etc.

According to Dr. Klaus (1994), R&D management can be defined as a function where the tasks of innovation management (i.e., creating and commercialising inventions) meet the tasks of technology management (i.e., external and internal creation and retention of technological know-how). This function spans across basic research from conceptualisation to deployment covering both product and process developments. R&D management does not end with proving a technology concept but works to realise it through prototyping, market trials and large scale manufacturing. Other R&D management functions include activities related to managing R&D projects portfolio, identifying areas of technology transfer. The areas excluded from R&D are technology licensing, intellectual property (IP) management or acquiring technology through mergers, acquisition of buy outs.

According to Pisano (2012)[4], there is no single issue today which is higher on the agenda of senior management than improving innovation performance. Accordingly, the role of R&D management has become very important for any organisation especially those which are competing on technology and have to face challenges of global marketplace. In a seminal article, Nobelius[5] described various stages of R&D management which have matured over a century. R&D

[4]Gary P. Pisano. Creating an R&D Strategy. Harvard Business School, Working Paper 12-095. 24 April 2012.

[5]D. Nobelius (2003). Towards the sixth generation of R&D management. International Journal of Project Management xxx (2004) xxx–xxx

management is not confined within the people of the enterprise but has crossed the boundary of the enterprise. The current 5th generation of R&D management is about cross-boundary alliances covering integrated internal functions and external participants. In addition, both technology development and product development have become integrated to address increased pressure of time to market, precision and innovation. This article widely cited the development of Bluetooth technology in 2003 which was developed by over 1600 companies participating under the banner of special interest group Bluetooth SIG[6] where Ericsson played the catalyst.

6.6 INTELLECTUAL PROPERTY MANAGEMENT AND INNOVATION PROTECTION

In a fiercely competitive world, the role of producing, maintaining and protecting intellectual property cannot be under emphasised. Intellectual properties are those technologies, formulas, manufacturing methods, design and other creative work which companies meticulously maintain and vigorously protect. There is legal angle to the protection process that we will discuss later in this chapter but before that let us understand what is the definition of IP, what all fall under this definition, how this is important to encourage the internal team to produce, maintain and protect.

According to a definition from WIPO (World Intellectual Property Organization), intellectual property is creations of human mind which include scientific inventions, work of literature and art, designs of products, methods and other works such as symbols, names of the companies or product and images used in commerce. IP protection is enforceable by law, provided suitable actions such as to register the intellectual property with appropriate authorities have been done. This means that companies and individual who have possession if such IP need to register their IP so that in case of any infringement or violation by others, law can enforce penalties and protect the interest of the holder of IP. Typically, various types of IP falls under broad categories of patents, copyright and trademarks which can be registered with suitable national and international bodies who will grant recognition and authority to the holder of such IP rights to seek financial as well as recognition benefits. For example, in writing a book if I quote a sentence or two verbatim from another author, I must recognise the author. However, if there is a substantial contribution by another author say a chapter or two, then I have to share the financial benefits such as royalties with the co-author. However, the purpose of IP protection is not just to grant the rights of creativity to its creator but also keep in mind wider public interest so that a right environment can be created to promote creativity and innovation.

Broadly, intellectual property is divided into two main subcategories:

- Intellectual properties related to industries: This covers patents for inventions, companies trademarks, logos and design or products and tools. In some cases, methods of manufacturing is also patented.
- Copyright for literary and creative work such as books, novels, poetry, plays, film, music compositions, works of art, drawings, paintings, photographs and sculptures. Recordings of radio broadcasts as well as television broadcasts fall under this category. If an artist is giving live performance, then the recording of the event will be covered under the copyright protection.

---

[6]Original Members of this group were Bluetooth SIG members include 3Com, Agere, Ericsson, IBM, Intel, Microsoft, Motorola, Nokia and Toshiba.

What exactly the IP rights to its owner are: Like physical properties both immovable and movable where the owner has the rights to own them and anyone else trying to use or take away will be liable under the law. IP rights ensure that its creator (or owners who have made investment in its creation) derive the financial as well as benefits of recognition under law. The misuse or any infringement can be challenged under the law. IP rights are covered in Article 27 of the Universal Declaration of Human Rights. IP rights were granted its first protection in 1883 under Paris Convention for the Protection of Industrial Property which was followed at Berne Convention for the Protection of Literary and Artistic Works in 1886. These treaties are maintained by WIPO.

In order to bring discipline across countries in the area of IP protection, WIPO was formed in 1970. This organisation helps in ensuring the rights of creators and owners of IP throughput the world. By its efforts, the holders of IP can seek recognition and reward for their work.

We will focus our discussion on IP management for technology-related products, designs and methods. The rights on products design and methods are granted by obtaining a patent. The subsequent section will describe in detail what patents are, how it is obtained and the rights of its holder are enforced by the rules of law. Similar procedure will also be followed for copyrightable items which will be described later in the section.

Patent, obtaining and enforcing: Patent is usually attached with an invention. The invention could be a new product, design or method of doing something. A solution to technical problems also falls under this category. By obtaining a patent for its work from a competent authority, its holder can claim financial rights for its use and also recognition. Patent is granted for a limited period about 20 years after which the product design or method becomes available for use without any rights for general public. It is evident that by allowing inventors reap its reward in terms of financial as well as reputational, the patent process encourages more inventions by inventors and a suitable climate is created that helps improving society.

Once patent rights are granted to its holder, no one can use or commercially exploit by making similar product using patented design or method. Such infringement can be fought in the court (see the case *Apple* vs *Samsung*) and reward be obtained in addition to restraining the violators. After specified period (20 years), the rights of its holder expires and the patented subject is called off patent.

By granting patent, the society and authorities recognises its inventors. We are all thankful for Edison and Swan for electric bulbs and Kodak for photo films. By public disclosure of the details of invention in the form of patent, the inventor can help further creativity and invention. Patent is granted by the Registrar of Patents and copyrights authority in every country. In India, it is a Controller General of Patents, Designs & Trade Marks (CGPDTM), United States Patent and Trademark Office (USPTO) in America and in Europe and Africa, European Patent Office (EPO) and the African Intellectual Property Organisation (OAPI), respectively.

6.6.1 Indian Laws Facilitation IP Protection

For patents, designs and trademarks: Indian government has set up a Controller General of Patents, Designs and Trade Marks. (CGPDTM) which is a body under union government department of Industrial Policy and Promotion under the Ministry of Commerce. This body follows and manages acts such as:

Patents Act, 1970 as amended
Designs Act, 2000 and
Trade Marks Act, 1999

Geographical Indications of Goods (Registration and Protection) Act, 1999 under the CGPDTM. Further details about each of these acts can be obtained from its website http://www.ipindia.nic.in/. Readers are also advised to study all available acts and laws from the website http://www.ipindia.nic.in/IPActs_Rules/IPActs_Rules.htm.

Copyrights for creative work: In case of creative work, no formal registration is required unlike in the patent registration. As soon as a work of art or literature gets created, its copyright becomes enforceable. However, the work can be registered in the Register of Copyrights Office of the Department of Education. Copyright Office is headed by a Registrar of Copyrights and applications in duplicate along with a copy of the work can be made to this authority who will grant copyrights to the requestor. Notable copyrights acts in India are:

- The Copyright Act, 1957
- The Copyright (Amendment) Act, 2012

Further, details on the process and procedure of copyrights can be obtained by accessing the website http://copyright.gov.in/.

6.6.2 IP/Patent Management Process

Invention can be protected by a variety of means. The way to protect the IP is through patent, copyright, trademark or service mark, or just by keeping it hidden from the world as trade secret. Examples of trade secret are the formulations of most of the cola drinks, perfumes, etc. Filing and obtaining patent is a way to protect the invention that any person or company has come out with. However, it is a complex process that requires completing several formalities and applying before the patent granting authorities in respective countries. It is also an expensive process and may need (in most cases) help of an attorney who specialises in patent and IP protection laws. By filing patent, the intent is to make the world aware of the invention and also to seek financial reward by letting others use it.

The first and foremost step of filing a patent is to ascertain whether such a patent has already been filed by someone in some country. A thorough search of publically disclosed patents within the country and other countries should be conducted. This is one of the tasks where a patent attorney may be able to help. Also the patent for the subject should be owned by the company or person not by someone else. A typical three-part test is conducted to ascertain whether the patentable subject is new, useful and is not so obvious. US Patent Office (USPTO)[7] defines three types of patents which can be granted. They are Utility, Design, and Plant. As per USPTO, utility patent is for new and useful process, machine, product and its improvement. Design patents are granted for a new original, and ornamental design for an article of manufacture. Finally, the plant patent is for any distinct and new variety of plant[8].

[7]http://www.uspto.gov accessed 14 Jun. 2015.
[8]http://www.uspto.gov/patents-getting-started/patent-process-overview#step1 accessed 14 Jun. 2015.

Based on the type of patent to be applied, the company or concerned person will have to apply in a proper format with all the necessary details. An applicable patent fee will also have to be paid. Once the application is complete in all respect and is submitted, patent office will assign an examiner who will examine the application. The examiner may ask for more information or clarification and decide to accept or reject. In case the patent application is accepted and the examiner notifies its acceptance which is called Notice of Allowance which contains patent issue and publication fee. Once the applicant pays these issue fee and any required publication, the patent office will grant a patent number and issue date. Details of these steps can be obtained from the respective patent office website in the country where the patent application is being filed. Multiple applications at all the countries where the said product is going to be marketed will have to be filed.

6.6.3 Case of IP Infringement Apple vs. Samsung

Both Apple and Samsung fought a protracted legal battle over patent of design of their smartphones since 2011. Apple filed several patent infringement suits on its rivals such as Samsung and Motorola. The patent war was also being fought to gain market supremacy by these players in the multibillion dollar smartphone markets. By August 2011, Apple and Samsung were fighting 19 cases in nine countries, number of such lawsuits increased to 50 around the globe. Some of these cases were won by Apple and some were ruled in the favour of Samsung. While several cases were fought by these two giants, it was the Apple design patent which led preliminary injunction on Samsung's Galaxy 10.1 tablet. The "ordinary observer test" which is used for testing design patent infringement was first laid down by the United States Supreme Court in 1871 in Gorham Co vs. White. The same logic was applied in this case also. Representative images of Apple and Samsung product can be seen to understand the stark similarities that led to Apple winning the case. This case also forced designers to think in a manner so that they are not dragged in the court cases for copying design of other products. A website report[9] details out the failed talk between the CEOs of these two organisations.

6.7 ROLE OF GOVERNMENT IN TECHNOLOGY DEVELOPMENT

There is little doubt that the development and welfare of the country is hugely dependent upon use of new and emerging technology. The famous White Revolution[10] carried out in India led by Dr. Vegies Kurian saw increase of milk production 17 million tonnes in 1950–51 to 88 million tonnes during 2002–03 (GOI, 2003). This was a direct result of using technology-led innovation to usher the year of self-sufficiency in milk production. So was the case of Green Revolution where a large scale use of technology in India to produce high yielding variety of seeds and new farming methods lead to self-sufficiency in their food production. While market dynamics will prompt technology-led product and process innovation to take place, yet the role of government to influence through policies and regulations always has a critical role to play. Take the case of technologies that promote green energy. Many may be costly to develop and use and these areas does require governmental incentives to promote them. Government's role is necessary

[9]http://www.cnet.com/news/apple-samsung-ceos-speak-but-fail-to-reach-settlement/accessed 29 May. 2016.

[10]http://www.fao.org/3/a-x6170e/x6170e2z.htm accessed 19 May. 2015.

to produce economically and environmentally sustainable technologies. Another area where government's role includes is to seek technology to solve some of the social issues; for example, water and air pollution management, transportation, food and agriculture, etc. Government's role is recognisable in accelerating the process of technological innovation to develop new energy sources.

The role of government in technology innovation can take place at two levels called push or pull. Through good policies and incentives will lead to pull for technologies innovation to commercialisation. Medicinal innovation, health care is a good example where incentives lead to more technologies to reach to commercialised stage. In other areas such as defence, environmental protection, weather forecasting and ecosystem management, technology innovation will follow the push approach through governmental investment in R&D and resorting to public private partnership. Both these approaches would need a significant role of government in educating the masses, developing skills pool, introducing training programmes, etc. Many researchers have argued that a combination of pull and push approach by the government is much more useful than just one of them.

Government role can be summarised in terms of the following activities:

(a) Through suitable policies to encourage technological innovation. Suitable policies help provide incentives that may add to the cost of the tax payers but ultimately it will lead to greater goods.

(b) Policies could be to both promote and restrict. Automobile companies are routinely pushed by the government to design engines that conform to higher fuel efficiency and stringent emission norms.

(c) Incentives to user environmental friendly sources lead to development and widespread usage of these technologies. Policy incentives can be both monetary and non-monetary. In the case of former incentives like tax credits, subsidies, direct funding in the form of loan or grants are most prevalent. In the case of later, efforts for education, award and recognition, technical assistance, etc., are included.

6.8 PRODUCT DEPLOYMENT STRATEGY

Deployment is military term referring to pressing soldiers into duty. In the case of new product development this refers to the stage when product is given in the hands of the actual users or used in service. This is last stage of the New Product Development Process also called Launch stage. At this stage the remaining activities for product release to market is done. We must recognize the fact that unless a product arising out of a technology innovation is properly used by its users its success would not come. So this part of the strategy is very crucial. Effective deployment strategy covers when to launch the product, its pricing, distribution, marketing and licensing it for further reproduction. The production volume is ramped up, detailed marketing and distribution plan is implemented. When the actual sales takes place the user/customer is given necessary education for its usage. Finally process for after sales support is drawn up. Depending upon the technology type different alternatives can be chosen for product deployment. We briefly summarize them as follows:

- **Timing strategy:** This covers decisions such as when the product has to be launched. Timing of entry is decided based on where product stands on technology development S-curve cycle or any seasonal considerations such as New Year or Diwali. Timings has impact on product availability with respect of firm's production capability. Timing also takes into account if the new product would warrant stopping earlier product (or technology). Finally the timing of deployment is related with a firm's preparedness.
- **Touch strategy:** A product may be of low or high volume, standard or customised and the strategy looks at the aspects of marketing, user education, field installation, customer handholding so that the product is accepted in the market. This is shown in Figure 6.5.

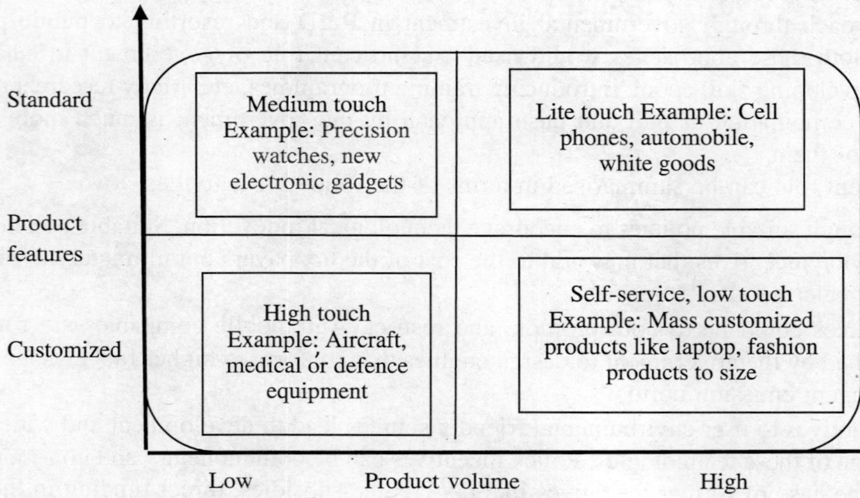

FIGURE 6.5 Touch alternatives during technology deployment.

- *Low volume custom deployment:* This type of product deployment means hands-on, manual deployment, where you deploying products at few places in customisation mode. Examples of their type is aircrafts, defence equipment's, high tech medical equipment which are customised. If the technology is new and requires lot of onsite customisation, for example installing solar panels at home or offices then this strategy works.
- *Low volume standard deployment:* This type of product deployment means very little interaction with the customer as customer may be aware of how to use them. Examples of these are precision watches, new electronic gadgets etc.
- *High volume standard deployment:* This is used for products that does not require any customisation and can be released in the market as customer may be using similar products in past and has very less need for training regarding using it. For example automobile, white goods. Electronics item. Here you need very lite touch with the customer.
- *Customized high-volume deployment:* This strategy requires limited interaction during deployment. Interaction occurs at the beginning of the installation, but the remainder of the process is automated. Mass customized products like configurable laptops, Medical equipment, machine tools etc. follow this method.

- **Distribution strategy:** Distribution is an important activity than can make a product deployment successful or if not done properly may lead to failure. A product can be sold directly or through distributors and retailers network. While the former may give better control the later would require less organization responsibility and quicker. In case of choosing a distribution channel suitable alliances can be developed with distributors. Take the case of some recent Mobile phone launches which were done prior to certain festival season and done through a popular e-commerce site.
- **Marketing strategy:** This covers those activities that help promote the product or technology in the market and build awareness in the minds of the its customer. Several strategies chosen for marketing during new product or technology deployment are providing free usage or trials to its prospective customers, use of social media, viral marketing or word of mouth publicity. Organizing event over web or on television is part of the marketing strategy.

  Marketing strategy has to be adopted for different types of customers some of which may be innovators, some early/late majority or laggards. While Innovators and Early Adopters prefer detailed technical inputs in marketing communication, others would like to more reassurance that product/technology has been used by others and has been found useful.

6.9 AI/GEN AI IN PRODUCT LIFECYCLE MANAGEMENT (PLM): FROM CONCEPT TO DISPOSAL

Product Lifecycle Management (PLM) encompasses the entire process from conceptualization, through design, engineering, development, manufacturing, and finally after-sales service and disposal. AI and Generative AI are profoundly transforming every stage of this lifecycle, enabling unprecedented levels of efficiency, innovation, and optimization.

In the **conception and design** stages, Gen AI facilitates rapid ideation and the generation of novel design options. Engineers can use AI to create dozens of design alternatives overnight, optimizing parts for lighter weight or improved performance. This accelerates early-stage ideation and facilitates 3D rendering. The use of AI-assisted design tools allows for a much broader exploration of the design space than human designers could achieve alone.

During **prototyping and validation**, AI enables the creation of "digital twins"—virtual replicas of physical products or systems. These digital models allow for real-time simulation and optimization throughout a product's entire lifecycle, minimizing costly physical prototypes and accelerating testing. This convergence of the physical and digital worlds transforms PLM from a sequential, document-driven process to a dynamic, data-driven, and continuously optimized system, revolutionizing product quality and efficiency.

In **manufacturing**, AI optimizes processes and enhances automation. AI-powered robotics streamlines warehouse operations, eliminating unnecessary movements and boosting efficiency. AI algorithms can predict equipment failures, enabling proactive maintenance and reducing machine downtime by up to 50%. This integration leads to more efficient production, lower costs, and improved quality control.

Finally, in the **service and maintenance** phase, AI-driven predictive maintenance allows for proactive servicing, extending product lifespan and reducing operational costs. Even at the **end-of-life** stage, AI can assist in material recovery and proper disposal by identifying recyclable components and optimizing recycling processes, contributing to sustainability. This comprehensive integration of AI across PLM stages signifies a shift towards a "cyber-physical" product lifecycle, where continuous data feedback and AI-driven insights optimize every phase.

6.10 AI-ASSISTED DESIGN, PROTOTYPING, AND MANUFACTURING

AI and Generative AI are fundamentally reshaping how products are designed, prototyped, and manufactured, moving towards a more integrated and co-creative process.

In **design**, Gen AI can generate a multitude of design options based on specified parameters and constraints. This capability accelerates early-stage ideation and facilitates 3D rendering, allowing designers to visualize hypothetical products quickly. AI can optimize designs for various factors like weight, cost, or performance, leading to innovative solutions that humans might not conceive. For instance, Siemens engineers use AI to create lighter parts and complete projects faster. This shifts the design process from purely human-led to a human-AI collaboration where AI acts as a powerful co-creator.

For **prototyping**, AI tools enable rapid visualization of ideas and virtual testing without the need for expensive physical models. Digital twins, virtual replicas of physical systems, allow for comprehensive simulation of process changes and prediction of outcomes, significantly reducing development time and costs. This means companies can iterate on designs much faster, leading to more refined products and a higher rate of design innovation.

In **manufacturing**, AI plays a crucial role in automation and optimization. AI-powered robotics enhances efficiency and accuracy in warehouse operations, performing tasks like sorting, picking, and packing. Predictive maintenance, enabled by AI, monitors equipment through sensors and analyzes real-time data to predict failures, triggering just-in-time maintenance and minimizing disruptions. This integration allows manufacturing processes to be dynamically adapted based on AI-generated design iterations and real-time operational data, blurring the lines between design and production and leading to more optimized physical products.

6.11 TRANSFORMING NEW PRODUCT DEVELOPMENT (NPD) TEAMS WITH AI/GEN AI

New Product Development (NPD) has always been a complex, multidisciplinary endeavor. With the advent of AI and Generative AI, the composition, skills, and collaboration models within NPD teams are undergoing significant transformation. AI is increasingly functioning as an intelligent assistant, augmenting human performance rather than simply replacing it. This means NPD teams are not just using AI tools; they are working *with* AI in a symbiotic relationship.

The integration of AI into NPD teams shifts the human role from being the sole ideator and executor to becoming an "orchestrator" and "refiner" of AI-generated content. This requires a new set of "human-AI collaboration" skills. For instance, while AI can rapidly generate novel concepts and prototypes , human team members are essential for critically evaluating AI outputs, providing context, and refining ideas to ensure strategic alignment and customer desirability. This necessitates new training programs focused on prompt engineering (the art of crafting effective inputs for AI models), evaluating AI-generated ideas, and integrating AI outputs seamlessly into workflows.

Cross-functional teams, already a hallmark of effective NPD, become even more critical. These teams now need members with AI literacy who can leverage AI tools for accelerated ideation, experimentation, and iteration. AI's ability to automate repetitive, data-intensive tasks frees human NPD team members to focus on activities that require uniquely human attributes, such as creativity, critical thinking, emotional intelligence, and complex problem-solving. This strategic reallocation of human capital allows NPD teams to achieve higher levels of innovation and efficiency, fundamentally changing team dynamics and leadership styles from directive to facilitative.

6.12 AI/GEN AI IN RESEARCH AND DEVELOPMENT (R&D) MANAGEMENT

Research and Development (R&D) is the engine of innovation, driving the creation of new products, processes, and knowledge. Generative AI is fundamentally accelerating and transforming R&D management by automating critical steps and enhancing the very nature of scientific inquiry.

AI agents are now specializing in various R&D tasks, significantly expediting the discovery process. For example, AI tools like Crow and Owl can automate literature reviews, quickly retrieving and summarizing vast amounts of scientific information. Other agents, such as Phoenix and Finch, can assist in chemical synthesis design and data-driven discovery in biology, respectively. This capability streamlines complex R&D workflows, allowing researchers to process and synthesize information at a scale and speed previously unimaginable.

More profoundly, AI is contributing directly to the intellectual core of scientific discovery by generating and evaluating hypotheses and enhancing experimental design. This moves R&D from a purely human-driven, often trial-and-error process, to a more automated, data-driven, and potentially faster path to breakthrough discoveries. For instance, AI is predicted to systematically discover over 30% of new drugs and materials by 2025, offering significant cost and time reductions in pharmaceutical and materials science industries. This implies an exponential increase in the pace of scientific progress, with profound implications for how R&D is funded, managed, and collaborated upon, and even raising questions about the nature of scientific authorship and the validation of AI-generated insights.

6.13 PROTECTING INTELLECTUAL PROPERTY IN THE AGE OF GENERATIVE AI

Intellectual Property (IP) management, encompassing patents, copyrights, and trademarks, is crucial for protecting the creative and innovative output of firms. However, the rise of Generative AI introduces significant new challenges and complexities to existing IP frameworks.

One major concern is **copyright infringement from training data**. Gen AI models are trained on massive datasets, often scraped from the internet, which may contain copyrighted material without explicit permission or attribution. This raises questions about whether the outputs generated by these models constitute derivative works and whether the act of training itself infringes on copyrights. There are currently no verifiable data governance and protection assurances for confidential enterprise information when using public AI tools, meaning users must assume data entered into such tools may become public.

Another challenge is the proliferation of **"deep fakes" and product copies**. Gen AI can produce highly realistic images, videos, and text that mimic existing content or designs, making it difficult to distinguish original from AI-generated or potentially infringing content. This creates new avenues for misuse by threat actors, including the generation of artifacts for complex scams.

Furthermore, the **lack of transparency** in how Gen AI models arrive at their outputs (the "black box" problem) and the difficulty of tracking **data lineage** complicate efforts to audit for IP compliance or identify the source of potential infringement. The "unclear ownership" of AI-generated content also challenges existing IP laws, which were primarily designed for human creators. This necessitates a re-evaluation of legal frameworks and potentially new models for attributing authorship, licensing, and compensation in a world where machines can "create." Organizations must implement robust data governance practices, including strict data security measures, careful data classification, and access controls, to protect sensitive or personally identifiable information used within Gen AI models. This proactive approach is vital to mitigate IP risks and ensure compliance in a rapidly evolving legal and technological landscape.

6.14 SUMMARY

This chapter was devoted to articulate product and process development and role of technology in these processes. In this chapter, we examined the product lifecycle and product development process at conceptual level. We started our discussion by understanding product lifecycle management process which is also popularly abbreviated as PLM, a useful concept to chart out various stages of development of a product or product family. We explained that process of PLM is partially physical as well as informational and detailed out its various stages such as conception, design and prototype, manufacturing and finally the sell, serve and maintain stage. All products (or products family) will and should go through a last phase called discard and dispose off, a phase which many companies do not consider but has become increasingly important from environmental perspectives. We outlined that PLM is an integrated process and explained various technologies at its various stages. We further explained that new product development (NPD) process is not simple and requires deep preparation and meticulous execution. A well-orchestrated and well-thought NPD process ensures that the NPD initiative is successful and this lead to our inquiry of how successful companies run the critical new-product development process. We discussed linear, non-linear approaches to build the concept. Predictably our next discussion was on selecting a right NPD process. Followed with the examination of a role of technology in product development.

The next important concept discussed was about the team characteristics and best practices in the new product development process. Several popular team structures and characteristics of a good NPD team were also discussed for NPD.

The next elaborations were on concept on the linkage between technology, development and competition and managing of research and development (R&D) process. This was followed up with the topic of intellectual property management and innovation protection. The brief insight of patents grating authorities in India and the prevalent Patent laws were also given to aid student's knowledge on this subject. In addition, a brief description of IP/patent management process was given along with the role of government in facilitating the rights of the inventors and holder of IP.

CASE STUDY

Grameen Shakti

This is unique case from Bangladesh where the micro lending institution called The Grameen Bank of Bangladesh, through its non-profit subsidiary started giving loans to marginal farmers and workers to use photo voltaic solar home systems for their commons household use. This effort was recognised and a Global Environment Facility grant through International Finance Corporation's Small and Medium Enterprises Program helped Grameen Shakti to give better credit facilities to its thousands of customers. (*Source:* www.gshakti.org.)

Questions

1. Why newer developments in rural areas are being led by startups and not by established firms who have greater strength and ability to come out with newer innovation? Answer your response based on the case above and other similar stories.
2. What are the similar technology-led opportunities in rural areas that are still to be tapped? Give at least three examples for Indian masses.

Key Terms: PLM, NPD, R&D, IP

REVIEW QUESTIONS

1. Define various stages of the product lifecycle. What is product lifecycle management (PLM)? Give examples to show your understanding. **Answer:** Section 6.2
2. How companies run new-product development process? What are the precautions taken to ensure that new product development is successful? How can a company select the right NPD process? **Answer:** Sections 6.3, 6.4 and 6.5
3. What are the characteristics of a good NPD team? Explain in brief. **Answer:** Section 6.8
4. What is the linkage between technology, development and competition? How are companies able to establish them seamlessly?
5. Describe in brief the process of management of Research and Development (R&D) function. **Answer:** Section 6.9
6. What is the need of intellectual property management and its role in protecting innovation? **Answer:** Section 6.10
7. What is the role of Government in Technology Development? Explain with examples. **Answer:** Section 6.12

ADDITIONAL READINGS

1. Akgun, Ali E., Gary S. Lynn and John L. Byrne (2004), Taking the Guesswork Out of NPD: How Successful High-Tech Companies Get that Way, *Journal of Business Strategy,* 25(4), pp. 41–46.
2. Crawford, Merle E. and A. Di Benedetto, *New Products Management,* 7th ed. New York: McGraw-Hill/Irwin, 2003.
3. Clark, Kim B. and Steven, C. Wheelwright, *Managing New Product and Process Development: Text and Cases.* New York: The Free Press, 1993.
4. Calantone, Roger, Rosanna Garcia and Cornelia Drőge (2003), The Effects of Environmental Turbulence on New Product Development Strategic Planning, *Journal of Product Innovation Management*, 20(2), pp. 90–103.
5. di Benedetto, C. Anthony (1999), Identifying the Key Success Factors in New Product Launch, *Journal of Product Innovation Management*, 16(6), pp. 530–544.
6. Narver, John C., Stanley F., Slater and Douglas L. MacLachlan (2004). Responsive and Proactive Market Orientation and New Product Success, *Journal of Product Innovation Management*, 21(5), pp. 334–347.
7. Muller, Amy, Liisa Valikangas and Paul Marlyn (2005), Metrics for Innovation: Guidelines For Developing a Customized Suite of Innovation Metrics. Strategy and Leadership, 33(1), pp. 37–45.
8. Pullman, Madeleine E., William L. Moore and Don G. Wardell (2002). A Comparison of Quality Function Deployment and Conjoint Analysis in New Product Design. *Journal of Product Innovation Management*, 19(4), pp. 354–364.
9. Taylor, Ernest (1996), T302 Innovation Design Environment and Strategy, Block 1 An Introduction to Innovation, Section 1 (pp. 4–39) *Invention and Innovation*, Milton Keynes, The Open University.
10. Dyer, J. and Gregersen, H. (2011), *The Innovators DNA: Mastering the Five Skills of Disruptive Innovators*, Harvard Business Press Books.

Chapter 7

Technology and Business Model

A disruptive innovation is a technologically simple innovation in the form of a product, service, or business model that takes root in a tier of the market that is unattractive to the established leaders in an industry.

—Clayton Christensen

At the end of this chapter, we will learn:

- What business model is
- Why business model is significant in the modern business
- The different types of business models to choose from
- Role of technology in formulating business model
- How to build sustainable business model
- Appraising business models
- Growing and maintaining business model over times

7.1 INTRODUCTION

In this chapter[1] we will focus on understanding the role of technology in business model innovation. After defining what a business model is in the simple terms, we will survey various definitions given by leading researchers. The objective of this chapter is to build foundational concepts for technology manager to define and outline their right business model so that they can be successful in their enterprise. We will also bring out the steps to be followed to develop any enterprise business model and then maintain and enhance it over time to take it to its success path.

7.2 BUSINESS MODEL DEFINED

Management literature is full of various definitions about business model. Some define it as how a firm makes money, some associate with strategy a firm adopts but a comprehensive definition of business model includes all aspects of a business. Michael Lewis in his book *The New New*

[1]Some part of this chapter was published as a chapter in the Book *Entrepreneurship*, written by the author.

Thing: A Silicon Valley Story[2] refers the phrase "business model" as a term of art that was central to Internet boom during the turn of the century. He also added that this term glorified all manner of half-baked plans to run any new business. This term gained enormous popularity because it brought new ways to run the business yet it needed more exploratory definitions. Peter Drucker, the legendary management author and consultant defined Business Model as the "assumptions about what a company gets paid for" in his article "The theory of the business" published in 1994 in HBR.[3]

This term has evolved over the years and now it stands for a larger meaning covering the business architecture, customer segments the firm addresses and ways through which it creates value for them and ultimately gets paid, directly or indirectly. The latter is the phenomenon which has come up during the internet era where the actual users of the product or services may not be paying to the company that provides the services but there are other means to recover the money. The most famous business model example of the last century was the free e-mail services launched by Hotmail which was ultimately sold by its promoters for over 400 million USD to Microsoft. The revenue was generated through the advertisement and other means such as selling data of its users for mass marketing campaigns.

In simple yet comprehensive terms, business model is defined as the methods enterprise usages to serve its customers and make money. Please note that both aspects of serving the customers as well as making money are interdependent. Unless we have compelling value proposition in the form of product or services, we would never be able to attract the customer. Yet we also have to think creatively as to how the product and services will have to be priced. If we take the example of any e-commerce site like Amazon or Flipkart, they don't make any product. All they do is to facilitate delivery of thousands of products from several manufacturers to our home and offices. We do not have to visit any shop for buying any of these products from these e-commerce sites. In the process they service their customer with convenience and to the supplier they enable reduced cost of holding the inventory. This is a win-win business model that e-commerce companies have evolved and perfected over the years.

Business model includes all activities that the firm has to think and plan in order to deliver what it promises to the customer. This may include manufacturing, design, sourcing logistics and finally distribution and selling. It is like blueprint of the business, depicting how the business runs, who are its target segments of customers and how the revenue generation happens. Business model is used to visualise and answer questions like how the firm will compete in the marketplace. An enterprise will have many internal players such as employees and managers and it will also have to deal with external entities such as customers, suppliers and investors, who would like to understand how the firm works and this answer is provided by a comprehensive business model. The business model also includes operational ideas such as how it will produce goods or services. The firm may decide in part or in full not to make a product but just do branding, marketing and selling. The pros and cons will have to be explained in the business model document of the firm.

---

[2]W.W. Norton & Company; 1 edition (January 6, 2014), p. 256.

[3]https://hbr.org/1994/09/the-theory-of-the-business.

7.3 WHY DO WE NEED A BUSINESS MODEL?

Businesses have been in existence for ages. So it is a pertinent question to ask as to why a discussion and so much of importance about the business model. The answer to this question lies in the new challenges as well as the opportunities modern day businesses are facing. It is no longer the age old way of doing business where you sell your product through your own channel or shops in the neighborhood. The price is not dictated by the cost plus margin but what competitors are going to offer. The globalisation and internet-based economy has made it possible to try and implement a variety of combination to make, distribute, sell and generate revenue of your goods and services from any part of the world. As producers from around the world are flocking to sell to the customers in your vicinity, you also have to sell in theirs. This is precisely why the business model discussion became a buzzword during dot com boom at the end of the last century. A good articulated business model increases confidence in your abilities among the investors and customers, suppliers and other stakeholders and finally leads to create better returns on its investments.

According to Alex Osterwalder[4], a noted researcher in Business Model area, a business model helps to define assumptions or hypotheses of the enterprise and how it is going to achieve its objectives. Another seminal article on this subject by JoanMagretta[5] states that "Business modeling is the managerial equivalent of the scientific method—you start with a hypothesis, which you then test in action and revise when necessary".

A clearly articulated business model also helps in continued feasibility analysis or new direction that a firm may be taking in course of its expansion. It enables the technology manager to focus attention on how all the elements of a business fit together. In addition, it properly describes how suppliers, distributers and business partners would work together to make a business idea viable.

An agile business model which is capable of adapting the situation as it demands or lowering the risk is likely to find more favours from the investors over time. Such business model will yield better returns and prevent the firm from going out of business after making huge losses. For a technology manager having a sound understanding of business model concepts helps to prevent losses and encourages seeking requisite support from its investors and other supports. Business model also helps to convey your vision and operating mechanism to your employees, customers and suppliers.

In short, some of the key components of a business model include:

- **Purpose of the organisation:** It covers its mission, brands, its ability to serve a target marketplace and of course its unique differentiators.
- **Strategy:** This helps organisation to achieve the purpose of its existence. This is the action part of the organisation where it is converting its desire into results. Strategy is further articulated in terms of its goals, timelines, resources required and how it will measure its success.
- **Assets:** Business model includes the assets the organisation possesses; it may be raw material or innovation ideas, capital or the strong credential of the team. This will lead

[4]https://hbr.org/2015/01/what-is-a-business-model accessed 25 Mar. 2015.

[5]Joan Magretta. "Why Business Models Matter". https://hbr.org/2002/05/why-business-models-matter accessed 25 Mar. 2015.

to what all products and services it will produce. This also includes how the organisation is structured, geographic locations, roles and responsibilities. The business model covers other assets such as financial and intellectual property as well.

- **Value proposition:** This answers why a customer should chose us over the competitive offerings and how we can make it difficult for competitors to emulate it.
- **People:** They cover the stakeholders of the firm including promoters, founders, customers, suppliers and most importantly employees. These components are shown in Figure 7.1.

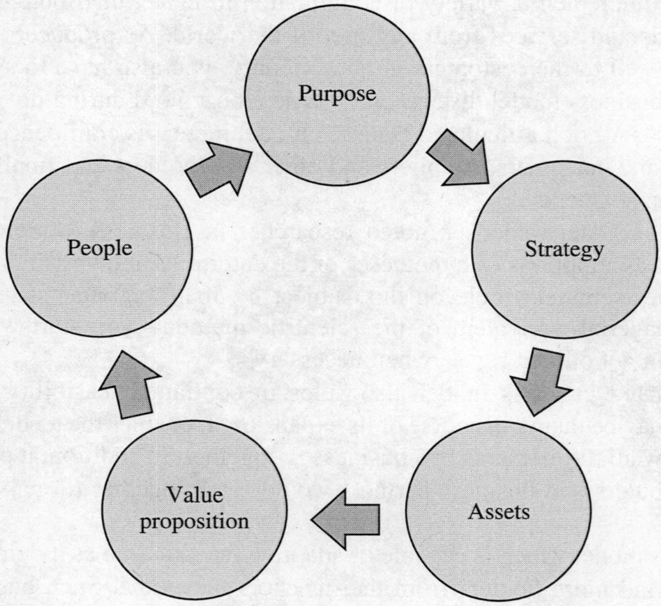

FIGURE 7.1 Components of Business Model.

7.3.1 Business Model as New Tool to Beat Competition

In the internet economy where many businesses are converging and are taking advantage of power of connectivity, superior business model is becoming a tool for gaining competitive advantage. No one would have imagined that Amazon would become the biggest provider of Cloud-based IT infrastructure services. Amazon which started selling books and music CDs online, offers pay as you use IT infrastructure services to its customers who can provision requisite disk space or CPU for their application on need basis. The recent success of Uber or OLA in India is an example where a new innovative model is leading the company to reach out to new customer segments providing better services at a reasonable or lower cost. Companies through business model differentiations can protect or increase their margins. It is no longer product or services features that count to beat the competition as more and more innovation in them would be hard to come by. A noted researcher Kay Plantes[6] opines that most successful companies have used

[6]http://www.innovationmanagement.se/imtool-articles/why-business-model-innovation-is-critically-important-today/accessed 20 May, 2015.

business model innovation to their advantages. The business model innovation helps the leading companies to offer a unique and difficult to emulate value proposition that resonates with changing customer needs leading to higher profits yet at a lower cost structure so that competitors cannot easily copy them.

7.3.2 Business Model is Not Static but Changes Over Time

An important aspect of business model is to articulate how the company will weave in the revenue generating stream over changing time. Companies like Gillette sell their Mach III razor handle at a lower cost and recover it through razor refills. Similar is the case of personal printers where the cost of printer is low but that of the refill cartridges allow the firm to make money. Nescafe installs coffee vending machines free in offices but makes money through selling each cup of coffee and its coffee mix. When digital camera replaced the film-based cameras, Kodak created a digital printing centre for users to print pictures of digital camera on genuine Kodak paper. You may be surprised that General Motors makes 60% of its earning from finance repayments, not from auto sales.

7.4 SUCCESS FACTORS FOR BUSINESS MODEL

Having a sound business model is important to ascertain if the business being planned or currently being run will be able to scale up or not. In addition, be clear that any business model that is not able to provide benefits to society in the long-term will not survive and will never grow up. Do not get confused with the short-term success of Ponzy schemes, creating paper companies doing nothing but seeking investments from gullible investors. All these are not enterprise in the stricter sense as they do not produce any goods to the society. We will exclude any such discussion or reference from our concept building task on business model.

While designing a successful business model, we must consider some of the key factors that help test the robustness of the business model. We will enumerate some of the key ones here.

(a) **Product or services offering:** The product and services offering could fall under the category of pull products or push products. The former refers to those products which are already in the market and the new enterprise is offering it at better price, better features, etc. Automobile, mobile handset, kitchen appliances and all the remaining existing products fall under this category. The latter, i.e., push category would be those products or services that do not really exist or do not have any wider acceptance at that point in time. Solar powered automobile, most of the new feature mobile/internet or new technology-based offerings or products fall under this category. This new category usually creates a new market and tap the hidden demand or needs of the customer. Taxi booking applications like OLA and Uber fall under this category of enterprise that creates new services for the customer. Similar products are launched in the area of health care, supporting the disabled, etc., where there was no market in the past but new products or services are redefining the markets.

(b) **Support or challenges from the ecosystems:** While defining business model, one must consider if the responsibility lies with the enterprise to manage the part of the ecosystem or it will depend on the existing ecosystem to expand its enterprise. Legal challenges, cultural issues and the acceptance from the customers on a particular market fall under this category. The good example is the adoption of vegetarian burgers by McDonald for Indian market.

(c) **Readiness of the firm:** This is yet another important factor for sustained business model. If the product or services is not able to live up to the promises it is bound to fail. When in 2007 Microsoft launched Windows Vista, it did not get the expected success despite huge marketing expenditure. The sole reason was its compatibility and performance problems that distracted some of the long-term users of Microsoft products. Another product called Mosquito Magnet designed to use carbon dioxide to attract mosquitoes into a trap was initially successful but did not scale up as its quality drooped when the mass manufacturing was shifted to China[7].

7.5 BUILDING SUSTAINABLE BUSINESS MODEL

This thought is to build business model that does not damage the environment and helps in preserving the natural resources. Sustainability refers to balancing local and global efforts to meet basic human needs without destroying or degrading the natural environment. So any business that is addressing these aspects like reducing carbon emission, not wasting non-renewal resources, preserving water or forest are considered sustainable. So while designing a sustainable business model one must consider if the proposed business is taking care of all these issues.

The factors to be considered are:

- **Enterprise must preserve and stretch natural resources:** This can be done if the enterprise is helping in increasing the efficiency of natural resources by an order of magnitude. The enterprise should consume less resources and energy from the earth's crust.
- Enterprise must invest in maintaining and restoring natural resources while it is expanding its business.
- **Reuse/Recycle material and resources:** Sustainability demands the end of the life products be reused. Companies should produce less waste either in material form or through reduced consumption of energy products, etc.
- **Responsible consumption:** Consume only what is necessary and aim to reduce the consumption over time. A good example given is about tree that produces more energy than what it consumes. Even when Tree's life is over it turns out into useful waste and becomes food for animals, nutrients for earth.

A sustainable business model is good for the enterprise, society and the environment.

7.6 ROLE OF TECHNOLOGY IN BUSINESS MODEL DEVELOPMENT AND INNOVATION

With the rapid advancement of information and communication technology especially internet, social media and several other related ones like mobile computing, it is natural to look up to

[7]https://hbr.org/2011/04/why-most-product-launches-fail accessed 26 Mar. 2015.

technology to strengthen and innovate a business model. Technology innovation is always linked with business model innovation.

Baden-Fuller and Haefliger (2013)[8] consider business model relationship with technology as a two-way process. Firstly, business models mediate the link between technology and firm performance and secondly, having the right technology helps in deciding business model for openness and user engagement. Technology development is known to facilitate new business models. Examples from technologies such as steam engine leading to rail road transportation and internet technology to facilitate e-commerce engine is well discussed. However, business model may work without technology as well, example of which being the famous Just-in-time business model developed by Japanese enterprise.

Technology and business model interact with each other in a seamless manner. The recent example of Amazon's success is not the new business model but enhancing the existing mail order-based business model through internet. Now they are selling their IT capabilities to lend computing capacity on rent (popularly called cloud computing) to generate new business model. Yet the Google's search engine was a new technology that led to an entirely new business model called Adwords to link advertisement to the key word search, thus giving new opportunities for Google. So it may be simple to say that while business model uses technology for execution, technology enhances and develops new business models. This has been shown in Figure 7.2.

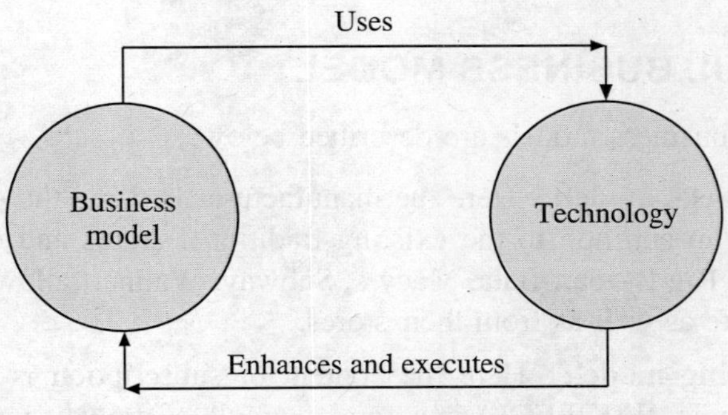

FIGURE 7.2 Business Model and Technology Interplay.

Technology impact of business model is manifold. Some of the impacts captured here are as follows:

(a) **Identifying new customer segments:** Technology increases the reach of the firm and therefore helps in identifying new customer segments. Caller tune is one example where mobile companies found new customer segments for the popular songs which the mobile users can download and make their caller tune.

(b) **Increased customer engagement:** The success of popular mobile apps bases taxi aggregators shows that technology enhances customer engagement and leads to increased revenues. When a taxi user sees the nearest taxi available on his mobile

[8]Charles Baden-Fuller and Stefan Haefliger. Business Models and Technological Innovation, Long Range Planning, Volume 46, Issue 6, December 2013, pp. 419–426. Managing Business Models for Innovation, Strategic Change and Value Creation.

phone, the confidence and urge to hire at any time increases. Making sure that the drivers are trained, electronic billing possible, feedback solicited and given leads to increased customer engagement.

(c) **Enhanced value delivery:** The earlier example can also be seen for an example of enhanced value delivery using technology. A user of such taxi hiring application can obtain a record of travel and a copy of the bill which can be used for subsequent actions such as seeking reimbursement from my employer if it is an official travel. This is an enhanced value which is offered to the customer. Another good example of enhanced value delivery is the rapid popularity of MOOC (massive open online course) courses which deliver online lectures almost free for larger populations to take benefit from.

(d) **Facilitates monetisation:** One of the most important aspects of any business model is to realise the money. This is also called value capture or monetisation. Here again technology comes to help business model to facilitate various sources of revenue not just from customer who pays but from advertisement and other means. Gmail and Google earn massive revenue from advertisement and selling customer behaviours pattern to marketing companies. Gaming companies that release online games earn money through numbers of hits and downloads. For example, Zynga, makers of popular game FarmVille, earns money from cross-selling and advertisement.

7.7 SUCCESSFUL BUSINESS MODEL

Some of the successful business models are described below:

(a) **Bricks and clicks model:** Here the manufacturer is using the online version to sell their products in addition to the existing traditional stores and distribution network. All stores like Big Bazaar, Bata, Macy's, Subway, Walmart allow customers to buy at their online site as well as from their stores.

(b) **Crowd sourcing model:** Here the content or subscription is sought from a wide number of people. WIKIPEDIA is a good example of crowd sourcing the content and Aam Aadmi party in New Delhi is another to source election funding from the crowd. Another example is Quirky.com that helps inventors who can crowd source ideas or Kickstarter.com for startups funding.

(c) **Lead generation also called Affiliate Marketing model:** In this the site generates leads for other companies. Classified search company justdial.com helps generate leads and offers discounts on restaurants and other services by directing traffic or selling phone numbers of the people who called Just Dial for seeking information about movie theaters, courier service, hotels, etc. The revenue is generated only when these leads get converted into a sale.

(d) **Multilevel marketing:** Here one of the users or consumers is prompted to bring more customers in a chain linked basis and earn revenue for every purchase from below the chain. Good examples are Amway and many other companies who incentivise people to expand their network.

(e) **Selling user profile data:** Many online companies collect data about the customer, name, address, other profile information and mobile/home phone numbers, and sell the data to prospect searching companies for marketing new products. Credit card companies usually sell segmented data about customers based on the spend pattern and earn money.

(f) **Open source model:** Here the software and products are given free including the source code for people to modify. Examples of this model are RedHat and MySql.

(g) **Advertisement based models:** Here the company put up content and lets its use as free but the revenue is generated through the advertising revenue. This is one of the first widely used internet based models which has huge success like YouTube, Google, Yahoo. MSN, etc. The revenue can be generated based on the display of ads or banner ads where the advertiser is charged based on number of ads displayed. Alternatively, as Google and other search engines do, the charges to the advertiser is done when the ad is clicked. Finally, for voice or video based services, e.g., Spotify.com, Pandora.com or YouTube, the ads are played before the user is allowed to access the content. In this case, the user is forced to watch or listen to the ads.

(h) **User Subscription based model:** In this model, a monthly or annual fee is charged of every registered user. Software companies are earning revenue software based on annual subscription on the number of user basis. This is also called SaaS, i.e., software as service. In this category, Salesforce.com is one good example. The only disadvantage of using this model is that as a user you may be locked in with the service provider as your data would reside with them unless you have set up an agreement to transfer the data to new sites as and when you desire to do so.

(i) **Frugal or strip down model:** Here the bare minimum feature of an established product is used to release a new product which is much cheaper. Low-cost airlines like Indigo and Spice Jet and automobile like Tata Nano fall under this category.

(j) **Mobile Apps-based model:** Here comes the applications written for mobile applications which are usually given free but are charged after you have become used to it. WhatsApp and most mobile games fall under this category.

(k) **Volume aggregation model:** This is where the aggregator gives a huge discount to attract a large number of customers for a particular product. This helps the seller with huge volume and customers are happy with the discount. Companies like Groupon, SnapDeal.com, Google offer, fall under this category. The biggest challenges for this model include lack of barriers to entry and enormous customer acquisition costs.

(l) **Razor and blades model:** In this model, the main product is sold cheap and money is made through supplies or complementary products. Most Gillette razors are sold at low price but money is made through refill sale. Apple's iTunes and Android Appstore generate lower revenue but lead to higher sale of iPhone.

(m) **Creating an online brokerage or marketplace model:** This model is hugely successful in the online world where the purpose of portal or website is to connect buyers and sellers. The money is made on the commission for every successful sale. It could use fixed or variable price or auction. The success of this model lies in the scale and the wide attractiveness of its users. The various options of having a marketplace could be just selling physical goods, like Amazon, or renting physical goods. The latter example is Airbnb.com or other time sharing sites where you rent a physical property for short-term vacation. All financial institutions, banks and brokerage firm have been creating financial market place to sell mutual funds, insurance policies, etc. In addition, services like job posting examples of which are Monster.com and Naukar.com or various matrimonial sites fall under this category.

(n) **Reverse action:** One of the successful models of reverse action is to sell a product or services at the lowest price possible where the users of the service quote the lower price. This model is very useful for extremely price-sensitive buyers. One of the early examples is Priceline.com that offers budget travellers hotel rooms, rental cars or air ticket without letting them choose who is the service provider but meets criteria like location, type of ticket, travel time or type of car.

(o) **Attempt aggregating demand:** This is a popular model adopted by e-commerce firms which give them a platform to bring host of buyers and sellers together. Started with eBay, this model is very successful with almost all e-commerce sites which aggregates demand.

(p) **Sell at lowest price to gain market share:** Many mobile handset manufacturers have adopted this model by dropping price of their handsets to gain market share.

(q) **Person to person exchange for services:** The popular cab aggregators like OLA and Uber is following this model where they are connecting drivers/cab owners with users on real time basis using mobile apps. Uber valuation is proving of success of this model that has raised \$1.2 billion at a \$40 billion valuation[9].

(r) **One day one deal:** This model has been used by companies like Woot, Groupon, LivingSocial, Moolala, etc., who make one product at limited quantity available at a very low price each day and thus start transforming the market.

(s) **Just-in-time (JIT) model:** This was first prompted and adopted by TOYOTA and later followed by Dell to keep the lowest inventory levels and attempt make-to-order rather than make-to-stock. Dell combined JIT method with direct ordering from the consumers of their product using a web-based interface proved to be dynamic business model. This helped Dell to cut out distributers and all the part of the expensive distribution chain and started selling directly to the consumer who has a choice to select their configuration and customise in their order. This helped to reduce the cost of distribution, freedom of choice for the consumer as well as faster service. Once customer orders its configuration, Dell would source necessary parts from suppliers to assemble the customised Laptop or Desktop. Dell would pay their suppliers at the end of the month but it would collect money upfront from the customer.

[9]http://www.wsj.com/articles/ubers-new-funding-values-it-at-over-41-billion-1417715938 accessed 27 May, 2015.

(t) **P2P business model:** Peer to Peer model is one of the most successful business models in the internet space. Some of the examples are Etsy which is the world largest buying and selling of handmade or vintage items, art and supplies. This connects the buyers and craftsman together. The other example is Kickstarter which is the world's largest funding platform for creative projects for film, music, art, theater, games, comics, design and photography. Paypal facilitates a faster, safer way to transfer money. OLX is one of the largest used goods marketplaces which also offers free local classified ads in India.

(u) **Freemium business model:** This model allows users to use free services for basic features but if you want advanced/special features then you have to pay extra. Examples are like Dropbox, Gmail, etc., where up to a certain limit, the services are free but when the limit increases or you want extra features, then you will have to pay extra.

7.8 CRAFTING AND DOCUMENTING BUSINESS MODEL

Traditionally, the firms used to adopt value chain concepts for defining a business model. The value chain shows how a product is converted from raw material to final product and taken through manufacturing and distribution, and finally to the end user. By drawing a value chain, a technology manager can identify ways to create additional value and ascertain, if necessary, capabilities that exist to create the stated or target value. This analysis helps in finding new opportunities as well. This analysis also helps to further identify the interfaces between one stage of the value chain and another such as one function with other.

Developing and Documenting Business Models have always been tricky. Noted researcher Alexander Osterwalder[10] has proposed a structured method to develop and document business model in a framework called The Business Model Canvas. This is a visual chart which allows the business model developers to capture an enterprises business model covering value proposition, infrastructure, customers and finances.

Osterwalder's Business Model Canvas has nine sections. Each section represents a set of activities that the business model developer should examine and put. The process of developing Osterwalder Business Model Canvas is iterative and goes through various imaginative and corrective phases. There are tools available for drawing the business model canvas or it can be drawn using paper and pencils and post it notes during the discussion phase. The nine blocks of Business Model Canvas as shown in Figure 7.3(a) are described here.

The first three are the internal infrastructure that the company will be using. This includes key activities, key resources and key partners. The key activities section include what the firm intends to do and key resources stands for what all resources such as human resources, money, material, etc. In addition, key partner includes which all suppliers and other companies who would be making the company's job easier.

The fourth important block is defining the value proposition of the firm. Osterwalder defines value proposition as those features that distinguish itself from its competitors. This may be new

[10]2010. Business Model Generation, A. Osterwalder, Yves Pigneur, Alan Smith, and 470 practitioners from 45 countries, Wiley published.

features, new level of service capabilities or material quality used. It could also include band convenience and usability of the product.

The next three segments on the right hand side is related with customers. This includes customer segments, distribution channels and customer relationships. The last one is related to what type of relationship the company would like to establish with the customer. This may include self-service, dedicated assistance or automated service. The company may create communities of customer for using them in co-creation of its products/services.

The last two blocks refer to cost and revenue streams of the firm. The business model will dictate these two areas. In terms of cost, the company may have to decide whether it is low cost player or a niche or premium players. Cost structure will include fixed as well as variable costs. In case of revenue streams, the company can adopt various ways to generate revenue, some of which has already been discussed in earlier sections of this chapter.

The latest addition to the business model canvas are two blocks at the bottom one representing social cost and other social benefit (Figure 7.3(a)).

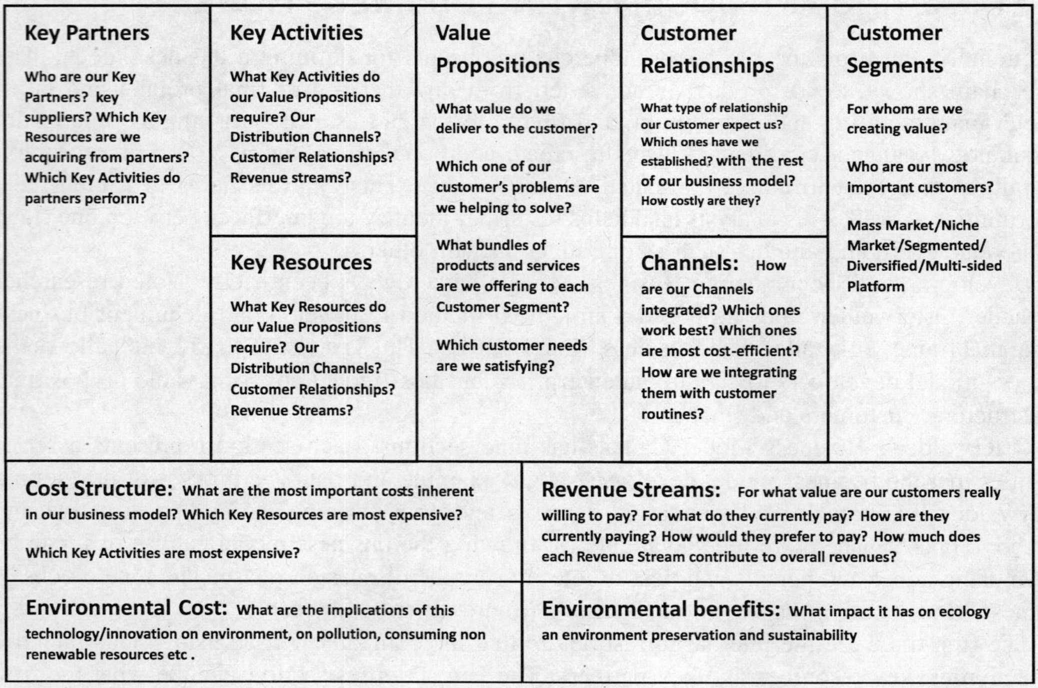

FIGURE 7.3(a) Business Model Canvas: Nine Box Business Model Building Blocks, Osterwalder, Pigneur et al. 2010.

The most important and difficult part of Business Model canvas[11] is to identify the value proposition. For this Osterwalder suggested creating Value Proposition canvas. The purpose of drawing value proposition canvas is to help in precisely defining customer profiles and Visualizing

[11]https://www.strategyzer.com to download the templates and other resource material.

the value the firm creates. This will make a proper Product-Market fit based on the insights gained from customer needs.

This is simple diagram as shown in Figure 7.3(b) which has two major blocks depicting customer and products and services.

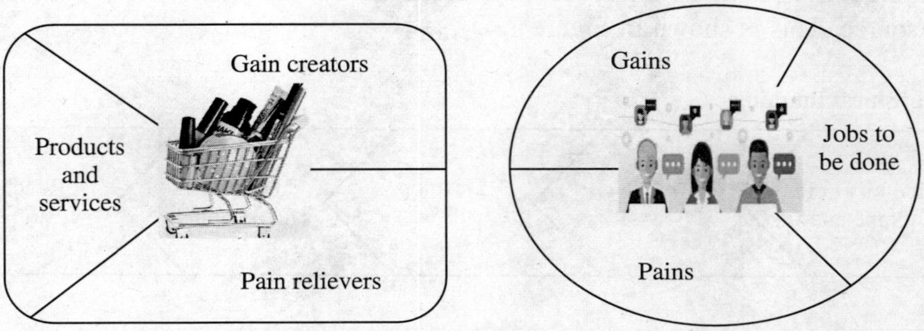

FIGURE 7.3(b) Value proposition canvas.

The right hand side block is populated first which covers:

1. Jobs to be done as needed by the customer: This could be social, emotional, and functional tasks that a customer wants to perform.
2. Pains that the customer undergoes while doing this job. This block is easy to fill up.
3. Benefits or gains customer expects by doing the job. This the toughest Part of the VPC. Gains are not opposite to pains and are the hidden ambitions of people which may be above and beyond pain relievers. One has to have an innovative designer's mind to identify them. So having any car may solve the job of traveling and removing the hassles of commute while using public transport but a car with sleek design and convertible roof gives extra image its owner.

This individual sub blocks are matched by the left hand side blocks with corresponding blocks such as

- Products and services that help in doing the jobs
- Pain relievers
- Gain creators

Once VPC is drawn well then the filling up Business Model canvas becomes easier.

7.9 REVERSING THE VALUE CHAIN FOR BUSINESS MODEL INNOVATION

Dubey in his book *Innovation with IT*[12] has brought out a concept of reversing the value chain for innovating the business model. Instead of starting by first defining the core competency and developing processes, products, services and channels to reach the customers in the traditional

[12]Sanjiva Dubey, Innovation with IT. 1st ed., McGraw-Hill Education India (2008).

way, reversing the value chain starts by focusing on the customer needs first. Once that need is established, various channels through which can be delivered to custom products and services are identified. The next step is to expand the portfolio of products or services that will satisfy the needs. Then the flexible processes are developed to meet these products and services objectives and are combined in a seamless whole. Finally, decisions are taken whether to make, do it in-house or outsource. This is shown in Figure 7.4.

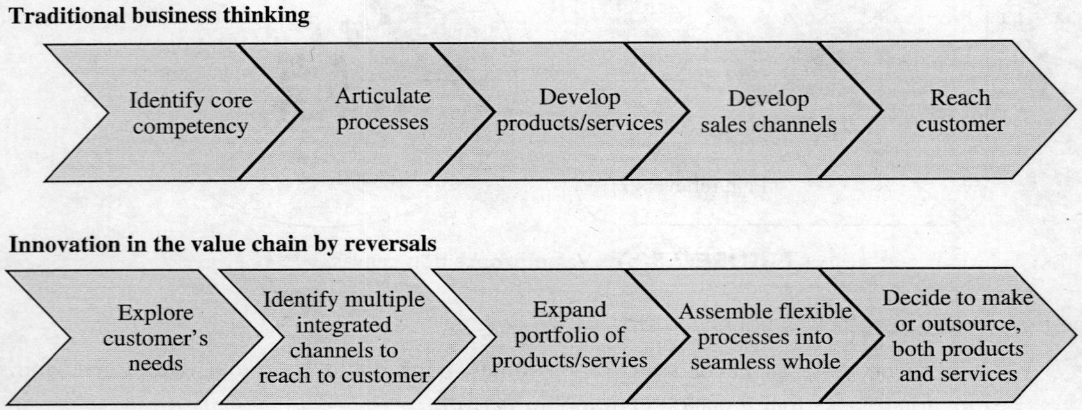

FIGURE 7.4 Reversing the Value Chain.

When Apple came out with the iPod, they were reversing the value chain. Apple was not in music business nor in making consumer electronics products like Walkman does that SONY is known for. But they had already created by then the iTune platform for their Macintosh. A cute little device which can store music for few hours was aimed at improving customer experience for listening to music while on the move. See the story behind the iPod Development in SALT 7.1.

SALT 7.1: Development of iPod: Digital music came into prominence by late 1990s. During this period, Apple realised that it does not have deep capabilities in this area and took over SoundJam MP, a popular Mac MP3 player application along with three of its creators to work at Apple. This team simplified and added CD-burning features to create iTunes. This iTunes team wanted to let users to transfer songs from iTunes to the portable MP3 players of the day which were in use since mid 90s. Since most of Apple's engineers were tied up in Mac-related projects, Apple management invited Tony Fadell to explore Apple's portable digital player options. Apple offered Fadell a six-week contract as a hardware consultant and paired with Stan Ng, a veteran Apple product marketing manager. At the end of his six-week contract in mid-April 2001, he presented his prototypes one of which was accepted. Steve Jobs offered Fadell to continue his work. The original iPod, was finally launched in October, 2001.

7.10 EMERGING TECHNOLOGY ADOPTION AND EXPLOITATION

Any upcoming technology can give rise to an opportunity to enhance or tweak the existing business model thereby getting more customers, better revenue and edge over the competition.

Finding new opportunities with the help of emerging technology is a rigorous exercise that goes through the following stages as shown in Figure 7.5.

FIGURE 7.5 Framework for New Technology Adoption and Exploitation.

The first step is to assess the technology if it can be of any use for the firm. The advantages can come in the form of new products, services or process changes. The second step is to explore where all this technology can be used to impact. Sometimes investment may be required to perfect the technology for the firm's use. The next step is to use the technology to innovate products, process, services or business model. After innovation, the technology has to be optimised and used in an efficient fashion and drive the advantage through economy of scale or quickly going up the learning curve. Once that is done, the emerging technology is put to regular use.

In order to remember these stages, just remember that the first letter of these stages represent vowels, A, E, I, O and U.

7.11 BUSINESS MODEL APPRAISAL

Business model evaluation is an upcoming topic where a number of researchers are working to identify as to how a success of business model can be predicted. We will attempt to demystify this topic using a simple 5 C approach of

- Clarity of purpose: Purpose of the organisation and why it should exist in society
- Clarity of customer: Its needs and benefits
- Clarity of execution: How these products or services are delivered.
- Clarity of revenue stream: Who, when and how much will pay.
- Clarity of competitive advantage: How is this business model different and better than the competition and how will it remain so.

A simple scoring table can help identify the preparedness. This can be done within a select group of stakeholders and their rating/scoring be summarised. A sample scoring sheet is shown in Figure 7.6.

	No clarity		Some clarity		*Absolute clarity*
Clarity of purpose	**1**	**2**	**3**	**4**	**5**
Firm has a strong vision and purpose identified	☐	☐	☐	☐	☐
The objective is for the betterment of society	☐	☐	☐	☐	☐
Product/Service is not violating laws	☐	☐	☐	☐	☐
Clarity of customer	**1**	**2**	**3**	**4**	**5**
Customers has a need	☐	☐	☐	☐	☐
Customer segment is identified	☐	☐	☐	☐	☐
Product and services will be needed for long time	☐	☐	☐	☐	☐
Clarity of execution	**1**	**2**	**3**	**4**	**5**
Process of manufacturing/sourcing identified	☐	☐	☐	☐	☐
Logistics and distribution identified	☐	☐	☐	☐	☐
Skills and other resources identified	☐	☐	☐	☐	☐
Clarity of revenue stream	**1**	**2**	**3**	**4**	**5**
Sources of funds identified	☐	☐	☐	☐	☐
Revenue stream identified and can be realised	☐	☐	☐	☐	☐
Expenses and cost identified	☐	☐	☐	☐	☐
Clarity of competitive advantage	**1**	**2**	**3**	**4**	**5**
Product/Service is different and useful	☐	☐	☐	☐	☐
Existing competition has identifiable weaknesses	☐	☐	☐	☐	☐
We have necessary means to sustain competition	☐	☐	☐	☐	☐

FIGURE 7.6 Business Model Appraisal Scoring Sheet

Once the scoring is done by the stakeholders in group workshop, their feedback is collated and plotted on radar chart as shown. The spread of the points towards the outer most ring will convey that the business model is well balanced.

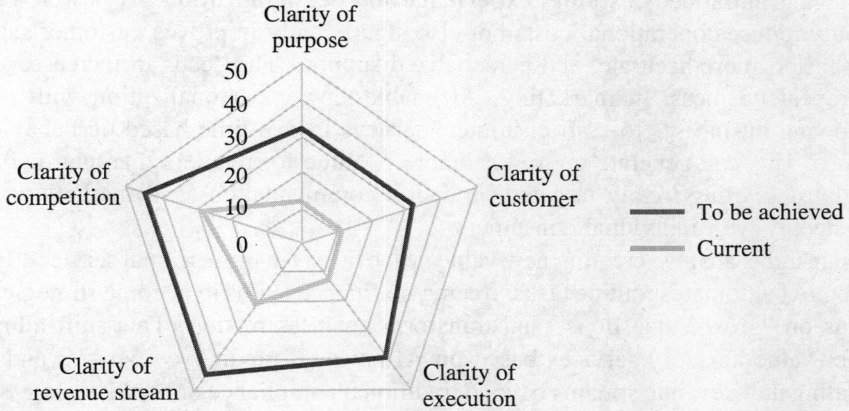

FIGURE 7.7 Business Model Appraisal: Plotting Results.

7.12 AI/GEN AI AS A DRIVER OF BUSINESS MODEL INNOVATION

A business model defines how an enterprise serves its customers and generates revenue. In the contemporary landscape, AI and Generative AI are not merely tools within existing business models; they are fundamental drivers of entirely new business model innovations.

Gen AI enables new business models by allowing companies to "personalize and customize at scale". This capability transcends traditional market segmentation, allowing for hyper-tailored products, services, and experiences that foster deeper customer engagement and loyalty. This mass personalization can drive innovative business models that were previously unfeasible due to the cost and complexity of individual customization.

Furthermore, AI's ability to automate complex processes and "knowledge work" is transforming service-based business models. AI agents can now perform tasks that were once exclusively human domains, such as navigating multiple applications, generating code for API integrations, or accessing and updating databases and CRMs. This moves beyond simply digitizing services to creating "AI agents" that can autonomously deliver value, potentially disrupting traditional professional services like consulting, legal, and finance. For example, AI-powered customer service assistants can handle millions of conversations, freeing human agents for more complex, empathetic tasks. This automation not only drives efficiency and reduces costs but also creates new revenue channels by enabling the delivery of services at scale with unprecedented personalization. The integration of AI fundamentally reshapes how firms create, deliver, and capture value, making AI strategy synonymous with business model innovation.

7.13 NEW REVENUE STREAMS AND VALUE PROPOSITIONS ENABLED BY AI/GEN AI

The transformative power of AI and Generative AI is creating entirely new revenue streams and enhancing value propositions across industries. Beyond traditional cost savings, AI enables businesses to unlock significant new growth opportunities.

One key area is **enhanced customer experience and personalization**. AI-powered customer service not only reduces operational costs but also significantly improves customer satisfaction by providing faster, more accurate, and personalized support. This leads to increased customer loyalty and repeat business. In marketing, AI enables hyper-personalization with predictive analytics, allowing businesses to craft customer journeys in real-time based on behavioral data and preferences. This can generate up to 40% more revenue for retailers than non-personalized experiences, by delivering highly targeted product recommendations and marketing messages that resonate deeply with individual consumers.

AI-driven insights are also creating new value propositions in professional services. In finance and accounting, AI automates routine tasks, freeing up finance teams to become strategic advisors who can focus on "growth questions" and transform business models. This shift allows firms to offer higher-value advisory services based on AI-powered predictive analytics and scenario planning, creating new revenue streams beyond traditional compliance or bookkeeping. Similarly, in scientific discovery, Gen AI's ability to accelerate drug and material discovery creates immense value, leading to faster market entry for life-saving therapies and novel materials. The shift towards "hyper-personalization" as a core value proposition implies a move from product-centric or segment-centric value to individual-centric value. This requires businesses to collect and analyze vast amounts of individual data ethically, pushing the boundaries of privacy and data governance, which in itself becomes a critical component of value creation.

7.14 APPRAISING AI-DRIVEN BUSINESS MODELS

Appraising the robustness and potential of a business model is critical for strategic decision-making. In the context of AI-driven business models, this appraisal requires adapting traditional frameworks like Osterwalder's Business Model Canvas to explicitly account for AI's pervasive role. AI is not merely a technology *within* the business model; it is a fundamental *shaper* of the model itself, permeating every aspect of value creation and delivery.

When appraising an AI-driven business model using the Business Model Canvas, each of the nine building blocks must be re-evaluated through an AI lens:

- **Key Activities:** How are core operations transformed by AI agents and automated processes?
- **Key Resources:** What AI models, data pipelines, and specialized AI hardware constitute critical assets?
- **Value Propositions:** How does AI enable hyper-personalization, predictive insights, or entirely new creative outputs?
- **Customer Segments:** Does AI allow for targeting of new, previously uneconomical, niche segments?
- **Customer Relationships:** How do AI chatbots and personalized interactions redefine customer engagement?
- **Channels:** How do AI-powered search and digital twins impact distribution and customer touchpoints?

- **Cost Structure:** How do automation and optimized processes driven by AI impact fixed and variable costs?
- **Revenue Streams:** What new AI-driven services or monetization strategies are enabled?
- Key Partners: How do collaborations with AI platforms and specialized AI firms shape the ecosystem?

Beyond these operational considerations, appraising AI-driven business models must also extend to ethical and societal impacts. Given the potential for bias, privacy concerns, and environmental footprint, a successful AI business model must demonstrate not only financial viability but also adherence to responsible AI principles. This necessitates a holistic AI strategy that permeates every aspect of value creation and delivery, moving beyond a narrow financial view to encompass broader stakeholder value and long-term sustainability. A simple scoring table can help identify the preparedness and balance of such a model, assessing clarity of purpose, customer understanding, execution, revenue streams, and competitive advantage, with AI's role explicitly factored into each criterion.

7.15 SUMMARY

This chapter was devoted to understand the role of technology in business model innovation. We first defined business model as the method an enterprise uses to serve its customers and make money. We further explained the activities included in a business model. The next concept developed was to focus on the need of a business model. We emphasised that globalisation and internet-based economy can be a source of advantage for growth for a good articulated business model. It enables the technology manager to focus attention on how all the elements of a business fit together and makes the business more agile. We then described the key components of a business model. The next discussion was as to how business model has become a new tool for business to survive in the competitive world. Business model innovation helps the leading companies to offer a unique and difficult to emulate value proposition that resonates with changing customer needs leading to higher profits yet at a lower cost structure so that competitors cannot easily copy them.

We postulated that business model is not static but changes over time and further outlined the success factors for a business model such as product or services offering, support or challenges from the ecosystems and readiness of the firm.

Subsequently, we discussed the steps for building sustainable business model. Business model should also focus on aspects like reducing carbon emission, not wasting non-renewal resources, preserving water or forest.

An important input at this stage was to articulate the role of technology in business model development and innovation. We opined that technology impact of business model is manifold and these impacts were captured and elaborated. This was followed with some of the successful business models of the current times. After this we outlined the steps for crafting and documenting business model using Osterwalder's Business Model Canvas which was explained in sufficient depth. This was followed up with the concept of reversing the value chain for business model innovation articulated by Dubey.

Finally, we gave a short input on how to embrace technology while designing business model using emerging technology adoption and exploitation model. Finally we presented a framework for Business Model appraisal.

REVIEW QUESTIONS

1. What is business model? Why business model is significant in the modern business? **Answer:** Sections 7.3, 7.4
2. What are the activities included in a business model and why we need to develop a business model? **Answer:** Sections 7.3, 7.4
3. Explain why and how a good articulated business can be a source of competitive advantage and growth of the firm? **Answer:** Section 7.5
4. What are the key components of a business model? **Answer:** Section 7.4
5. Is business model static over time? What are the success factors for a business model? **Answer:** Sections 7.6, 7.7
6. Outline the steps for building sustainable business model. Why do we need to consider sustainability while designing business model. **Answer:** Section 7.8
7. What is the role of technology in business model development and innovation? Articulate some of the successful business models of the current times. **Answer:** Sections 7.9, 7.10
8. How do we craft and document business model? Explain it by using Osterwalder's Business Model Canvas framework. **Answer:** Section 7.11
9. How can we reverse the value chain for business model innovation? Explain by using Dubey's framework. **Answer:** Section 7.12
10. What are the steps for embracing technology while designing business model using a framework that can be abbreviated by five vowels? **Answer:** Section 7.13

ADDITIONAL READINGS

1. Afuah, A., Tucci, C.L., 2000, *Internet Business Models and Strategies: Text and Cases.* Irwin/McGraw-Hill: New York.
2. Amit, R., Zott, C., 2001, Value creation in e-business, *Strategic Management Journal,* 22: 493–520.
3. Chesbrough, H., Rosenbloom, R. 2002, The role of the business model in capturing value from innovation: evidence from Xerox Corporation's technology spinoff companies. Industrial and Corporate Change, 11: 529–555.
4. Magretta, J., 2002, Why business models matter, Harvard Business Review, May 2002: 86–92.

Chapter 8

Technology and Innovation Implementation

You can plan hundred things but if you don't execute it well it does not look good in the field.

—Mahendra Singh Dhoni, India's T20 Cricket Captain[1]

At the end of this chapter, we will learn:

- What constitutes implementation processes that a firm should adopt
- Who should be responsible and accountable for Timings of technology implementation
- How to measure the success of implementation

8.1 INTRODUCTION[1]

This chapter is all about implementation aspects of the process of technology and innovation management. While one cannot undermine the importance of good planning in any new initiative yet the implementation of these ideas are equally important. A number of articles have been written and several research projects have been published covering planning aspect of new projects, especially, to introduce new technology and innovation. However, implementation aspects have been not well researched as it is always managed by practitioners who have little time or energy to document the good or poor practices for subsequent learning.

Finally, implementation is left to the wisdom of a few people on the ground and success is always a suspect. This chapter will demystify the process of implementation for technology and innovation management and present them in a succinct manner.

But before that we will also build concepts on a few important topics to understand the goals and objectives of TIM implementation and its relationship with the firm's goals and objectives.

[1]After winning a crucial T20 World cup match with Bangladesh with one run in the last ball during after match presentation.

8.2 FIRM'S BUSINESS GOALS, TECHNOLOGY AND INNOVATION PROJECT IMPLEMENTATION AND OUTCOME OBJECTIVES

Let us understand the relationship between these three terms to understand the role TIM has to play for the success of the enterprise.

According to a definition[2], implementation is the carrying out, execution, or practice of a plan, a method, or any design, idea, model, specification, standard or policy for doing something. As such, implementation is the action that must follow any preliminary thinking in order to make something actually happen. All implementations realise a plan, deliver what is thought and accomplish goals and strategy of a firm. The objective of any implementation, including technology and innovation management, is to accomplish the organisation's strategy through technology and innovation projects.

There is shade difference between implementation objectives and outcome objectives. In the case of implementation objectives, the firm defines its targets for implementing TIM programme (e.g., an automobile firm may define its business goals as launching five new models in the next two years or replacing existing technology by 2020, etc.). But outcome objectives define the ultimate realisation of the targets (e.g., at least 5 of the new models would cross 1,00,000 sales volume in the next one year since their launch). While implementation objectives define internal under control objectives, the outcome objectives are result driven and prove that TIM is working! Remember the outside world is more interested in your outcome objectives and how much you have been able to achieve. Please note that implementation objective is subservient to outcome objectives and you cannot achieve the later unless the former (i.e., implementation objectives) is achieved.

Finally, it is important to understand the linkage between implementation objective and outcome objective with the firm's business goals. Refer to Table 8.1 to clarify this.

TABLE 8.1 Example of Relationship between Firm's Goals, Implementation and Outcome Objectives

Firm's goal	Implementation objective	Outcome objective	Measures of success
Get market share of 30% or more from current 10% in three years	1. Launch new models every quarter in the next 3 years	Success of new model	Sale of one thousand vehicles in the month of launch
	2. Ensure 1000 hrs of testing before every launch	Zero new model field complaints in first six months	Number of complaints in the first six months
	3. Develop a consortium for new fuel efficient technology	Release of new fuel efficient technology in 3 years	Fuel efficiency of the new technology
	4. Adopt recycle philosophy in product design	80% parts can be safely recycled	% of parts being recycled

[2]http://searchcrm.techtarget.com/definition/implementation accessed 27032016

8.3 TIM IMPLEMENTATION PROCESS

Figure 8.1 explains the implementation management process. All innovative ideas after going through rigorous stage gate selection process of the innovation funnel are selected for implementation using appropriate technology.

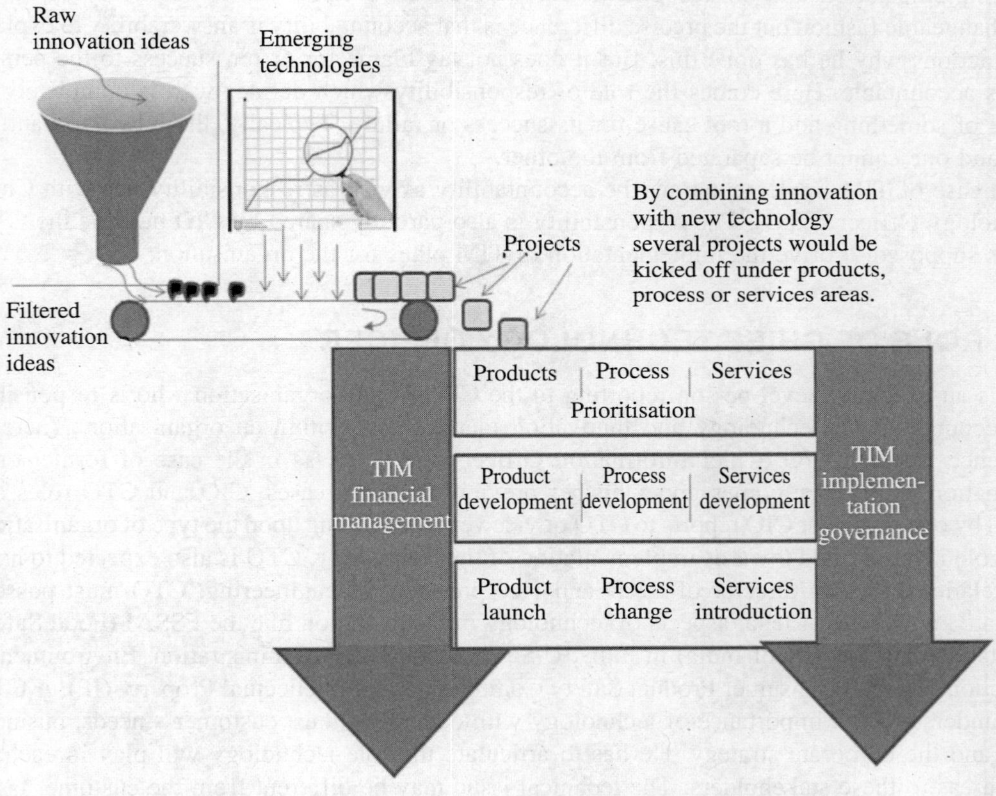

FIGURE 8.1 TIM Implementation Process.

The conveyor belt symbolises that innovation ideas and emerging technologies are mixed together to convert into projects. These projects are grouped as

(a) Product development: These follow Product Lifecycle (PLM) process.
(b) Process development: These projects are taken through process improvement process.
(c) Services development: These projects are taken through services development process.

The TIM governance process and TIM financial management process run all through as two guiding rails to convert product ideas into new launched products, processes or services.

TIM implementation governance process includes review of progress by a steering committee, members of which are drawn from various functions and possess varied expertise. TIM Steering committee is usually chaired by the CEO who authorises new projects, evaluate progress of existing projects and monitor returns from the recently launched projects.

8.4 TIM IMPLEMENTATION RESPONSIBILITY AND ACCOUNTABILITY

It is important that the responsibility and accountability of driving TIM implementation be defined in the organisation. There has to be a set of people who should be responsible to drive TIM implementation and be accountable for it. These two terms are sometimes used in an interchangeable fashion but the precise difference is that accountability is answerability to explain one's actions why he has done this. But it does not lay blame for or pin success to the person who is accountable. Here comes the role of responsibility which defines who is completely in charge of something and a root cause for its success or failure. Typically, these two go hand in hand and one cannot be separated from the other.

In case of TIM implementation, the accountability as well as responsibility lies with Chief Technology Officer (CTO). The responsibility is also partially shared by CIO but it is the CTO who is supposed to drive the implementation of TIM plans for the organisation.

8.5 ROLE OF CHIEF TECHNOLOGY OFFICER

CTO is an executive-level person reporting to the CEO in any organisation who is responsible and accountable for technology and innovation management within an organisation. There is difference between CIO (Chief Information Officer) and CTO, as in the case of former only information technology comes under his/her preview. In some cases, CIO and CTO roles are played by one person or CIO reports to CTO or vice versa depending upon the type of organisation. CTO role is more tilted towards implementation of the technology. CTO is also expected to have peer relationship with director of R&D and vice president of engineering. CTO must possess adequate knowledge of legal aspects of technology implementation like the FSSAI (Food Safety and Standards Authority of India) in India, U.S. Food and Drug Administration, Environmental Protection Agency, Consumer Product Safety Commission and Intellectual Property (IP). A CTO must understand the importance of technology with other functions, customer's needs, business value and the corporate strategy. He has to articulate the role technology will play in each of these areas to these stakeholders. The technical issue may be different from the customer issue but CTO should understand the implication in the larger context.

As technology has become increasingly important to gain strategic advantage for the company, the CTO role becomes very important. This role will further evolve as organisations are able to buy and acquire technology from outside and integrate with internal technology development efforts. CTO's main objective is to identify the strategic value of an emerging technology and convince CEO/CFO for making investment to develop or acquire emerging technology. For this CTO may have to seek support from their peer executives like Chief Marketing Officer, Chief Operating Officer, etc. At this time, CTO becomes an evangelist of new technology. The new technology will often require discarding of the old one including discarding old processes and acquiring new skills sets. All this will bring extra strain on the existing teams and CTO roles shift to that of change agent. CTO is also the chief innovation officer either in the same role or supporting it as a peer. CTO job is also to champion innovative ideas. You may realise that this role is not an easy one to perform. By definition it may look a very specialised role but in reality it is a role that has multiple facets and requires broad skill set.

Technology adoption also has a legal angle where the creating, acquisition and use of intellectual property is involved. The choice is between acquiring knowhow or developing it in-house. Sometimes it looks easy to adopt (or copy) but it may lead to unwarranted consequences. Examples of fast changing technology companies in fiercely competitive market getting into serious legal fight are not uncommon where each sue the other with million $ patent infringement suits (SALT 8.1). But paying for each a patent and waiting for the competitor to release the patent for use and loosing the market share in the process is also a sure recipe of disaster. The CTO's role is to understand the legal angle of this entire IP conundrum and yet be practical to steer ahead of competition in expediting its own patent process. CTO during acquiring a technology has to act like a tough negotiator. However, while spinning off a technology which has been developed in-house, he acts like an ace marketer. Finally, during technology and innovation implementation phase, a good CTO charges up the team to gallop the expectation divide and acts like a passionate motivational guru!

8.6 CTO CHALLENGES AND SUGGESTED BEST PRACTICES

Some of the CTO challenges and best practices followed by leading CTOs are as follows:

1. Given the fact that the rate of change of technology is very fast, it is very difficult to keep up-to-date with newer technology. CTO should set up a small team to constantly evaluate new technologies for the organisation use.
2. CTO must understanding the firm's business and communicating the benefits of the new technology to the business leaders. Typically, CTOs are groomed in technology discipline all their life and they find it difficult to articulate their thoughts in a manner that appeals to the business peers. Any CTO without support from their business peers and leaders, will not be effective.
3. Establishing credibility is incredibly important among the peer group so that CTO is not seen to promote technology just for the sake of it or for motives hard to explain. CTO must gain respect from peer group who should value his judgment and leadership. Credibility building requires CTO to have demonstrated honesty and integrity.
4. CTO must have a right balance between technical depth and business width in his thinking process. CTO may come up with technology with huge value of cost saving but should not lead the firm getting under the scrutiny of pollution control board.
5. Understanding laws around intellectual property is necessary otherwise the company may get pulled in legal battle.
6. Managing expectation during growth phase: When the company grows faster, then expectation for newer technology increases. Companies want newer models to be launched and want to incorporate new innovations faster than before. In such situation, a CTO may find it difficult to manage without a supporting team who are equally capable. CTO should not become a bottleneck for newer ideas. Many CTOs have made this mistake by making the organisation too dependent on him and did not create a strong second line. In short run, it might have made their job more secured but in long

run it would have back fired. Such approach will harm the individual as well as the organisation.

7. Ability to integrate with external world: As more and more companies are cooperating with the external world directly or indirectly for technology as well as innovation development, the CTO's role is converted to become an orchestrator of various groups. Many participants may dislike each other or even fight yet the orchestrator has to make them work together and get the best out of them for the organisation's benefits. Sometimes such professional rivalry stifles the growth of the company as the established technology group does not let new voices to come up and take visible positions. Many technology acquisitions have gone bad as the existing organisation could not integrate the new team. Ultimately, this rivalry led to either cannibalising the new team or surrendering their advantage. Companies find it hard to balance between imbibing the new vs. retaining the old and converting them into new common for business advantage.
8. Ability to bring in collaborative influence: The CTO's role is also to collaborate and influence those people who still may not be a part of his team. Creating a right vision and ensuring that everyone else is aligned with it is important and for this the ability of CTO to bring collaborative influence is the most useful.
9. Ownership of any failure of the team: CTO has to act as a good coach and hard taskmaster while practising, but supportive during failure. He also has to step in to overcoming the shortcomings of the team. Late Dr. Abdul Kalam shared an anecdote about Prof. Satish Dhawan, the Head of Indian Space Research Organisation (ISRO). In 1979 when the SLV 3 Satellite could not be successfully launched to its orbit, it was Prof. Satish Dhawan, the leader of the organisation ISRO, who conducted the press conference in front of the world media. Prof. Dhawan took responsibility for the failure—he said that the team had worked very hard, but they needed more technological support. While Dr. Kalam was the project director of the SLV projects, it was the chairman of ISRO Prof. Dhawan who decides own responsibility for the failure. Later in July 1980 when the next satellite launch was successful Prof. Dhawan called Dr. Kalam aside and told, "You conduct the press conference today." To quote Dr. Kalam "I learned a very important lesson that day. When failure occurred, the leader of the organisation owned that failure. When success came, he gave it to his team."
10. CTO also has to set goals for each technology project. These goals should be consistent with the corporate and business goals not just for the departmental benefit.
11. CTO should establish a mechanism of measuring success for each technology projects by conducting major gate reviews and minor sub-gate reviews. CTO should also conduct monthly programme management reviews and earned value reporting as appropriate. Before a project starts, its outcome and success criteria should be defined along with a tentative timeline and compared with industry benchmarks.
12. CTO should capitalise on the team's strengths where every member of the team must contribute at the highest level.

13. Create an environment of output generation like a production unit; this type of atmosphere is required to be created else people get swayed by wild futuristic ideas and start idling on unrelated projects.
14. Adapt with change and accept mistakes: Many good CTOs have shown the mettle to change and accept mistakes. This attitude helps them to overcome their own shortcomings and learn for the failure.

Story and Learning Task

SALT 8.1 Lawsuit between Apple and Samsung

Apple and Samsung are the two leading names in the mobile handset Industry. While Apple has its own constituency of loyal customers who swore by Apple and nothing else but Samsung rules the rest of non-Apple world dominated by android and other operating systems (like Symbion and few others). Leading market research and analysis firm IDC pegs Samsung and Apple share around 21 and 13%, respectively in 2015[3].

This battle of marketplace has also extended to courtroom battle between the two giants. In 2011, Apple filed a suit against Samsung for patent infringement. In 2011, the number of such suits went up to more than 50 lawsuits around the globe. Each one claimed billions of dollars in damages from each other. While Apple got victory in the U.S. courts, Samsung got victory in South Korea, Japan and the UK. Samsung also obtained limited ban from the U.S. International Trade Commission on sales of certain Apple products as after the commission, it was found that Apple had violated a Samsung patent, later vetoed by U.S. Trade Representative[4].

The news of their court room battle keeps grabbing the business press headline and will continue for some time for sure.

Discussion Questions

1. What is the role a CTO has to play to prevent such legal issues?
2. What capability CTO must have to protect the interest of its firms from court room battle?

(SALT) 8.2 How Microsoft has changed under Satya Nadella.

Microsoft, the technology giant, named its new CEO Satya Nadella in 2014 after a rigorous search to replace Steve Ballmer, a long-term CEO under Chairman Bill Gates. Satya was an internal candidate but his induction came as a surprise to many. Some expected Microsoft fortune to go but some were hopeful that he will bring about the needed change. The group's optimism about Satya's success was proved right after a year since he took over according to a report published in *CXO Today*[5].

[3]http://www.idc.com/prodserv/smartphone-market-share.jsp accessed 25 Mar. 2016.
[4]https://en.wikipedia.org/wiki/Apple_Inc._v._Samsung_Electronics_Co. accessed 25 Mar. 2016.
[5]http://www.cxotoday.com/story/what-makes-microsoft-ceo-satya-nadella-so-successful/accessed 27 Mar. 2016.

Most large technology companies find it difficult to leave their legacy of success. Their flagship product which brings in the maximum revenue dominates on all other newer developments. The hegemony of the success is so powerful that it stifles the growth of any new development. There have been many examples where a firm delayed adoption of something new as it was not willing to antagonise the successful big brother. The situation according to industry analyst was something similar in Microsoft where it was dominated in thoughts and deeds by its flagship product WINDOWS.

A year later, under CEO Satya's reign, Microsoft has changed its focus to become more relevant in the new tech world which is dominated by Apple and Google. Satya has done this by doing certain things right. Nadella began with a clean slate and brought in new energy. Microsoft is no longer protecting Windows at all costs. Microsoft lost out to iPhone, Google and Android leading to near absence in mobile-cloud area. Nadella has repositioned 'mobile first, cloud first' strategy. In the process, he is also bringing in cooperation and not confrontation with rivals like Apple and Google. By releasing released Office for the iPad and Android devices and giving free Outlook app for both, he has shown that together the industry can grow the pie of business and help the customer. Microsoft under his leadership is now supporting open source software applications on its cloud. He surprised many by giving Windows 10 as a free upgrade to users of Windows 7 and Windows 8. By providing free Microsoft Office on iPad and Android platform, it can have access to the mobile universe. He is being credited to increase inter-divisional cooperation within Microsoft, an example of which came from the success of Skype Translator which needed several teams to work together like Skype team, the Azure team and the Office team. He also admits his mistakes, sincerely apologizes and moves on. Nadella too believes, 2015 is more of a reinvention and re-strategising year for the company. "This year, we will see the company making a whole lot of innovation in the areas of mobile and cloud," he said according to the report[6].

Discussion Questions

1. Identfy various characteristics of Satya from the list of desired characteristics for a CTO.
2. Identify the changes brought about by Satya in Microsoft to keep pace with new realities.

8.7 TIMINGS OF TECHNOLOGY INTERVENTION

The timing of technology intervention or new innovative ideas is a complex decision. Lack of timing or speed of adoption impacts performance, competitiveness, productivity and growth of the firm. Some authors[7] even attributed this for the slowdown of US productivity growth in the early 1970s when generation and exploitation of new technology had huge time lag. Technology adoption does not happen instantaneously as seen by several examples. Such adoption of basic oxygen furnace (BOF) in the process of steel-making which was in 1949, but by 1968 only 12.2% of the US manufacturer adopted it and this adoption increased 80% only by 1980. But this is no longer true in other technologies. In many cases, especially, electronics and IT, the adoption rate is much faster. Even in automobile products, the design cycle has shrunk to 24 to 36 months

[6] *Ibid.*

[7] Krugmann, P., 1994, Peddling Prosperity Network, Norton.

from average 60-month lifecycle a decade ago. The chart drawn by Nicholas Felton of the New York Times as shown in Figure 8.2 shows how various categories of product, from electricity to the Internet, try to achieve different penetration levels in US households.

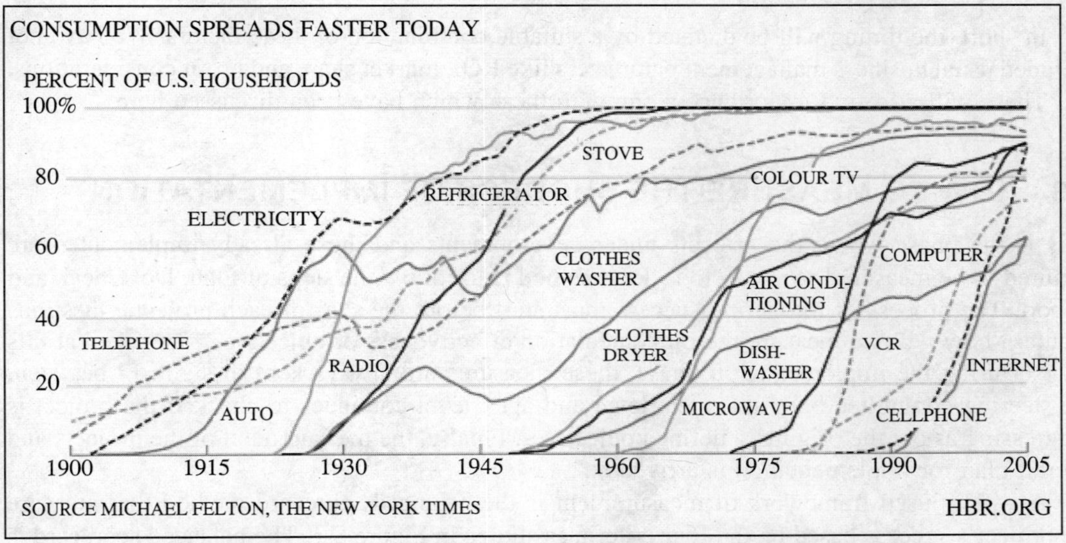

FIGURE 8.2 Adoption Rate of New Technology by US Household[8].

For any firm, the timings of adopting a new technology will depend upon several factors such as:

(a) **Preparedness:** How much the firm is prepared to absorb the technology in its work streams. This also means discarding the old and along with the old discarding assets, re-skilling people, etc.

(b) **Pressure from peers:** Most technology adoption happens due to peer pressure. If 4G is adopted by one telecom operator, then others in the same region have to follow, the same is applied for automobile, computers, mobile phones, etc. While preparedness or lack of it can drag or expedite the technology launch, the peer pressure always pushed the firm to adopt the new technology. This may be counterproductive as without sufficient preparation one can fail to perform and invite the wrath form the customer and bad press.

(c) **Regulations, incentives from the government:** Especially in the areas of environmental protection, the governments give incentives to launch early or force firms to adopt newer technology by certain date. Failure to adhere may lead to work stoppages and closure of business.

(d) **Proactive leadership:** This factor acts more with the technology leaders and innovators who take risk, redefine the market with newer technology introduction. Remember this factor is also guided by what the firm's style of management is and their appetitive to take risk with new technology.

[8]https://hbr.org/2013/11/the-pace-of-technology-adoption-is-speeding-up/accessed 29 Mar. 2016.

(e) **Standing of the firm in the market:** Certain firms have to live up to the standing and reputation they enjoy in the marketplace and this creates expectations in the minds of the customer. For example, in mobile handset business, launching new improved products every year or 9 month has become an expectation from customers.

In short, the timing will be dictated by a suitable combination of these factors. We have not included usual business management parameters like ROI, market share and profit considerations, etc. These will also find importance along with these which have been discussed here.

8.8 HOW TO MEASURE THE SUCCESS OF IMPLEMENTATION

This is the phase where the projects under developments and those already implemented are required to be measured. An easy to follow method is to follow the steps of Plan, Do, Check and Report. The process of measuring success must start before the start of each project. Questions such as "how will we measure the implementation effectiveness or objectives" are asked at this stage. During the implementation phase, these measures are always kept in sight. In between, the steering committee both at project level and apex level continues to check if the project is progressing as per the originally defined objectives. Finally, the measurement of the projects and overall plan for implementation is arrived at.

A widely used framework of measurement is the balanced scorecard method that measure the project's success based on the four criteria as shown in Figure 8.3. The balanced scorecard is used extensively and align business activities to the vision and strategy. This was developed by Robert Kaplan (Harvard Business School) and David Norton who added strategic non-financial performance measures such as innovation, customer satisfaction and operations to traditional financial metrics as shown in Figure 8.3.

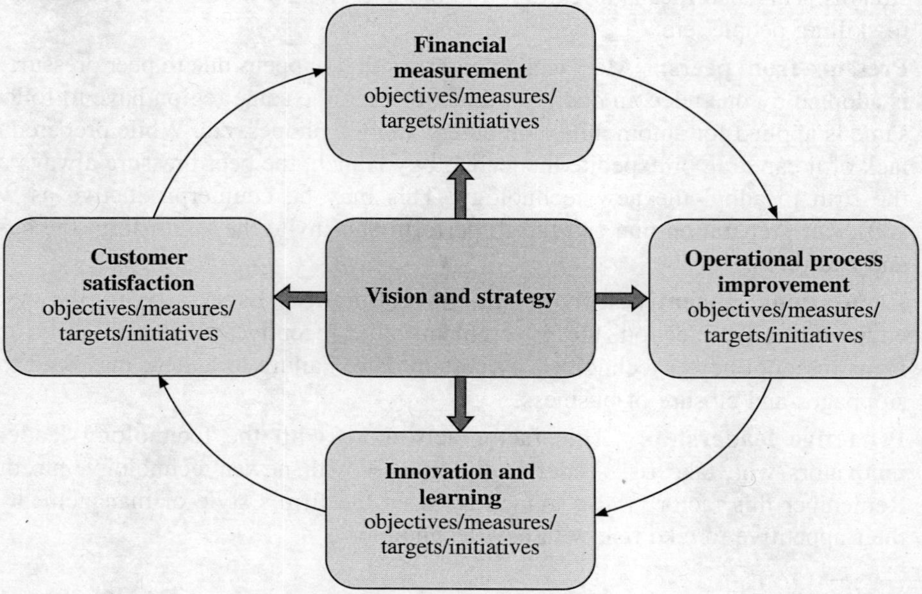

FIGURE 8.3 Balanced Score Card.

8.9 IMPLEMENTING AI/GEN AI PROJECTS: GOVERNANCE, RESPONSIBILITY, AND ACCOUNTABILITY

Implementing technology and innovation projects requires meticulous planning and execution, with clear responsibility and accountability. AI and Generative AI projects, however, introduce unique challenges that demand specialized governance frameworks and leadership.

Key implementation challenges include:

- **Data Quality and Bias:** Gen AI models are heavily reliant on the quality of their training data. Inaccurate, unrepresentative, or biased data can lead to biased or harmful outputs. Rigorous data preparation, bias identification, and continuous mitigation are essential.
- **Technical Expertise:** Implementing Gen AI effectively requires a high level of technical expertise, often necessitating internal team development or partnerships with external specialists.
- **Integration with Existing Systems:** Seamless integration of new Gen AI tools with legacy technology stacks and complex data flows can be challenging due to compatibility issues.
- **Change Management:** Preparing employees for the changes and opportunities presented by Gen AI technology, including new workflows and skill requirements, is critical for successful adoption.

Effective implementation of Gen AI projects requires strong executive sponsorship, as demonstrated by AWS's emphasis on executive champions to drive vision, address concerns, and implement risk mitigation strategies. Cross-functional teams are also crucial, combining domain expertise with technical AI knowledge to ensure comprehensive planning and execution.

The emphasis on "Responsible AI" from the outset of implementation is a significant shift. This includes ethical considerations, bias mitigation, transparency, and accountability. This signifies a move from purely technical or financial success metrics to a broader definition of successful implementation that includes societal well-being and trust. Governance frameworks must evolve to include "Responsible AI" principles, and implementation teams need training in ethical AI and data governance to navigate these complexities. The Chief Technology Officer (CTO) or Chief AI Officer (CAIO) bears primary responsibility and accountability for driving these implementations, ensuring strategic alignment and ethical deployment.

8.10 MEASURING THE SUCCESS OF AI/GEN AI IMPLEMENTATIONS (BEYOND ROI)

Measuring the success of technology and innovation implementations is crucial for validating investments and guiding future strategies. However, traditional Return on Investment (ROI) metrics often fall short for AI projects. AI's impact frequently compounds over time, and its value is derived from intangible benefits like enhanced efficiency, accelerated innovation, and improved risk reduction, which are difficult to quantify directly in financial terms. A narrow focus on ROI can lead to short-term thinking and the premature abandonment of potentially valuable AI initiatives.

The inadequacy of traditional ROI for AI highlights a deeper challenge in organizational performance measurement: how to quantify the value of strategic, long-term, and transformative initiatives that do not fit neatly into existing financial models. This necessitates a shift towards a more adaptive and multifaceted measurement framework. A balanced scorecard approach, which incorporates non-financial performance measures alongside financial ones, is particularly well-suited for AI implementations.

For AI projects, key metrics should extend beyond financial returns to include:

- **Operational Efficiency Gains:** Quantifying time and effort saved, reduction in manual tasks, faster decision-making, and improvements in employee productivity due to AI-assisted workflows.
- **Adoption and Usage Metrics:** Tracking how many employees actively engage with AI tools, usage patterns (e.g., strategic vs. basic tasks), and improvements in employee AI fluency over time. High adoption is critical, as AI's value is realized through effective utilization.
- **Business Impact and Innovation:** Measuring revenue growth directly attributable to AI-driven insights, improvements in customer experience (e.g., faster response times, personalization), and the successful launch of new business models or product innovations enabled by AI.
- **Risk Reduction and Compliance:** Assessing the reduction in compliance violations through automated monitoring, improved decision-making leading to fewer costly errors, and enhancements in cybersecurity through AI-driven threat detection.

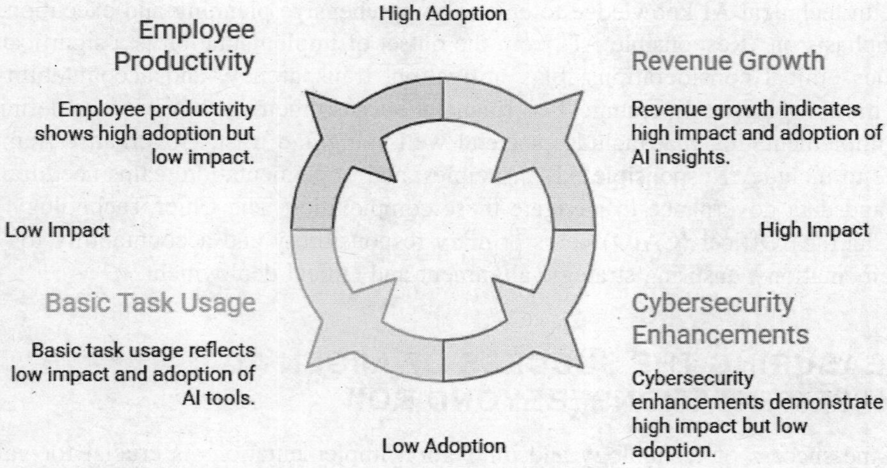

FIGURE 8.4 AI Project Metrics Prioritization

This comprehensive set of metrics provides a more accurate and holistic view of AI's value, allowing organizations to understand its strategic and transformative impact. It forces organizations to rethink their performance management systems and embrace a broader view of value creation that integrates strategic and operational KPIs with financial ones, ensuring that AI initiatives are not prematurely curtailed.

8.11 SUMMARY

We discussed in this chapter about implementation aspect of the process of technology and innovation management. We primarily focused to identify

(a) Implementation processes
(b) Fix responsibility and accountability
(c) Timings of technology intervention
(d) Metrics for implementation success

We started with building conceptual foundations on TIM implementation relationship with the firm's goals and objectives. We defined each one of them, established the linkage between implementation objective and outcome objective with the firm's business goals by giving representative example in a tabular form.

This was followed with explaining the implementation management process. By a suitable figure, the relationship of various process steps were explained. We explained how on the organisation conveyor belt of interaction, innovation ideas and emerging technologies get intertwined to get convert into projects. These projects could be for Product, Process or Services Development and they are taken through the implementation process. All these implementations are closely guided and supported by two processes called TIM governance and TIM financial management. The role of TIM Steering committee and its composition was briefly touched upon. The next discussion to follow was on who has the TIM Implementation responsibility and accountability. We explained the role of Chief Technology Officer, who is supposed to drive the implementation of TIM plans for the organisation. We also outlined the role challenges and the suggested best practices for CTO role. Two Stories and Learning Task (SALT) further elaborated the situation a CTO has to undergo in real life.

The next discussion was on timings of technology intervention, a complex decision which, if not performed well, can lead to negative impact on firm's performance, competitiveness, productivity and growth. We described factors such as preparedness, pressure from peers, regulations, incentives from the government, proactive leadership and standing of the firm in the market which are balanced to decide the timings of technology adoption.

Finally, we elaborated on measurement approach a firm can adopt to for identifying success of TIM. We closed the discussion of the chapter with a widely used framework of measurement called balanced scorecard method.

Key Terms: Chief Technology officer, Balanced Score Card.

REVIEW QUESTIONS

1. What are the four areas to concentrate for the success of TIM implementation?

Answer: Section 8.2

2. What is the TIM implementation relationship with the firm's goals and objectives? Explain it using a suitable example by drawing a table. **Answer:** Section 8.2
3. Explain the TIM implementation management process steps. How are innovative ideas and technology opportunities converted in to projects for product, process or services and managed through realisation? **Answer:** Section 8.3
4. Explain TIM governance and TIM financial management process. Explain the role of TIM steering committee and its composition briefly. **Answer:** Section 8.3
5. Explain the roles and responsibilities of Chief Technology Officer. What are the role challenges and the suggested best practices for a CTO role? **Answer:** Section 8.5
6. How is the timings of technology intervention decided? Describe factors which are to be considered for deciding the timings of technology adoption. **Answer:** Section 8.7
7. How do we measure success of TIM implementation? Describe Balance scorecard methods. **Answer:** Section 8.8

ADDITIONAL READINGS

1. Gowrisankaran, G. and Stavins, J. (2004), Network Externalities and Technology Adoption: Lessons from Electronic Payments, *Rand Journal of Economics*, 35, pp. 561–82.
2. Einav, L. (2003), Not All Rivals Look Alike: Estimating an Equilibrium Model of The Release Date Timing Game, mimeo, Stanford.

Chapter 9

An Overview of Existing and Emerging Technology

Any sufficiently advanced technology is indistinguishable from magic.

–Arthur C. Clarke

At the end of this chapter, we will learn:

- Technology used in business management such as ERP, MIS, DSS, ESS, Data Warehousing/ Data Mining, SCM and CRM
- E-business, E-commerce, B2B, B2C, Big data and Social Media Analytics
- Mobile computing, 3D printing Internet of things and other emerging technologies

9.1 INTRODUCTION

The objective of this chapter is to give students an overview about the most commonly used technologies. Primarily, it will cover technologies used in the running of business. The appreciation of these technologies is a must for any student undergoing graduate or post-graduate courses in Engineering and Business Management program irrespective of their specialisation. Our treatment to these technologies would be at the level of overall capabilities, suitability and their application for business. This chapter attempts to capture as many of them so that students, irrespective of the industry they may join, will get benefitted while they are planning, acquiring or just using technology for their day-to-day business needs.

9.2 TYPES OF INFORMATION SYSTEMS USED IN AN ENTERPRISE

Most managers and engineers use information systems and technology while performing their day-to-day task in the business context. As managers or executives in the enterprise, they have to perform certain business functions and processes which are supported by Information Systems. As a matter of fact, information systems includes much more than the hardware or software but includes data, processes and people who together make it work. In this section, we will take a quick look at the information systems used in the enterprise to perform various functions and try to categorise them by nature, purpose and usage.

A short definition of information system from business dictionary[1] is that it is a combination of hardware, software, infrastructure and trained personnel organised to facilitate planning, control, coordination, and decision making in an organisation. It is a combination of

- Technology components: Hardware, operating system and other related software and network components
- Application programs software, operating system software and other utilities software
- Data, data bases, data on the internet used by the enterprise
- People, who develop applications, manage IT infrastructure
- Process, of planning, development, implementation and management of information systems

These are shown in Figure 9.1.

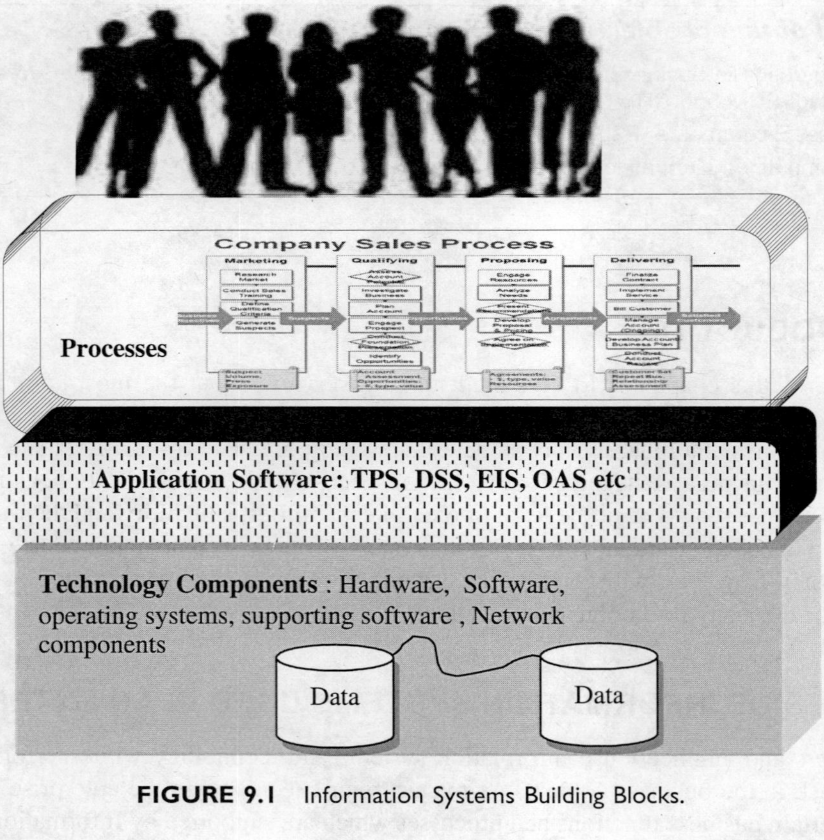

FIGURE 9.1 Information Systems Building Blocks.

[1]http://www.businessdictionary.com/definition/information-system.html accessed 20 Sep. 2015.

9.3 CATEGORIES OF INFORMATION SYSTEMS WITHIN THE ENTERPRISE

An enterprise is further organised into several layers of management performing different functions. Organisation itself is composed of many functions and they together perform several processes to produce goods, perform services as demanded by their customers. Accordingly, the nature of the information systems required by these managers at various levels of management would also be different and would vary according to the function they are performing. Table 9.1 shows various levels of managers and corresponding information systems used and required by them.

TABLE 9.1 Types of Information Systems Required at Various Levels of Management

Managerial level	Managerial focus	Information systems used
Top	Strategic	Executive Support Systems (ESS)
Middle	Execution Leadership, Performance management and control	Management Information Systems (MIS)
Subject matter experts, Information workers	Planning operations, Analysing historical data, Performance improvement, Process improvement	Decision Support Systems (DSS), CAD CAM, Simulation and Modelling
Operational	Day-to-day operations	Transaction Processing Systems (TPS)
All levels	Workplace productivity	E-mails, Office Automation Systems (OAS), Word processing, Presentation software, Spreadsheets, etc.

Brief explanation for each of these systems is given in the subsequent section.

(a) **Executive Support Systems (ESS):** Executive support systems are customised systems for senior executives of the organisation which primarily help in taking critical decisions. The purpose of ESS is to summarise data for senior executive, collected from various sources both internal and external and presented in graphical/pictorial form showing trends and key metrics. The key feature of ESS is to present the key trends in easy to understand form for busy executives. ESS should have strong reporting and drill-down capabilities (detailing out capability). ESS highlights trends of key parameters variables to monitor performance so that opportunities and problems can be identified ahead of time. ESS is also considered as part of Decision Support System (DSS) and has been influenced these days with business intelligence systems that are able to produce new insights from the vast amount of data.

(b) **Management Information Systems (MIS):** These systems support the middle level managers whose task is to plan and control the operations. These managers have to plan and deploy resources to achieve the plan. They need summarised data from transaction processing systems about consumption, and future needs. MIS are built on top of Transaction Processing Systems (TPS) and produce summarised reports for the middle level.

(c) **Decision Support Systems (DSS), CAD CAM, Simulation and Modelling:** These systems are specially developed to facilitate certain decision making. The rules and algorithm for particular application is built in the software and used by the knowledge workers. Take for instance, Computer-Aided Design (CAD), in which by giving certain key parameters, the design of the element is carried out by the CAD system. All simulation and modeling systems are categorised under DSS and also Computer-Aided Manufacturing (CAM) where software-aided machines perform operations using pre-determined instructions.

(d) **Transaction Processing Systems (TPS):** These are the systems used at the operational level to record activities and data related with every transition. Some examples would be like raising a bill, receiving payments, raising purchase order, shop order or recording customer complaints. Transaction processing systems are the back bone of enterprise IT systems as they are the one in which the most elementary level of data is captured in detail which become the basis on which MIS,DSS or ESS are built.

(e) **Workplace Productivity Systems:** These systems are used by almost everyone and include systems such as Emails and other collaborative platforms like Chat or instant messaging. In addition, there are Office Automation Systems (OAS) which are used for writing letters or preparing reports, such as Word processing software or creating presentation. Microsoft Office suits that provided Microsoft word and PowerPoint are examples of these systems. Google docs and software, Spreadsheets, etc. fall in this catogory.

9.4 ENTERPRISE SYSTEMS

While IT applications are built for functional areas in isolation, a need was felt to develop them in an integrated manner so that data duplication can be eliminated. This gave rise to systems that covered more than one functional area and were called enterprise systems. The primary aim of such systems is not only to cater to transaction processing requirements but to build MIS on top of the transaction processing module and also facilitate DSS functions. Many enterprise systems developed by independent software vendors also provide built-in ESS module. These enterprise systems are categorised as:

ERP: Enterprise resource planning (ERP) covering the needs within the enterprise.

SCM: Supply chain management (SCM) systems that is extended to suppliers and suppliers' supplier, logistics partners, warehouse and distribution centres.

CRM: Customer relationship management (CRM) systems that extends enterprise information to customers, distributors, retailers and logistics providers.

Figure 9.2 shows the relationship between these three enterprise systems in a pictorial form. Please note that all these types of systems do not work in isolation but are dependent upon each other and exchange data. We will now explain each of these systems in detail in the subsequent section.

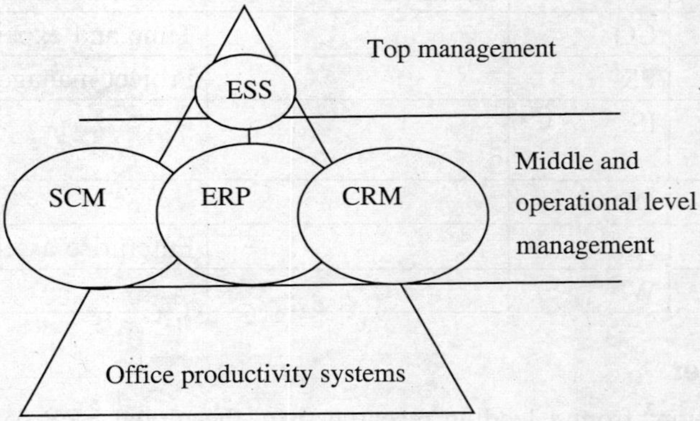

FIGURE 9.2 Enterprise Systems in Context.

9.4.1 ERP: Enterprise Resource Planning

ERP is a cross-functional enterprise systems that serves as a framework to integrate and automate many business processes. ERP software is a family of software that supports the business activities involved in back office processes. ERP software traces its origin in the manufacturing industry's MRP (material resource planning) software. The purpose of MRP was to generate net requirements of raw materials and sub-assemblies along with brought out components for each production cycle run in a mass production plant. Also called BOM (Bill Of Material processor), this software expanded the BOM into discreet component numbers and amount of raw materials needed to make them. Later on MRP took the form of ERP for covering all aspects of enterprise resources such as men, machine hours, money and others. ERP software has become all-pervasive across industries covering IT systems requirements from operations levels to middle management level. It also provides inputs to the senior management data requirements used in ESS and specialised requirements of DSS systems.

ERP comes in various modules each addressing the needs of particular function of the enterprise and covers the entire lifecycle of manufacturing, servicing, marketing, and sales, finance and human resources. A brief comparison of various modules of popular ERPs in the market are given in Table 9.2.

TABLE 9.2 Overview of Modules of Popular ERP

Module name	SAP name	Oracle name	People soft name
Sales and Distribution	SD	Marketing and Sales	Supply chain
Material Management	MM	Procurement	Supplier relationship
Production Planning	PP	Manufacturing	
Plant Maintenance	PM	Services	Enterprise services
Human Resources	HR		
Financial Accounting	FI	Financial	Financial management
Controlling	CO		Time and expense management
Project Systems	PS		Project management
Industry Solutions (specific to industry)	IS		
Quality Management	QS		
Asset Management	AM		Enterprise asset management
Workflow	WF		

ERP software market

According to a prediction[2] from a leading research firm, the global ERP software market will touch $ 41.69 billion by 2020, registering a CAGR of 7.2% during 2014–2020. The leader of the market is SAP which serves Fortune 1000, Global 5000 companies. The turnover of SAP in 2014 is €17.56 billion. SAP capabilities in accounting and distribution module is well-established. In addition, it is integrated modules, such as financials, manufacturing, human resource, and payroll and customer relationship management. The next company worth noting is Oracle which is second largest in the ERP world market. It acquired PeopleSoft (with JD Edwards) and Siebel Systems and is likely to acquire many more as per its strategy for growth. Other ERP worth mentioning is Epicor which is recognised by Aberdeen group, a leading analyst firm as the ERP to achieve lowest TCO (Total Cost of Ownership). In addition, companies like Infor is the third largest ERP after SAP and Oracle. Microsoft has become the ERP of choice for SMB (small and midsize business) organisations. Since 2000, Microsoft has ERP offering such as Great Plains and Navision which are very popular in SMB (small and medium business market), especially, in Europe and Asia Pacific.

9.4.2 Supply Chain Management (SCM)

SCM application serves the need of information exchange with the suppliers and partners. SCM is the management of the flow of goods and services and information. Since it involves the suppliers, its boundary is beyond enterprise. By using internet-based information technology connectivity,

[2]http://www.businesswire.com/news/home/20150513005351/en/Research-Markets-Global-ERP-Market-2015--#.Vcrqp0Z7twE accessed 20 Aug. 2015.

all enterprise in the supply chain can share data and can effectively manage business processes across them. SCM is not only cross-functional but works across enterprise to provide seamless flow of information between suppliers, consumers, business partners and all the stakeholders involved in the process.

Typically, SCM covers the following modules:

- Strategic Sourcing and Procurement
- Forecast and Demand Planning
- Customer Order Fulfilment/Service
- Distribution Network and Warehouse
- Production Logistics
- Transportation and Shipment Management

Figure 9.3 shows the various stages of the supply chain lifecycle.

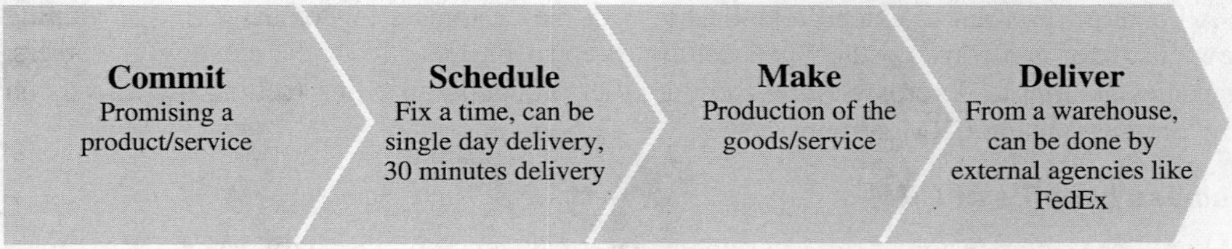

FIGURE 9.3 SCM Stages.

SCM software market

SCM software market, as predicted by leading market research firm Gartner, is likely to reach \$9.8 billion by 2018 and will grow at the healthy rate of 9.9%[3]. The market is led by SAP and closely followed by Oracle. SAP also acquired Ariba in 2012 which helped in this growth. Other players in the SCM software market is JDA software, Manhattan Associates and Epicor.

9.4.3 Customer Relationship Management (CRM)

All enterprises exist for customers and they need to serve their customers efficiently and effectively. The information need of customer service is met by CRM systems. CRM systems helps managers manage the complete lifecycle of customer services. It starts from prospecting the customer to finally rendering continued service CRM major functions are:

(a) Prospecting: At this step, the organisation wants to find out who could be new customers. These prospective customers are attracted by sending mailers, or making calls to them and educating them of the company's products and services. Majority of the call centres working on outbound calls are heavily engaged in customer prospecting and solicitation. The role of CRM systems is to maintain prospect data base, facilitate outbound calls and note down customer's feedback, response and proceed for the next step.

[3]http://www.supplychain247.com/article/2014_top_20_global_supply_chain_management_software_suppliers accessed 20 Aug. 2015.

(b) **Focusing:** At this stage, customers who have shown interest are further grouped under those who are more profitable and are likely to buy. Focused compaign is run to reach out to these prospective customers for soliciting business.

(c) **Acquiring:** At this stage, the customer order is accepted, price and delivery dates are confirmed and the customer order is passed on for further execution either by manufacturing or supplying from the existing stock.

(d) **Servicing:** At this stage, information systems is used to lodge customer service request that could be additional product, services or complaints received for already supplied products or services.

(e) **Relationship enhancement:** In this phase, customer is offered new products and services or opinions sought for improving the relationships. Programmes like loyalty points and offering special privileges are granted using the information systems.

All enterprises want to extend relationship with the customers for longer period as gaining a new customer is always costlier than getting a repeat business from the existing customers. Companies attempt to do cross-selling (selling other products) upselling (selling higher version of the products) using CRM systems.

Business benefits of CRM

CRM provides better customer services and increases call centre productivity. Using CRM cross-selling/upselling becomes more effective.

All CRM systems have typical modules categorised as:

(a) **Operational modules:** It covers all the transaction processing requirements while running the operational aspect of the CRM.

(b) **Reporting module:** It does most of reporting based on customer identification, customer segmentation and profitability reporting.

(c) **Analytical modules:** This module is used in predicting customer preferences based on modelling the earlier buying behaviour. This module heavily relies on data warehousing and data mining application that are described later.

(d) **Sales force automation module:** This module covers the automation and information support to the sales force team who are on the ground meeting customers and soliciting business.

CRM software market

According to a leading research firm[4], CRM market grew 13.3% in the last year, from $20.4B in 2013 to $23.2B in 2014. The leading providers of CRM software are Salesforce, SAP, Oracle and Microsoft. About 47% of total CRM software revenue in 2014 was generated from SaaS-based CRM applications. Salesforce leads the worldwide CRM market with 18.4% market share. Most CRM companies are using social media for extending their features and giving rise to a new

[4]http://www.gartner.com/newsroom/id/3056118 accessed 20 Aug. 2015.

type of CRM called Social CRM. The analyst prediction[5] is Global Social CRM Software market to grow at a CAGR of 38.1% over the period 2014–2019. Major companies occupying space in Global Social CRM Software Market are Jive Software, Lithium Technologies Inc., Oracle Corp. and Salesforce.com Inc. In addition, companies like Artesian Solutions, Bazaarvoice, Kana Software and Visible Technologies are also worth mentioning.

Figure 9.4 shows the interrelationship between SCM, ERP and CRM and e-Business systems. These systems are also covered and supported by e-Business.

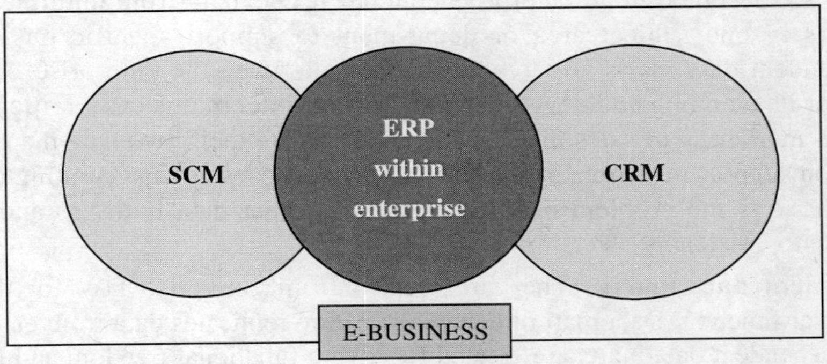

FIGURE 9.4 SCM ERP and CRM in Context.

9.5 DECISION SUPPORT SYSTEMS, DATA WAREHOUSE, DATA MART

Enterprise needs IT systems to support decision making based on certain algorithms, models and statistical analysis. IT applications supporting decision making process are called decision support systems. In order to help an enterprise in making decision based on past data of customers, suppliers, orders and other details, enterprise typically create a repository of data called data warehouse which facilitates storage of data in a summarised fashion for easy retrieval and analysis.

9.5.1 Data Warehouse

Data Warehouse (DW) keeps summarised data which are extracted from operating database and maintained along with certain predicted periodicity. For example, customer purchases are stored as monthly summary in the data warehouse on monthly frequency summarised out of several purchase transactions during the month. The transactions of each purchase by customer is maintained in the operational database. Data warehouse is a comprehensive data storage facility.

Typically, the data warehouse is distinguished with operational database by its nature of maintaining data. In data warehouse, all enterprise data are kept in an integrated manner over time frequency as explained earlier. The data kept in DW is not removed, therefore, it is called non-volatile (read only) database for decision making.

[5]http://www.researchandmarkets.com/research/9jhh9b/global_social accessed 20 Aug. 2015.

9.5.2 Data Mart

Smaller data warehouse dedicated to each function are called data mart. These are small, single-subject data warehouse subset that provides decision support to functional groups such as marketing, customer service, manufacturing, etc. Data marts could also be of two types, independent or dependent.

(a) **Independent (standalone) data mart:** It focuses exclusively on one subject area and is not designed in an enterprise context. It gets data from multiple transaction systems in one subject area or department to support specific business needs. Independent data marts are created in situation when the enterprise DW is not in place or its planning and development is taking time. In this case, critical functions, such as marketing or sales may go ahead and create their own data mart to meet the decision support requirement. The only issue that goes against creating independent data marts is the problem of integration with other data marts as and when they come into existence.

(b) **Dependent data mart:** They are created from enterprise DW for the use of a particular function. Data mart of dependent nature replicates data from enterprise DW. Such dependent data marts are created for giving functional freedom and faster access to individual functions.

Components of DSS: Decision support systems not only need data warehouse or data marts as data stores but have other components as well to facilitate data access and presentation. These components are

(a) **Data store:** It could be enterprise data warehouse, data marts or operational data bases.

(b) **Data extraction and filtering tools:** Most of the data for DSS purposes are extracted from the operational data bases. Sometimes data from external sources (for example, competitors sales data, prospective customer data, etc.) are also loaded in the enterprise DW or functional DMs. The process requires tools that can extract, summarise, filter and load them into DWs or DMs. Such tools are called ETL, Extract transform and Load Tools.

Figure 9.5 shows the relationship between all of them in a pictorial fashion.

(c) **End user query tool:** Once the data are available in DWs or DMs, they are ready for analysis and interpretation by the end users. Most DW software gives a feature called end user query tool using which a non-IT business user can extract data in a desired format. For example, if a business user wants to identify month by month history of sales by regions and product category then he can use the end user query tool to extract data.

(d) **End user presentation tool:** The example of extracting data for a particular nature as given above will be required to be presented in a formatted fashion, this could be in the form of bar graph, pie charts, etc. Most DSS software will have built-in tools to facilitate generation of graphs and charts. These are called end users presentation tools.

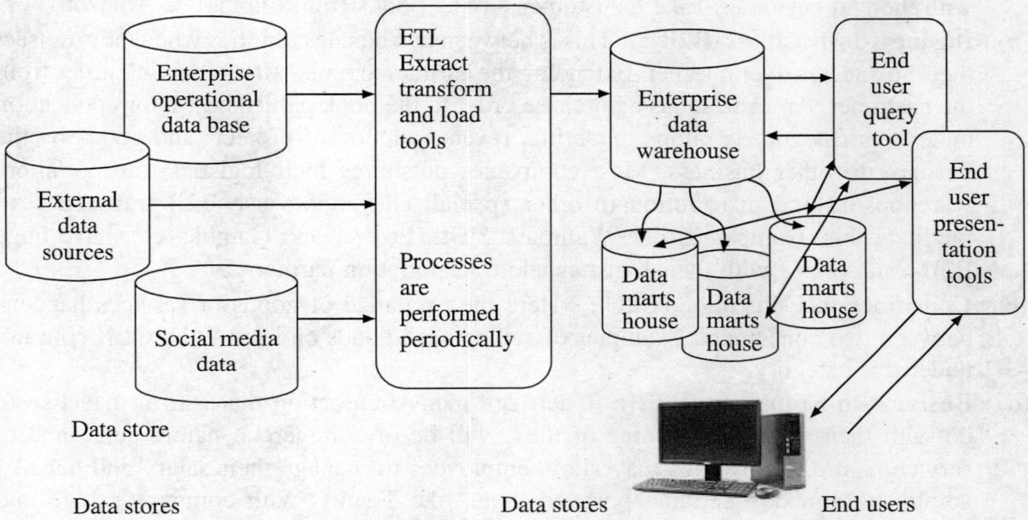

FIGURE 9.5 Schematic Representation of Data Warehouse and End User Query Tools.

9.6 E-BUSINESS

E-business is a generic term used to denote all activities of businesses which use electronic or digital communication to do transactions. So all usages of ICT (information and communication technology) in activities of business will be considered as e-business. In contrast, e-commerce is much narrower which covers only buying and selling over electronics medium that includes internet. The use of mobile phones in commercial activities gives a new definition of m-commerce which stands for use of mobile communication for commercial activities.

Figure 9.6 shows their relationship in a simpler form.

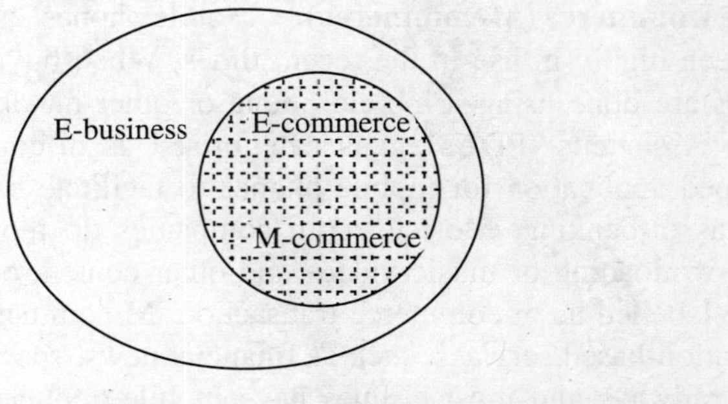

FIGURE 9.6 E-Business, E-commerce and M-Commerce Relationship.

9.6.1 Types of E-Commerce

(a) **Business-to-Consumer (B2C):** When buying or selling happens over internet directly with the end customer. Like a customer buying books from Flipkart or Amazon.

(b) **Business-to-Business (B2B):** This is between two business entities when they transact their businesses over internet. Extending the earlier example, after receiving order from the customer, Amazon sends a purchase order to the book publisher. Major application under this category is online tendering, reverse auction of projects and goods by the business to other business. Most companies outsource their logistics transportation, warehousing and distribution to other specialised vendors use B2B transaction to facilitate this. Companies like Wallmart, HUL, Procter and Gamble, etc. have huge B2B transactions with their logistics and transportation partners.

(c) **Consumer-to-Consumer (C2C):** Here the exchange of goods or services happens between two consumers. Examples of selling used goods on internet by OLX.com fall under this category.

(d) **Business-to-Employee (B2E):** There are many transaction that a firm may like to do with their employees. Some of these will be of commercial nature and some of service nature. Companies may allow employees to manage their salary and benefits administration, buy certain approved items like T-shirts with company's logo and other activities like e-learning, buying cheaper medical or health care insurance, travel packages, etc.

(e) **E-Government:** E-Government is a generic term used for the use of electronic medium for transacting government function. This means all functions within the government as well as its interfaces with the citizens. Issue of passports using internet website, payment of subsidy benefits using direct benefit transfer to bank accounts are all application of E-Government. Issue of Passport, Aadhaar card, ration cards, PAN cards using website or E-government portal will be further categorised as G2C, i.e., government to customer applications. Similarly, the cooperation between two government (either at country or government levels) could be further categorised as G2G, i.e., government to government. Exchange of data regarding travellers, suspected criminal or terrorists, trade-related information exchange are all classified under this category.

(f) **Mobile Commerce (M-commerce):** Mobile phones, especially, smart mobile phones have been highly in use in the recent times. When buying and selling of products or services are done using a mobile phone or other handheld devices such as Personal Digital Assistants (PDAs), it is categorised as m-commerce. Several banks have developed application for mobile phones to facilitate banking transactions which are called as m-banking. Most telecom companies do the billing, recharge of the talk time, downloading of music videos and other content over mobile phones which can also be labelled as m-commerce transaction. M-commerce is highly used for seeking information-based services, such as financial news, sports updates and traffic updates. Indian railways and most airlines have mobile applications for booking tickets and seek information on schedule, expected arrivals, etc. Most online stores have adopted m-commerce for buying and selling using mobile apps.

(g) Social Media: As one of the extensions of internet-based applications, social media has revolutionised the way people are interacting with each other. Social media facilitates instant interaction between groups of people using internet or intranet where one message posting by an individual can be seen by the connected group of people. The message could be just a text, video, voice or pictures. Famous example of social media of current times is Facebook, Twitter and LinkedIn. Each one of them has certain features and is popular among certain type of users. Social media usage is growing rapidly because it is easy to operate using mobile phones. It has now become an important part of everyone's life. There are many associated usages and benefits coming out of social media. On matters of public interest, social media is giving a free platform to build opinion and gather support. Social media is also said to be heralding next generation of web called Web2.0 where it has many interaction and participative development of content by design or just in an evolutionary way. Seeking information from unknown members through technical and non-technical forums is yet another innovative usage. Sharing of music, videos, slides and other knowledge content is widespread. Social media is also helping to unleash creativity of the masses and people are able to post their write-ups in blogs and music videos on YouTube. It is estimated that 150 million blogs are posted every day and over 100 million videos are viewed on a daily basis. Facebook claims[6] to have 968 million daily active users on average for June 2015, out of which 844 million users were active on mobile devices.

Social media applications are characterised by their properties of instant conversation, sharing of posts like comments, images, videos or voice and invites freedom of participation. It helps building informal community across geographies with known as well as unknown people. Some of the popular social media applications in the current times are:

1. Community/Networking sites like Facebook, LinkedIn
2. Hosting of contents like videos, voice, slides, e.g., YouTube, Slide share, Instagram
3. Content publishing also called Blogs
4. Microblogging, e.g., Twitter which is used to make comments and share pictures in shorter format
5. Podcast, speaking to a group using internet
6. Wikipedia, user generated contents on wide variety of subject
7. Voice and video calling using internet, e.g., skype, IM, Google talk
8. RSS (Rich Site Summary), also called RDF Site Summary, or Really Simple Syndication, helps in getting updated information on frequently published contents like blog entries, news headlines, audio, video, etc.
9. Widgets is a generic term for the part of a graphical user interface (GUI) which can display information and invite the user to act in a number of ways

[6]http://newsroom.fb.com/company-info/ accessed 20 Aug. 2015.

9.7 BIG DATA ANALYTICS

Social media is also giving rise to the generation of huge volume of wide variety of data. Earlier the data used to be generated and maintained mostly by the enterprise. This data also used to be largely in the text format. But with social media even a common person is generating wide variety of data pertaining to posts in the text, images, video or voice format. This is called big data, a term that represents a collection of data from traditional and digital sources inside and outside the enterprise. This large volume of data is giving rise to a new technology called big data analytics. This technology is used to analyse massive amount of data getting generated on the internet to reveal new patterns, trends, and associations. These trends are hitherto unknown especially with respect to consumers. With machine sensor generated data coming on the internet in future the role of big data in analysing hidden pattern is going to be much more significant. Even the technology to analyse the big data is being developed as the traditional database management software is no longer useful in this situation.

Some of the characteristics of big data are as follows:

1. Big data contains largely unstructured data such as Twitter tweets, and other social media posts.
2. The data format is multi-structured not just text, but a wide variety of data formats such as pictures, web logs and videos.
3. Big data volume is truly large. It is estimated[7] that just the volume of global consumer web usage, e-mails and data traffic is over 6,706 petabytes/month. It also estimates that 2.7 zettabytes of data exist in the digital universe and 35 zettabytes of data are likely to be generated annually by 2020.
4. Big data generated on social media is not hundred per cent accurate. It also contains unverified, erroneous or intentionally modified data by the people who post it.

Big data technology market is rapidly growing. According to the leading analyst firm IDC[8], big data technology market is expected to grow at a 26.4% compound annual growth rate to $41.5 billion through 2018, roughly six times the growth rate of the overall information technology market.

9.8 EMERGING TECHNOLOGIES

It may be pertinent to keep track of some of the emerging technologies which are impacting all types of businesses. Students are advised to also search for more such developments which are happening around the world at a rapid pace.

9.8.1 Internet of Things (IoT)

So far internet is being used primarily by the human beings. In some cases, computer generated

[7]http://www.unifiedsocial.com/blog/2015/03/12/ustats-bytes-and-billions-10-stats-you-need-to-know-about-big-data/#~pleE2zUXwrfR2f accessed 20 Aug. 2015.

[8]https://www.idc.com/prodserv/4Pillars/bigdata accessed 20 Aug. 2015.

scripts called BOT also access internet data to send sometimes spurious messages or track the interaction. However, the future is not going to be limited to interaction by human beings alone but machines with internet address will be able to exchange data with each other. For example, the machine sensors at various traffic interaction would be able to send data about traffic density which can be used to regulate traffic. Such a scenario where machines will be able to access internet, send and recover data through internet is coming to be a reality in very near future. This phenomenon is described as internet of things (IoT) where machine objects will be given unique internet address and will have the ability to transfer data over a network without requiring human-to-human or human-to-computer interaction. For example, a person sitting in the office can access the washing machine at home and start its functioning when IoT becomes a reality. International Telecommunication Union (ITU), the apex body that controls allocation of internet addresses and protocols, defines IoT as a global infrastructure for the information society, enabling advanced services by interconnecting (physical and virtual) things based on existing and evolving interoperable information and communication technologies.[9] The prime driver of IoT's to bring in addressable devices connected on the internet which can be remotely managed. More devices with Wi-Fi capabilities and censors built into them are being produced and the cost of making them is also going down. Finally, use of feature rich smart phone in almost every hand is a huge potential. According to an estimate by the year 2020, almost 26 billion connected devices will access internet. This will include from cars to cell phones, home appliances, such as washing machines and air conditioners and weather and traffic sensors, cameras, etc. Machines such as aircraft engines or drilling oil rig will be able to send performance data to a centralised control or monitoring stations without any human intervention by adopting architecture of IoT. IoT will facilitate relationship between machine, people and with other machines. The development of Internet Protocol version 6 (IPv6) will further help in meeting a large number of internet address requirement.

The credit for the term Internet of Things goes to a British entrepreneur Kevin Ashton in 1999 who visualised possibilities of machines getting connected and exchanging data over internet. The concepts of Smart Grid and Smart Cities can only be realised when the machines start communicating with each other and start taking appropriate action. A smart device worn by an individual can alter the person of his/her heart condition and his doctor as the case may be. Similarly, smart cars will take to the most congestion-free route based on the traffic flow information from the traffic management system in a smart city. Fire-fighters can use such embedded devices in search and rescue. The connected device on IoT are also expected to generate very large amount of data which can be used in prediction and analytics.

Like any other new technology, there are potential risks which are required to be managed. The important among them are security and privacy. According to Tim O'Reilly, the founder of O'Reilly Media founder and chief executive officer, security is a major concern for IoT as this will expose vast new attack surfaces[10]. For example, while we fly in the airplane, it is really being flown by the computer, controlled by ground navigation systems managed by computers,

[9]http://www.itu.int/en/ITU-T/gsi/iot/Pages/default.aspx Recommendation ITU-T Y.2060 accessed 20 Aug. 2015.

[10]http://www.mckinsey.com/Insights/High_Tech_Telecoms_Internet/The_Internet_of_Things_Five_critical_questions?cid=digital-eml-alt-mip-mck-oth-1508 accessed 20 Aug. 2015.

so any potential compromise on these systems by a hacker or cyber attackers can create serious issue. Yet IoT also offers safety, for instance, in a self-driving cars (driverless Metro trains are already running at several places. Data privacy is the next big issue that the industry thinkers have to resolve and agree on a common world-wide standards. While all data about people movement and transactions are being collected, the question does come up as to who Own the data and to what extent any other institution or agency can use or exploit. The next issue is that when such data are being misused against someone, then it is of deep concern. In the same article[11], Mike Olson, Cloudera cofounder cautions that sensorisation of the environment will lead to occasional security breaches that will leak important private information. The success of IoT will depend on not only eliminating or minimising these risks but also promoting open standards and interoperability across devices, seamless connectivity and exchange of data and focus on non-IP-encumbered technology.

9.8.2 3D Printing

3D printing which is also known as additive manufacturing is the latest technology that creates three-dimensional object from a digital image. Like we take out two-dimensional image in a photocopy, the same way a component, jewelry or a three-dimensional object is created through 3D printer. This is achieved by laying down successive layers of material confirming to the shape of the object. As against existing process of machining where an object is produced by removing the material by cutting or drilling. In 3D process, the material is just deposited as per the shape. This technology is now being extensively tried high value unique objects, such as medical/dental implants, jewelry, industrial spare parts amongst others.

A news item[12] on 3D printing got heightened attention where this technology was used to let a blind and expectant mother feel the image of her unborn son (Figure 9.7).

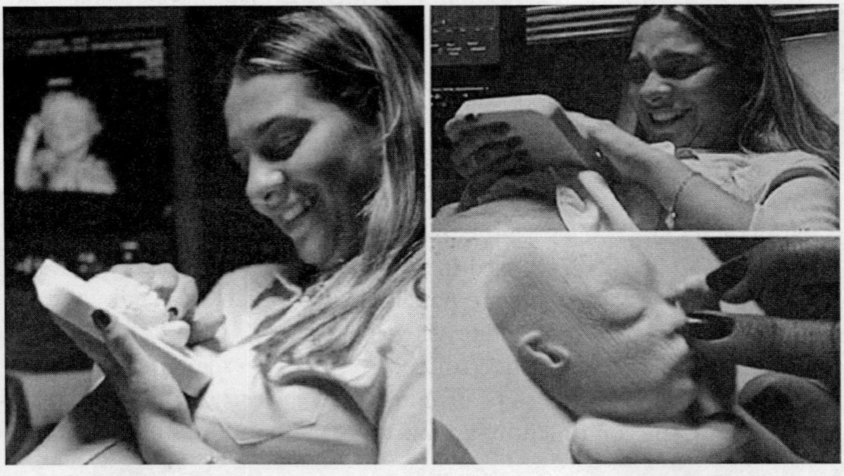

FIGURE 9.7 Blind Expectant Mother Meets Baby with 3D-printed Ultrasound

[11]*Ibid.*

[12]http://www.cnet.com/news/watch-emotional-moment-3d-printing-lets-blind-mom-to-be-see-her-unborn-son/

9.8.3 Nano-Architecture

Scientists across various research labs in the world are likely to come out with materials whose structures can be precisely tailored so that they are strong yet flexible and extremely light, predicts MIT study[13]. This will lead to lighter structural materials which would be more energy-efficient and versatile. For example, scientists of the research lab of Caltech have come out with a nano-architecture ceramic which is not brittle. We all know that conventional ceramics are strong, heavy and brittle but this development of ceramic is not only the strongest and lightest substances ever made but is also not brittle.

9.8.4 NeuroMarketing

Neuromarketing is a field of marketing research that studies consumers' sensorimotor, cognitive and affective response to marketing stimuli. Neuro-marketing uses functional magnetic resonance imaging, a brain-scanning device that tracks blood flow as we perform mental tasks. It helps in market research studies which are enhanced with brain-imaging technology. There are several platforms[14] which allow you to directly measure the brain's electrical activity, uncovering deeper consumer insights than those what a traditional market research method can find out.

As 90% of the decision making is done at the subconscious level, most of the marketing research tools only access the conscious level, which is only 10% of the actual response.

Neuro-marketing is the study of the brain's responses to ads, brands and the rest of the messages littering the cultural landscape. For conducting this study, a specially designed gadget (see Figure 9.8) has to be worn by the subjects covering part of the head and eyes. There will be several electrodes to sense the brain signals when the questions are asked or the subject is shown a visual. This is called BCI (Brain Computer Interface) headset[15] which is a brain–computer interfaces based on electroencephalography (EEG) technology. This captures non-conscious cues into the human-computer dialog to emulate human to human interaction.

The signals emanating from brain out of the reactions are analysed using Software Tool. These tools interpret subconscious behaviour whether the person is engaged, getting short- or long-term excitement, feeling frustrated or having positive feelings of carrying out deep emotional activity.

9.8.5 Near Field Communication (NFC)

Near field communication (NFC) is a set of short-range wireless technologies, typically requiring a distance of 4 cm or less to initiate a connection. NFC allows you to share small content of data between an NFC tag and another device. Similar to other proximity reader devices NFC also uses

---

[13]http://www.technologyreview.com/featuredstory/534976/nano-architecture/accessed 20 Feb. 2015.

[14]http://www.neurospire.com/accessed 18 Mar. 2016.

[15]Example of such product can be seen at the web site https://emotiv.com/insight.php Emotiv Insight - a sleek, 5-channel, wireless headset that allows

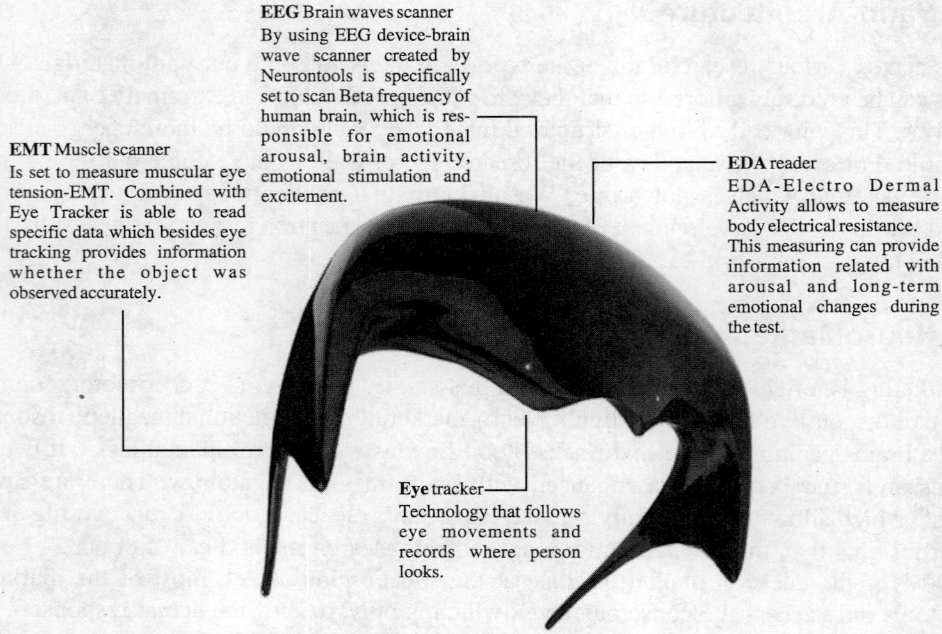

FIGURE 9.8 A Typical NeuroMarketing Gadget to Collect Response.

electromagnetic induction between two devices—say a smartphone and point of sale to exchange billing information and deduct balance. Some characteristics of NFC:

- Use RFID technology at 13,56 MHz
- Useful for data exchange up to a maximum of 10 cm
- Data exchange up to 424 kilobits/s
- NFC is complementary to bluetooth
- NFC can also works in dirty environment
- NFC does not require line of sight
- NFC has easy and simple connection method
- Provides communication method to non-self-powered devices

Some of the applications of NFC are smart key for mobile local payment, peer to peer communication, virtual connector, low cost solution to distribute information/services, e.g., by passive loops embedded in paper media.

9.8.6 Gamification

Getting insight of a customer mind, increasing engagements with the employees or just finding out tools that can enhance learning is always a mystery. There are many such situations where one cannot force someone to tell or act unless a conducive condition is created. Gamification tries to address these situations by using game thinking and game mechanics to solve problems and engage audiences. By using game playing activity where a player scores point in competition with others, these software/hardware combination tools try to unravel the mystery of human mind. The approach of gaming is applied in non-gaming contexts to engage audience in solving problems. The net result is enhanced engagement with customers, better understanding for marketing new products or services and improving learning process. Similar use can be found in other areas as well.

Gamification techniques exploit human instincts to compete in a social situation and display their skills and abilities. This human desire is converted into a game to enable its users in such a way that it also leads to some meaningful outcome. For example, the cardboard game of trade we all played in our childhood was able to impart the concepts of how a trade is conducted, profit and loss, etc. Now the games are designed using computer programs and played using mobile phones and other devices. The gamification process rewards the players with points, achievement badges or with virtual a currency.

A well-known author on the subject of gamification, Jane McGonigal[16] believes that games contribute powerfully to human happiness and motivation, give them a sense of meaning, and help in the development of community. She has used the power of gamification in her own recovery from illness and concludes that resilience in everyday life can be simply built by adopting a gameful mind-set. Being gameful means bringing the same psychological strengths we naturally display when we play games—such as maintaining optimism, using our creativity, displaying courage, and working with determination—to real-world situations.

Some of the applications for gamification are in marketing, learning, design and product market research. For example,

- Recruitment process by U.S. Army uses gamification
- Social Loyalty and Customer Engagement used by Samsung to get user-generated content by rewarding users for getting engaged with the community, participating in Q&A discussions with other users, watching videos, reviewing products, and other activities. In exchange for their participation, users are awarded with badges and progress through levels of achievement.
- Kaplan University has enhanced its curriculum using gamification.
- Crisco's The Binary Game, is used to teach people the basics of binary numbers.
- IBM has an interactive business process model simulation game, called INNOV 8 BPM[17]s. This game teaches the complex idea of business management. It gives students the responsibility to make decisions for a fictitious company, named After, Inc.

Analysts predict that the gamification market will grow to $2.8 billion by 2016. Gartner also predicted that "by 2015, 40% of Global 1000 organisations will use gamification as the primary mechanism to transform business operations"[18]

---

[16] Jane McGonigal books, Reality is Broken: Why Games Make Us Better and How They Can Change the World Published by Brilliance Audio; MP3 Una edition (July 31, 2015), and SuperBetter: A Revolutionary Approach to Getting Stronger, Happier, Braver and More Resilient-Powered by the Science of Games published by Penguin Audio; Unabridged edition (15 September 2015).

[17] http://www-01.ibm.com/software/solutions/soa/innov8/index.html accessed 19 Mar. 2016.

[18] Olding, E. (2012): "Engagification" of the Enterprise–Gamification and Employee Engagement. Gartner Research.

9.8.7 Apple Pay

This is combination of several existing technologies to make faster and secure payment using smartphones. This will eliminate credit card frauds that impair the secure payment and increases cost of transaction.

9.8.8 Project Loon

Search engine giant Google is investing millions of dollars in the project to perfect a reliable and cost-effective way to achieve internet connectivity using helium or hydrogen-filled balloons floating in the stratosphere in the sky. These hundreds of balloons, nearly twice the height of commercial airplanes will have a boxy gondola using solar-powered electronics and will make a radio link to a telecommunications network on the ground and beam down high-speed cellular internet coverage to smartphones and other devices. This approach will help reach of internet at remote places which are difficult to connect through ground-based networks of fiber optics cables of mobile towers.

9.8.9 Case: *Project Meghraj*

Project Meghraj is a Government of India initiative to utilise the advantages of cloud computing. With the focus on improving the IT infrastructure in the government department, this project has been conceptualsed. Meghraj is basically an Information and Communication Technology initiative with the intent to free up the capital so that the departments spend more on operational part rather than the installation and handling IT infrastructure. National Cloud services for Government under Meghraj is being implemented by NIC, the nodal agency for Government IT projects and programmes. Meghraj will help evolving strategy from cloud adoption in the Government sector and facilitate its implementation. Meghraj will have several cloud computing environments at various locations using existing as well as new IT infrastructure and follow common standards and protocols as issued by the Government of India from time to time.

9.9 SUMMARY

This chapter was indented to give a quick snapshot of various technologies both widely used one and emerging ones. The selection of these technologies was based on the criteria that they are used by a wide variety of industries. We started our discussion by covering major information technologies such as ERP, MIS, DSS, ESS, Data Warehousing/Data Mining, SCM and CRM. This list was expanded to include e-business, e-commerce, B2B, B2C, big data social media analytics as well. Finally, technologies such as mobile computing, 3D printing internet of things (IoT) and other emerging technologies were discussed. The purpose of this chapter is to equip students to get a bird's eye view and supplement their knowledge.

We also defined the types of information systems used in an enterprise. This covered information systems used at various levels of the management. This covered Executive Support Systems (ESS), Management Information Systems (MIS), Decision Support Systems (DSS), CAD

CAM, Simulation and Modelling. Further, transaction processing systems (TPS) and workplace productivity systems were discussed. A detailed description of enterprise systems such as ERP, SCM and CRM were provided as these are used by most enterprises in the current times. The next topic was around data management covering data warehouse (DW) and data mart with their subcomponents. Further, e-business and e-commerce were explained along with m-commerce in detail.

The next technology widely used is social media and how it is helping to unleash creativity of the masses and people was discussed. This is giving rise to big data analytics due to huge volume of a wide variety of data. Finally, other emerging technologies such as IoT (internet of things, 3D printing, nano-architecture, apple pay and project loon were discussed. Finally, a case study on Indian government cloud computing platform Project Meghraj was discussed.

Key Terms: FSS, MIS, DIS, TPS, IoT, Data Warehouse, Data Mart 3D-Printing NFC, CAD/CAM.

REVIEW QUESTIONS

1. Identify various levels of information systems for the company giving examples at each of the levels.
2. Explain the need of data warehousing or data mining for a retail company. What would be the benefits? What subjects would you select for creating data warehouse? What data mining activities are likely to yield what all for what typical possible patterns?
3. What are the basic supply chain management stages? Explain them by giving suitable examples.
4. Explain the need and benefits from customer relationship management (CRM) systems for any organisation such as airlines, banks or telecom service provider.
5. Write short notes on
   (a) Internet of Things
   (b) 3D printing
   (c) Driverless vehicles
   (d) Big data analytics
   (e) B2B and B2C
6. What is ERP? Why is it necessary for an enterprise? Can we implement e-commerce without ERP in a large manufacturing company?

ADDITIONAL READINGS

1. Unlocking the potential of the Internet of Things. McKinsey Global Institute report. Source: http://www.mckinsey.com/insights/mgi/research/technology_and_innovation accessed 22 Sept. 2015.
2. Disruptive technologies: Advances that will transform life, business, and the global economy: The McKinsey Global Institute, May 2013.

3. Dundas, Jitesh, "Machine learning helps software development," *Software Magazine*, June 2012.
4. Govindarajan, Vijay, and Praveen Kopalle, "Disruptiveness of innovations: Measurement and an assessment of reliability and validity," *Strategic Management Journal*, Vol. 27, Issue 2, February 2006.

The Global Information Technology Report 2014, Rewards and Risks of Big Data by Beñat Bilbao-Osorio, World Economic Forum, Soumitra Dutta, Cornell University, Bruno Lanvin, INSEAD, Editors http://global-indices.insead.edu/documents/GITR2014.pdf accessed 20 Sept. 2015.

Chapter 10

Human Aspects and Social Issues in Technology Management

The human spirit must prevail over technology.

— Albert Einstein

At the end of this chapter, we will learn:

- Integration of people and technology
- Organisational and psychological factors
- Organisational structure
- Technological change and industrial relations
- Technology assessment and environmental impact analysis

10.1 INTRODUCTION

Human aspect of technology and related social issues is an interesting topic that all technology managers must understand. So far we have studied technology and innovation from the economic/commercial angle, but this chapter will be devoted to consider the human angle and the impact of technology on a larger social platform. We will broad base our discussion to consider impact of technology in the development of quality of life, issues of ethics, impact on environment and a holistic perspective encompassing all. In short, our enquiry would be on the following key areas:

- How to assess the impact of technology from humanitarian and social angle?
- What are the current research, models and framework that can be used in this evaluation process?
- How to develop and prescribe an approach of technology development from human angle?
- Examples and case studies that have underlined some of issues of technology development where human angles were not taken into account and have reached a far reaching impact.

10.2 TECHNOLOGY AND HUMANITY

Whenever a new technology is discovered or attempted to internalise for commercial purposes, its evaluation is usually based on its commercial and economic viability. In the past, the technology or any scientific discovery was being questioned by religious or political angles. People found it difficult to absorb new realities and even castigated scientists. Many of these principles and discoveries faced challenges from the existing belief which were given support by the religious preachers or elderly generations. There are several examples where early scientific discoveries and postulations were questioned by religious leaders. Such inventors, theoreticians and followers of scientific principles (or users of technology) were condemned or even punished. Galileo Galilei (1564–1642), one of the greatest scientists of all times whose work of astronomy, improvement of telescope and postulation that earth is not stationary also called "heliocentrism", had to face severe criticism of Church. However, the modern society which has seen and enjoyed the fruits of science and technology has become less skeptical of new technology. The wide spread adoption of technology and new methods without questioning their larger impact on human society, environment and human value system is now forcing thinker to resist whether one should stop and think before adopting them. Nuclear disasters, environmental changes, greenhouse effect, pollution in the food chain and even natural disasters are being attributed to reckless development, wide spread consumerism and adoption of technology that are having severe side effects.

Even in the area of medicines, the after effects and side effects are being discovered much later by the time it has already caused irreversible damages to the individuals. Pollution in rivers and disposal of industrial waste in the rivers have created severe problems to the people living the downstream chain. Consumer goods, packaged food, health drinks, mobile phones, automobiles are few products, where technology has played important role in their development yet they have also caused severe damage to the environment, health hazards to individuals or ecology. In a seminal essay as the introduction the book[1], Morton Winston calls ethical and social problems as the children of inventions.

In order to address some of these issues, US National Science Foundation (NSF) in 1997 came up with two sets of evaluation criteria which have invited a lot of attention to understand the relationship between science and society[2]. While the first criteria is internal the other one is based on external factors.

Society is defined as, "the sum of social relationships among human beings" and technology as, "the body of knowledge available to a civilization that is of use in fashioning implements, practicing manual arts and skills, and extracting or collecting materials." Given these two definitions one can argue that Technology shapes our society in both positive and negative effects. Some of these technology has improved the social relationships and some has led to deterioration. IT has been used to predict imminent disaster and to give enough warning to prevent injury and save lives. Use of technology is always welcomed during disaster to help affected population. Yet we must be aware of the possible negative consequences of any technology and take necessary precautionary measures.

[1]Society, Ethics, and Technology Paperback–January 10, 2000 by Morton Winston (Author), Ralph Edelbach (Author) Publisher: Wadsworth Pub Co., ISBN-10: 0534505813.

[2]Assessing the science–society relation: The case of the US National Science Foundation's second merit review criterion J. Britt Holbrook, Technology in Society 27 (2005) 437–451 www.elsevier.com/locate/techsoc accessed 17 May, 2015.

In order to address some of these issues, US National Science Foundation (NSF) in 1997 came up with two sets of evaluation criteria which have invited a lot of attention to understand the relationship between science and society[3]. These criteria of evaluations for any technology are intellectual merit and broader impact. The former is an internal evaluation criterion but the later is external criterion. These criteria were applied largely for US government funded projects but are good starting points to understand the societal impact of technology for any organization or firm. So far in the book, we have focused on the former criterion about technology development and management but in this chapter we will focus our attention on the later. Let us understand them in detail.

1. **What is the intellectual merit of the proposed activity?** This internal criterion considers if the new technology of innovation is in the direction of advancing knowledge.
2. **What are the broader impacts of the proposed activity?** The second criteria of NSF for evaluating a technology is at times ignored or not given due importance. As result of which the damaging consequences are faced by the society. This criterion is used to evaluate if the technology and innovation has the potential to benefit society and contribute to the achievement of specific, desired societal outcomes.

Microsoft CEO, the legendary Bill Gates has questioned the negative aspects of Technology and said[3] "As more and more people store personal information on the internet, how will we ensure that information is kept secret? As our economy becomes more dependent on bits than atoms, how will we protect these resources from being damaged or devalued by hackers? As the barriers to information come down, how will we protect from negative and predatory influences? And, as the internet dissolves national borders, how will we help indigenous cultures co-exist with an increasingly homogenous global culture?" Every new technology needs to balance these two criteria (see Figure 10.1).

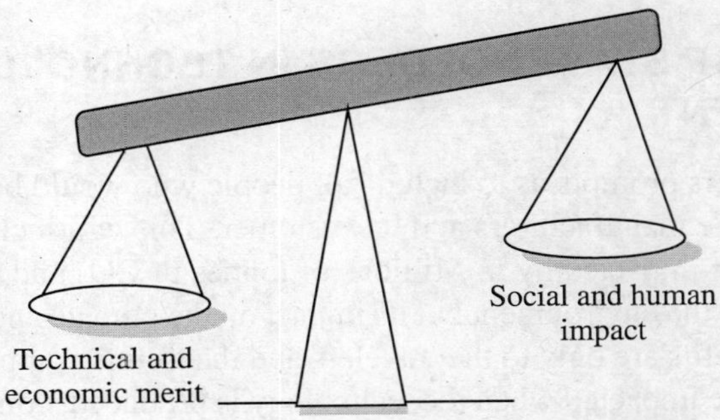

FIGURE 10.1 Balancing Technological vs Social Impact.

[3]https://www.academia.edu/10327940/Effects_of_Technology_THE_POSITIVE_AND_NEGATIVE_IMPACTS_TECHNOLOGY_HAS_ON_OUR_DAILY_LIVES.

10.3 UNDERSTANDING THE IMPORTANCE OF VALUES IN TECHNOLOGY AND DESIGN

Any technology or technology-induced design must consider what value it brings on the larger context of society. A term 'value sensitive design' has been coined to incorporate human values in technological design. Values are those aspects that are considered to be important from the social/human point of view. Norms are policies or standards that are formulated to realise the value. Finally, one need to establish design criteria to comply with the norm. For example, if the aimed value is to ensure environmental friendliness of the product, then the norm would be to prevent pollution of surface water. In order to achieve this norm, the design criteria would be to follow the standards for drinking water purification or any other context dependent criteria. Table 10.1 shows an example of value hierarchy for a real estate building or apartments. You may notice that one design criterion can help in meeting several norms. Similarly, for any technological product, there could be several value items and each one of them may have several supporting norms, some of these norms may be common with other value points.

TABLE 10.1 Value, Norms and Design Criteria Example of Real Estate Product

Value	Health and Safety		
Norms	Use of non-toxic products in construction/ maintenance	Prevent seismic risk	Environmental protection
Design Criteria	Select material which has no toxicity	Earthquake resistance building	Use of solar power
	Use of solar power		Garbage segregation and disposal

10.4 CONCEPT OF STAKEHOLDERS IN TECHNOLOGY MANAGEMENT

The concept of stakeholders prompts us to include all people who would be impacted /affected by the technology, not just the manufacturers and its customer. This will include society and people who are not connected yet impacted by it. Millions of tonnes of CO_2 and Nitrogen oxides (NOs) are released by aircrafts in the environment but its impact on the climate and environment is felt by everyone whereas its benefits are only to the travelers and the airline companies. Stakeholders are people who are going to be impacted when the technology is produced, consumed, retired whether successfully or if it fails. Nuclear fuel power plants are environmental-friendly as compared to the coal-based power plants, but in case of radioactive substance leak the impact is much higher for the people around the power plant. We will have to grade various stakeholders under several categories such as those who are the actual producers, distributers or users of the technology and those who either receive output or input to the technology. The latter will include suppliers or consumers. In case of railways, the secondary stakeholders would be suppliers of equipment and beneficiaries of the transported goods. In addition, there would be tertiary stakeholders who have no direct involvement but effected by its success or failure. For example, the inhabitants in villages and towns through which the new railway line passes.

10.5 THEORY OF TECHNOLOGICAL DETERMINISM

The impact of technology on society was given a new term "technological determinism" which is believed to have been coined by an American sociologist and economist Thorstein Veblen (1857–1929)[4]. Technological determinism theory presumes that technology drives the society culture and structure. This phrase also covers the influence of technology on human evolution and claims that technology determines who we are and how our world is structured. Heidinger[5] opines that mobile phones are the perfect example of technological determinism. In the last 20 years of their existence, they have become omnipresent in all walks of our life. Their good impact has been to reduce the connectivity problem, we can work from home, etc., but it now has given a tool in the hands of governments and corporations who can track our movements. Cellphone cameras have produced several sting videos and have helped revolutionaries to spread the message using social media sites which are now conveniently accessible from cellphones. Cellphones have music players and radios which youth listens while walking and several of them have met with accidents. Drivers call while driving, often compromising on their safety. Social media usage on cellphone and free texting apps have led to loss of concentration amongst students. According to Marshall McLuhan[6], technology creates new "spaces" that people adopt. The example of which is printing press giving us Gutenberg Bible, radio revolutionizing popular music, TV is giving us new content and off course couch potatoes.

The dark side of technological determinism theory is also leading the world into an "exitless dead-end"[7] such as in the case of nuclear disasters happened at Fukushima in Japan or Chernobyl meltdown in Ukrainian. These instances show that blindly following the technology with a belief that everything will be good may have far-reaching consequences. Some technology may be giving big profits to select few, but their failure may be costing a large number of unconnected people as well.

10.6 SOCIO TECHNICAL SYSTEMS AND MODELING

Socio Technical Systems (STS) approach is to understand the interaction between people and technology. This term also captures the relationship of society's complex infrastructures and human behaviour. This term was first coined by Eric Trist et al.[8] who dwelled on the interaction

[4] https://en.wikipedia.org/wiki/Technological_determinism accessed 18 May. 2015.

[5] http://biocitizen.org/technological-determinism-what-it-is-what-we-can-do-about-it accessed 18 May. 2015.

[6] Herbert Marshall McLuhan, (July 21, 1911–December 31, 1980) was a Canadian philosopher of communication theory and a public intellectual.

[7] http://biocitizen.org/technological-determinism-how-it-leads-to-exitless-dead-ends accessed 18 Jun. 2015.

[8] Eric Trist and H. Murray (Eds.) (1993) *The Social Engagement of Social Science*, Volume II: The Socio-Technical Perspective. Philadelphia: University of Pennsylvania Press. http://www.moderntimesworkplace.com/archives/archives.html.

of technology with other aspects of the society. Understanding of the impact of technology on society is done through Socio Techno modeling. There are several approaches which can be used depending upon the type technology. Some of these modeling methods are:

(a) **CUSTOM A:** A six stage process which first identifies the stakeholders and organisational context and maps their needs whether it is being met with the proposed technological systems or not.

(b) **Open System Task Analysis (OSTA):** This method of modelling focuses in task and is conducted in eight stages. All the identified tasks with their goals are considered in an external environment ascertaining its impact on physical, economic as well as political aspects. The model examines what all changes will be brought and what will be the impact on each of these areas. The specifications of new technical systems are then decided based on social and technical requirements.

(c) **Effective Technical and Human Implementation of Computer Systems (ETHICS):** Here the design teams working on separate technical solution merge their solution to develop a solution that meets social as well as technical needs.

(d) **Soft systems methodology:** Here the technical solution is not assumed, but the problem is considered from both technical and social angle and then solution is developed.

10.7 TECHNOLOGY IMPACT ON FUTURE OF EMPLOYMENT

Technology advancement has always been viewed with two lenses. While it brings in overall prosperity to the owners of new technology (and to those skilled to use it), it also results in reduced opportunities for those who are stuck with the old. When automobile came in as means of transport, it impacted the employment to people who were engaged in running horse-driven cart[9]. Rapid adoption of technology, robotics, mass manufacturing machines have already led to lower employment to factory workers. However, the job shifted to another area due to the arrival of new technology. The net result, however, was increased employment in the society. A study[10] in the U.S. shows that overall growth of employment was 10 times in the last over one hundred year touching 48% from just 21% a century ago. In the recent times, for nearly 50 years, the job shifted from physical labour to mental labour which caused massive employment opportunities in IT, ITeS, banking, financial and other knowledge economy industry. However, these industries are also getting impacted due to automation and building of smart hardware, microchips, etc., that is eliminating the need of human intervention. Metros in major cities run without any driver and traffic is all controlled by automated signaling system. A MIT study[11] points out that automation

[9]Hindi film titled Naya Daur (1957) starring Dilip Kumar, Vyjayanthimala depicted this the race between a tongawallahs and a bus service showed the economic fight due to technology.

[10]http://cs.stanford.edu/people/eroberts/cs201/projects/1999-00/technology-dangers/issues.html accessed 22 Jun. 2015.

[11]http://www.technologyreview.com/featuredstory/515926/how-technology-is-destroying-jobs/ accessed 22 Jun. 2015.

such as improved industrial robotics to automated translation services are in fact a reason for sluggish employment growth. While technology has always been increasing productivity, it was also helping in employment growth but not any longer. Since 2000, this study shows that while economic growth is happening it is not leading to a commensurate employment growth which the researchers label as "great decoupling." Back home in India, recent reports[12] in newspapers suggest that task automation in hugely successful IT services companies are leading to reduced intake of college graduates. Even Bill Gates, the legendary founder of Microsoft is quoted[13] to have said that in 20 years from now, labour demand for lots of skill sets will be substantially lower and the manual work will be replaced by software substitution ("bots" in tech slang).

Case of Kiva Robots

Amazon, the leading e-commerce giant, is using over 15000 Kiva robots across its 10 warehouses. This helps the pace of fulfilment of orders from its warehouses. Instead of workers going to the aisles and picking up goods for shipment, these robots bring in the goods to the shipment points. While these robots have expedited the productivity of Amazon's warehouses, the question remains as to how many jobs they have reduced in this process although Amazon claims that there is no job reduction. Earlier examples of Foxconn, a key supplier for Apple, was also in the news to replace employees with robots. Many experts predict that over half of the jobs human being are engaged in today would be replaced by robots in areas—health care, customer services, fulfilment, management of transport, toll gates and cleaning of homes.

10.8 TECHNOLOGY RISK MANAGEMENT

We all agree that our life would be too difficult without technology. The latest indispensable is our smartphone that remains with us at all times. Several researchers have opined about the possible risk from smartphones, laptops, mobile communications which we tend to ignore as their direct and immediate impact is not seen. Risks such as smartphone stress, radiation, transmitting of germs, accidents due to distraction, allergies, and wrist, back and neck pain are well-known. Many other inventions ended up being hugely risky while in peaceful use and enormously damaging for military use. Nuclear war heads have huge potential risk of falling in the hands of terrorists groups who are always in the look out to smuggle one such device and can threaten a large section of society. Even Einstein, the father of nuclear science, regretted having written a letter[14] to the U.S. President informing the likely use nuclear chain reaction for military purposes fearing German's ability to harness. Even accidents at peaceful installations such as nuclear power plants or submarines have led to irreparable damage. One case in point is

---

[12] Automation in IT companies reducing space for employees; puts question mark on future of IT grads http://articles.economictimes.indiatimes.com/2014-07-16/news/51600564_1_vineet-nayar-hcl-technologies-ganesh-natarajan accessed 22 Jun. 2015.

[13] http://www.businessinsider.in/Bill-Gates-People-Dont-Realize-How-Many-Jobs-Will-Soon-Be-Replaced-By-Software-Bots/articleshow/31969522.cms accessed 22 Jun. 2015.

[14] http://cdn.theatlantic.com/static/mt/assets/science/Einstein-Roosevelt-letter.jpg accessed 22 Jun 2015.

the Bhopal gas tragedy where thousands of innocent citizens lost their lives due to cyanide gas leak. The inventor of television Philo T. Farnsworth once opined that he had created kind of a monster, a way for people to waste a lot of their lives[15]. The inventor of AK 47 Kalashnikov regretted[16] that he designed a light weight rifle to defend his country, not for terrorists to use it.

In a seminal article[17], the noted German social scientist Ortwin Renn defines term risk as the possibility that an undesirable state of reality (adverse effect) may occur as a result of natural events or human activities. Therefore, the risk arising out of any human action, such as new technology adoption can be avoided or modified if the causal actions are avoided or modified. But then he asks two other questions. One is about finding appropriate criteria on which the risk should be evaluated and the second is how safe is safe enough. So when we evaluate any technology of its possible risk, we have to identify likely undesirable outcomes, its likely possibility and the degree by which our knowledge reflects the reality. If we know very little about the technology, then our identification of undesirable outcome and its possibility will be far too poor than if we know adequately about the technology. This is the reason why after 70 years of nuclear energy discovery we should evaluate its risk and its possibility much differently than what it would have been evaluated when the knowledge was much less.

Various researchers have worked on suggesting various aspects of technology risk management and all these risks can be categorised into the following:

1. **Technical risk:** This risk covers whether the proposed technical solution or product will succeed technically. The technology may not be adequate to meet the requirements and hence will carry a risk. When the first airborne vehicle was designed by Wright Brothers, no one was sure whether it will fly long distance and carry so much of load. The famous case of Motorola funded IRIDIUM project for satellite-based telephony did not succeed as satellite phones need line of sight and open sky to function hence not be useful indoors or during overcast sky.
2. **Economic risk:** Many technology may pose economic risk where it may not be cost-effective for the technology to be used. Solar powered cars fall under this category where the cost of building and maintaining using expensive batteries is outweighing its environmental friendliness and low cost of running.
3. **Environmental risk:** Our next chapter is more focused to bring such risk from technology. The inventors must consider ecological damage the new technology will do in entire lifecycle of usage from manufacturing to disposal. CFL bulbs though consume less energy has the potential to damage the environment if not disposed of properly. The e-waste disposal or lack of it is already seeking a lot of attention from environmentalist. Many may not be aware that a laptop weighing a kilogram might have consumed 2000 kilograms of natural resources in manufacturing, transportation and running of the laptop. It is estimated that nearly 60% of the energy is consumed in manufacturing the laptop and only 40% is balance which is consumed during its use.

[15]http://www.cracked.com/article_17186_6-geniuses-who-saw-their-inventions-go-terribly-wrong.html accessed 22 Jun 2015.

[16]http://motherboard.vice.com/blog/the-inventions-their-inventors-have-lived-to-regret accessed 22 Jun 2015.

[17]Concepts of risk: a classification. Renn, Ortwin (1992), Krimsky, Sheldon (Hrsg.): Social theories of risk, Westport, Conn.: Praeger, 1992. ISBN 0-275-94168-X, S. 53–79.

Some researches[18] point out that laptops connected to the power source consume 10% of residential energy in the United States and 1% of CO_2 emissions worldwide.

4. **Social risk:** This is related to the soft societal issues of use or likely misuse of the technology. We all know the disadvantages of miniature cameras which can now be carried without being detected has led to uncontrolled voyeurism, loss of privacy and crime. In addition Internet transactions are susceptible of fraud. This risk relates with issues of ethics, privacy and distortion of the social value systems. So as technology designers or propagators, we must think of the safety mechanism or warning systems from its misuse.
5. **Future risk:** When a technology is used for the first time, it may not pose such a huge risk to society but its widespread proliferation may. One of the reasons of Delhi being rated as a city of poor air quality is attributed to a large number of cars and other passenger vehicles. Some recent researches[19] have claimed a link between the declining honey bee populations and increasing cellphone radiation[20]. While some of these findings are yet to be conclusively proved, if damages do take place in the environment then the reversal would be far difficult. So it is the duty of the technology developers and managers to ascertain the future risks and accordingly take decisions. Figure 10.2 shows an example of plotting risk on two ordinates of impact magnitude and impact over time.

Given such risk potential form any technology leads to taking a concreted action to evaluate and plan for mitigation by the technology developers as well as users for example, if we are aware if the risk to human body due to excessive radiation of cell phone, then we must take adequate precaution. At the same time cell phone manufacturers should further make efforts to reduce rediation. The recent incidents (2016) of Samsung note 7 cellphone catching fine is a case in point which warrents that technology providers must take adequate precautions otherwise it will lead to serious loss of reputation as well as market share.

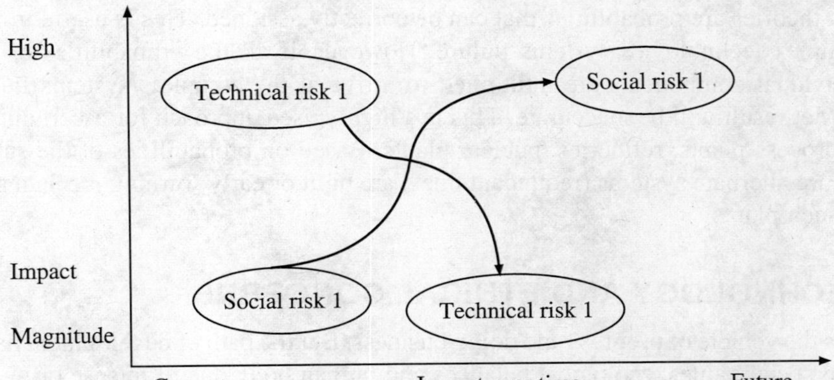

FIGURE 10.2 Risk Impact Assessment on Scale of Magnitude and Over Time.

[18] http://www.betterworldbetty.org/why-your-laptop-sucks/ accessed 24 Jun. 2015.
[19] http://naturalsociety.com/is-the-cellphone-killing-the-honeybee/ accessed 24 Jun. 2015.
[20] http://naturalsociety.com/is-the-cellphone-killing-the-honeybee/#ixzz3dyJXJh8o accessed 24 Jun. 2015.

10.9 TECHNOLOGY RISK ASSESSMENT AND MITIGATION

Technology risk assessment is an inherent task for technology managers, users and developers. Whether they are developing, inventing or innovating new technology or they are just using it in their product and process cycle. This task has to be performed with meticulous detail and with care. In his relevant book, Author Alan Randal argues that there is a justifiable role for the precautionary principle in a risk management framework that integrates precaution with elements of the standard risk management model. We cannot consider everything in the negative and will have to manage the risk while taking benefit of the technology advancement.

10.9.1 Technical Risk Assessment

There are several models used for technical risk assessment. We will describe some of the widely used approaches.

1. **Actuarial approach:** In this approach, the risk is ascertained based on the past occurrence where harm was done to the environment. This approach assumes that we have sufficient information about the past events and can use the past data to predict the future. Airline accident or failure midway is one such example where risk is considered based on past data. Automobile insurance rates of different segments of society uses this approach. This approach does not help in solving or address the risk. It does give facts summated over a period of time.
2. **Toxicological or epidemiological approach:** This approach identifies causes that lead to the undesirable events. In this order, this approach is an improvement over the earlier one. The underlying assumption of this approach is that the causes can be explained by using existing theory and models. If a correct theory or model is not applied, then the risk prediction and its cause can go wrong.
3. **Probabilistic approach:** Here the probability of the risk is ascertained based on models such as fault tree or event-tree analysis based on logic. This approach assumes that theories are probabilities that can be correctly assigned. This is useful in predicting complex technologies systems failure. However, if all the probabilities of failure of individual components are multiplied to arrive at the complete systems failure, then the net result will be inaccurate. This is a highly used approach for ascertaining failure in process plants, refineries, nuclear plants. Based on probabilities of the sub systems failure alternate systems (redundant ones) are built or early warning mechanism is built in such plants.

10.10 TECHNOLOGY AND ETHICAL CONCERNS

Technology is the vehicle of progress and doing business. But the path of development has dangers of damages to social values, ecological balances and human body due to misuse or overuse. Let us look at some of the burning questions to understand the relationship between technology and ethical concerns.

- Can ethics and technology ever go hand in hand to carve out a better world without damages described above?

- What harms will happens if ethics is not considered during technology adoption?
- What are the benefits to the mankind when ethical principles are used in technology development and adoption?
- What principles should be adopt to ensure technology is not causing any harm?

These and some other related questions plague the minds of social scientists who feel that without a deep respect of ethical practices the end result from technology will be nothing more than a disaster. In an article in Scientific American[21] Nayef Al-Rodhan argues that many advancements are likely to cause problems of unknown magnitude. The reasons for walking is such dead end alley is that technologist do not visualize the ethical consequences while introducing technology. The issue is not their reluctance but perhaps the ignorance.

Take the case on internet, social media, YouTube, WhatsApp and many such widely used technologies. The over use of these by masses has led to loss of privacy, increasing financial frauds, crime against weaker section especially women and erosion ethical values. While we must welcome technological innovation for its benefits but must exercise restraints if it leads to inequality, loss of human dignity and erosion of inclusiveness. Egbert Schuurman[22], another thinker in her article Ethics of technology cautions about the dark side of questionable technology which leads to the environmental problem or the cultural distortions. We are often mesmerized by technology's phenomenal growth, our challenge is to also continuously visualize potential of any disastrous consequences. As we become more and more dependent on the economics of technology, we tend to forget its ethical consequences. Profit before planet and people concern is not a good idea for long-term survival of our world. Increasingly many companies are considering all the three Ps (also called Triple bottle line or 3BL) in adopting technology or extending their business.

So what is the solution? Shall we shun technology and return to the medieval age? Perhaps, not. We need to understand the relationship between ethics and technology to understand this topic better.

First of all any new technology brings a good degree of uncertainty. Technology also changes hence lack experience of its possible misuse or adverse impact. In the past we have been able to draw few lessons which can be extremely valuable. Our apparent inability or ignorance of using new technology makes understanding of ethics of technology challenging. Some people see no reason to question the inevitability of technology developments. But technology ultimately is a human action hence its positives as well as negatives is our responsibility.

We know that ethics is a theoretical discipline that embodies good or responsible actions of human beings. Ethics is not a specialized science but multidisciplinary or interdisciplinary endeavor. An ethics of technology is aimed to ensure people's good or responsible conduct in and with technology for actions covering legitimate motives, sound values, and norms. Technology is not just a tool that we use to help our day to day work. Technology is dynamic system with larger ramifications. Technology leads business and profit which leads to power and politics. Hence any technology that enables me to get profit and power is welcomed with considering its cost some one lese may be paying.

---

[21]The Many Ethical Implications of Emerging Technologies, Brain like computer chips, smart pharmacology and other advances offer great promise but also raise serious questions that we must deal with now, By Nayef Al-Rodhan on March 13, 2015, accessed 24122016.

[22]http://www.metanexus.net/essay/technology-and-ethics-responsibility

Leading researchers have advocated certain guiding principles for injecting ethical disciple in technology and innovation management. Some of these principles are as follows:

- **Priority principle:** This principle states that any technology must define its priority and why it should be developed and used. It should also consider the likely potential of misuse and weighed carefully before advocating its proliferation. New drugs, several of them were hailed as solution of certain diseases were later on banned when it was found to have side effects. Burgeoning cola industry is causing ground water depletion in several countries.
- **Life principle:** Human and other lives on the planet are the most precious objects that should not be threatened by any new technology howsoever profitable it may be. Technology must preserve biodiversity, take responsibility for clean water and air, keeping and making the soil fertile, and improving the living environment. It should not harm preserve dangerous emissions. Technology must preserve nature and maintain its diversity.
- **Social principle:** Technology should preserve the social fabric of the society. It should maintain and promote community spirit, respect individual's privacy and dignity, ensure equitable justice, civility, mutual care and social welfare in general. Technology should promote harmony between people, nature and society.
- **Safety principle:** This principle aims to evaluate all possibilities that may lead to dangerous situations to harm human and ecological system during or after the use to the technology. It also considers all possible dangers due to technology malfunctioning. For example if the internet connection does not work what will happen to the driverless car? Will it run safely?

All technology development must consider these principles before embarking on future development. If the damages are minor then ways to mitigate should be found out. In such cases people should be asked to take necessary precaution while, cautioned for overuse or malfunction. For example, consider electricity as technology. It has several good use and scored well on first three principle but needs proper care for safety principle. Precautions such as not touching a live wire, installing fuse and protections needs to be exercised.

SALT: The story of Emission fraud by a leading Automaker

In the third week of September 2015, the world had woken up with the news of emission fraud committed by the world leading automaker Volkswagen. The emission scandal of German automaker Volkswagen Group came to light in September 2015 when United States Environmental Protection Agency (EPA) issued a Notice of Violation of the Clean Air Act. Apparently, the automaker has programmed their vehicles using deceptive software code in diesel engines that could detect when they were being tested and then modify the performance to improve results. In actual conditions, their cars were found to produce 35 times more NOx than what they showed during the test conditions. Volkswagen has produced and sold nearly eleven million cars worldwide between 2009 and 2015. While Volkswagen has accepted this act and has announced recalling of almost 5,00,000 cars in the U.S. alone, the total estimated fine can go as high as about $18 bn as per newspaper reports.

Newspaper reports also mentioned that Volkswagen U.S. chief executive blamed "individuals" for using software to cheat on diesel emissions. The law makers in U.S. House of Representatives questioned federal environmental regulators for failing to catch the fraud for years. This emission scandal has already reduced the Volkswagen market value by one-third and seen exit of several executives including the CEO. Volkswagen's U.S. CEO apologised before a congressional subcommittee for his company's decision to surreptitiously rig diesel cars to beat emissions tests and acknowledged that it's "hard to believe" top VW officials didn't know about the scam.[23]

10.11 TECHNOLOGY AND ETHICS RESEARCH

There is raging debate on ethical aspects of technology. Some of the research agencies and organisations working on the social and human aspects of technology are as follows:

1. The European Group on Ethics in Science and New Technologies to the European Commission (called EGE) http://ec.europa.eu/epsc/ege_en.htm: This is a group of eminent individuals who are entrusted to evaluate ethical questions pertaining to science and new technologies and advise European Commission to formulate legislation or policies.
2. U.S. National Science Foundation http://www.nsf.gov/: This is a U.S. federal government agency established by an act of Congress in 1950. This agency helps to promote science and technology for health and community welfare and funds projects for basic research in American universities. In 2015, it had a budget of $ 18 bn and funds only those projects that have better impact on taxpayers money.
3. Internet resources: A blog Technological Citizen http://thetechnologicalcitizen.com/?page_id=2 is worth considering.
4. Society, Ethics, and Technology Paperback – January 10, 2000 by Morton Winston (Author), Ralph Edelbach (Author) Publisher: Wadsworth Pub Co; ISBN-10: 0534505813

Readers are advised to examine the content on these sites.

10.12 THE FUTURE OF WORK: HUMAN-AI COLLABORATION AND WORKFORCE TRANSFORMATION

Technology has always influenced the nature of work, often leading to job displacement in some sectors while creating new opportunities in others. In the age of AI, the prevailing perspective on the future of work emphasizes human-AI collaboration and augmentation rather than wholesale replacement. AI is increasingly functioning as an intelligent assistant, enhancing human performance and creating a more productive, innovative, and fulfilling work environment. AI excels at tasks that are repetitive, data-intensive, and rule-based, such as data entry, report generation, and invoice processing. By automating these mundane chores, AI frees human

[23] http://www.usatoday.com/story/money/cars/2015/10/08/volkswagen-us-ceo-michael-horn-congress-testimony/73572476/ accessed 09 Oct. 2015.

workers to focus on activities that require uniquely human attributes: creativity, critical thinking, emotional intelligence, complex problem-solving, and interpersonal communication. This strategic reallocation of human capital allows employees to dedicate their energy to more engaging and impactful work, boosting job satisfaction and sparking innovation.

AI enhances decision-making by processing vast amounts of data and identifying patterns and insights far beyond human capacity, providing comprehensive and accurate information for faster, more informed strategic choices. In customer interactions, AI chatbots and virtual assistants handle routine inquiries, seamlessly handing off complex or sensitive cases to human agents with full context. Generative AI tools accelerate innovation and creativity by assisting designers, writers, and artists in generating ideas and drafting content. AI also improves training and development by personalizing learning experiences and enabling immersive simulations.

The shift towards human-AI "symbiosis" implies a fundamental redefinition of job roles and skills. It is not just about upskilling for AI literacy, but about cultivating a workforce that can effectively "partner" with intelligent machines. This requires a focus on developing uniquely human capabilities that complement AI, leading to new forms of productivity and job satisfaction. However, it also presents new challenges in managing this hybrid workforce, including ensuring fair labour practices, addressing potential skill gaps, and fostering a collaborative culture where humans and AI play to their respective strengths.

10.13 ETHICAL AI: ADDRESSING BIAS, TRANSPARENCY, AND ACCOUNTABILITY

The rapid advancement and widespread adoption of AI necessitate a deep consideration of its ethical implications. The concept of "Responsible AI" has emerged as a critical practice, emphasizing human oversight and societal well-being in the development and deployment of AI systems. This encompasses broader ethical implications, governance, legal considerations, and long-term repercussions.

Key principles of ethical AI include:

- **Human agency and oversight:** AI should augment human decision-making, uphold human rights, and allow for human intervention.
- **Technical robustness and safety:** AI systems must be secure, resilient, accurate, and reliable, with contingency plans to prevent unintentional harm.
- **Privacy and data governance:** Systems must fully respect privacy, regulating the quality, privacy, and legitimate access to data.
- **Transparency:** AI systems must be traceable, clearly marked as AI, and their capabilities and limitations effectively communicated. This addresses the "black box" problem, where AI's decision-making processes can be opaque. Explainable AI (XAI) is emerging to provide clear reasoning for AI conclusions, enhancing trust and accountability.
- **Diversity, non-discrimination, and fairness:** AI should avoid promoting bias, support diversity, and ensure equal accessibility. Bias in AI systems, often stemming from biased training data, can lead to discriminatory outcomes. Responsible AI development practices

include assessing model training data, causal analysis, counterfactuals analysis, and implementing fairness in machine learning to identify and mitigate biases.

- **Societal and environmental well-being:** AI systems should benefit all human beings, including future generations, and must be sustainable and environmentally friendly.
- **Accountability:** Mechanisms must be in place to ensure responsibility for AI systems and their outcomes, including auditability and accessibility.

FIGURE 10.3 Ethical AI Principles Overview.

Current emphasis on "explainable AI (XAI)" and "auditability" highlights a critical tension between AI's complexity and the human need for understanding and trust. As AI becomes more autonomous and impactful, the ability to understand *why* AI makes decisions becomes paramount for trust and accountability. This pushes the ethical discussion beyond just preventing harm to actively designing for transparency and human comprehension, which is a significant technical and philosophical challenge for technology managers.

10.14 PRIVACY AND SECURITY CONCERNS IN AI/GEN AI DEPLOYMENT

The deployment of AI and Generative AI introduces a new layer of privacy and security concerns that fundamentally challenge traditional cybersecurity and data privacy frameworks. The flexible nature of AI interfaces, particularly those allowing natural language interaction, introduces new attack vectors like prompt injection and accidental data exposure. Sensitive information can inadvertently become embedded in neural networks when models are trained on large datasets, creating hidden vulnerabilities that standard security audits might miss.

The "exponential data complexity" associated with managing AI data grows rapidly with increasing adoption, making comprehensive testing for edge cases prohibitively expensive and outputs potentially chaotic. This necessitates a proactive, AI-specific data governance strategy that integrates security, privacy, and ethical considerations from the design phase.

Best practices for data governance in AI models include:

- **Data Security:** Implementing strict data security measures to protect sensitive or personally identifiable information used within Gen AI models. This involves following best practices for data encryption and access controls.
- **Data Quality:** Establishing rigorous validation processes to ensure the accuracy, completeness, and consistency of training data. Poor data quality directly impacts AI model performance and can propagate errors.
- **Data Lineage:** Maintaining comprehensive tracking of data sources, transformations, and dependencies across AI pipelines to ensure transparency and rapid identification of issues.
- **Compliance:** Ensuring AI systems meet evolving regulations such as GDPR, CCPA, and new AI-specific legislation. The regulatory landscape is rapidly changing, necessitating proactive rather than reactive compliance frameworks.
- **Ethical Considerations:** Implementing bias detection and fairness testing to prevent discriminatory outcomes, as AI systems can perpetuate historical biases present in their training data.

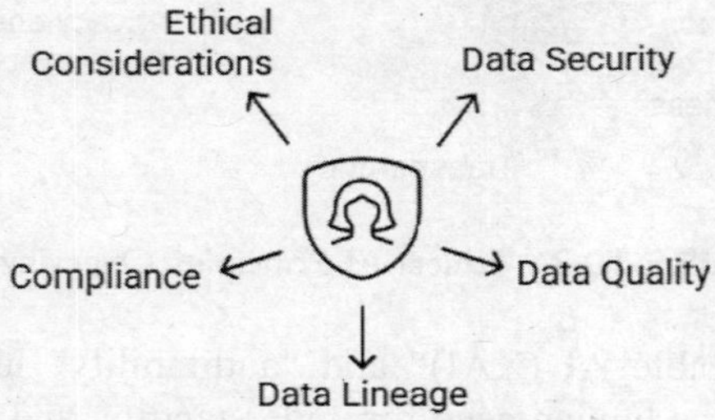

FIGURE 10.4 Data Governance in AI Models.

The unique challenges posed by AI's data demands require a structured approach to data governance, including organizational data stewardship, metadata labeling for sensitive data, access permissions tailored for AI workflows, continuous monitoring, and iterative improvement based on audit results and user feedback. This specialized approach is critical to mitigate risks and build trust in AI systems.

10.15 NAVIGATING THE EVOLVING AI REGULATORY LANDSCAPE

The rapid evolution of AI technologies has outpaced the development of regulatory frameworks, creating a complex and fragmented landscape globally. Governments worldwide are grappling with how to regulate AI, with approaches varying from comprehensive legislation like the EU AI Act to more fragmented, targeted policies in the United States.

The challenges in regulating AI are significant:

- **Speed of Technological Advancement:** The "breakneck speed of technological advancement in AI" makes it difficult for regulators to keep pace with emerging risks and capabilities.

- **Heterogeneity of AI:** AI is not a single technology but a diverse set of methods and applications, making a one-size-fits-all regulatory regime impractical.
- **Lack of Consensus:** There is often "bitter disagreement" among AI experts and policymakers regarding the most pressing risks and appropriate regulatory approaches.

This inherent dynamism of AI technology creates a fundamental tension with the inherently slower pace of legal and regulatory development. Consequently, AI regulation is likely to remain dynamic and adaptive, focusing on outcomes and "risk tiers" rather than rigid prescriptive rules. The EU AI Act, for instance, pioneers a model that sorts AI applications into tiers (unacceptable, high, limited, minimal risk), each bearing different regulatory burdens. This outcomes-based approach allows for flexibility while still imposing controls on high-risk applications.

For firms, this evolving landscape requires continuous legal and ethical vigilance. They must proactively monitor and comply with regulations, understanding that the regulatory environment will likely remain a "patchwork" of specific policies that are regularly updated. This necessitates developing internal AI governance structures that are equally agile and capable of adapting to new legal requirements, rather than just complying with fixed rules. Companies that embrace a proactive approach to responsible AI and engage with policymakers will be better positioned to navigate this complex regulatory environment and build public trust.

10.16 SUMMARY

We took up the human aspects of technology and related social issues in this chapter. Our goal was to assess the impact of technology from humanitarian and social angle taking advantages from current research, models and framework so that we can develop and prescribe an approach of technology development from human angle.

We first established the relationship between technology and humanity by choosing two sets of evaluation criteria for any technology for its intellectual merit and its broader impacts of the proposed activity. We then established the impacts of technology on humanity and society by understanding the importance of values in technology and design and with the concept of stakeholders in technology management. We touched upon the theory of technological determinism which presumes that technology drives the society culture and structure. We also cautioned our readers with the dark side of technological determinism theory which may lead the world into a "exitless dead-end" such as nuclear disasters.

Our next step was to establish the sociotechnical systems and modeling approach to understand the interaction between people and technology. We discussed some of the modeling methods such as CUSTOM: A Open System Task Analysis (OSTA), Effective Technical and Human Implementation of Computer Systems: (ETHICS) and Soft systems methodology.

We then focussed on the technological impact to society such as future of employment. We then explained the concept of technology risk management and how to do risk impact assessment on scale of magnitude and over time.

Our next discussion was around technology and ethical concerns and whether and how new technologies should be used. We followed this up with technology risk assessment and mitigation.

We then examined the role of technology and ethics along with case studies.

CASE STUDY

Incidents of Technology led fraud in Banks and Financial markets are rising

In a study commissioned by The Associated Chambers of Commerce and Industry of India (ASSOCHAM) in July 2015 and conducted by PwC, a leading consulting and auditing firm brought of several interesting and alarming facts of rising incidents of fraud in banking and financial sector. The industry body ASSOCHAM estimated that financial fraud is leading to a whooping 20 billion USD losses every year and the actual number may be still higher. This is acting as a deterrent to increase in FDI inflows into India. The report opines that the new technologies adopted by financial institutions are making them increasingly vulnerable to various risks such as phishing, identity theft, card skimming, vishing, SMS, phishing, viruses and Trojans, spyware and adware, social engineering, website cloning and cyber stalking. PwC Global Economic Crime Survey 2014 pointed that cybercrime reported in organisation around the world including India. According to Norton Report of 2013 India ranked amongst the top 5 countries in terms of cybercrimes such as ransomware, identity theft and phishing attacks. If we account for black money, then the total amount of illicit money moving out of India rose to 439.59 billion USD (28 lakh crore INR) from 2003 to 2012. Minister of Communications and IT, Government of India, cyber fraud cases worth 497 crore INR have been reported by the RBI and CBI since 2011. Even National Crime Records Bureau Statistics shows that the total number of cases of cybercrime registered in India in 2013 rose to 4,356 and total number of arrests made were 2,098. An analysis revealed that 80% of all fraud cases were valued for less than 1 lakh rupees and the total amount involved was only around 2% of the total amount involved. Incidentally, frauds worth 11,022 crore INR were unearthed in public sector banks in India between April–December 2014; 2,100 cases of fraud were reported to the RBI.

Experts opine that the only way to fight the fraud is to follow and adopt new and up-to-date technology. Organisation can prevent fraud by methodically accumulating and quickly analysing large amounts of data to identify any symptoms of potential fraud. Organisation must have regular risk assessment to determine potential hazards and the likely outcome. After which the mitigation plan for potential loss and probability of occurrence is worked out. Wherever human beings are involved, background checks of employee is a good idea.

Some of the tools and methods used in cybercrime preventions are:

- **Data analytics:** By screening and analysing a large volume of data through data analytics tools, financial institutions and banks are able to identify and report fraud attempts quickly. IT solutions exist which can do real-time transaction screening and also provide a visual representation of complex data patterns which could point towards a possible fraud or do forensic analysis of already committed fraud.
- **Behavioural analytics:** This is another specialised discipline where fraudsters disguised as customers are identified by understanding their behaviour, preferences, etc. This is also used in real time as well as post-mortem situations.
- **Deep learning:** This is a unique approach using a combination of artificial intelligence and machine learning to identify if there are any complex patterns getting established cybercrime and online fraud.
- **Conducting regular internal audits:** The old internal audit is now giving way to new technology based audit activity using extensive forensic and data analytics solutions to establish if there are adequate controls exits and are being followed.

Questions

1. Do you think that cyber crime will ultimately slow down the use of IT in the banking sector? Give your answers with reason.
2. Is this a problem of people not finding useful jobs that they turn towards cyber crime or is it just a personality problem?

Key Terms: Technology determinism, Technology risk management, Technology risk assessment and mitigation.

REVIEW QUESTIONS

1. Do you believe that cyber crime act could have been committed by few rouge software engineers without the knowledge of the top management?
2. What price will the company and in turn the employees and other stakeholders pay for the act of cheating in the long run?
3. What will be your recommendations to prevent such acts of cheating within a firm that you lead?
4. What is the relationship between technology and humanity? Explain this by choosing suitable evaluation criteria? **Answer:** Section 10.2
5. Describe the impacts of technology on humanity and society keeping values of technology and design and the stakeholders. **Answer:** Section 10.3
6. What is the theory of technological determinism? What are the dark sides of technological determinism theory? Explain with examples. **Answer:** Section 10.5
7. What is the sociotechnical systems and modeling approach to understand the interaction between people and technology? Write short notes on some of the modeling methods such as:
   (a) CUSTOM:A
   (b) Open System Task Analysis (OSTA)
   (c) Effective Technical and Human Implementation of Computer Systems
   (d) (ETHICS) and Soft systems methodology. **Answer:** Section 10.6
8. What is the technological impact on society on areas such as future of employment? **Answer:** Section 10.7
9. Explain the concept of technology risk management. How will you do risk impact assessment and develop mitigation strategy? **Answer:** Sections 10.8 and 10.9
10. Discuss the relationship between technology and ethical concerns, giving suitable examples. **Answer:** Section 10.10

ADDITIONAL READINGS

1. http://humanitiespolicy.unt.edu/hum pol/our work/science-1.pdf.
2. Sarewitz Daniel Frontiers of illusion: science, technology, and the politics of progress. Philadelphia: Temple University Press; 1996.

Chapter 11

Technology and Sustainability

We do not inherit the Earth from our Ancestors, we borrow it from our Children.

—An Ancient Indian Proverb

At the end of this chapter, we will learn:

- About three perspectives of technology and sustainability
- To develop enterprise green technology strategy
- About role of IT in greening the enterprise
- About diffusion of green technology and IP right

11.1 INTRODUCTION

The objective of this chapter is to discuss environmental impact of technology, possible risk from its adoption and ways and means to mitigate them. By understanding the risk and potential dangers of any technology, managers and professionals can choose the right ones to maintain environmental balance and reduce damages, if any, from its use. This appreciation is increasingly necessary for any manager as the world is facing serious challenges on the environment from the use, misuse or overuse of various technologies. It is no longer disputable that various economic activities are leading to emission of hazardous gases, erosion of water table, reduction in forest cover and generation of toxic elements in the atmosphere. Technology plays an important role in the economic activities such as manufacturing, services, entertainment, transportation, etc. and it makes enormous impact on the environment. We have described in our initial chapters that technology is primarily used to address the 4 Cs, i.e., for cost control, customer satisfaction, compliance management and competitive advantage. These 4 Cs are the basis on which any technology adoption is evaluated and those which figure high in achieving that these are adopted. In this chapter, we are adding another C for climate considerations while planning about any technology. Technology must now be developed, adopted and deployed which leads to cleaner and greener climate. Sustainability is a complex concept. According to UN Bruntland

Commission: "Sustainable development is development that meets the needs of the present without compromising the ability of future generations to meet their own needs." Keeping this view in mind, the technology development must meet the needs of the present but should not damage the environment of the future.

11.2 THREE PILLARS PERSPECTIVE OF TECHNOLOGY AND SUSTAINABILITY

We will adopt three perspectives to understand technology and sustainability issue. The first perspective is largely applicable to governments, policy makers and international bodies and their roles and responsibilities for the greener world using advanced technology. This perspective will examine aspects of cooperation and interventions around formulating climate-friendly policies, ratings technology products and encouraging and incentivising adoption of green or sustainable technology.

This perspective also includes transfer of green technology at an affordable rate and protection of intellectual property but giving the world its larger benefits. Undoubtedly, sharing the newer greener technology with the rest of the world for making our world greener would require a change in mindset. Unless governments of the world come together, create a mechanism and get motivated to share green technology IP with competing countries, greening of the world will be slow and painful. Nature or environment is like a common boat on a rough sea in which we are all sailing together. If countries or companies continue to resist sharing knowhow, technology transfer to facilitate greener world or dump the obsolete and hazardous ones to less wealthy nations, then we all will not survive. Here the role of international bodies to force companies to adopt green technology, encourage cooperation and knowledge sharing to protect the environment is very important.

The second one is for technology providers and R&D firms to plan and invest in technology that has greener impact on the environment. They have to be aware of questions such as, if this technology is leading to the production of more Green House Gas (GHG), emission consuming depletable resources, oil for example, and producing waste which is harmful. Environmental considerations have to be set, right from design, exploration and R&D stages of any technology till its deployment and finally disposal.

The third perspective is for firms and individual users of technology. This perspective will make them aware of the risks of wrong choices and guide them to choose the right one. Any technology will always have a choice between a greener one and the less green one. The later may be cheaper, convenient or just a habit arising out of ignorance. Unless the desire to choose the green technology and resistance to reject the environments hazardous one comes from the users of technology, the world will not change. We are showing these three analysis perspectives in Figure 11.1.

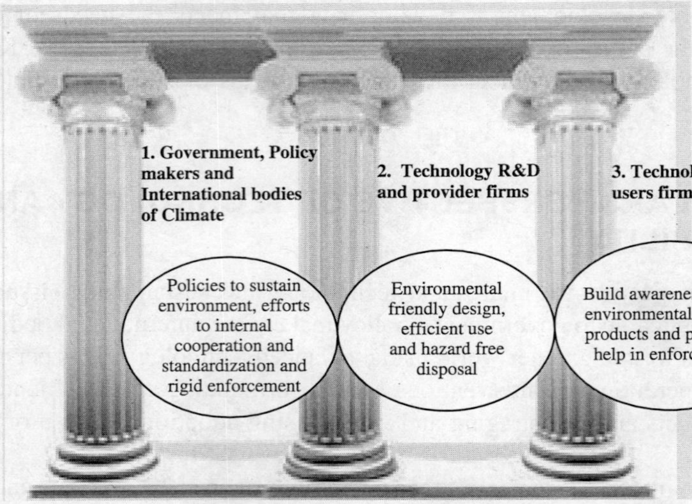

FIGURE 11.1 Technology and Sustainability: Three Pillars Perspective.

11.3 GOVERNMENT AND POLICY MAKERS PERSPECTIVE

Fortunately, governments around the world have become sensitive to the sustainability issue and have enacted several legislation in many countries to reduce automobile exhaust emissions, lower pollution through the traded carbon credit programme, energy ratings, etc. Many international and national bodies like United Nations Environment Programme (UNEP), United States Environmental Protection Agency (USEPA), The Ministry of Environment and Forest, Government of India are the prominent ones among many. They are supported by nonprofit organisations, think tank groups having deep interest. But their role is much larger than enacting a few legislations and releasing occasional white papers. Governments are representative of the society in a legal form who have to preserve its environmental assets for the future generation. Economic growth is necessary but the path of economic growth must be paved with green and ecofriendly policies, technologies and sincere efforts of implementation. We will discuss the role of government in formulating and implementing green technology policies along with their counterparts in other nation and world bodies like United Nations.

11.3.1 Various Government Actions for Green Technology

Government initiatives for environmental preservation go at several levels. It starts with promoting green energy, providing incentives for its use and finally enacting legislations to nab delinquents. We will describe some of these initiatives in brief.

(a) **Green energy production:** According to a recent report[1], the Government of India has decided to harness 100 GW from solar and 60 GW from wind energy by 2022 which

[1]http://timesofindia.indiatimes.com//articleshow/51518376.cms accessed 23 Mar. 2016.

has a huge 125 billion dollars investment opportunity. Several initiatives like National Solar Mission and state solar policies have come up to encourage use of alternate fuel for environment protection. Government is encouraging technologies for energy storage and efficient transmission infrastructure, wind and solar power generation, other energy efficiency technology and services to help Indian government's ambitious clean energy targets of installing 175 GW by 2022. These initiatives are especially necessary to support 'Make-in-India' mission for high-tech industry which will require fault-free, high-quality and reliable power. For example, energy storage enables the efficient integration of renewable energy, can replace conventional peaking generation capacity and reduce the need for investment in transmission and distribution.

(b) Building SMART cities: Cities are necessary for the growth of civilisation but they also bring in concentrated population, tons of garbage, cars, crime, reckless consumption and pollution. A United Nations report[2] quotes that global population will increase from the current 7.3 billion to 9.7 billion in 2050 and 11.2 billion in 2100. Another report says that while 54% of the world's population resides in urban areas in 2014 it will increase to 66% by 2050. Incidentally, the urban population was just 30% in 1950. Such growth and concentration into urban areas will demand more energy, food, water and other resources leading to more strains on the environment and natural sources. In short by 2050, twice the resources will be needed by cities of the world that the whole Earth can ever supply. The answer to growing urbanisation by cleaner and more habitable cities is the concept of SMART cities using Information and Communication Technology (ICT). Technology can play a massive role in making our cities more livable and less polluting to the environment.

ICT in the future will be a key driving force to ensure full and efficient use of the limited natural resources on the earth. SMART cities initiatives will be able to lay down a new, sustainable and efficient infrastructure with safety, security, efficiency and equality of society. SMART city concept would transform them into a habitable city without worry which is safer to live, greener, more efficient, and more livable. For example, if we want our cities to be safer from crime and terrorist attack, then our urban infrastructure management agencies, local and regional governments should have better information sharing and open communication which can only be ensured by ICT among public safety agencies. Safety is best achieved by preventing crime and catching perpetrators. SMART cities would have CC TV cameras located at vantage points in the city. By monitoring these CC TV cameras, curbing and prevention of organised crime and maintaining citizen safety, especially for women, old and children can be ensured. Collaboration technology will further ensure effective implementation. SMART cities would be ecofriendly. From energy to transportation, from human capital to raw information, the solutions must be adept and flexible enough to respond to challenges during each stage of development.

By using biometric recognition technologies, such as face recognition will track and trace unwanted elements on the watch list. Using sensors at locations will help in saving energy or providing emergency services in the event of any man-made/natural disasters.

[2] www.un.org/en/development/desa/news/population/2015-report.html accessed 23 Mar. 2016.

Face Recognition System (FRS) applications in addition to an aid for surveillance can also be used for forensics and employee management and access control.

(c) **Curbing automobile emission:** Automobile emission norms are popular and effective methods by which governments force automakers to improve engine efficiency. In India the current emission standards are Bharat Stage V.

(d) **Forming, adopting and enforcing green standards:** This includes giving energy star rating for technology products, giving guidelines of not using certain hazardous chemicals or material and also laws around their disposal.

(e) **Developing international cooperation for green technology transfer**

(f) **Policies for incentivisation and promotion of green technology**

(g) **Indian Government Actions for Environmental protection** by forming bodies such as[3]

(i) Compensatory Afforestation Fund Management and Planning Authority (CAMPA)

(ii) Capacity Building for Industrial Pollution Management (CBIPM) project: This project is to establish a National Program for Rehabilitation of Polluted Sites (NPRPS) and help state pollution control boards (SPCBs) to do environmentally sound remediation of polluted sites.

(iii) The National Green Tribunal was established under the National Green Tribunal Act, 2010 for effective and expeditious disposal of cases relating to environmental protection and conservation of forests and other natural resources. It has judicial powers to enforce and punish delinquent firms and agencies by giving relief and compensation for damages. It is a specialised body equipped with the necessary expertise to handle environmental disputes involving multi-disciplinary issues.

11.4 TECHNOLOGY PROVIDER PERSPECTIVE

Every new technology may be presumed to be profitable to some individuals and/or firms but many are not equally beneficial to the society[4]. Technology developers, R&D staff and planners must consider its effects on the environment before putting it to commercial use. They are the most knowledgeable among all three and have to share the most responsibility as they are the central pillar. While technology is required to make the lives of the people easy and enjoyable, but at what cost to the environment? Designing a fuel guzzler, fume emitting car that may serve the purpose of few and may fill the coffer of the car manufactures is almost a criminal act of snatching the future health of our next generation. We read routinely stories about firms disposing off their hazardous affluent to the neighborhood river impacting the lives of the people who live nearby and contact incurable diseases like cancer. Technology developers must also take into account the side effects of the technology.

An ideal technology would be not only saving labour, capital and pushing the demand so as to get economic growth but also pollution-reducing. Unfortunately, such ideal is rarely achievable, in practice, because tradeoffs have to be made between these objectives. This is the precise role

---

[3]Source http://www.moef.gov.in/ accessed 25 Mar. 2016.

[4]http://www.insead.edu/facultyresearch/research/doc.cfm?did=1071 accessed 23 Mar 2016.

of policy makers and industry leaders to select and adopt technology that has less risk to the environment by making suitable tradeoff.

Technology is also useful for promoting sustainability especially replacing a technology that is causing harm with some other that is greener and promotes sustainablity. Solar power is one such example which can minimise the carbon emission and pollution due to coal fired power plants. Telecommunication enables video conferencing and is reducing the need of business travel thereby reducing the carbon emission which otherwise could have happened due to air or ground travel. A technology which is also sustainable should also be highly efficient, have good impact on health, and be renewable, reusable, socially affordable, etc. as few needed criteria. Yet we have to remember that some of the current day's technologies are also partially responsible for today's problems. We have become so used to it that we cannot avoid them in our day-to-day work. As long as the environmental impact is lesser than the benefits it provides, we may have to continue using them. We know that many non-renewal resources no longer will be available to our future generations so it is in our interest that we preserve them, use less by using technologies that are efficient.

This leads to the interesting relationship of technology with sustainability. On one hand, some technologies are impacting sustainability and, on the other, some new technologies are preserving and promoting sustainability. This dichotomy of relationship is likely to continue and that is why this chapter becomes important for our managers to think about any new technology from the angle of sustainability before adopting, investing and promoting it.

Technology may turn good!: Take the case of synthetic ammonia production using atmospheric nitrogen and hydrogen. It was German physical chemist Fritz Haber (Nobel Prize for Chemistry in 1918) who through his research made ammonia making economically feasible through synthetisation of atmospheric hydrogen and nitrogen. Further Carl Bosch, an industrial chemist (Nobel Prize in 1931 with Friedrich Bergius) developed its mass production method. Haber-Bosch process is the most economical method of fixation of nitrogen was incidentally developed for war usage in World War I for weapons. However, this technology is now extensively used in fertiliser production which helps in increasing food output from farms to sustain growth in global population. This is an example of technology turning good for the mankind though its initial use was in war for enemy destruction.

Technology that has bad side effect: Another example of a technology that led damage to environment comes from a totally new area but this time from ship building. World War II led the development faster and efficient ships and sea vessels. However, it also increased the ability to do deep sea fishing from oceans at a large scale leading the damage of the ecosystem.

11.5 DEFINING ENTERPRISE GREEN TECH STRATEGY

Enterprise exists within the society, run by the constituents of the society and ultimately has to serve the society. It takes nourishments from the environment and nature and hence must take responsibility of its presentation. Enterprises have to observe environmental stewardship by discharging its responsibility for meeting global climatic challenges and preserve natural resources. The terms like "global warming", "greenhouse gases" and "carbon footprint" pop up in newspaper stories almost on a daily basis. Most think that it is more of an academic discussion that may not impact their day-to-day life. But this is not true. Early signs of environmental impact manifested into erratic weather pattern in the form of flash floods, continued drought, unexplained snow besides heightened level of pollution in our congested cities leading to health problems to its inhabitants are already seen time and again. The green initiatives are not for a few NGOs or school children to make placards on their annual day but have to be adopted by enterprises which are drivers of economy and individuals who are ultimately going to be impacted.

In order to do this effectively, all enterprises must establish green strategy. This is a larger umbrella term of which Green Technology Strategy will be a component. Technology, being the prime driver and powerful executor of overall business strategy, will also drive a firm's green strategy. Green strategy will help enterprise to meet not only legislative obligations and social responsibilities, but also help in reducing cost through better energy saving, reduced consumption of material and generation of waste. Enterprise green strategy is applicable for all types of enterprises whether it is public or private, government or commercial, profit or non profit. It will be a supporting strategy to other strategies such as overall business, operations, marketing or IT. It is not one of those nice-to-have strategies which should be printed in colourful paper and bound in an expensive folder to be filed in the cabinet and occasionally dusted to show to the world in the Earth day! It has to be internalised, executed and revised with time, assessing new challenges. Green strategy must be a part of all these strategies and all departments of the enterprise must make their strategies that have positive impact on the environment. Green strategy should and in most cases make great business sense as well. We will limit our discussion largely within the technology domain of the enterprise green strategy, i.e. Enterprise Green Technology Strategy (EGTS).

11.5.1 Enterprise Green Tech Strategy (EGTS) Development

Developing a comprehensive EGTS requires a series of concerted efforts to be taken by the senior management. At this point in time, most organisations may not have green champion till the time Chief Green officer role emerges. Such role will be ideally played by the CEO or MD of the company who has to drive the green adoption philosophy within the enterprise. The series of steps required in developing EGTS would be as follows (Figure 11.2):

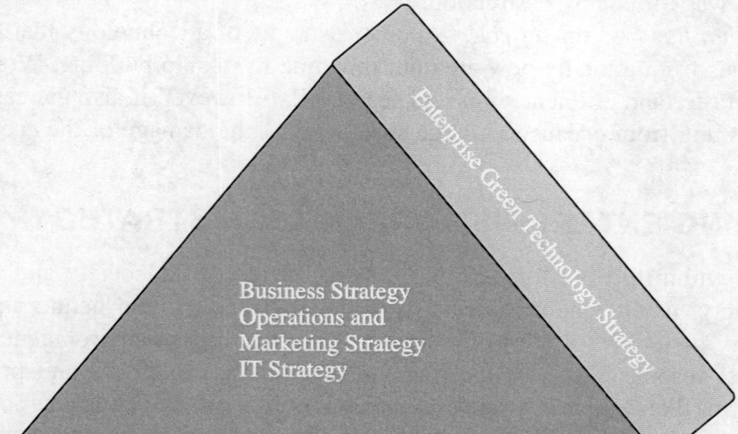

FIGURE 11.2 Enterprise Green Technology Strategy.

(a) **Create a green culture:** Sensitising the organisation towards green philosophy is the first step of EGTS success. The leadership has to reinforce behaviour by providing appropriate tools and training. Leadership must ask this question before every decision if it is also green? Small actions like turning off the lights when the last person leaves the conference room also requires a simple tool in the form of a single switch outside the conference room for powering off all lights. Movement sensitive features to turn on or off the lights are also in use but they will cost some more and more useful for corridors hallways and open space. Using a combination of photocopier, printer and fax machine which is centralised in every floor is another simple but effective idea for encouraging green culture. Green culture can be reinforced by providing training to employees on environmental issues and follow through newsletters, display boards and sharing success stories. Some of the useful best practices to reinforce green culture are:

(i) Walk the talk
(ii) Communicate often
(iii) Invest in tools and training
(iv) Measure effectiveness--for example, recycling weight/percentage effluent discharge quality and quantity, air pollution index, etc.
(v) Instances of published success stories

(b) **Assess the current green initiatives:** This activity is required to baseline the current status of enterprise green readiness. A comprehensive audit and review will expose the gap with respect to emission standards, lack of compliance from the existing as well as proposed regulations and opportunities for action.

At this stage, the use of Green Technology maturity model can be used to ascertain where the organisation stands in terms of its green technology maturity.

Green technology maturity model is defined at five stages that any organisation may fall under. The ultimate goal for any organisation should be to reach the level five (5) of full maturity, however, it has to take appropriate steps to go from their current level to the next level. These levels and their characteristics[5] are defined in Table 11.1.

TABLE 11.1 Green Technology Maturity Model

Level	Description	Characteristic
0	Unaware /unconcerned	Ignorant of the risk and dangers of environmental pollution and hazard due to technology. Has taken no initiatives for green technology adoption.
1	Informed	Aware about the risks of environmental hazards due to non-green technology. Has started to educate people and managers to think green initiatives projects, select green technology.

(Contd.)

[5]Creating an enterprise-level ''green'' strategy Eric G. Olson, *Journal of Business Strategy*, Vol. 29 No. 2, 2008, pp. 22–30, Emerald Group Publishing Limited, ISSN 0275–6668, part of the concepts have been referred from this article.

TABLE 11.1 Green Technology Maturity Model (*Contd.*)

Level	Description	Characteristic
3	Planning and developing	The organisation has several key programmes in place, technology selection and this is done based on 4th C, i.e. climatic considerations. Policies of waste disposal, recycling are getting in place, people are sensitive to over use and conserve energy, do not waste unnecessarily.
4	Implementing and perfecting	Policies are being practised, successes are being published and adopted, people/teams are being rewarded.
5	Leading and optimising	Taking proactive steps to prevent environmental damages. Proactive is R&D for green technology, sharing expertise and knowledge with the rest of the community.

(c) **Envision a future green state for the enterprise:** This step lays down the actions required to achieve the green preparedness. The organisation defines its green technology vision and mission for example[6].

(i) *Vision:* To better our environment by being the global leader in premiere green technology, offering wholesome alternative solutions to global environmental issues.

(ii) *Mission:* To provide ecologically-friendly and sustainable solutions, that is, efficient and economical. To deliver consistently outstanding and reliable services globally.

(d) **Select product, process and technology which are green:** This is a continuous exercise. Use standards such as EPEAT and ENERGY STAR while buying any technology products.

(e) **Develop compelling cost effective alternatives:** To choose from newer technology. The initiatives towards green do not mean working against the principles of existence of the enterprise. It only demands innovative thinking and running the extra mile to find where and how the greener technology is better than the existing one and justifying its business ROI. Attractive value propositions that are cost-effective as well have to be found out. It is a well-known fact that the newer technology always comes with better efficiency and features, if it is also environment-friendly, then it should be adopted. But discarding the old and adopting the new will be an extra cost that has to be justified through the potential benefits. Generally, EGTS should be cost-effective to meet or exceed regulatory requirements yet articulating the benefits not just in qualitative but in quantitative terms is required. In many cases, this can be justified to ward off the potential risk. An enterprise gets extra benefits by adopting a greener option, for example, by choosing an efficient server which is also compact and consumes less energy will save floor space and air-conditioning cost. Governments are routinely incentivising firms in the form of carbon credits to adopt such improvements. Evaluating greening proposals may require some different methods of comparison, for example, they may have initial higher cost but lower ongoing cost. Electric car is one

[6]http://www.ecospec.com/mission accessed 25 Mar. 2016. Vision and Mission of a technology company.

such example. While the time for break-even return is longer, such products are more differentiated and easier to sustain. Other benefits such as social prestige, community accolades, good press, employee morale and customer support will be in addition to these.

11.6 TECHNOLOGY USER PERSPECTIVE

Some of the concepts discussed in the earlier section for technology provider perspective will also be applicable for the technology users. In addition, we will discuss how the concepts of using green technology for sustainability can be deployed by the users of technology in these sections.

Typically, these initiatives can be grouped under three major heads:

(a) **Choose green over non green:** Choose technologies that are efficient, recyclable, less hazardous, i.e., green. If they have energy rating, much better.

(b) **Green your output:** Be sensitive to the waste and output from the operations. Take initiatives such as waste recycling plants, water treatment plant, proper disposal of the e-waste as much as possible.

(c) **Use green source and less resources:** Here the enterprise uses solar power, wind turbine and other green form of energy and attempts to reducing direct consumption of energy and other natural resources such as water.

Some of the green initiatives technology users can take are:

(a) One of the latest developments is connected machines with internet, also called "Internet of Things." These devices can be remotely controlled even using a mobile application, allowing users to put them off remotely to reduce energy consumption.

(b) Use energy-efficient lighting and lighting controls such as LED, use motion sensors to turn off office lights when they are not in use.

(c) Multi use of PCs and laptops, don't oversize the machine for the task.

(d) **Address Heating, Ventilation, And Cooling (HVAC):** Control the use and misuse of air-conditioning, heaters, insulate the walls and windows, use dedicated cooling for data centres.

(e) Consolidate common infrastructure like your fax, printer, copier, and scanner and properly dispose the consumables, install duplex printers which can print on both sides by default, recycled paper, recycled toner cartridges are the few actions that will immediately create a sense of responsibility among the employees.

(f) Large servers are required to run IT applications. For them, energy usage is one of the biggest causes of concern. Most large IT dependent companies find innovative ways to reduce their energy consumption. This can be done by using efficient systems management, virtualisation and IT infrastructure consolidation, liquid cooling and other energy-efficient technologies to reduce energy consumption by as much as 40%.

(g) Technology equipment after their useful life are dumped at landfill sites causing environmental hazard. By recycling some of the components, extending the life or multi-tenancy usage their adverse impact on environment can be reduced. As early as 1990,

Xerox implemented a take-back programme for their copiers which they used as a source of material for new machines. This was universally welcomed by the customers as it freed them of the worry about machine disposal. It also led over hundred million dollar savings annually for Xerox. They almost reused 70-90% (by weight) of old machines and diverted 144 million pounds from landfills (2003). Popularly called ARM, Asset Recycle Management[7] incorporated environmental and remanufacturing considerations into its product delivery process. This helped them realise higher financial returns and helped their customers.

(h) **Green IT infrastructure:** The IT infrastructure for any company will need large energy requirements. If that is optimised, then it will help in protecting the environment systems. Software Defined Infrastructure (SDI) helps transforming a static IT infrastructure into a dynamic resource whose workload can be optimised by deciding where is the appropriate IT resource which could be tapped from. It could be a local server of space in cloud computing environment or a mix of these two (hybrid).

(i) **Green supply chain management:** Green supply chain management (SCM) entails optimisation of transportation, storage and material waste during production. Use of environment-friendly material, which are recyclable and are recycled through a process is part of Green SCM.

(j) **Telecommute or virtual working/meeting:** Here the employees are asked to work remotely or to the nearest office thereby saving energy in transportation as well as personal time. According to a Telework Research Network (TRN) report[8], if an employee works half-time away from the office, then it saves the company about $10,000 a year on infrastructure cost of space, lighting, etc., and the employee up to $6,800. This report estimates that from widespread adoption of telecommuting could cut greenhouse gas emissions nationwide by as much a 53 million metric tonnes. Similarly, using the concept of virtual meeting instead of face to face meeting using Skype, Telepresence, audio conferences and other tools can vastly reduce business travel and the need of in-person meetings, even with customers. Many other tools like MURAL, Central Desktop and Zoho, facilitate collaboration such as file sharing, collaborative document editing, etc., to facilitate highly distributed work teams to function smoothly.

11.7 ROLE OF IT IN GREENING THE ENTERPRISE

The relationship between IT and the environment is complex. IT is one technology that has become ubiquitous and all-pervasive. It can be a source of taking green initiatives and/or it can all add to the green woes. IT can add to environmental impact through production, use, and disposal of IT products. The term "Green Information Technology" attempts to reduce IT's environmental impact through IT products. However, using Information Systems (IS) in key areas can help

[7]http://infohouse.p2ric.org/ref/02/01568.pdf accessed 23 Mar. 2016.

[8]http://www.workshifting.com/downloads/downloads/Workshifting%20Benefits-The%20Bottom%20Line.pdf accessed 23 Mar. 2016.

establish eco-sustainability of businesses and society. This is the solution perspective of IT. Both these perspectives are shown in Figure 11.3.

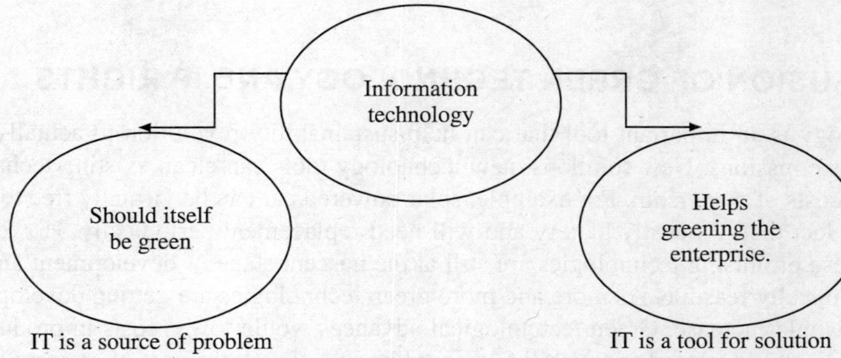

FIGURE 11.3 Two Perspective of Green IT.

Many recent reports are pointing that IT industry is generating similar levels of carbon emissions as the aviation industry which will actually double in the next few years. Some of the Green IT initiatives are:

(a) **Increase data centre temperatures:** American Society of Heating, Refrigerating and Air-Conditioning Engineers recommends that data centres can run as warm as 81 degrees without damaging equipment, compared to 68 degrees less than 10 years ago. This should be adopted.

(b) **Locate data centres at cooler locations:** This will facilitate natural air cooling to lower the energy costs.

(c) **Remove dead equipment from the network:** Large corporations typically have hundreds of servers, many of them become redundant either due to new technology or applications have come to use, yet they are not taken off as soon as they become redundant. Efforts should be taken to routinely take inventory and take off such dead/non-used equipment.

(d) **Use the power of virtualisation:** We all know that newer computers are more powerful yet consume less energy and can replace several low powered computers. In addition, using the principles of virtualisation, they can be used by many users all at the same time. This will result in a greener IT due to saving in power, air-conditioning and lower waste due to efficiency.

(e) **Adopt Cloud computing model:** This is a new way of addressing the peak requirements and take advantage through multi-tenancy. It facilitates scalability, rapid deployment and minimal upfront capital. Using cloud is also cost-effective as you pay only what you use.

(f) **Reduce e-waste through extension of life or recycling components:** This is a problem due to increased personal computers, mobile phones tabs, portable computers like notebooks, laptops and notebooks. Instead of discarding them early, they should be recycled and used for prolonged period. If they reach to land-fill site, they release toxic chemicals that find way to environment. Care should be taken with proper recycling and stringent legislation for protecting workers and the environment for its hazardous exposure is required to be enacted.

11.8 DIFFUSION OF GREEN TECHNOLOGY AND IP RIGHTS

Green technology is an important tool that can help sustainability revolution to actually reduce greenhouse gas emissions. New solutions, new technology tools can clean existing technologies and lower the costs of ownership. For example, solar powered car can be virtually free to operate other than the fact that it's costly battery and will need replacement periodically. However, the majority of these promising technologies are still at the nascent stage of development and yet to become economically feasible. As more and more green technologies are getting developed their adoption rate would increase. Green technological advances would lower costs in production or processing leading to increased accessibility. According to a report, the cost of an installed solar cell system has fallen from US$58 per watt in 2004 to approximately US$ per watt in 2010 and the goal is to bring it down to US$1 per watt in 2017.

Such improvements obviously have happened and would happen due to extensive research and development which will lead to a prominent questions as whether the developers (and the investors) would like to share their intellectual property for the larger goods of the society. Normally, any technology is transferred under a commercial license and patent rights are protected, but can such development be shared across the world because this would be one of the ways to save it from environmental damages. These are some of the questions we will examine in this section. The underlying thought is that the benefits of green technology goes beyond organisation and country limits borders and benefits all others whereas the pollution in one country adversely affects others.

Ironically, when the world is facing acute challenge on the environmental front, one of its instruments of growth called intellectual property rights has become a hurdle. For a developer (or investor) in any new technology research, IP rights are the means to get rewards and returns through its licensing. But in the context of green technology, not letting the IP to be used by those who cannot afford would not only mean denying an opportunity to clean air and clean environment to them but the ill-affect of this denial will be felt by all others. Global access to green technology becomes important as through universal access the world can mitigate climate change and be addressed as a global effort. The importance of universal access (or flexible access) to green technology has been recognised by The United Nations Framework Convention on Climate Change (UNFCCC) as its fundamental framework component. Kyoto Protocol[9] to the UNFCCC laid down that all signatories will cooperate in the development, application and diffusion of green technologies and take necessary steps to promote, facilitate and finance. They would also provide transfer of or access to environmentally sound technologies, their knowhow, practices and processes especially to developing countries.

2010 Bali Action Plan of UNFCCC Cancun conference established a technology mechanism comprised of a Technology Executive Committee (TEC) and the Climate Technology Centre and

[9]http://unfccc.int/resource/docs/convkp/kpeng.pdf accessed 26 Mar. 2016.

Network (CTCN) to promote these objectives. UNFCCC is working towards cooperation by all countries to give access to green technology. For example, cooperation in the development in solar energy technology will achieve as much as 25% of the world's energy leading to avoiding potentially 7,250 MT of carbon emissions per year. Similarly, wind power is aimed to yield 20% of the world's energy resulting in a potential savings of 5,600 MT of carbon emissions per year.

It is well-known that research and development will be pursued seriously if there are financial rewards to do so. Intellectual property rights help in ensuring the fruits of the labour is not fritted away. According to a report on climate change, it would be economically impossible without technology Research, Development, Demonstration, Deployment and Diffusion (RDDD&D) and Induced Technology Change (ITC), to stabilise GHG concentrations at a level that would prevent dangerous anthropogenic interference with the climate system. Obviously, intellectual property laws guarantee such financial rights to technology developers both government and private companies, and collaborating universities. So mechanism must be found to provide incentives to the technology developers and also enable its use by those who have not participated. The World Intellectual Property Organisation (WIPO) has a platform (WIPO GREEN) which aims to facilitate adaptation, adoption and deployment of green technologies. It also facilitates climate-friendly technologies, especially, for developing countries and emerging economies.

Jonathon[10] argues that intellectual property rights have both positive and negative impacts on the green technology development. However, government and international bodies should take supportive steps and also remove some of the challenges. In terms of supportive steps, the government and world bodies should:

- Encourage Innovation by Incentives
- Discourage Delay in Investment and Technology Transfer
- Improvement of the Intellectual Property System, speed up the process
- In terms of ironing out the roadblocks the steps would be to remove
- Restrictions of usage of green technologies as far as possible
- Delays to Technology Transfer Acceptance

However, assuming that most technology development takes place at developed country is not entirely true. Brazil is one of the world's leading producers of biofuels whose 93% of new vehicle run gasoline or ethanol and by 2020, 81% of all its vehicles (old and new) will be flexible fuel vehicles. China dominates in the use of photovoltaic and wind power.

Global efforts for environmental protection can only succeed by formulating suitable policies, necessary mandatory education, cooperation among the participants and adopting changes of basic habits worldwide.

11.9 THE ENVIRONMENTAL FOOTPRINT OF AI/GEN AI (ENERGY, WATER, E-WASTE)

While AI and Generative AI offer immense benefits, their rapid growth comes with a significant and growing environmental footprint, posing critical challenges to global sustainability efforts.

[10]Developing and Diffusing Green Technologies: The Impact of Intellectual Property Rights and their Justification Jonathan M.W.W. Chu, Washington and Lee Journal of Energy, Climate, and the Environment Volume 4 | Issue 1 Article 4 1-1-2012.

The primary environmental impacts include:

- **Energy Consumption:** AI computing is far more power-intensive than traditional computing. AI server racks consume significantly more electricity (30 to 100 kilowatts) compared to standard servers (7 kilowatts) due to their reliance on high-powered hardware for complex calculations. A substantial portion of AI's total energy use (60-70%) comes from inference (running AI models in real-time), not just training. The International Energy Agency (IEA) predicts global data centres could consume up to 1,000 TWh of electricity in 2026, a 400% increase from 2022. Carbon emissions linked to AI are also expected to double between 2022 and 2030.
- **Water Consumption:** AI data centres require extensive cooling systems to maintain optimal operating temperatures, leading to high water consumption. For example, generating a 100-word email with ChatGPT-4 consumes approximately 519 millilitres of water. This puts increasing pressure on local water supplies, with AI's projected annual water withdrawal expected to reach 6.6 billion cubic meters by 2027.
- **Electronic Waste:** The AI boom increases demand for specialized hardware, resulting in more discarded processors and server parts. The manufacturing of IT equipment and chips for data centers contributes significantly to AI's environmental footprint.

The "AI arms race" and escalating competition among AI developers to scale model parameters further amplify energy demand and the overall environmental burden. This implies that market forces alone may not drive sustainable AI development, necessitating stronger policy intervention and industry-wide benchmarks for energy efficiency and emissions reporting. The challenge lies in balancing the immense economic and societal benefits of AI with its growing environmental cost.

11.10 AI'S ENVIRONMENTAL FOOTPRINT AND MITIGATION STRATEGIES

Impact Area	Quantifiable Data (Examples)	Mitigation Strategy	Value and Significance
Energy Consumption	AI server racks: 30-100 kW vs. 7 kW for traditional servers; 60-70% of AI energy from inference; ChatGPT-4 training: 5.7M kgCO_2; Global data centers: up to 1000 TWh by 2026.	Optimized hardware (e.g., Google's TPUs over NVIDIA GPUs); Smarter cloud computing (choosing data centers powered by clean energy); More efficient training mechanisms (model pruning, knowledge distillation); Renewable energy sourcing for data centers.	Reduces carbon footprint, lowers operational costs, and aligns with corporate sustainability goals.

Water Consumption	ChatGPT-4: ~519 ml water per 100-word email; Projected annual water withdrawal: 6.6 billion cubic meters by 2027.	Efficient cooling systems for data centers; Locating data centers in regions with abundant water or sustainable water management.	Minimizes strain on local water supplies and addresses water scarcity concerns.
Electronic Waste	Increased demand for specialized hardware leading to more discarded processors and server parts.	Designing for recyclability; Implementing circular economy principles for hardware; Responsible disposal and recycling programs for e-waste.	Reduces landfill burden and promotes resource conservation.
GHG Emissions	AI's wider industry category (ICT) generates at least 1.7% of global emissions; Carbon emissions linked to AI expected to double by 2030.	Stronger policies and benchmarks (e.g., requiring AI developers to report carbon impact); Incentivizing transparency in emissions; Complying with ISO 42001 (AI management) and ISO 14001 (environmental management).	Ensures accountability, drives industry-wide change, and fosters a company-wide sustainability culture.

This table provides a systematic overview of AI's environmental challenges and actionable mitigation strategies, serving as a practical guide for technology managers and policymakers.

11.11 LEVERAGING AI/GEN AI FOR SUSTAINABLE DEVELOPMENT AND GREEN INITIATIVES

Despite its environmental footprint, AI can also be a powerful tool in combating climate change and promoting sustainable development. This dual nature creates a complex ethical and strategic dilemma for firms, implying that a "green AI" strategy must not only mitigate its own footprint but actively leverage AI to solve broader environmental challenges, turning a potential liability into a strategic advantage.

AI's positive contributions to sustainability include:

- **Data Analysis and Insights:** AI can quickly and effectively analyze significant volumes of data to provide insights into climate trends, the effectiveness of emissions reduction strategies, and a greater understanding of extreme weather risks, leading to faster action.
- **Resource Optimization:** AI algorithms can optimize energy distribution grids, predict peak demand, and reroute energy flows to prevent outages, enhancing grid reliability and reducing energy waste. In supply chains, AI optimizes energy consumption patterns across manufacturing and logistics, identifies inefficiencies in transportation routes to reduce fuel consumption and emissions, and improves waste reduction through enhanced demand forecasting.
- **Renewable Energy Integration:** AI algorithms analyze weather data, solar and wind patterns, and energy consumption trends to optimize the integration of renewable energy

sources into the grid, ensuring efficient harnessing of clean energy and reducing reliance on fossil fuels.

- **Sustainable Material Development:** AI can expedite the development of new sustainable and energy-efficient materials by simulating molecular interactions and predicting properties, accelerating innovation in green chemistry and engineering.
- **Circular Supply Chain Models:** AI plays a crucial role in enabling circular supply chain models, which prioritize resource reuse and waste minimization. AI allows businesses to track product lifecycles and optimize reverse logistics for efficient collection and redistribution of used products, reducing reliance on raw materials and environmental impact.
- **Environmental Monitoring:** Gen AI analyzes data from remote sensors, satellites, and ground measurements to detect changes in air quality, monitor emissions, and assess ecological impacts, enabling timely interventions to mitigate damage.

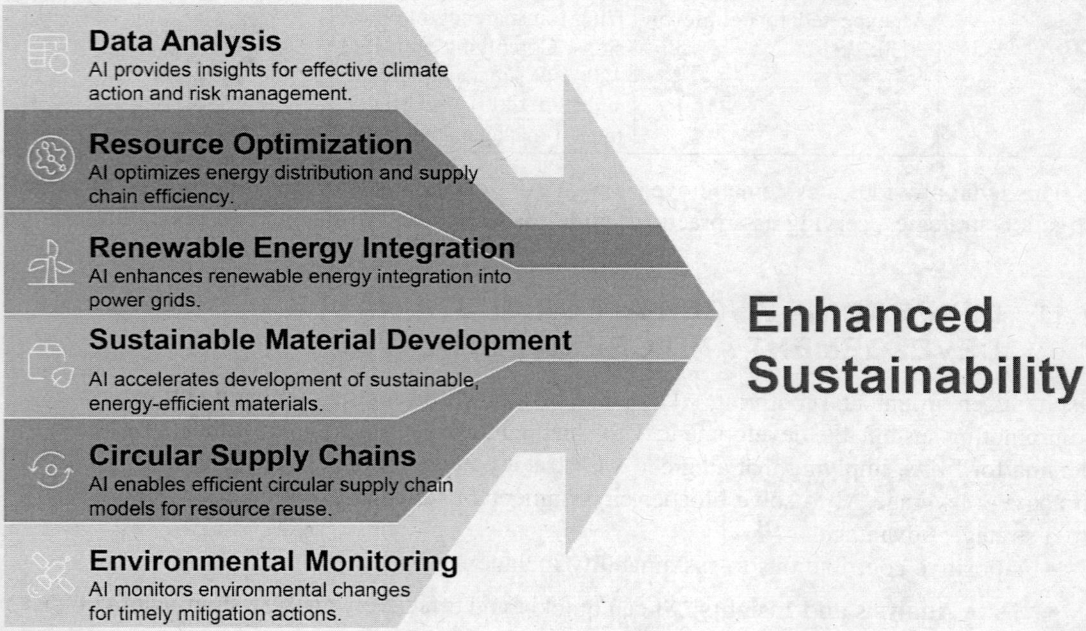

FIGURE 11.4 AI's Role in Environmental Sustainability

Leading organizations are already investing in these areas, with companies like Google and Microsoft committing to carbon-free electricity goals and investing in AI model efficiency and data center energy consumption. This demonstrates that AI, when developed and deployed responsibly, can be a powerful ally in the fight against climate change, fostering a more sustainable and environmentally conscious future.

11.12 SUMMARY

We discussed in this chapter the environmental impact of technology, possible risk from its adoption and ways and means to mitigate. Taking a cue from our initial chapters that technology is primarily used to address the 4 Cs, i.e., for cost control, customer satisfaction, compliance management and competitive advantage, we added another C for climate considerations while planning about any technology. We outlined our three pillars Perspective of Technology and sustainability to understand technology and sustainability issue. The first perspective was to understand the role of governments, policy makers and international bodies for the adoption of green or sustainable technology. The second one was for technology providers and R&D firms to plan and invest in technology that has greener impact on the environment. And finally, the third perspective was for firm and individual users of technology.

We discussed the role of government and international bodies to balance between economic growth, green and ecofriendly world. Various government actions for green technology such as green energy production, building SMART cities, curbing automobile emission, forming, adopting and enforcing green standards, developing international cooperation for green technology transfer and policies for incentivisation and promotion of green technology were discussed. Indian government actions for environmental protection by forming several bodies were also outlined.

The technology provider perspective covered the development of Enterprise Green Tech Strategy as the first building block. Enterprise Green Tech Strategy (EGTS) development requires a series of concerted efforts to be taken by the senior management. We detailed out the process of EGTS development.

The third perspective was that of technology users and initiatives they can take which were grouped under three heads: choose green over non-green, green your output and use green source and less resources. We also added some of the successful initiatives taken by companies.

Our next discussion was focussed on the role of IT in greening the enterprise. This is one technology that has become ubiquitous and all-pervasive. We postulated that IT can be a source of taking green initiatives and/or it can all add to the green woes. We discussed the term "Green Information Technology and Green Information Systems (IS)" which can help establish eco-sustainability of businesses and society.

Another important discussion was the challenge as to how green technology can be diffused in accelerated manner and whether the existing policy of IP right will help in impeding this process. We took the balance view of this subject and outlined several initiatives by world bodies to help in this process. We discussed universal access (or flexible access) efforts of The United Nations Framework Convention on Climate Change (UNFCCC), Kyoto Protocol and Bali Action Plan of UNFCCC Cancun conference. We brought out both positive and negative impacts of IP on the green technology development.

Finally, this chapter concluded that global efforts for environmental protection can only succeed by formulating suitable policies, necessary mandatory education, cooperation among the participants and adopting changes of basic habits worldwide.

CASE STUDY A

Green Technology Master Plan of Government of Malaysia

Malaysian government has taken unique efforts to promote green technology. They call it as green technology base lining and The Green Technology Master Plan (GTMP). The GTMP[11] covers green technology applications and action plans into four stages:

- GTMP framework based on six (6) key enablers, viz., human capital, financial incentives, infrastructure, regulatory framework, innovation and branding
- Conduct Techno-Economic Modeling Analysis
- Identify prioritised green core technologies and businesses
- Prepare comprehensive action plans and identify relevant implementing agencies. The GTMP can also be demonstrated through identification of potential
- Entry Point Projects (EPPs) or existing EPPs with GT applications. The diagram below shows the output of the baseline study.

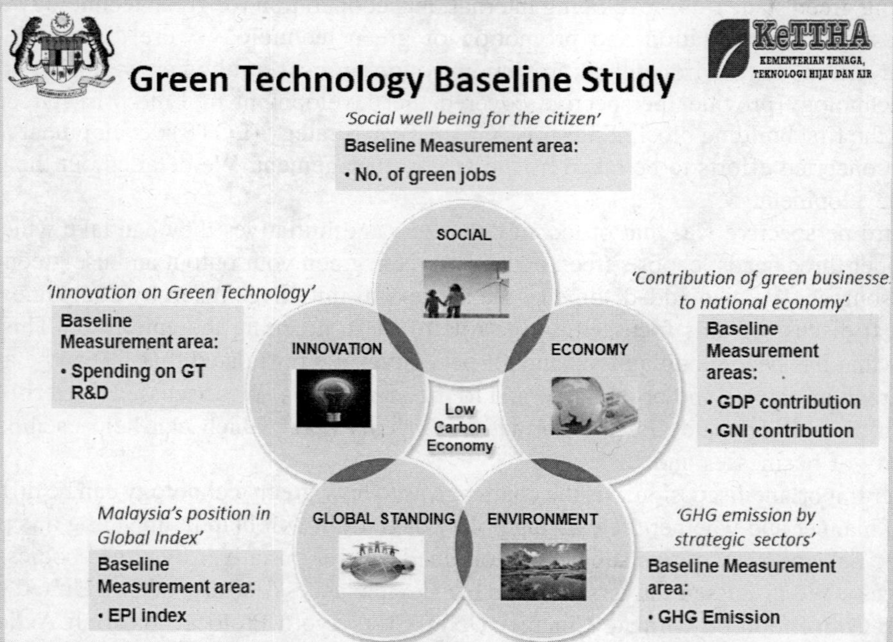

FIGURE 11.4

Questions

1. Which are the initiatives that Indian state and Central Government can adopt?
2. What are the lessons for Indian corporations?

[11] http://home.jeita.or.jp/greenit-pc/activity/asia/file/8_Green%20Technology%20Presentation_Malaysia.pdf accessed 23 Mar. 2016.

CASE STUDY B

Tirupur First to Arrive at Zero Liquid Discharge Technology[12]

Tirupur is a small city of South India called Tirupur also known as the 'Knit City'. Its 700–odd dyeing units were ordered to be shut down by the Madras High Court in 2011 on a petition moved by the Farmers Association in the area. The arguments of the farmers were that these units were discharging hazardous dyes and chemicals into the Noyyal River and into the surrounding farmlands. This led river water and farmlands to become toxic causing skin problems, livestock deaths after drinking water and impacting field cultivation due to highly coloured groundwater. The Total Dissolved Solids (TDS) of the effluent were found to be in the range of 4000–5000 ppm, well above the legal limit of 2100 ppm. This closure impacted the USD 1.8 billion industry in this area and loss of jobs to thousands of workers.

However, by using 100% Zero Discharge Technology implemented at both Common Effluent Treatment Plants (CETPs) and Individual units, the industry has resumed operations. According to a press release[13] by the ministry, more than 50% of total units are running. Approximately, 494 dyeing units and 162 bleaching units were there before closing down due to court order. There are 16 CETPs under operation out of 18 now.

After successful implementation of ZLD at Tirupur, it is being adopted for cleaning of Ganges which is also due to polluting industries along its coast. ZLD's advantages include protection of the surrounding soil salinity and absence of groundwater or river pollution. This also helps in conservation of water resource and salt due to re-use. Some of the ZLD disadvantages include that it uses higher amount of chemicals in wastewater treatment and extra energy in treating water. It also generated enormous amount of hazardous sludge and other solid waste. Finally, it costs an upward of 25–30% on the manufacturing cost.

Tirupur's ZLD success story has led to Indian government releasing a draft regulation on 22nd October 2015 to make ZLD mandatory for textile units having wastewater discharge of more than 25 KLD (kilolitres per day). According to Apparel Export Promotion Council (AEPC), Tirupur is the first textiles cluster in India to arrive at the Zero Liquid Discharge Technology in Dyeing & Processing Technology. At present, all dyeing and processing units are using 100% zero discharge technology. This textile hub of southern India also created and generated more than 2000 MW in Wind Mill Energy.

Key Terms: Sustainability, GHG (Green House Gas), SMART city, EGTS (Enterprise Green Tech Strategy), Green IT

REVIEW QUESTIONS

1. What are the three perspective of Technology and Sustainability? Describe giving real life examples. **Answer:** Section 11.2
2. What is the necessity and process of Enterprise Green Tech Strategy (EGTS) Development? Do you recommend that start-up companies should consider strongly to adopt EGTS before embarking on new Business ? **Answer:** Section 11.4.1

[12]http://nimkartek.com/blog/zero-liquid-discharge-a-solution-to-zero-discharge-of-hazardous-chemicals/ accessed 25 Mar. 2016.

[13]http://pib.nic.in/newsite/PrintRelease.aspx?relid=90033 accessed 25 Mar. 2016.

3. Describe Green Technology Maturity Model in brief. **Answer:** Section 11.4.1
4. Describe the role of IT in Greening the enterprise. **Answer:** Section 11.7

ESSAY QUESTION

Question 1: Discuss the environmental footprint of AI and Generative AI, focusing on energy consumption, water consumption, and electronic waste. What strategies can organizations adopt to mitigate these impacts, and how can AI itself be leveraged for broader sustainable development initiatives?

Hints for Answer:

- **Environmental Footprint:** Detail the primary environmental impacts.
- **Energy Consumption:** AI computing is far more power-intensive (AI server racks 30–100 kW vs. 7 kW for traditional servers; 60–70% of AI energy from inference; IEA predicts global data centers could consume up to 1,000 TWh by 2026; carbon emissions linked to AI expected to double by 2030).
- **Water Consumption:** AI data centers require extensive cooling, leading to high water consumption (e.g., ChatGPT-4 generating a 100-word email consumes ~519 ml of water; projected annual water withdrawal of 6.6 billion cubic meters by 2027).
- **Electronic Waste:** Increased demand for specialized hardware leads to more discarded processors and server parts.
- **Mitigation Strategies:** Discuss actionable steps organizations can take, such as optimizing hardware (e.g., Google's TPUs over NVIDIA GPUs), smarter cloud computing (choosing data centers powered by clean energy), more efficient training mechanisms (model pruning, knowledge distillation), implementing stronger policies and benchmarks (e.g., requiring AI developers to report carbon impact), and fostering a company-wide sustainability culture.
- **Leveraging AI for Sustainability:** Explain how AI can be a powerful tool in combating climate change and promoting sustainable development. Examples include data analysis and insights into climate trends, resource optimization (e.g., energy distribution grids, supply chains), renewable energy integration, sustainable material development, enabling circular supply chain models, and environmental monitoring.

ADDITIONAL READINGS

1. On green technology: A Framework for Evaluation, Robert U. Ayres, Centre for the Management of Environmental Resources INSEAD Fontainebleau, France September 1999.
2. Harro Van Asselt, et al., Nationally Appropriate Mitigation Actions (NAMAS) in Developing Countries: Challenges and Opportunities 21 (2010), ("In February 2007, the Intergovernmental Panel on Climate Change concluded with 90% certainty that human activities contribute to the increase in the global average temperature").

Chapter 12

Innovation Driving Industry 4.0 and Fourth Industrial Revolution

It was the best of times, it was the worst of times, it was the age of wisdom, it was the age of foolishness, it was the epoch of belief, it was the epoch of incredulity, it was the season of light, it was the season of darkness, it was the spring of hope, it was the winter of despair.

—Charles Dickens, *A Tale of Two Cities*

At the end of this chapter, we will learn:

- Role of technology and Innovation in the era of fourth Industrial revolution and Industry 4.0
- Five Laws of Emerging Technology and trace their Combined effect
- Changes in Innovation paradigm with I4.0
- Approach for Ushering Innovation 4.0
- Societal value of Innovation 4.0
- Leadership traits expected in the fourth industrial revolution

12.1 INTRODUCTION

As we look around at the end of the second decade of the twenty-first century it is like living the famous lines of Chares Dickens novel ***A Tale of Two Cities***. This is new chapter has been added in the Book Technology and Innovation Management, encapsulating the latest trends in the area of Technology and Innovation management driving a phenomenon called Industry 4.0 or fourth industrial revolution.

We had argued in our earlier chapters that Technology and Innovation have been interdependent and synergistic in many ways. That remains true and proven beyond doubt. In this chapter we will address some the recent trends of technology development that will be useful to our readers.

12.2 INTRODUCING FOURTH INDUSTRIAL REVOLUTION

The term fourth industrial revolution was first introduced by Prof Klaus Schwab, the founder and executive chairman of the world economic forum in an article published in Foreign Affairs[1],

[1]https://www.foreignaffairs.com/articles/2015-12-12/fourth-industrial-revolution accessed 30052019

December 12, 2015 issue. This was followed up with the World Economic Forum Annual Meeting 2016 in Davos-Klosters, Switzerland with the theme of "Mastering the Fourth Industrial Revolution". Prof Schwab also published a book titled The Fourth Industrial Revolution in 2016 by World Economic Forum.

However this was not the only thought but similar initiatives were undertaken elsewhere as well. Germany, a country known for manufacturing excellence in 2011 took a similar initiative under the aegis of its Ministry of Education and Research (BMBF) and the Ministry for Economic Affairs and Energy (BMWI) named "Industrie 4.0" (Industry 4.0 (I40)) to drive digital manufacturing forward by increasing digitisation and the interconnection of products, value chains and business models. BMBF and BMWI jointly funded approximately €200 million for this purpose. The underlying philosophy was to attain Digitalization of production using technologies such as the Internet of Things, machine-to-machine communication and global connectivity make more intelligent manufacturing facilities.

As a nation Germany took this initiative to create its manufacturing ecosystem innovation using digital technologies and set up *Plattform 4.0 Industrie 4.0*[2] with the overarching goal to secure and expand Germany's leading international position in the manufacturing industry. This platform was available across participating companies, academician, policy makers, political leadership, trade unions, associations and other stake holders to discuss appropriate and reliable framework to achieve this holistic goal. This platform is aimed to develop core concepts in working groups to arrive at concrete recommendations for academics, companies and politicians. Small and Medium companies (SMEs) were enabled with specific service offerings, use cases, online library and support infrastructure. This platform also promoted national and international exchanges through numerous bilateral and multilateral cooperation addressing issues of IT security and standardisation.

In simple terms such massive and disruptive transformation cannot just happen for one organization or two, but has to happen across the ecosystem where all stake holders have to wholeheartedly participate and put their own contribution to embrace and make it success.

Before we explain this fourth revolution is and how it is different than the earlier ones, let us review the word revolution. This is to ensure that the revolution we are trying to explain and prepare ourselves for does qualify with all the necessary and sufficient attributes of a revolution.

First and second industrial revolutions: Revolution means a dramatic and wide-reaching change in conditions, attitudes, or operations. It is not a small incremental change but unanticipated dramatic change. Breaking away from the past and disrupting the present is the mainstay of any revolution. This word is more associated with political upheaval, regime changes and change of guards at the position of power. Yet it could also be associated with silent ones that engulfs the masses within no time with or without a leading force.

The term Industrial Revolution was first made popular by Arnold Toynbee (1852–83), an English economic historian who traced Britain's economic development from 1760 to 1840. Britain during this period changed from an agrarian and handicraft economy to one dominated by industry and machine manufacturing. The main factor behind the **first industrial revolution** was use of coal, and steam engine to power machines which could be used in many applications

---

[2]https://www.plattform-i40.de/PI40/Navigation/EN/Industrie40/WhatIsIndustrie40/what-is-industrie40.html accessed 30052019

such as rail road locomotives, waterways steamships, or for running machines in factories. Transportation and Textile industries were largely impacted due to mechanization which was largely earlier manual and cottage industry. Due to First Industrial Revolution factories and public mechanized transportation using steam fuelled by coal became possible. It led to urbanization where people from villages started to move to the new cities. While few owners of machine and factories could earn more the working class working conditions were very difficult.

The period 1870–1914 is labelled by historians as **Second Industrial Revolution** which witnessed the massive adoption of electricity, petroleum and steel. This led to led to the introduction of public automobiles and airplanes. Electricity became publicly affordable and available by paying just usage charges. It brought lights to homes and small establishments which were dependent upon candles and gas lamps. Electricity fundamentally changed the way people worked and lived. In 1881, Great Britain was the very first country to install a public power station. Further in 1876, Alexander Graham Bell invented the telephone and Thomas Edison came out with a better design of the light bulb in 1879. By 1880, electric streetcars began to replace horse-drawn carriages in major European cities. The most significant innovation of Second Industrial Revolution was the internal combustion engine. As liquid fuels, such as petroleum became a reality it led to the development of automobiles and airplanes. Without the internal combustion engine flying would have been impossible. The primary difference of second with the first industrial revolution is the beginning of mass production in manufacturing and consumer goods. The new source of power as electricity and petroleum led to wider impact across other industries. While the working conditions were still bad for the working class, some improvements were seen in sanitation.

But everything that happened in the earlier two revolutions were not all good. The Second Industrial Revolution fuelled the Gilded Age. While few accumulated great wealth the rest were subjected to inhuman conditions in factories with long hours and no compensation for injuries, no pensions, and low wages. The new system established the virtue of skills which can be sold at a price.

Second industrial revolution is also credited with the induction of Mass production, popularized by Ford in 1918, as a way of producing large amounts of standardized material goods. Instead of one person or the group doing everything from beginning to the end the task was standardized and divided into many steps, each performed one after the other by different people. The product moved on an assembly line where individual parts were added until it reached the end of the line as a finished product. In a way this was new philosophy to divide the work into standardized steps producing standards parts and performed by people who acquired skills and proficiency in doing that very steps. The results of this approach, perhaps one of the first Management principles, was a low cost automobile Ford Model T which was standard and famously said to have a choice of colours as long as it is black!

Second industrial revolution in itself is criticized for bringing in several negative effects to the society. Both first and second industrial revolutions were fuelled by laissez-faire capitalism as an economic system where government control was supposed to be minimum. This led to poor working conditions of the labours, massive use of child labour, under wages and of course pollution to river and damaging natural resources. Exploitation of labour by the factory owners is chronicled in several literary work. This also led to protest, trade union agitation and social revolution. Every now and then horror stories of factory building collapse, child labour abuse and pollution came up across the world especially form less development countries. These inhuman treatments have spread in the white collar space as well where workers complain for long hours without compensation and working in odd hours (popularly called "Ghost shift") in call centres and IT support companies in the current times.

12.3 THIRD INDUSTRIAL REVOLUTION ALSO CALLED DIGITAL REVOLUTION

By the second half of the 20th century thought leaders recognised a new change taking place with the rise of electronics, computers and miniaturization. While nuclear energy gave a new potential source of energy during this period, the rise of telecommunications and computers led to white collar productivity improvement. This era also saw high-level automation in production using programmable logic controllers (PLCs) and industrial robots. This is the period which witnessed rise of computers from punched cards machines to PC and hand held computers, rise of internet, and automation of back office functions across industries. India was largely a followers or late adopter in almost all these three industrial revolution. Only during the third industrial revolution, India became a leader of IT service business due to low wages and highly skilled manpower.

A seminal work produced by Noted author and economic theorist Jeremy Rifkin titled *The Third Industrial Revolution: How Lateral Power is Transforming Energy, the Economy, and the World, Palgrave Macmillan 2011*, outlined that internet technology and renewable energies are have created a powerful infrastructure for a Third Industrial Revolution (TIR). He argued that in the coming era, hundreds of millions of people will produce their own green energy and share it in an "energy internet", just as we now generate and share information online.

Jeremy Rifkin opines[3] that great economic revolutions in history occur when new communication technologies converge with new energy systems. While in the first and the second revolution the sources of energy were steam/coal and oil respectively, he argues that for third Industrial revolution is about renewable sources, the signs of which is being witnessed these days. Consequently the digital, internet and other technology confluence with eco-friendly transport component would see driverless cars, solar powered vehicles.

Yet there are few other notable characteristics of third industrial revolution. The younger generation also called millennial generation[4] have different thinking process much different than the earlier generation. They are much more globally connected, aspirational to the core, have no past baggage and have ability for more risk taking. They are nomadic, migration prone, easy to form or drop out from relationship and don't believe in long term commitment either with companies, profession or in personal life! Call them the entitled generation, they are more rational and above racial and political biases. Their likes and behaviour has given rise to sharing Economy that started with social media post and photo or status sharing but has moved to other parts likes sharing accommodation, workspace and rides. Technology encapsulated in the acronym SMAC — i.e. Convergence of Social media, Mobile, Analytics and Cloud further fuelled the third industrial revolution.

---

[3]https://www.worldfinancialreview.com/the-third-industrial-revolution-how-the-internet-green-electricity-and-3-d-printing-are-ushering-in-a-sustainable-era-of-distributed-capitalism/ accessed 11092019

[4]Nielsen Media Research defines millennials as between 21 and 37 years old in 2018

Third Industrial Revolution (TIR) also underlines the new digital manufacturing technologies such as 3D printing. A basic 3D printer costing a few hundred dollars can promote industrial paradigm of a decentralized society. 3D printing has unforeseen potential. Automobile manufacturers may soon produce all its models using 3D on the same production line sooner than later.

Rifkin advocated use of distribute renewable energy production and sharing it through energy grid or intranet across regions. He received good support from European Union countries to work in this direction. Like Internet, which is a networked communication technology without any centralized control, so would be the renewable sources of energy production. It will Citizens produced goods, services and energy through digital production technologies and distributed renewable energy resources, the surplus of which will be shared with the community. Citizens and micro-businesses led productive efforts will lead to information, societal and economic power, redistributed bottoms up. This is leading to the creation of niche markets with glocal (global & local) cultures, "immaterial" and creative economy, leading to a combination of individualism and communities ("indocollectivism").

All this will be possible due to ubiquitous nature of internet, connecting everything and everyone which included people, sensors, machines and natural resource meters. According to Castells (1996)[5] internet symbolizes isomorphism[6] where different cultural expressions, institutions and spheres of life are morphed into each other.

Ironically the impact of the earlier revolutions is still skewed and patchy. About 1.3 Billion of people which is nearly 17% of the world population remain in dark. Digital revolution which is nearly 50 years old still remains alien to 4 billion people, from the developing world who lack affordable internet access.

12.4 FOURTH INDUSTRIAL REVOLUTION

It would be a fair to say that like earlier industrial revolutions, the fourth revolution is driven by technology component. There are a set of emerging technologies such as AI, ML, Big Data, Block chain iOT/ iiOT, cloud, Platform economy, Robotics, 3D printing and many others which are the main driving force. Yet the difference of fourth industrial revolution with earlier revolution is its pervasive impact across geography and depth covering various strata of the society. The fusion of technology with other a parts of our live is convergence of physical, digital and biological systems.

The digital technologies mentioned above are impacting physical systems like autonomous cars, Smart Machines, 3D Printing, and Advanced Robotics. On Biological level this revolution is leading to development on Human Genome, Synthetic Biology, Bioprinting etc. Its impact is and will be felt across the aspects of human life–work, business, home, Governments and Society. Fourth Industrial Revolution shows the potential to raise global income levels and improve the quality of life for populations around the world. Like all other revolutions the ill effects of change are yet to be fully understood and precautions taken off.

In short, Fourth Industrial Revolution is amalgamation of the physical, digital, and biological worlds using advances in cloud computing, artificial intelligence (AI), Big Data Analytics, robotics, Iot/IIoT, 3D printing, AR/VR, genetic engineering etc, Figure 12.1 shows all the four Industrial Revolution in a pictorial fashion.

---

[5]http://www.citi.columbia.edu/B8210/read2/Castells.pdf accessed 01062019

[6]similarity in organisms of different ancestry resulting from convergence

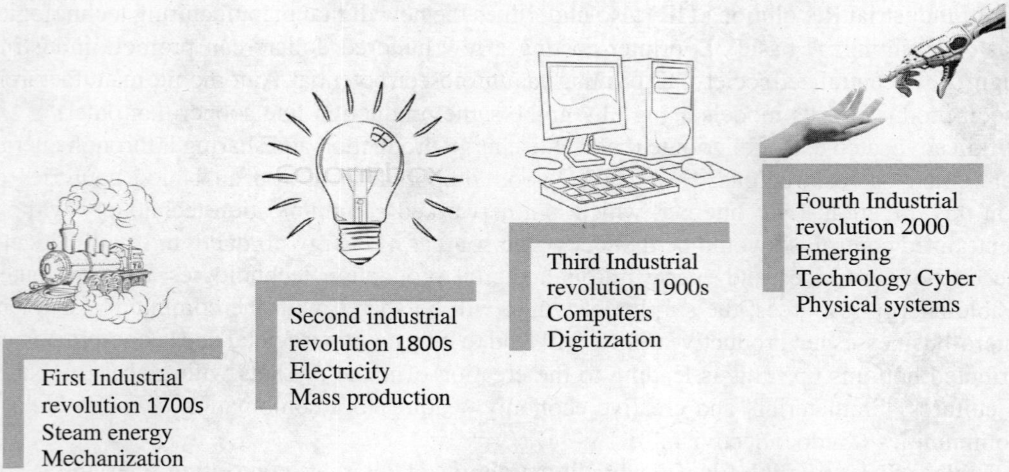

FIGURE 12.1 Industrial Revolution Passage Over Time.

Our modern life is increasingly dependent on these technologies. For example when we use Google map for navigation using GPS, we also search the next restaurant using voice assistant like Apple Siri or OK Google to call a friend while we are still driving. We also keep an eye on our home looking after aging parent's Blood pressure or playing young children using CCTV and connected through Internet to our mobile phone. If the need be we can also switch off/on Air conditioner remotely, an application of IoT. While watching Amazon prime or Netflix we get suggestions based on our past viewing. Police routinely use mobile locations to catch criminals or offenders and facial recognition or bio metrics to locate their past history.

Fourth Industrial Revolution has transformative impact on lives and almost every business sector at an unprecedented, whirlwind pace. All this has happened due to certain advancement of technology which can be explained by Digital Transformation laws.

12.5 INDUSTRY 4.0, IS THIS DIFFERENT?

Industry 4.0 and fourth Industrial revolution is sometimes used interchangeably. However Industry 4.0 is one part of Fourth industrial revolution that has wider impact across industry and society, for example smart cities. Using Industry 4.0 approach machines are augmented with wireless connectivity and sensors so as to be connected with each other and governed by a system for autonomous working. This included technologies such as data exchange from machines, cyber-physical systems (CPS), industrial internet of things (IIOT), cloud computing, cognitive computing and artificial intelligence. All these concepts are also encapsulated in the term Smart Manufacturing or smart factory. Smart factories have cyber-physical systems to govern physical processes, create replica of the physical world and make decentralized decisions. These cyber-physical systems interact with human and with other similar systems.

12.6 FIVE LAWS OF EMERGING TECHNOLOGY

Five laws that are worth understanding to gauge the impact of the pace of change usher by emerging technology and how the changes are different than the earlier changes and revolution.

(a) **Amara's law:** One of the first useful "law" (a rule of thumb!) named after Roy Amara (1925–2007) a Stanford University computer scientist and long-time head of the Institute for the Future. While he himself never named this as law, his observation is attributed to him. According to Roy Amara we tend to overestimate the impact of a new technology in the short run, but we underestimate it in the long run. The same is true with many new happenings in the recent times.

Amara's law explains the reality of disappointments in short term and underestimation in long term, something that the mutual fund investors understand. William Gibson's 1984 novel Neuromancer, coined "cyberspace" of connected world of computer which did not happen in next 10 years but became a reality nearly 20 years after 1984.

The Amara's law can be very well explained by the following simple curve.

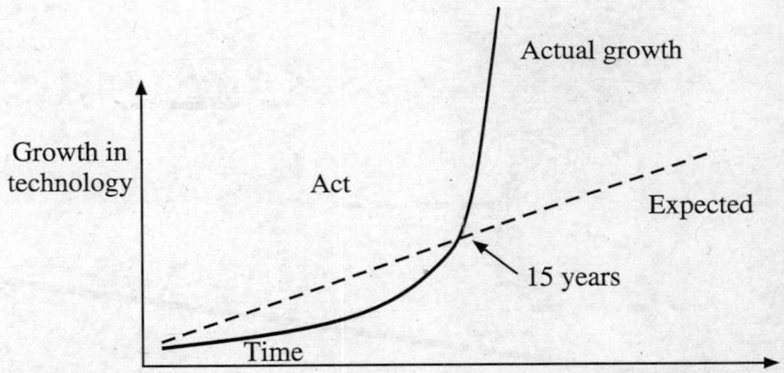

FIGURE 12.2 Amara's Law explained.

Leading Analyst firm Gartner (www.gartner.com) also presents technology forecasting using Hype cycle which covers similar philosophy of short term disillusionment and long term bewilderment with technology. Gartner Hype cycle curve also plot emerging technology across the curve stating the time required for a technology to become a reality or become extinct due to new technology taking over or not found useful by the masses.

(b) **Moore's law:** The second law named after Intel cofounder Gordon E. Moore was published in an article April 19, 1965 in Electronics Magazine states that the computing power will double every eighteen months. This law encapsulated the miniaturization of electronics technology and packing of chips and thus processor speeds, or overall processing power for computers will double about every 18 month. This means that the cost of computing would drastically get reduced every 18 months.

(c) **Gilder's law:** is attributed to George Gilder, prolific author of several books including Telecosm (2000), The Silicon Eye (2006). He is also known as a prophet of the new technology age, who said that the total bandwidth of communication systems doubles every six months. So the computing power will double every 18 months, the network capacity would grow six times during the similar period. This is the underlying assumption of exponential use of network for business and entertainment.

(d) **Metcalfe's law:** was proposed by Robert Metcalfe founder of 3COM.Metcalf law states the impact of a telecommunications network is proportional to the square of the number of connected users of the system (n2). The end nodes can be computers, servers and/or connecting users. As a network grows, the value of being connected to it grows exponentially, while the cost per user remains the same or even reduces. So if I have only one mobile phone it is worthless but more and more people have mobile phone then they can talk easily and the number of combinations mathematically as the triangular number n(n–1)/2, which is asymptotically proportional to n2. Most social media sites usefulness is explained by this law where greater number of users with the service, the more valuable the service becomes. This is perhaps the reason why the new start up focus on customer acquisition even though they may not be earning real money.

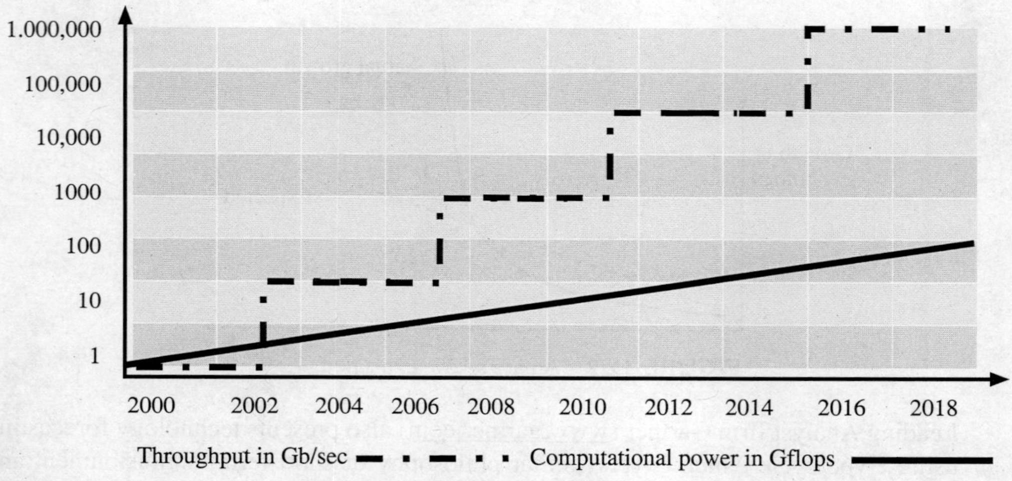

FIGURE 12.3 Moore's and Gilder Laws.
(*Source:* Gaivoronski, Svetlana & Gamayunov, Dennis (2013). Hide and Seek: Worms Digging at the Internet Backbones and Edges. 10.15514/SYRCOSE-2013–7–16).

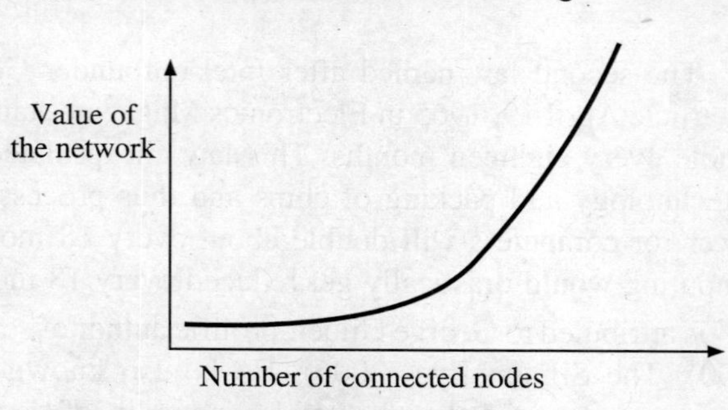

FIGURE 12.4 Metcalfe Law.

(e) **Hal Varian law:** is attributed to Hal Varian Google's chief economist Hal Varian who said that "A simple way to forecast the future is to look at what rich people have today; middle-income people will have something equivalent in 10 years, and poor people will have it in an additional decade"[7]. Hal Varian argues in the same breath that while today, rich people have chauffeurs, in 10 years or less, middle-income drivers will be able to afford robotic cars that drive themselves. Take the case of smart phone once considered luxury item is now readily and affordable to masses.

12.7 COMBINED EFFECT OF ALL THESE LAWS

The combined effect of all these laws are dramatic and compounded and give a spiralling impact. Kocovic(2008)[8] argues that they together produce spiralling effect. That is why some changes which seem to be at nebulous stage become so rapid that it takes a disruptive proportion impacting industries, people and society. For example social media platform Facebook, founded in 2004 by two Harvard University students Mark Zuckerberg and Eduardo Saverin has over 2.4 B active users (2018) and its Net income is $5.14bn for the third quarter of 2018. Its IPO raised $16 billion, making it the third largest in U.S. history and catapulted as the 4th most valuable brand in the world with a value of $94.8bn. It has spent well over $22.4 billion buying competitors such as Instagram, WhatsApp, and Oculus. It has become not only the platform of sharing personal news and photographs but a platform for gaming and business. It also came into criticism for sharing (or leaking[9]) user data which were used to impact several national election results.

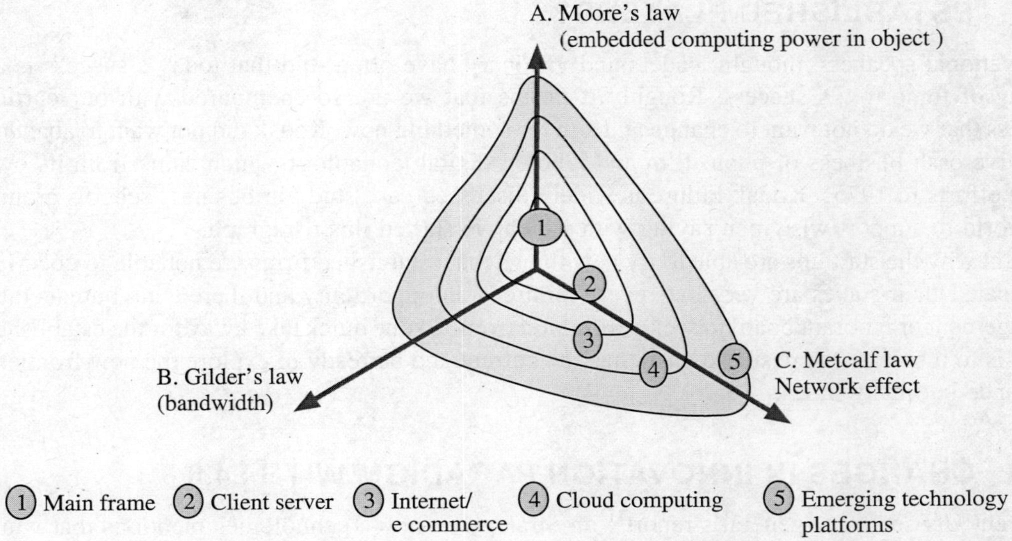

FIGURE 12.5 Combined effect of three laws, Moore's, Gilder and Metcalf.

---

[7]https://foreignpolicy.com/2011/08/15/micromultinationals-will-run-the-world/ accessed 14092019

[8]http://www.scielo.org.mx/pdf/jart/v6n3/v6n3a1.pdf accessed 17062019

[9]https://timesofindia.indiatimes.com/india/over-half-a-million-indian-facebook-users-may-have-been-affected-in-data-breach/articleshow/63625675.cms accessed 22082019

The combination of Emerging technology such as AI ML IOT and many others which we will describe in our subsequent chapters have created a truly spiralling effect for new entrants such as Facebook, Alibaba and many others. It has stunned the old economy companies and led to possible closure of many if not losing their market share.

Take another case of Alibaba[10], a Chinese company started in 1999 named after the character from Arabian Nights. Alibaba created a history by becoming the second Asian company to cross the $500 billion valuation ($527 billion) in January 2018. It is world's largest and most valuable retailer crossing the likes of Walmart, Amazon, and eBay. Alibaba business of B2B is now grown beyond ecommerce and covers movie production, music and movie streaming, online learning, microblogging, travel booking, mobile apps, online maps, and so much more. A new star is born in China.

India also has its success story of rapid growth and market expansion. Flipkart in ecommerce space which has been now acquired by Walmart, Paytm now funded by Alibaba founder Jack Ma, OYO rooms, OLA cab aggregator, Zomato and many others.

The question which remains unanswered is that why these start-ups are able to do such miracles which the established companies in each of these domains are not able to do. This is a topic of discussion to suggest how any company can usher similar changes using the concepts and practices of Digital Transformation. We will also need to understand what capabilities are required to be build or rebuild within any firm to be able to drive the transformation process.

12.8 IS IT ADVANTAGE TO STARTUPS OR HANDICAP TO ESTABLISHED PLAYERS?

Motivational speakers, thought leaders and visionary have often said that today's success is an enemy of tomorrow's success. Roughly it means that we are so enamoured with our current success that we do not want to change and aim for something new. Kodak did not want to abandon lucrative cash business of photo film and ignored digital technology which came from its own R&D efforts in 1975!. Kodak failure is widely discussed case study in business schools around the world to support wise men saying with which we started this paragraph.

But why the start ups are able to try new things that established firms are not able to do? May be because their stakes are very low, every failure is an opportunity and there is no bureaucratic management or ignorant board to seek permission from. So one quick take away for the established firms is to inculcate the desire to challenge the current and be ready to explore the new frontiers. Not once but many times.

12.9 CHANGES IN INNOVATION PARADIGM WITH I 4.0

A recent UN secretary-general's report[11] on Strategy on new Technologies mentions that while New and rapidly developing technologies such as artificial intelligence, biotechnology, material sciences and robotics hold incredible promise for the advancement of human welfare. They also hold the potential to generate more inequality and more violence.

[10] https://yourstory.com/2018/02/the-story-behind-the-alibaba-group accessed 22082019

[11] https://www.un.org/en/newtechnologies/images/pdf/SGs-Strategy-on-New-Technologies.pdf accessed 11092019

Accordingly the new technology must ensure the following:

(a) Protect and promote global values
(b) Foster inclusion and transparency
(c) Work in partnership
(d) Build on existing capabilities and mandates
(e) Be humble and continue to learn

Emerging technologies have great potential for increased productivity and growth. However, it is time to consider seriously its impact on human well-being as well. The new wave of Innovation, call it Innovation 4.0, must also ensure reduced disruption and potentially destabilizing effects on society. A Mckinsey report[12] gives emphasis on innovation-led growth and careful management of the workforce and other transitions related to technology adoption and diffusion.

Arguably, the purpose of technology and Innovation is to bring betterment in the society. Yet in the past its negative effects did undermine the positives it brought. Nuclear energy once considered a source of world power in the future is no longer a preferred choice due to environmental and health hazards as well at unforeseen damages during any man made or natural disaster. Many manufacturing and mining towns have become depleted as it shifted base to low cost countries like china and Philippines. Reckless automation may bring heightened risks of unemployment and social change. Technology and innovation must consider how to downside effects of technology adoption, both in the short and longer term.

12.10 USHERING INNOVATION 4.0

Reaching Innovation 4.0 stage is not just applying few emerging technology at few places and touting them in newspaper interviews but fundamental change in the way firms have to operate. The most important change of inculcating the desire for doing social goods has already been mentioned. Because if there is no desire to transform for social goods no amount of effort is going to help the society.

One could argue that the Innovation 1.0 was about closed innovation of isolated products, services or processes using limited technology using a controlled closed group of people. People are the source of innovation and the scale at which we utilize their innovative capability determines the usefulness and adoptability of the innovation. At the most primitive level in legacy firms typically the R&D section, Methods study department, few research scholars would bring about innovation. The rest would be asked to implement and adopt whatever may be the consequences. These restrictive approached of the past were challenged by adopting Open innovation also called Innovation 2.0. The role of technology in innovation is enabler, facilitator, sometime idea generator and invariably as implementer. Further progress in this direction took place to seek the wisdom of crowd which included stakeholders such as consumer, supplier and sales channel partner. The innovation can and should happen across the value chain of any firm and the sources of good ideas can come from any quarter. This development is called Innovation 3.0.

As we progress further, the next wave which is waiting to take over is the about larger inclusive perspective of innovation inclusive of social and environmental issues. So it is now the

---

[12] https://www.mckinsey.com/~/media/mckinsey/featured%20insights/future%20of%20organizations/tech%20for%20good%20using%20technology%20to%20smooth%20disruption%20and%20improve%20well%20being/tech-for-good-mgi-discussion-paper.ashx accessed 12092019

innovation of the eco system and society involving all stake holders in not only generating idea but participating in all the stages of the innovation journey. Call it Innovation for social good or Innovation 4.0, this phase is the next likely phase which is being promoted by few national government and industry associations.

The role of technology also changes from just being a support and facilitator to driver and disruptor. It is already happening in some industries like Retail, Media, Travel and Transportation but likely to be all pervasive. Technology has made impressionable improvement on products and processes. Information technology in particular was more effective on process innovation. With Services being the mainstay of our society, Information Technology became an integral part of the services value chain and source of innovation. While it was being used in isolated manner which changed over the years to integrated support and digitization of functions. The latest wave commensurate to cyber physical system also called Industry 4.0 is about using IT for transforming the enterprise, also called Digitalization or Digital Transformation or Innovation 4.0. IT is no longer a just a support infrastructure but the mainstream function for most progressive firms across industries.

Innovation 4.0 is no longer an isolated phenomenon which is the preserve of few people or organization. Given a proper stimulus, building skills and training using right methodology and support infrastructure Innovation can lead to transformation, a total change.

Our target of innovation is also shifting from Products to process and largely to services. Disruptive innovation are seen as ecosystem innovation that define new boundaries, new players and new rules of the game. The services innovation is the order of the day as more and more products are being consumes as services which need innovated processes. But disruptive innovations like solar or battery powered autonomous cars can bring about unbelievable ecosystem changes.

Finally as we progress further the innovation has to lead to ecosystem innovation where the degree of transformation and the commensurate benefits would be much higher.

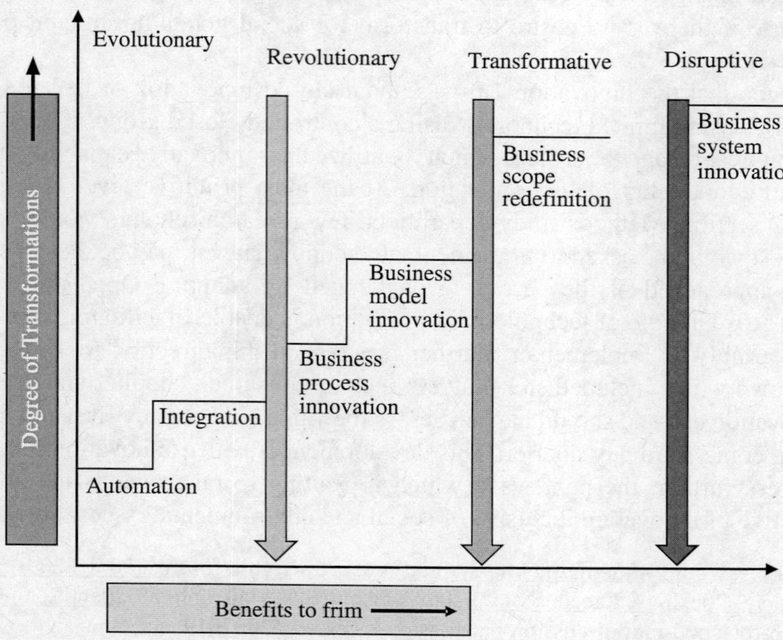

FIGURE 12.6 Stages of Technology Led Innovation.

Establishing an innovation culture is the key: Remember organization Digital Transformation of 4.0 variety assumes that technology would play a major role to institutionalize the innovation process supported by leadership. You can read the Story and Learning Task (SALT 10.1) and find why Google despite being big is able to behave like a start-up and able to innovate in totally Diverse areas such as solar-powered contact lenses to pills that search your body for disease as well as driverless cars. Such projects not only highly ambitious but if they succeed it will make game-changing impact on humanity for the better.

SALT 12.1: How Google despite its size continues to innovate relentlessly?

By visiting google website[13] one gets some interesting insight. You find Google founder and chairman Eric Schmidt saying "The story of innovation has not changed. It has always been a small team of people who have a new idea, typically not understood by people around them and their executives". True to this philosophy, Google outlines the following mantra's for Creating a Culture of Innovation.

(a) **Think 10x:** In order to achieve true innovation try to improve by 10 times rather than by 10%.

(b) **Launch, then keep listening:** Like soft launch of a restaurant business where they invite friendly people in to learn and improve. Google resorts to beta launches (soft launch) and makes rapid iterations to improve

(c) **Share everything you can:** This means collaboration is essential to innovation and by sharing information openly.

(d) **Hire the right people:** Easier said than done, but Google is working hard to attract right people to tackle big problems by structure hiring process to tap the "wisdom of the crowd" during referral, screening and interview process.

(e) **Use the 70/20/10 model:** Google project mix is 70% of dedicated to core business, 20% related to core business and 10% unrelated to our core business. The last one helps them to bring in new opportunities for future.

(f) **Look for ideas everywhere:** Google routinely crowdsources innovation ideas to improve. A case improving quality of Google Maps, Google created a platform where users could provide the missing data (Google Map Maker), to make changes to Google Maps.

(g) **Use data, not opinions:** Google uses data for making every choice, for example Googlegeist, an anonymous survey tool with over 90% of Googlers respond collects data about broad range of issues—like employee wellbeing, culture, managers, compensation, work-life balance, diversity and career opportunities.

(h) **Focus on users, not the competition:** Google penchant for relentless desire to improve the lives of users. They believe that any product can be improved by simply focusing on how to make life even better for users, simple!

[13]https://gsuite.google.co.in/intl/en in/learn-more/creating a culture of innovation. Accessed 10092019

12.11 SOCIETAL VALUE OF INNOVATION 4.0

One must not forget that the companies and businesses exist for the society and any such change howsoever useful on the face must have necessary safe guards respecting individual, society and environmental concerns. Some of the use and misuse of the technology in public life has created huge uproar from the community leaders and social activity groups. No society is without aberration or differences but as far as human values are concerned profit cannot be put before people interest. This book is not about arousing dangers of technology led innovation but about positives of it. Yet it may suffice to say that all technology may have its negative consequences if used improperly, excessively or by ill motive. I recommend technology innovators to consider necessary safeguards, even if it is just a warning sign, to be built while releasing the products. The larger users are ignorant of the consequences of new technology and tools and they should not the pay the price of being victims who forced corrections and safeguards.

The new approach for tackling the complex challenges our society faces by combining government, industry, academia, and civil societies to participate, share multidisciplinary viewpoints through team working, collaboration and the sharing of ideas. This is also described as quadruple helix approach that benefits all participants of the innovation ecosystem as shown in Figure 12.7.

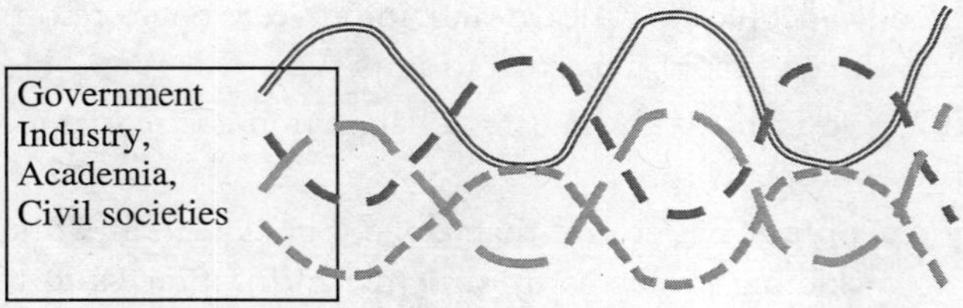

FIGURE 12.7 Quadruple Helix approach.

In the process of mad rush to innovate and use technology for commercial success, we should not forget the very purpose of technology and innovation, which is to cause good for the society in all respect. Businesses have ignored society as its prime stake holder and have focused on profit and profit alone, ignoring other stakeholders. It is the society in which any business comes from and business have to work for its benefit. Unfortunately emerging technology have largely ignored the aspects of misuse and protecting the ignorant users from ill effects. The physical technology is well known for causing damages to environment and eco system and much has come in the purview of laws and regulation, some heavily punished for their misdeeds.

There are many lurking dangers of emerging technology that is being hailed as disruptive and leading to obscene profits for few (there are many such examples in the recent past), yet the ill effects are neither visualized nor adequate safe guards are built from any ill consequences.

It is like designing a fastest car without adequate and powerful break, seat belts, air bags and many other safety features that have become mandatory as human race and governing authorities have learnt lessons and acted wiser. Emerging technologies are fast growing, ill effects not yet understood, cautionary systems not yet in place (remember the Skull and crossbones sign for 440 volt current !) but being readily promoted by all. It is like releasing untested drugs without any authentic clinical trial or body implants being put without knowing how it can be safely extracted should it mismatches with a human body.

12.12 LEADERSHIP IN FOURTH INDUSTRIAL SOCIETY

World economic forum report[14] on fourth Industrial revolution underlines the changing role of leadership. Not only the leadership has to be inclusive and balanced towards all stakeholders of the business including society but also to show the path to its team to follow the same. It describes the six dimensions of the leadership covering.

(a) Responsibility and accountability towards all stake holders,
(b) Developing a shared vision and collaborative action across world/ecosystem
(c) Understanding and harnessing the unprecedented impact of Technology
(d) Entrepreneurial mind set in all deeds.
(e) Adaptive leadership which relies on experimentation, learn faster than the world, abandon old behaviours, habits and beliefs. Instead of "pilot and perfect" model the better choice make "progress than look for perfection."
(f) Shaping societies by allowing inclusive participation to positively impact by proactively address rising concerns about inequality, social tensions, political fragmentation and the protection of the environment.

12.13 SUMMARY

This chapter was to examine the role of technology and Innovation in the era of fourth Industrial revolution and Industry 4.0. We defined the term fourth industrial revolution and Industry 4.0 by pointing out the difference and the philosophy behind them. We underlined that such massive and disruptive transformation cannot just happen for one organization or two, but has to happen across the ecosystem for its benefits. We also traced the evolution of initial three revolutions and what were the underlying factors. All revolutions including the fourth revolution, are driven by technology component. The latest one is driven by emerging technology impacting across various aspects of human life–work, business, home, Governments and Society. Fourth Industrial Revolution is amalgamation of the physical, digital, and biological worlds using advances in cloud computing, artificial intelligence (AI), Big Data Analytics, robotics, Iot/IIoT, 3D printing, AR/VR, genetic engineering etc. Industry 4.0 and fourth Industrial revolution is sometimes used interchangeably. However Industry 4.0 is one part of Fourth industrial revolution that has wider impact across industry and society, for example smart cities.

We then examined the Five Laws of Emerging Technology and traced their Combined effect. The combination of Emerging technology such as AI ML IOT and many others have created a truly spiralling effect for new entrants such as Facebook, Alibaba and many others. It has stunned the old economy companies and led to possible closure of many if not losing their market share.

We then explained the Changes in Innovation paradigm with I4.0. Here the concept of keeping the larger role of society was underlined. Because the emerging technology potential impact and concerns are equally daunting. Emerging technologies has great potential for increased productivity and growth. However, we must also ensure its reduced disruption and potentially destabilizing effects on society.

[14]http://www3.weforum.org/docs/WEF_Leading_through_the_Fourth_Industrial_Revolution.pdf accedd 12092019

This was followed by describing the approach for Ushering Innovation 4.0. We identified further progress in this direction to seek the wisdom of crowd which included stakeholders such as consumer, supplier and sales channel partner called Innovation 3.0. Finally the next wave Innovation 4.0 waiting to take over is the about larger inclusive perspective of innovation inclusive of social and environmental issues. Here the role of technology also changes from just being a support and facilitator to driver and disruptor of the eco system. Innovation 4.0 is no longer an isolated phenomenon which is the preserve of few organization.

We further established that creating an innovation Culture is the key. And gave example as to how Google despite its size continues to innovate relentlessly.

The Societal value of Innovation 4.0 was discussed further. We discussed the new approach for tackling the complex challenges our society faces by combining government, industry, academia, and civil societies to participate, share multidisciplinary viewpoints through team working, collaboration and the sharing of ideas.

Finally we concluded with a short inputs of leadership traits expected in the fourth industrial revolution.

Key Terms: Fourth industrial revolution, Industry 4.0, Innovation 4.0, Quadruple Helix, Amara's Law, Moore's law, Metcalf law, Gilder's law, Hal Varian's Law.

CASE STUDY A

Paytm growth in India 2000–2020: A case of continuous eco system innovation

India during the first decade of this century underwent a major mobile revolution. There were many operators and the country was divided into 23 telecom circles or service areas as of July 2018. These circles are further grouped into 4 groups. Densely populated cities like Delhi, Kolkata, and Mumbai are called 'metro circles' and then 'A', 'B', and 'C' circles. A telecom circle covers the entire state normally but exceptions do exit like Mumbai which includes Goa. Jharkhand is a part of the Bihar zone but Uttar Pradesh is divided into east and west zones. Delhi circle includes Gurgaon and Faridabad of Haryana and Noida and Ghaziabad from Uttar Pradesh.

India's total mobile subscribers base as on December 2002 was barely 10.5 millions. But growing competition and proactive initiatives taken by regulators and licensors this base led to rapid expansion to over 929 million subscribers as of May 2012. In 2019 May this number has swelled to 1.161 billion.

Mobile phones which were originally thought to be a means of voice communication not only become affordable, thanks to lowering of call rates by the operators to woo customers but also became a source of several innovation. Indians are known to find innovative applications the simplest one is leaving a missed call from your registered mobile number of your bank account to a designated number of the bank which will respond with account balance. Some other services like ordering a cheque book by making a missed call to another designated number of the bank from your registered mobile number falls under this category. As he technology moved to 3G and 4G and more and more value added services started to come up like downloading ring tone of your choice or setting up a caller tune of your choice by paying a small fee to the telecom operator.

Most of these value added services (VAS) were the creative output of start-up companies. In order to reach their target customers these companies would have to approach the telecom operators who would let them use their infrastructure and share the revenue at times in 60 : 40 percentage where the lower share will be given to the start-up companies.

In March 2013 Idea Cellular launched a balance transfer facility – BUDDY RECHARGE. This allowed friends to transfer their prepaid balance to their friends at small fee. For each ₹5 transfer Idea started charging ₹2.[15] The seed of payment wallet has just been sown only it took some time to become legally accepted as means of payment to merchants.

A brief look at Paytm a well-known mobile wallet and now a full-fledged M commerce platform reflects the trajectory of Mobile revolution in India.

Mr Vijay Shekhar Sharma founded Paytm in August 2010 with an initial investment of $2 in Noida (NCR New Delhi). Mr Sharma came from a humble background of school teacher parents and studied his schooling in Hindi. While he could get admission in Delhi College of Engineering, a prestigious institute, he was at a loss to meet the educational standards as all teaching was in English medium. Through sheer hard work he found solution to cope up with English language challenge. This also forced him to spend a lot of time in the Computer Room, browsing the internet and dreaming about being in Silicon Valley entrepreneur. He built his first company-'XS Communications', created Content Management Systems.

The initial services of Paytm was prepaid recharge for prepaid mobile and DTH. Further it added data card, post-paid mobile and landline bill payments by 2013. Paytm wallet was launched in January 2014 where one could buy railway tickets and pay for Uber rides. They did not stop here but continued to add new services such as bus ticketing (2015), paying education fees, metro recharges, and electricity, gas, and water bill payments. 2016 was major turnaround year for Paytm who launched movies, events and amusement parks ticketing along with as well as flight ticket bookings. By 2016 its user base more than 100 million, and its travel business alone over $500 million in annualised GMV. Using prompt presence of mind and past advertisement experience of Mr Sharma welcomed Government of India's demonetization announcement with full front page newspaper advertisement the next morning of the announcement in Nov 2016. Paytm become synonymous to the mobile wallets in India and its advert. with tag line PayTM karo (i.e. do Paytm) was much talked about by the masses.

In 2017, Paytm crossed over 100 million app downloads and became the first company to achieve this feat. It continues its innovated addition of services like online Gold purchase for as little as ₹1. It soon metamorphosed into Paytm Payments Bank when it received a license from Reserve Bank of India. It allowed merchants to accept Paytm, UPI and card payments directly into their bank accounts at 0% charge. Paytm further launched its M commerce market place where its subscribers can buy from 1.4 lakh registered sellers. Paytm has investors such Alibaba Group and SAIF Partners in March, 2018 and it was awarded with Outstanding Start-up of the Year Award at Forbes Leadership in 2016.

Questions:

1. What are reasons which are responsible for Paytm growth? Identify them as external factors as well as internal efforts to innovate.
2. Research the internet and read some of the start-up innovators story.

---

[15]https://telecomtalk.info/idea-launches-buddy-recharge-share-your-balance-with-friends-free-facebook-data-to-nokia-asha-205/105435/ accessed 09092019

CASE STUDY B

Creating a Global Edutech start-up from India, Byju

Affordable quality education in India is still a distance dream. A widely large geography with rural and semi urban population located at far flung places often face the challenges of providing even basic education. Many small school going children have to walk few kilometres and at time cross small rivers or hilly areas. The proximity aside the schools in rural areas struggle with lack of good quality teachers and trainers. The good part is that Indian parents have strong desire for their children to study and support them beyond their means in most cases.

Under class 12 education (K-12 kindergarten-Class XII) is highly competitive in India. Admission in good colleges and universities are through competitive examinations where the seats are limited. On an average and IIT admission test will have over 10 lacs students appearing for approximately 30 thousand seats.

One change has happened in the recent past which was due to massive growth of Mobile phones usages. With cheaper data connectivity the access to content using mobile phones has increased manifold. According to a published report nearly 20 million children between Classes VI and XII in India have access to the Internet and take private coaching classes. Such students can use on line classes with an addressable market opportunity of about $2.5 billion.

This is an opportunity that the innovative entrepreneurs like Khan Academy and Byju targeted and have become a house hold names in education sector.

Byju Raveendran story of foraying into edutech start-up has several twists and turns. His induction into coaching and training was purely by accident when in 2003 he was back in India while working UK-based shipping firm on vacation for few months. Initially his desire was to help some of his friends appearing for Combined Admission Test for IIMs (CAT) in Bangalore which prompted him to take exam, and he scored amazingly 100 percentile.

Buoyant with the success he continued teaching informally his friends, and appeared in CAT again 2005 without any preparation, and scored a perfect 100 percentile. While he also cleared the interview of IIM-A, B, C but his inner calling was in the potential in teaching students how to crack CAT. Through word of mouth publicity the number of students grew and he started teaching 1000 students in an auditorium back in 2007. In an interview[16] he said that they had to innovate their teaching through visualisation and conceptualisation predicting what kind of doubts may have in the minds of the students as the interaction was not possible for such a large audience. By 2009 his coverage increased to 9 cities where he travelled regularly.

Byju formed his company for under K-12 education in 2011 using online format. The app-based format took 4 years to create these products. They made the learning interesting with interactive videos.

The app-based model has several advantages as the app also begins to understand the student learning behaviour and make it more personalised learning. Now it is used across India, not just limited to metros, but also small towns. Byju app works on use freemium business model where certain content is free but for accessing all one has to pay a charge. His company Think and Learn Pvt. Ltd, has raised $204 million from venture investors Aarin Capital, Chan Zuckerberg.

---

[16] https://www.firstpost.com/tech/news-analysis/the-story-of-byjus-from-a-small-village-in-kerala-to-creating-a-global-edutech-startup-from-india-3688455.html accessed 09092019

It had more than 320,000 active users and those buying premium service is growing every month as claimed by the company. If they tap early they will have a four to seven-year association with the same user.

Byju says "I am of the opinion that a business cannot be driven by the passion to make money. The passion to change society is far more important." Noble thought indeed!

Questions:

1. How do you see spotting the innovative opportunity in the success story of Byju?
2. What is the role technology has played in Byju's success? Do you think this is like any other technology use? Answer your question after viewing Byju's app.

REVIEW QUESTIONS

1. Trace the development of Fourth Industrial revolution and the underlying elements that have led to this development.
2. What is Industry 4.0 and how it is different from Fourth Industrial revolution?
3. What are likely dangers of emerging technology and how can we mitigate their risk?
4. What is concept of quadruple helix and why is it used?

ADDITIONAL READINGS

1. http://www3.weforum.org/docs/WEF_Leading_through_the_Fourth_Industrial_Revolution.pdf
2. Dreams and Details (Hardcover) – 2018 by Jim Hagemann Snabe (Author), Mikael Trolle

Chapter 13 Design Thinking for Innovation

If a picture is worth a thousand words, a prototype is worth a thousand meetings.

—IDEO.org

At the end of this chapter, we will learn:

- What is Design thinking and why is gaining so much of popularity in the recent times.
- Brief history of evolution of Design thinking concepts
- Design thinking process and its unique characteristics
- Success stories and case studies
- Challenges and remedial measures while adopting Design thinking

13.1 INTRODUCTION

Design thinking has caught attention of managers and management thinkers in the recent times. As the world is becoming increasingly competitive, customers want more and more innovative products, services and processes. Those companies that marketed innovative products or services after gaining good insight of customer requirement did better than the rest of the industry peers. Apple is credited to have used Design thinking approach[1] while coming out with path breaking iPhone and other iSeries products.

This chapter will explain various aspect of Design Thinking as a discipline to steer innovation in an organization. We will discuss how Design Thinking is no longer confined to just design products features but can be used much widely. Design Thinking is an accepted disciplined approach to innovate various functions of the business right from Business Strategy, Planning, Process resign, product and process innovation and many others.

Design Thinking adoption is rapidly growing across industry verticals like manufacturing retail, health care, education and many others. We will discuss various prevalent Design Thinking approaches followed by leading researchers and practicing organization and would recommend

[1]https://www.designorate.com/design-thinking-case-study-innovation-at-apple/ accessed 09102019

our readers to take the best suited for their organization. Finally we will outline the challenges and mitigation strategies while adopting Design Thinking.

13.2 HISTORY OF DESIGN THINKING

The discipline Design thinking has gained momentum in the recent times due to some very prominent use cases led by leading companies and thinkers. However, the origin of Design thinking can be traced to 50s and 60s when R. Buckminster Fuller[2] an American architect-inventor at MIT published several papers and books on Design Sciences. His work as a 'comprehensive anticipatory design scientist' to solve global problems was noticed by the scientific community.

Later Scandinavian famous Utopia project[3] (1981–1985), where Co-operative Design involving users at very early in the design process was advocated. This was later reincarnated as Participative design.

As shown in Figure 13.1, Design thinking is the culmination of several research projects across the world over that last 50 years where the importance of design method as tool for improvement is advocated bringing along many disciplines such as Industrial design, social sciences, economics, Strategy, computer sciences and information architecture.

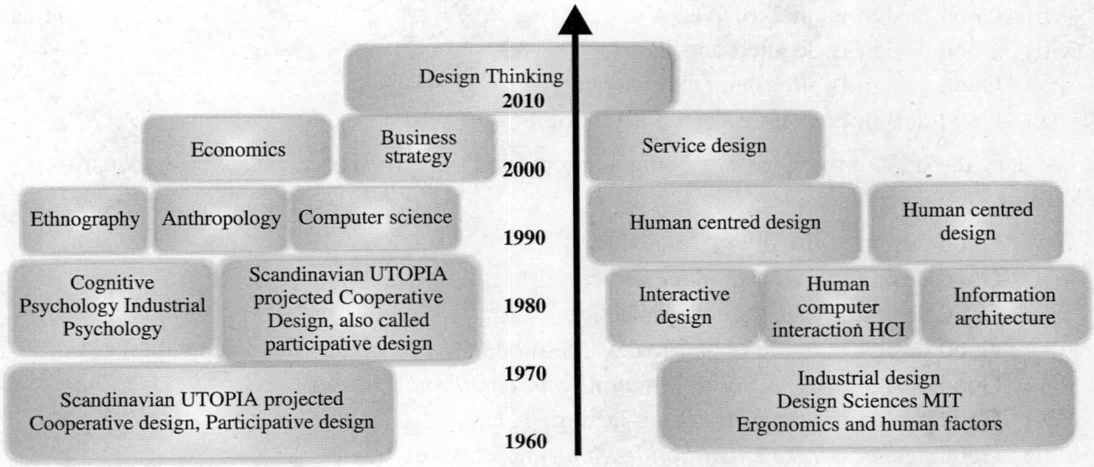

FIGURE 13.1 History of Design Thinking.

13.3 WHAT CONSTITUTES A GOOD DESIGN?

The reinvention of Apple from being desktop/laptop company to premium smartphone designers and manufacturer (marketer!) in early 21 century also underlines that good design of product is no longer a nice to have feature but a sustainable competitive advantage. Start-up companies

---

[2]https://medium.com/@szczpanks/design-thinking-where-it-came-from-and-the-type-of-people-who-made-it-all-happen-dc3a05411e53 accessed 29092019

[3]https://www.researchgate.net/publication/237225075 Cooperative Design-perspectives on 20 years with' the Scandinavian IT Design Model accessed 29092019

have shown that with prowess of good design they could disrupt existing business and become most loved by their customers and stakeholders. These companies like Uber, Airbnb, OLA, OYO and many others thought innovatively to serve the customers using similar functionalities already available but offering creatively design services without making any massive investment of capital in acquiring assets.

Defining "good design" becomes hugely important in current times, however this definition is also hard to achieve as design always remains subjective. In 1970, Dieter Rams (b.1932) a leading German industrial designer, credited for the innovative success of German brand Braun, and pioneer of functionalism movements of the industrial design, proposed 10 principles of good design, widely acclaimed as ten commandments of good design by designer community and researchers. These ten principles are.

(i) Good design is innovative
(ii) Good design makes a product useful
(iii) Good design is aesthetic
(iv) Good design is intuitive and makes the product understandable
(v) Good design is honest
(vi) Good design is long-lasting
(vii) Good design is unobtrusive
(viii) Good design is detailed and thorough
(ix) Good design is environmental friendly
(x) Good design is as little design as possible

Of late the 1970 principles are being reinterpreted[4] to suit the current world scenario as follows:

(i) Good design is *disruptive* (innovative).
(ii) Good design makes a product *addicting* (useful)
(iii) Good design is *A/B testing* (aesthetic)
(iv) Good design is intuitive and makes the product *collect data* (understandable)
(v) Good design is *agreeing to the terms and condition* (honest)
(vi) Good design is *temporary* (long-lasting)
(vii) Good design is *Like silent notification* (unobtrusive)
(viii) Good design is a prototype (thorough – down to the last detail)
(ix) Good design is environmental friendly
(x) Good design is as little design as possible

13.4 A GOOD DESIGN ALWAYS SURPRISES A CUSTOMER AND MEETS UNSTATED NEEDS

We usually get attracted by a product or services when we find that it is taking care of some of our unstated needs. Take the case of additional feature of a parking assistant in the high end cars.

[4]Source Tobias VAN SCHNEIDER @vanschneider Designer, Maker & Founder http://Semplice.com

While most cars are designed for the primary task of driving from point A to B, safety and fuel economy, the customer would want more features than those meeting these primary needs. So car manufacturers added features like Air-conditioning, Air bags, side bars, rear view mirrors, fuel gage etc. Yet there are many needs that still remain unstated and unmet. Voice operated side window or parking assistance are latest addition. Voice operated side window helps the passenger to raise or lower the window in hands-free mode and parking assistant helps to park car in a narrow space. Collision detecting proximity sensors beep when the car comes closer to an object to prevent collision. Such features are huge hit amongst non-proficient car drivers who are not skilled enough to navigate in the smaller space as well as a proficient drivers who now have an additional features to make their driving easier.

13.5 WHAT IS DESIGN THINKING?

In simple terms Design thinking is applying innovative ideas to solve problems and find opportunities to delight the customers. Design thinking involves following a disciplined approach to seek solution to end user needs and while doing so challenge the assumptions and redefine them in an attempt to identify alternative strategies and solutions which may not be very apparent initially. But all this is done in an iterative, visual and participative process involving a diverse set of team members who bring different perspectives to solve the problems or find hidden opportunities.

The interesting aspect of Design Thinking is that it not only to be used by the designers as the name may sound but can be used across industry and people with various expertise. Design Thinking is effective in technology products development, education curriculum development, designing various types of services or manufacturing. This process leads to new product and services for customers or improved processes and ensures productivity gains for the organization. The Design thinking process can help transform various functions of the organization such as Manufacturing, services, HR, finance, sales and marketing.

David Kelley who founded IDEO, a leading global design firm widely known for the popularizing Design thinking approach says[5] that design thinking is a human-centred approach to innovation that draws from the designer's toolkit to integrate the needs of people, the possibilities of technology, and the requirements for business success. Design Thinking approach combines people, technology and business aspect while designing any solution. Ultimately the products and services must be developed to address customers explicit as well as implicit needs, the innovative use of technology is needed to achieve the business benefits.

Design thinking has once again underlined the customer as the starting point of any innovation journey of developing solutions. Some of the values imbibed by design thinking approach is empathy, diversity, and allowance for ambiguity. Design thinking approach advocates using multidisciplinary teams while arriving at a solution. One of the central theme of design thinking approach is experimentation and acceptance of failure as necessary part of experimentation.

Design Thinking seeks to find a solution to problems by developing greater understanding of the people for whom products or services are being developed. This approach helps in making keen observation and develop empathy with the target user.

[5]https://www.ideou.com/pages/design-thinking accessed 210919

Interactive Design Foundation[6], an organization devoted to promote Design thinking explains that Design Thinking Process is a blend of Heart, Head and Hand. It includes vision, customer needs, emotion and feeling as the component of heart during empathise phase. This is followed with cognitive processing of ideation and evaluation. Finally the use of hand is depicted by practical creation of a workable product and services.

13.6 WHY DESIGN THINKING APPROACH?

For most of us innovation or creativity is an act of serendipity. Either one is born with creative instinct or not. Even major scientific discovery is often attributed to chance factor when an inventor comes across something unusual while trying to discover something else. Scientific community is full of anecdotal account of how such and such discovery happened just because something else unexplained happened. Sony Walkman is attributed to a missing recording feature of a product lot of record players or Post-it was discovered by 3M when a weak composition of glue was accidently developed.

Yet innovative minds have always been interested in streamlining the process of innovation through a rigorous practice so that a predictable outcome can be obtained. While creativity will still be spark of a moment in one's mind yet it needs to kindle through a method of questioning or stimulation. This is precisely the reason of using approaches like Design Thinking.

Design thinking enable people to become creatively confident as they practice a process and see the results for themselves. The methods and techniques of design thinking enable the minds to energize in new way of thinking. This confidence helps people to work through ambiguous situations and tackle complex (wicked!) problems.

Design Thinking is not a fad or likely to be passed over soon. It will remain relevant till the time creativity remains the mainstay of successfully navigating a complex world.[7] Design thinking is not a recipe book following which one can find creative conclusion quickly to the problems. It is a rigorous practice that orients the organization to think innovatively in an customer centric manner while addressing problems or seeking new opportunities. In a recent HBR article[8] Jeanne Liedtka summarizes why design thinking a successful approach by narrating following reasons.

(a) By including user inputs while designing solutions it's likely to succeed more but most cases user themselves would not know what is right for them.

(b) Diversity improves solution due to better probing and improvisation. Care should be taken to ensure that Debate should not get unproductive or divisive.

(c) The gap between research and roll out gets narrower.

(d) Once insight of customer is gained then the team can agree on design criteria to arrive at solution. Critical success criteria need to be tested with deep realistic trials.

(e) Design thinking approach included in firm strategy brings focus to the customer as their goal to win over. Design thinking can be used as process to improve all products, processes and services.

---

[6]https://www.interaction-design.org/literature/article/design-thinking-a-quick-overview access 05102019

[7]IBM survey https://www-03.ibm.com/press/us/en/pressrelease/31670.wss accessed 21092019

[8]https://hbr.org/2018/09/why-design-thinking-works accessed 21092019

(f) Companies alike IDEO, Apple, Google and many others are using design thinking for their various activities. But it is not limited only to big companies alone, many small and medium enterprises are immensely benefited.

13.7 IDEO'S DESIGN THINKING APPROACH

In Dec 2012 Harvard Business Review article titled Reclaim Your Creative Confidence,[9] the authors Tom Kelley and David Kelley motivate its readers to ignite the creativity to solve pressing complex problems. Tom is the partner of famous design Firm IDEO and David its chairman and partner and founder of the Hasso Plattner Institute of Design at Stanford, where he is the Donald W. Whittier Professor in Mechanical Engineering. The current Design thinking discipline advocated by IDEO and its popularization is largely attributed of the work done by these two thinkers.

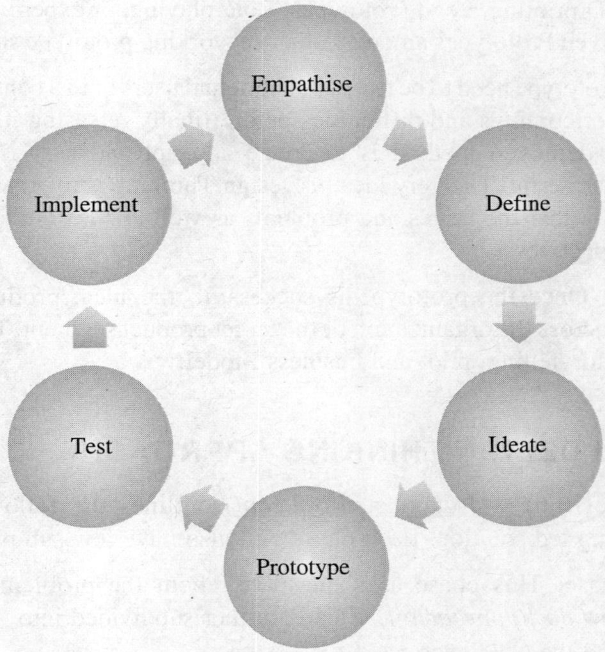

FIGURE 13.2 IDEO Design Thinking Stages.

Figure 13.2 shows the various stages of IDEO Design Thinking , However is iterative in nature.

1. **Empathise:** Understand the end customer needs and the way they operate and live. This phase can be further broken into three phases of Understand, Observe and creating a point of view. Using techniques like surveys, interviews, observation, demographic statistics, secondary data research and by conducting focus groups session the Design Thinking team develops empathy with customer problem and needs.

[9]https://hbr.org/2012/12/reclaim-your-creative-confidence accessed 29092019

2. **Define:** At this stage the team prioritizes the information collected in the first stage to aim at opportunities for improvement. The team uses techniques such as empathy maps, customer journey maps, Personas, or service blueprints.
3. **Ideate:** Now that the needs and opportunities have been identified and prioritized, the team ideates for possible solution. Thus is the time to generate ideas addressing customer needs both apparent and hidden as well as existing pain points.

   This stage usually is a group activity where the team brainstorms ideas and then prioritizes them. All technique that challenge the current situation is used to open up creative thinking like brainstorming, worst possible idea, Six thinking hats of Edward Debono, collaborative sketching, and product box.
4. **Prototype:** Now the time is to create a working prototype a reduced and inexpensive versions to implement the ideas captured at the earlier stage. The prototyping stage should be fast and inexpensive. Using a paper or cardboard models, low quality wireframes, 3D printing, Lego Prototypes, Role-playing, or experiential prototyping or even User-Driven Prototypes amongst others a working prototype should be developed.
5. **Test:** The prototype need to be tested by the actual users or in a controlled environment to find out shortcomings and difficulties before finally releasing it to larger audience. A commonly deployed method is to create a script and user is asked to perform according to the script. The very idea of Design Thinking is to create multidisciplinary group to ensure that the issues and problems as well as the solutions are tested from different perspectives.
6. **Implement:** Once the prototype is successful, the idea, product or services are implemented across the organization or the target product segment. This phase is further divided into storytelling, pilot and business Model.

13.8 STANFORD DESIGN THINKING APPROACH

Stanford Design School (https://dschool.stanford.edu/) outlines the following five steps to undertake design thinking led solution. Each phase will also have few sub phases. They are

(i) Discovery phase: This phase asks questions about the problem. It says *I have a challenge. How do I approach it?* This is further subdivided into
   (a) Understand the Challenge
   (b) Prepare Research
   (c) Gather Inspiration

(ii) Interpretation, here the questions asked are *I learned something. How do I interpret it?*
   (a) Tell Stories
   (b) Search for meaning
   (c) Frame Opportunities

(iii) Ideation: questions asked at this stage *I see an opportunity. What do I create?*
   (a) Generate Ideas
   (b) Refine Ideas

(iv) Experimentation: questions asked at this stage *I have an idea. How do I build it?*
   (a) Make Prototypes
   (b) Get Feedback
(v) Evolution: questions asked at this stage *I tried something new. How do I evolve it?*
   (a) Track Learnings
   (b) Move Forward

Stanford Design institute website has good resources available to help conduct workshop and process for design thinking, typically done by a diverse team all sitting together using charts and diagrams.

13.9 IBM DESIGN THINKING APPROACH

Like many adoptions of Design Thinking available, IBM's design thinking approach suggests a variation of the stages. IBM states that its Design Thinking methodology is a new way to solve today's problems at scale which is adapted for the unique needs of the modern enterprise. IBM thinking was that for large organization like them their need to tweak the IDEO approach which was considered more suitable for Small and medium size companies.

As shown in Figure 13.3 IBM stages of Design Thinking process has three major stages depicted in the form of continuous loop. These stages are:

- Observe to improve understanding about the problem
- Reflect on acquired knowledge on your own knowledge to adapt it into a plan
- Make, here covert the understanding gained into a prototype and an outcome

The recommended three principles are:

- Focus on user outcomes: by putting user needs as the priority a good design can be achieved
- Diverse Empowered Teams: ensures the participation of stockholders in the organization leading to faster and smarter output. IBM considers teamwork as source of developing Empathy: first with each other within the team and then with our users.
- Restless Innovation leads to using an iterative process to build prototyping solutions keeping in mind that nothing is perfect and hence a subject of restless iteration and development.

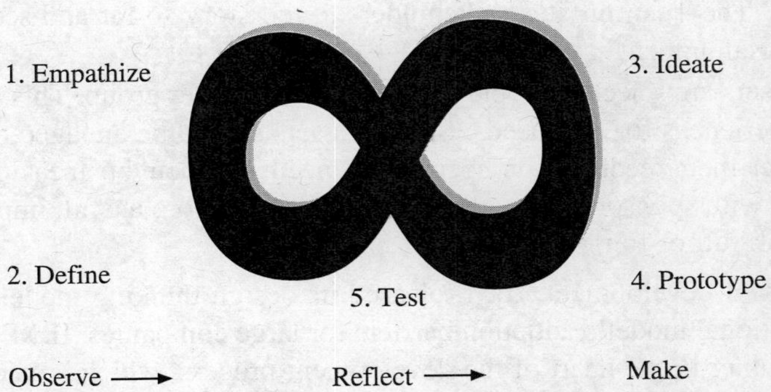

FIGURE 13.3 IBM's Design Thinking Continuous Loop.

IBM Design Thinking continuous loop is represented by a horizontal number 8 which entails understanding the present and envisioning the future through endless cycle of observing, reflecting, and making. It further recommends the following principles.

- Explore possibilities by identifying what works and what does not work by continuous churn of ideas.
- Communicate ideas using diagram or pictures so that people understand it.
- Prototype concepts to validate or invalidate hypotheses and assumptions. By using simple prototype, ideas can be simulated and hypothesis tested.
- Drive outcome when the idea is acceptable. It may not be picture perfect yet worth moving. The correction will be done as the things progress.

13.9.1 IBM Design Thinking Additional Features

While the loop approach is good for small projects, complex problems need collaborating across organization which have with complex teams.

IBM model aims for scalability and hence it proposes thee more techniques for scalability that can be used in large organization to make Design Thinking successful. These techniques are Hills, Playbacks, and Sponsor Users.

(a) The first technique is Hills which helps in clearly defining the objectives to the team by articulating "who," "what," and "wow." Late President John F. Kennedy of United States (USA) articulated the goal of moon mission as "landing a man on the Moon and returning him safely to Earth within a decade". Not only this defined who will do (American), "what" (man on the moon and returning back), and "wow" (safely within a decade).

(b) The Playback is the second technique to align an integrate teams to achieve the project target through regular meetings with the stockholders. Here stakeholders are involved reflect together the specific goals. This can be done for various stages such as for project Hills (Hills Playbacks), for proposed solution (Playback Zero) and for measuring progress delivery (Delivery Playbacks). Playbacks involving customer is called "Client Playbacks." Playback can be done in various forms such as one-on-one or with a larger group. Feedback is essential part of the Playback outcome which can be achieved using discussions, diagrams or demos. There is no frequency set but should be done at regular milestones. The Team invites stakeholders to tell story so far and seeks feedback and areas of misalignment.

(c) Sponsor Users are selected people from actual target user group. This will lead to better design experiences for real needs. Sponsor users should be engaged on a regular basis so as to get their feedback on specialized needs of their business domains. A good interaction with sponsor users will make the product more useful, implementation easy and the task full of fun.

After three years of development, IBM released its design thinking model with the goal of overcoming the traditional model's adoption barriers for large companies. IBM's design thinking model puts the consumer in the heart of the development process, which is known as the Loop. The Loop principles and techniques provide a practical approach to how to solve complex project problems with the consumer in mind, regardless of the size of the problem, the project, or the number of stakeholders.

13.10 UNIQUE CHARACTERISTICS OF DESIGN THINKING

The Design thinking process is not unique just for its process or rigor but the philosophy or spirit of the entire exercise. Author Daniel Ling who wrote a very successful book *Complete Design Thinking Guide*[10] summarizes the unique aspect of design thing as Design thinking utilizes both left and right brain thinking together in equal proportion. It combines logical, analytical functions, with imagination, creativity and emotions.

The 7 key unique characteristics of design thinking suggested by Daniel Ling are:

(i) It can be used by anyone across diverse background and profession, right from school students to industrial designers or civil servants. Basically they all wanted to solve a complex problem in an innovative way.

(ii) Its method enables empathy with people and understanding their problems which is the heart of Design Thinking process.

(iii) It gives more importance to first define the problem and then seek solution. Famous Quote of Albert Einstein states that out of 1 hour to solve problem he would spend 55 minutes defining the problem. Design thinking is not a series of steps to execute a solution but using these steps to energize the mind to understand a problem.

(iv) The solution is gradually ideated and explored using analysis ad synthesis. Here you first create divergent views to create various choices but finally converging on a solution.

(v) It is collaborative and involves iterative prototyping by creating a culture to encourage creativity and radical collaboration of people from diverse background.

(vi) It can be used to address problems of many different types which are human-centric and hard to defined problem. It also considers larger social and sustainable goals as well while creating solution.

(vii) The process is hugely interesting and fun to ensure people are light hearted mood and retain their creativity.

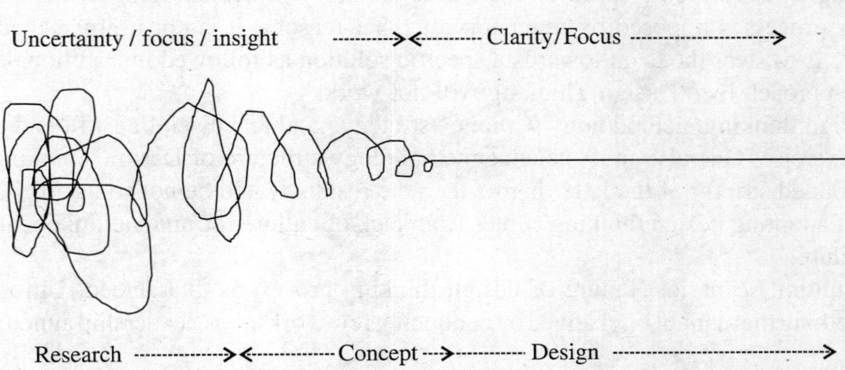

FIGURE 13.4 Progress of Design Thinking Process-exploratory to Clarity.

---

[10]https://www.amazon.in/Complete-Design-Thinking-Successful-Professionals-ebook/dp/B01BT3HT2I accessed 29092019

13.11 SUCCESS STORIES OF DESIGN THINKING

Noted author Jeanne Liedtka opined in a HBR Article[11] that Design thinking has the similar potential to do for innovation, exactly what TQM [total quality management] did for manufacturing. The success stories of Design Thinking lead projects are many. We will point out few of them for our readers' benefits but they are not exhaustive in nature.

(a) Apple various products have come out of Design thinking process, the latest being the ear bud for hands free hearing and blue tooth connectivity with iPhone
(b) IBM has embraced design thinking and made their enterprise design thinking assets available to everyone.
(c) Uber Eats approached their food delivery service with a design thinking mind-set.
(d) Salesforce.com, a cloud-based customer relationship management (CRM) product company transformed the online consumer engagement for Adidas by combining data and technology to personalize content at scale using concepts of design thinking.
(e) PepsiCo under the leadership of CEO Indra Nooyi inducted Mauro Porcini[12] as chief Design officer to redesign PepsiCo's user experience. They prioritised user-specific solutions, designed human-centric products.
(f) IDEO the design thinking pioneer has several success stories right from designing several Apple products to furniture, health case services, education etc. (more details can be obtained from www.ideo.com.
(g) Airbnb using Design Thinking Transformed itself from a almost failed Startup to a Billion Dollar Business.

13.12 CHALLENGES AND REMEDIAL MEASURES WHILE ADOPTING DESIGN THINKING

While Design thinking is applicable at very wide variety of situations yet like all other creative and problem solving process Design Thinking is also not recommended in certain situations. Design thinking by definition is open ended and exploratory in nature. Hence where there are constraints for processes imposed by regulatory or other reasons, it is not useful. Alternatively if the objective is to steer the team towards a specific solution as followed in traditional strategy development approach then Design Thinking will not work.

Using design thinking methodology without a strategy, goal and discipline will end up being a superficial exercise. One also must balance methodology structure of Design Thinking but do not feel constrained strictly. If the latter is true then the results would be not so useful. The main impediment of adopting design thinking comes from lack of culture for innovation, openness and respect for failure.

In such cultural scenarios, failure of design thinking process is guaranteed. Unfortunately culture is something that cannot be changed by conducing few workshops, leadership announcement

[11] https://hbr.org/2018/09/why-design-thinking-works accessed 08102019 HBR September–October 2018 issue

[12] https://www.linkedin.com/in/mauroporcini/ accessed 08102019

or motivational sessions. It requires concerted and long term effort. The biggest stumbling block is the lack of trust and respect for dissent.

However, radical thinkers should not be allowed to highjack the agenda and criticise every idea just to prove their point or show one-upmanship. Another constraints in design thinking process is when organization does not allow playfulness, an environment that allows people to be more creative.

13.13 SUMMARY

We started this chapter by defining what is Design thinking and why it is gaining so much of popularity in the recent times. In simple terms Design thinking is applying innovative ideas to solve problems and find opportunities to delight the customers. The interesting aspect of Design Thinking is that it not to be used by the designers only as the name may sound but can be used across industry or area of expertise. Design Thinking is not a fad or likely to get passed over soon, it will be useful till the time creativity remains the main stay of successfully navigating a complex world.

We then explained the brief history of evolution of Design thinking concepts. We summarized 10 principles of good design, widely acclaimed as Ten Commandments of good design by designer community and researchers. This chapter also covered some of the prevalent Design thinking approaches of IDEO, Stanford design School and IBM while using concepts of design thinking.

At the end we summarized covering some of the success stories and challenges that one may encounter during Design thinking practices.

REVIEW QUESTIONS

1. What is Design thinking and Why it has become highly in demand these days?
2. Explain the Design thinking approach of IDEO, Stanford and IBM. Draw similarities and differences between them.
3. What are the possible challenges of design thinking implementation? How it can be overcome?

ADDITIONAL READINGS

1. *Change by Design: How Design Thinking Transforms Organizations and Inspires Innovation* by Tim Brown.
2. *The Design Thinking Playbook: Mindful Digital Transformation of Teams, Products, Services, Businesses and Ecosystems,* Paperback—22 May 2018 by Michael Lewrick, Patrick Link, Larry Leifer.
3. *Value Proposition Design: How to Create Products and Services Customers Want*, Paperback—5 Jan 2015 by Alex Osterwalder, Yves Pigneur, Greg Bernarda, Alan Smith, Trish Papadakos.

Chapter 14

Generative AI Impact on Business

At the end of this chapter, we will learn:

- Core capabilities of AI and its evolution
- Overview of Foundation Models and Large Language Models (LLMs)
- Economic Implications and value creation using AI /Gen AI
- Creating an AI native organisation

14.1 DEFINING GENERATIVE AI: CORE CAPABILITIES AND EVOLUTION

14.1.1 What is Generative AI?

Generative AI (Gen AI) represents a paradigm shift in the field of artificial intelligence, moving beyond systems designed for analysis or prediction to those capable of creating novel content. At its essence, Generative AI is a type of AI that learns from vast quantities of existing data to produce new, original, and realistic artifacts that reflect the characteristics and patterns of its training data, rather than merely reproducing it. This capability distinguishes it fundamentally from discriminative AI, which typically classifies, predicts, or identifies patterns within existing data. The emergence of Gen AI signifies a profound leap in AI's capabilities, enabling machines to engage in what was once considered exclusively human domains of creativity and invention.

The scope of content that Generative AI can produce is remarkably broad, encompassing diverse modalities and applications. This includes, but is not limited to, human-like text, compelling images, dynamic video clips, original music compositions, synthesized speech, functional software code, and even intricate product designs. The ability of Gen AI to "create" rather than just "analyze" fundamentally shifts the value proposition of AI from mere efficiency and prediction to innovation and augmentation. This implies that businesses can leverage Gen AI not just to perform existing tasks better or faster, but to engage in entirely new activities and develop novel offerings, opening up previously unfeasible business models and avenues for value creation. This transformative potential requires a re-evaluation of how organizations approach innovation, product development, and market engagement.

14.1.2 Key Capabilities: Content Generation, Natural Language Interaction

At the core of Generative AI's transformative power lies its ability to generate diverse content and its intuitive natural language interface. Gen AI models excel at producing a wide array of content in response to natural language requests, effectively democratizing access to powerful AI capabilities by eliminating the need for complex coding knowledge for end-users. This means that business professionals, marketers, designers, and even general employees can interact with and leverage Gen AI directly, using conversational prompts to achieve desired creative or analytical outputs. This intuitive interaction fundamentally changes human-computer interaction in the workplace, making AI a more accessible and integrated partner for a broader range of tasks.

Beyond basic content creation, Gen AI's capabilities extend to several sophisticated applications:

- **Written Content Augmentation and Creation:** It can produce draft text in a desired style and length, manipulate text tone (e.g., softening language or professionalizing text), summarize lengthy conversations, articles, emails, and webpages, and simplify complex content by breaking down titles, creating outlines, and extracting key information. This significantly accelerates content production and refinement for various business functions.
- **Classification:** Gen AI can classify content for specific use cases, such as sorting by sentiment or topic, enabling more efficient data organization and analysis.
- **Chatbot Performance Improvement:** It enhances chatbot performance through better "sentity"(specific entities within a conversation) extraction, whole-conversation sentiment classification, and generating journey flows from general descriptions, leading to more natural and effective customer interactions.
- **Software Coding:** Gen AI can generate, translate, explain, and verify software code across various programming languages. This capability significantly boosts developer productivity, with reports indicating 10-30% productivity gains for software developers using Generative AI. Developers using tools like Copilot have reported being 55% faster in general, 88% more productive, and 96% faster with repetitive tasks.
- **Emerging Use Cases:** Long-term impacts include creating medical images to show disease development, generating synthetic data for data augmentation, bias mitigation, and privacy preservation, and proactively suggesting actions and information to users. Gen AI can also assist in modernizing legacy software code.

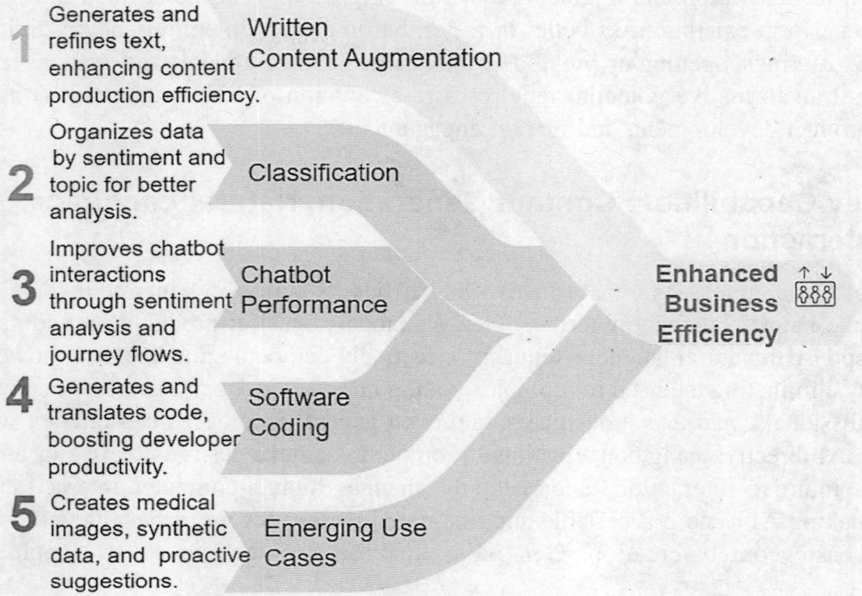

FIGURE 14.1 Gen AI's transformative impact.

The natural language interface of Gen AI is a critical enabler for widespread business adoption, lowering the technical barrier for non-programmers. This implies a future where business users can directly interact with and leverage AI for creative and analytical tasks, fundamentally changing human-computer interaction in the workplace and leading to more pervasive AI adoption across all functions.

14.1.3 Foundation Models and Large Language Models (LLMs)

Generative AI's capabilities are primarily powered by advanced AI architectures known as **foundation models**. These models are trained on extensive, diverse, and unlabelled datasets, allowing them to learn broad patterns and representations that can then be fine-tuned for a wide variety of downstream tasks. This approach signifies a new modularity in AI development, where a single, powerful base model can be adapted for numerous specific applications without needing to build AI from scratch for each use case.

Large Language Models (LLMs) are a prominent type of foundation model, specifically designed to understand and generate human language. These models achieve their remarkable linguistic capabilities by having "read the whole internet"—billions of books, articles, websites, code repositories, business reports, legal filings, technical manuals, and more. Through this massive exposure, LLMs become sophisticated pattern-recognition engines capable of complex language understanding, generation, and reasoning. Popular enterprise-grade LLMs include OpenAI's GPT-4, Anthropic's Claude 3.7, Google's Gemini, and open-source alternatives like Meta's LLaMA and Mistral.

The concept of foundation models and their ability to be fine-tuned for diverse tasks implies a new economic and technical model for AI development. Businesses can now *consume* powerful AI capabilities via APIs or fine-tune existing models for specific needs, rather than investing heavily in foundational AI research and development. This significantly accelerates deployment and reduces initial investment costs. However, it also creates a new layer of dependency on model providers and introduces strategic considerations around model choice, data privacy (as sensitive data might be processed by external models), and the long-term implications of relying on third-party AI infrastructure. The continuous evolution and competition among these models mean organizations must stay abreast of advancements to select the optimal fit for their strategic objectives.

14.1.4 The AI Hardware Revolution: TPUs, GPUs, and Wafer-Scale Engines

The rapid advancement of Generative AI is inextricably linked to a parallel revolution in specialized computing hardware. The complex mathematical operations underlying neural networks, particularly the dense matrix computations required for training and inference in large AI models, demand immense processing power and memory bandwidth.

Graphics Processing Units (GPUs), primarily pioneered by NVIDIA, have become central to the AI revolution. Originally designed for rendering complex graphics, GPUs offer massive parallel processing capabilities that are highly efficient for the matrix multiplications characteristic of AI workloads. NVIDIA's latest architectures, such as the H100 and Blackwell platforms, are purpose-built "AI factories" designed to deliver the scale, efficiency, and return on investment required for high-level AI inference and training. Innovations like NVFP4 4-bit precision enable ultra-efficient, high-accuracy inference while significantly reducing power and memory requirements, making it possible to deploy trillion-parameter LLMs in real-time. NVIDIA's extensive software stack (CUDA platform) further optimizes these GPUs for AI development, supporting millions of developers worldwide.

Beyond GPUs, companies like Google have developed custom-designed **Tensor Processing Units (TPUs)**. These Application-Specific Integrated Circuits (ASICs) are specialized for accelerating Machine Learning workloads, particularly those leveraging Google's TensorFlow software. TPUs are optimized for dense matrix computations and feature a systolic array architecture that allows for high-computational throughput on neural network calculations by minimizing memory access during multiplication processes. Google Cloud offers Cloud TPU services, providing developers access to these high-performance resources for training and inference of Generative AI models.

Pushing the boundaries even further, companies like Cerebras Systems have introduced **Wafer-Scale Engines (WSEs)**. The WSE-3, for instance, is the world's largest AI chip, measuring 46,255 mm and containing 4 trillion transistors, delivering 125 petaflops of AI compute through 900,000 AI-optimized cores. This architecture aims to eliminate traditional bottlenecks like GPU memory bandwidth and communication overhead, enabling record-breaking inference speeds for large models. For example, Cerebras AI Inference Cloud achieved 3,000 tokens per second output speed for OpenAI's gpt-oss-120B model, significantly reducing wait times for high-intelligence AI reasoning use cases.

The rapid evolution of specialized AI hardware indicates that computational infrastructure is a critical, often overlooked, driver of AI's transformative power. Organizations' ability to leverage Gen AI effectively is not just about software and data, but also about strategic investment in or access to cutting-edge computational infrastructure. This reliance on high-performance, energy-intensive chips and specialized data centers creates new competitive divides, as firms with superior hardware capabilities can train larger models faster, deploy more complex AI applications, and achieve greater efficiency in their AI operations.

14.2 ECONOMIC IMPLICATIONS AND VALUE CREATION

14.2.1 Projected Economic Impact and ROI

The economic implications of AI and Generative AI are projected to be monumental, signaling a new era of global economic growth. The scale of this impact suggests that AI is not merely an incremental technological improvement but a fundamental driver of economic transformation, comparable to past industrial revolutions.

Global Cumulative Impact: IDC predicts that investments in AI solutions and services are projected to yield a global cumulative impact of $22.3 trillion by 2030, representing approximately 3.7% of the global Gross Domestic Product (GDP)[1]. This projection underscores the profound and widespread influence AI is expected to have across all sectors of the global economy.

Annual Economic Impact: McKinsey projects an annual economic impact of $6.1-$7.9 trillion from AI. This substantial figure highlights the immense value that AI is expected to unlock each year through various applications and efficiencies.

GDP Growth from Gen AI: Goldman Sachs predicts that Generative AI alone will raise global GDP by 7%, equating to a staggering $7 trillion.[2] This specific projection for Gen AI emphasizes its unique potential to drive new economic value through its creative and transformative capabilities.

Investment Multiplier Effect: The significant multiplier effect of AI investments is a crucial indicator of its economic power. For every new dollar spent on AI solutions and services by adopters, an additional $4.9 is expected to be generated in the global economy. This underscores AI's capacity for accelerating productivity and business growth.

The sheer scale of these projected economic impacts suggests that AI and Generative AI are becoming a macro-economic imperative. Nations and firms that fail to adopt and strategically leverage AI risk being left behind in the global economic landscape. Governments, industries, and educational institutions must prioritize AI adoption and development to maintain or gain competitive standing, making AI a matter of national strategic importance for future prosperity.

14.2.2 Beyond Cost Savings: Driving New Revenue and Growth Opportunities

While AI is undeniably powerful in enhancing operational efficiency and reducing costs, its

[1]https://hatchworks.com/blog/gen-ai/generative-ai-statistics/ accessed 09082025

[2]https://vlinkinfo.com/blog/ai-for-business-to-solve-problems/ accessed 09082025

true transformative potential lies in its ability to unlock entirely new growth opportunities and revenue channels. The value generated by AI extends far beyond simple cost-cutting measures, positioning it as a strategic profit driver.

- **Unlocking New Growth Opportunities:** AI allows organizations to go beyond mere process optimization and discover exciting new avenues for growth. This includes the faster creation of new products, the systematic discovery of new drugs and materials, and the enhancement of customer experiences. For instance, Generative AI is predicted to systematically discover more than 30% of new drugs and materials by 2025, a significant leap from zero today, offering substantial cost and time reductions in drug discovery.
- **Worker Augmentation and Talent Optimization:** Generative AI augments workers' abilities to draft and edit text, images, and other media; summarize, simplify, and classify content; and generate, translate, and verify software code. This frees employees from repetitive, mundane tasks, allowing them to engage in more complex and creative work. This shift not only makes the work environment more stimulating but also boosts job satisfaction, sparks innovation, and provides actionable insights for better decision-making. Employees will be increasingly distinguished by their ability to conceive, execute, and refine ideas, projects, processes, services, and relationships in partnership with AI, accelerating time to proficiency and greatly extending worker competency.
- **Process Improvement and Value Extraction:** Generative AI can derive real, in-context value from vast stores of content that may have previously gone unexploited, fundamentally changing workflows. This leads to significant improvements in operational efficiency, such as reducing errors in reports by 40%, cutting analytics time, and accelerating decision-making by 50%.
- **Risk Mitigation:** AI's ability to analyze and provide broader and deeper visibility of data, such as customer transactions and potentially faulty software code, enhances pattern recognition and the ability to identify potential risks to the enterprise more quickly. This proactive risk management contributes to long-term financial stability and reputation.

The "multiplier productivity and business acceleration effect" of AI investments indicates that AI is shifting from a cost centre to a profit driver. This necessitates a change in how firms' budget for and evaluate AI initiatives, moving from a narrow focus on short-term ROI to a strategic, long-term perspective on value creation. AI's capacity to create entirely new revenue streams and accelerate business growth fundamentally changes the financial calculus for technology investments.

14.2.3 AI-Native Organizations: Characteristics and Advantages

The emergence of "AI-native" organizations signifies a new competitive paradigm in the business world. Unlike traditional businesses that attempt to integrate AI functionalities into existing, often outdated, systems, AI-native companies are fundamentally designed with AI at their core. This means that AI is engineered intrinsically from the ground up, becoming a pervasive and inseparable component of all operations and services.

Key Characteristics of AI-Native Organizations

- **Foundational AI Integration:** AI is not an add-on but the central architecture around which the entire system is built. This allows for seamless incorporation of advancements in AI technology and rapid adaptation to new innovations and market changes.
- **Data-Driven, Knowledge-Based Ecosystem:** AI-native applications leverage a data-driven, knowledge-based ecosystem, rapidly replacing static, rule-based systems with the ability to learn and adapt when needed. They are optimized for AI functionalities, absorbing and comprehending data to bring new AI-based functionalities to life.
- **Continuous Adaptation and Innovation:** This foundational integration positions them as leaders in innovation and adaptability. They are built to proactively identify issues, automate tasks, and optimize processes.
- **Trust and Fairness:** AI-native systems manage the lifecycle of AI-based functionalities, ensuring trust and fairness by making operations transparent, explainable, and trustworthy. They also implement AI safety and control mechanisms.

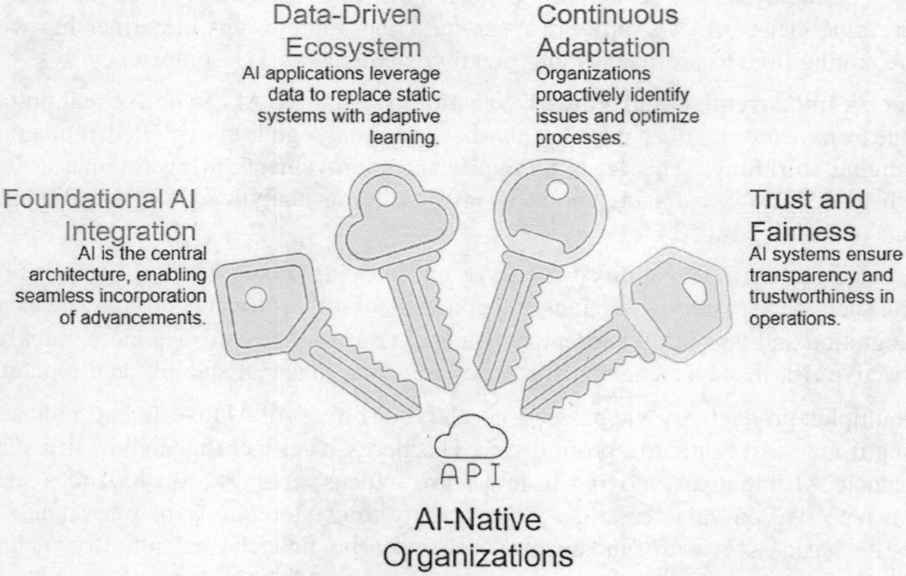

FIGURE 14.2 Core attributes of AI-Native organizations.

Advantages of AI-Native Organizations[3]

- **Enhanced Efficiency and Performance:** AI-native solutions improve network traffic routes, allocate bandwidth optimally, and minimize latency, leading to unprecedented speed and dependability. They proactively schedule maintenance and repair issues, reducing downtime and optimizing resource utilization.

---

[3]https://aisera.com/blog/ai-native/ accessed 09082025

- **New Business Models:** By leveraging AI to its fullest potential, AI-native architectures can drive transformational changes across industries, enabling new business models that were previously unfeasible. For example, AI-native strategies in banking enhance customer interaction, improve fraud detection, and optimize loan processing. In healthcare, they enhance diagnostic accuracy and personalize patient care.
- **Cost Savings:** Automation of network management and other operations replaces costly manual observation and intervention, leading to significant cost reductions.
- **Scalability and Flexibility:** AI-native networks are built to adapt to scaling workloads and incorporate new devices without manual reconfiguration, offering superior scalability.
- **Improved Security:** By proactively identifying issues and automating threat detection and response, AI-native systems enhance security.

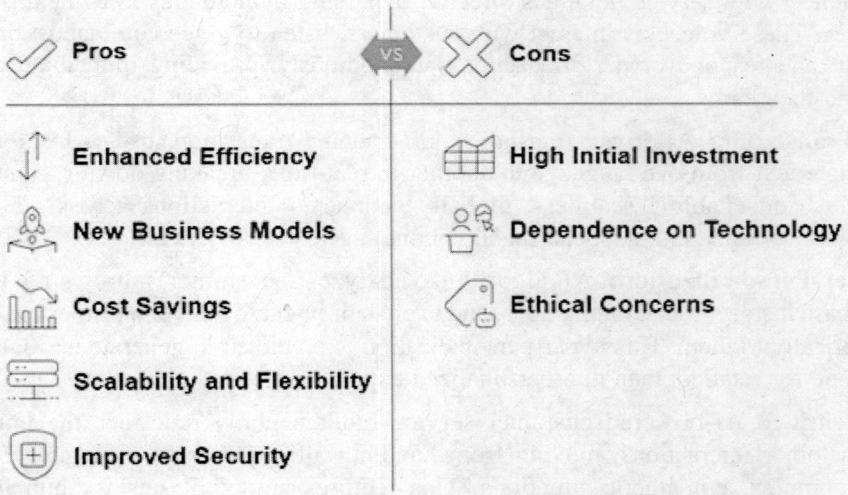

FIGURE 14.3 AI-Native organizations.

The rise of AI-native organizations signals a new competitive divide: firms that can fundamentally redesign their operations around AI will have a structural advantage over those trying to retrofit AI onto legacy systems. This implies a need for radical organizational transformation, impacting culture, skills, and strategic priorities for long-term survival and competitiveness.

14.3 TRANSFORMING BUSINESS FUNCTIONS WITH GENERATIVE AI

Generative AI is not merely an incremental improvement for existing business functions; it is fundamentally transforming how these functions operate, creating new efficiencies, capabilities, and strategic opportunities.

14.3.1 Customer Service

Generative AI is revolutionizing customer service by enabling proactive engagement and enhanced multimodal support. Advanced AI models are adept at understanding nuances, context, and even emotions, leading to more natural and personalized support interactions.

- **AI-Powered Assistants:** Companies like Swedish fintech Klarna have implemented AI assistants that handled two-third of all customer chats in just one month, managing 2.3 million conversations—equivalent to the work of 700 human agents. This drastically reduced customer wait times from 11 minutes to under 2 minutes and decreased repeat questions by 25%. This frees human agents to focus on complex issues requiring empathy, where human touch remains critical.
- **Voice-Based AI Assistance:** AI voicebots offer 24/7 customer support, allowing clients to connect with service helplines directly, bypassing monotonous IVR menus and long queues. These voicebots interact with customers, listen to voice commands, understand intent, and respond or perform actions autonomously, providing immediate responses around the clock.
- **AI Translation:** AI-driven translation, or machine translation, uses AI algorithms to translate text from one language to another in real-time, breaking down communication barriers and enabling seamless, globally connected interactions across all customer touchpoints (chat, email, social media, phone).
- **Hyper-Personalization:** AI algorithms analyze a customer's browsing behavior, purchase history, social interactions, and even their intent to deliver an experience tailored specifically to them. This hyper-personalization is predicted to generate up to 40% more revenue for retailers than non-personalized experiences.
- The shift to AI-powered customer service fundamentally redefines the human role in customer interactions, moving from handling all inquiries to managing exceptions and complex, empathetic situations. This requires new skill sets for human agents, emphasizing emotional intelligence and complex problem-solving, and a re-evaluation of customer service training.

14.3.2 Marketing and Sales

Generative AI is redefining creativity, efficiency, and strategy in marketing and sales.

- **Content Generation:** Gen AI tools like ChatGPT and Midjourney can generate captivating content, including articles, product descriptions, and advertisements, by analyzing vast datasets of text, images, and video. This saves time and ensures consistency and relevance, enabling effective audience engagement. At many companies, these smart systems now write 30% of marketing materials, finishing work almost twice as fast while cutting content costs by 30-50%. For instance, Bayer saw an 85% jump in clicks and paid 33% less per click when using AI for their marketing.
- **Personalized Marketing and Targeted Advertising:** Gen AI optimizes advertising by leveraging data analytics and machine learning algorithms to reach the right audience

with the right message. Meta, for example, has announced Gen AI features for advertisers that allow quick generation of subtitle copy and design tweaks for efficient A/B testing.

- **Gen AI-Powered Search:** This is steadily impacting organic web traffic. Gartner expects a 50% or more drop in organic website traffic as more customers opt for generative AI search and search engines roll out AI-assisted search engine result pages (SERP). This implies a fundamental shift in digital marketing strategy from traditional SEO to "AI-citation optimization," forcing brands to rethink their content and distribution strategies.
- **Top-of-Funnel Automation:** AI has evolved from co-pilots to agents, handling tasks like identifying ideal prospect profiles, targeting companies, finding contacts, and personalizing outreach via email, phone, and text. This leads to a leaner and more efficient lead generation process, diminishing the traditional role of sales development representatives (SDRs).
- **Go-to-Market Engineers:** Many companies are shifting away from traditional sales operations roles in favor of "go-to-market (GTM) engineers" who focus on internal automation, efficiency, and optimizing sales workflows through technical solutions and custom automations.
- **Streamlining Hiring and Training:** AI streamlines hiring and training processes in sales through AI-driven role-playing scenarios, resume screening, and candidate assessments, making it easier to identify and onboard talent.

The impact of Gen AI on marketing and sales moves beyond optimization to a fundamental re-architecture of customer acquisition and engagement. This necessitates a strategic pivot for brands, as they must now optimize for AI search engines and adapt to new models of customer interaction.

14.3.3 Supply Chain Optimization

Artificial intelligence is transforming supply chain management by building more resilient, agile, and intelligent logistics networks that can adapt to an increasingly volatile global market.

- **Predictive Analytics:** AI-powered predictive analytics is revolutionizing supply chain management by enabling businesses to anticipate demand and optimize inventory levels with remarkable accuracy. It analyzes historical data, real-time market trends, supplier reliability, equipment performance, and external factors like weather or geopolitical events to identify potential disruptions before they occur. McKinsey research highlights reductions in logistics costs by 15%, improvements in inventory accuracy by 35%, and service level enhancements of up to 65%. IBM's cognitive supply chain, for instance, achieved a 100% order fulfillment rate during the COVID-19 pandemic by leveraging AI and IoT.
- **Generative AI for Communication and Models:** Gen AI streamlines procurement and sourcing by analyzing vast datasets and learning from patterns. It transforms supply chain communication by automating content creation like reports, emails, and updates, ensuring consistent messaging across stakeholders. Furthermore, Gen AI facilitates the design of

innovative supply chain models by simulating various scenarios and creating probabilistic models for inventory management, optimizing stock levels and reducing waste.

- **Advanced Automation and Robotics:** AI-powered robotics is revolutionizing warehouse operations by enhancing efficiency and accuracy. Autonomous robots perform tasks like sorting, picking, and packing, minimizing errors and reducing processing times. Amazon Robotics exemplifies this trend, utilizing AI-driven systems to streamline order fulfillment.
- **AI-Driven Sustainability:** AI tools analyze energy consumption patterns to optimize energy use across manufacturing and logistics, identify inefficiencies in transportation routes to reduce fuel consumption and emissions, and improve waste reduction through enhanced demand forecasting and inventory replenishment. AI can reduce greenhouse gas emissions by 5% to 10% in supply chains.
- **Digital Twins:** AI-powered digital twins create virtual replicas of physical systems to revolutionize supply chain simulation. These models simulate process changes, predict outcomes, and optimize overall supply chain processes, enhancing preparedness and stability.

The integration of AI, automation, and IoT in supply chains creates a "self-optimizing" supply chain, moving from human-managed, reactive logistics to an autonomous, predictive, and adaptive system. This fundamentally changes the role of human oversight and decision-making in logistics, requiring new skills in data science and AI ethics for supply chain professionals.

14.3.4 Human Resources and Talent Management

AI is rapidly transforming Human Resources (HR) and talent management by streamlining processes, automating routine tasks, and providing data and analytics to enhance decision-making.

- **Talent Acquisition and Recruiting:** AI is most commonly used in recruiting, with 51% of organizations employing AI for these efforts. AI generates job descriptions (66% usage), screens resumes (44%), automates candidate searches (32%), customizes job postings (31%), and communicates with applicants (29%). This saves significant time (89% of HR professionals report time savings) and reduces recruitment costs (36%). AI-powered Applicant Tracking Systems (ATS) use natural language processing (NLP) and machine learning to parse resumes, match candidates, rank them, and schedule interviews. This automation frees up HR teams to focus on high-value tasks like relationship building, candidate engagement, and strategic workforce planning.
- **Onboarding and Performance Management:** AI-powered onboarding tools, such as personalized video welcome programs, streamline administrative tasks and training for new employees. AI assists with performance management by supporting goal setting, feedback, and reviews, providing data-driven insights into workforce trends.
- **Learning and Development (L&D):** AI tools create personalized professional growth programs and custom training paths, and identify skill gaps for real-time training improvements. AI-powered analytics can synthesize data from performance reviews and

learning management systems to identify high-potential talent and design customized L&D curricula.

- **Employee Experience and Retention:** AI-driven employee experience platforms foster a positive workplace culture through recognition and communication tools. AI-powered tools identify disengaged employees through behavior analysis, allowing HR to implement targeted retention programs and reduce turnover. AI also streamlines offboarding processes.

AI in HR shifts the HR function from administrative and reactive to strategic and predictive. This allows HR professionals to become more strategic partners in talent acquisition, development, and retention. However, it also introduces critical ethical challenges related to algorithmic bias in hiring and performance evaluations, requiring HR professionals to develop expertise in ethical AI and data governance.

14.3.5 Finance and Accounting

Artificial intelligence and automation are profoundly redefining the accounting and corporate finance professions, transforming them from traditional record-keeping roles to strategic advisory functions.

- **Automated Financial Processes:** Automation has become a nearly universal practice in accounting, with 95% of accountants leveraging it. AI finance tools are capable of processing invoices, reconciling accounts, and inputting data with near-perfect accuracy. AI-powered robotic process automation (RPA) tools enable real-time processing of thousands of transactions simultaneously and integrate seamlessly with ERPs and CRMs to keep financial records continuously updated. Machine learning algorithms automatically spot anomalies in transactional data, helping to flag potential human errors or fraud before they escalate. This automation enhances productivity and accuracy, freeing finance teams from manual tasks.
- **Predictive Analytics for Strategic Planning:** AI-driven predictive models analyze historical data, real-time financial metrics, and external market trends to provide customized, actionable forecasts.These models enable companies to simulate various business scenarios, proactively plan to reduce risk, inform decisions, and capitalize on opportunities. They integrate directly with financial and operational data, making forecasting a more widespread practice. AI-powered predictive analytics tools can even leverage natural language processing (NLP) to analyze news, market reports, and social media sentiment, offering a more comprehensive view of factors influencing the business landscape. A significant 93% of professionals are now using AI to deliver higher-value strategic business advisory services, moving beyond mere compliance.
- **Transparent, Explainable AI (XAI):** As AI takes on a greater role in driving business decisions, the need for transparency and accountability grows. Explainable AI (XAI) addresses this by enabling decision-makers to understand and verify how AI models reach their conclusions. Unlike traditional "black box" AI systems, XAI offers clear reasoning, ensuring that insights are both actionable and trustworthy. In corporate

finance, XAI will transform practices such as credit scoring, risk management, and investment recommendations by providing detailed explanations of the factors influencing calculations, rather than just a simple risk score. This transparency builds confidence among finance leaders and helps ensure compliance with regulatory standards and ethical guidelines.

The integration of AI in finance fundamentally elevates the finance function from transactional processing to strategic value creation. Finance professionals, freed from manual tasks, can now focus on higher-level analysis, scenario planning, and advising on business model transformation, requiring significant upskilling in AI literacy and data interpretation.

14.3.6 Scientific Discovery and R&D

Artificial intelligence is accelerating scientific discovery and transforming Research and Development (R&D) by automating critical steps and enhancing the very nature of scientific inquiry.

- **Automating Research Workflows:** AI platforms are designed to automate many critical steps on the path toward scientific progress. These platforms consist of a series of AI agents, each specialized for tasks such as information retrieval, information synthesis, chemical synthesis design, and data analysis. For instance, tools like Crow (formerly PaperQA) retrieve and summarize information in scientific literature, while Owl (formerly Has Anyone) helps scientists determine if specific experiments or hypotheses have already been explored. Phoenix assists researchers in planning chemistry experiments, and Finch automates data-driven discovery in biology.
- **Accelerating Discovery and Hypothesis Generation:** Gen AI can expedite scientific research, drug discovery, and materials science by generating and evaluating hypotheses, models, and experiments. This capability can lead to breakthroughs that would be extremely challenging or time-consuming for humans alone. AI is predicted to systematically discover over 30% of new drugs and materials by 2025, offering significant cost and time reductions in pharmaceutical and materials science industries.
- **Enhancing Experimental Design and Data Analysis:** AI enhances experimental design, streamlining complex R&D workflows. It empowers R&D professionals to gain new levels of efficiency and insight from their data, by analyzing vast datasets to identify patterns that human perception might miss.

AI's role in generating hypotheses and designing experiments fundamentally changes the nature of scientific inquiry, moving beyond human-led intuition to AI-driven exploration of vast possibility spaces. This could lead to an exponential increase in the pace of scientific discovery, making industries reliant on R&D highly dependent on AI capabilities. It also raises questions about the human role in scientific creativity and validation, and the very definition of "discovery."

14.3.7 Case Studies of Gen AI Impact across Industries

The pervasive influence of Generative AI is evident across a multitude of industries and business functions, driving both efficiency gains and novel opportunities. The following tables consolidate key capabilities and their applications, providing concrete examples of how Gen AI is transforming the business landscape.

TABLE 14.1 Generative AI capabilities and business applications

Capability	Business Function/ Industry	Specific Application	Example Company/ Project
Content Generation (Text, Image, Video, Code)	Marketing & Sales	Generating marketing copy, product descriptions, social media posts, ad iterations.	Bayer, Monks/Hatch
	Software Engineering	Generating, translating, explaining, and verifying software code; automating testing.	GitHub Copilot, Katalon, CodeGPT
	Entertainment & Content Creation	Creating original music compositions, visual art, stories, poems, video clips, and animations.	Midjourney (for sci-fi film footage), Duolingo (Role-play feature)
Natural Language Interaction	Customer Service	AI-powered chatbots and virtual assistants for instant support, handling queries, and providing contextual assistance.	Klarna (AI assistant handling 2.3M chats)
	HR	Communicating with applicants, providing chatbot support for onboarding and offboarding.	
	Finance & Accounting	Streamlining data analysis and simplifying complex data interactions using AI Query.	
Predictive Analytics	Supply Chain	Anticipating demand, optimizing inventory levels, identifying potential disruptions (supplier reliability, equipment performance, external factors).	IBM (cognitive supply chain), DP World (CARGOES TOS+ system)
	Healthcare	Personalized treatment plans based on medical history, lifestyle, genetic data; predicting patient response to medications.	HCA Healthcare (extracting info from physician-patient conversations)
	Banking	Offering tailored financial products/services; predicting fraud patterns; risk assessment in lending/investment.	
	Finance & Accounting	Actionable forecasts, simulating business scenarios, reducing risk, informing decisions, capitalizing on opportunities.	

(*Contd.*)

TABLE 14.1 Generative AI capabilities and business applications (*Contd.*)

Capability	Business Function/ Industry	Specific Application	Example Company/ Project
Automation	HR	Generating job descriptions, screening resumes, automating candidate searches, payroll processing, benefits administration.	
	Finance & Accounting	Processing invoices, reconciling accounts, data input with high accuracy; robotic process automation (RPA).	
	Operations (General)	Automating repetitive, mundane tasks to free up employees for creative work.	
AI Agents	Sales	Identifying ideal prospect profiles, targeting companies, finding contacts, personalizing outreach, managing cadences.	
	Scientific Discovery & R&D	Automating information retrieval (Crow), chemical synthesis design (Phoenix), data-driven discovery in biology (Finch).	FutureHouse (Crow, Owl, Falcon, Phoenix, Finch)
Digital Twins	Customer-Facing Operations	Creating virtual copies of customers to test new ideas and spot fraud patterns.	Clothing retailers (outfit suggestions), Banks (virtual customer accounts)
	Supply Chain	Creating virtual replicas of physical systems to simulate process changes, predict outcomes, and optimize supply chain processes.	
Hypothesis Generation & Experimental Design	Scientific Discovery & R&D	Generating and evaluating hypotheses, models, and experiments; enhancing experimental design.	
Image Processing & Visuals	Advertising & Marketing	Creating on-brand content, product images, social media posts, lifestyle scenes, reducing photo shoot costs.	
	Retail & E-commerce	Visual search functionality (finding products by analyzing images/patterns).	Snapchat (visual search for Amazon products)
	Healthcare	Creating medical images to show disease development.	

This table provides a comprehensive, at-a-glance overview of Generative AI's practical applications across diverse sectors. It demonstrates the pervasive impact of Gen AI, making the theoretical concepts tangible for readers and highlighting its role in driving both efficiency and innovation.

TABLE 14.2 AI's Impact on Key Business Functions: Quantifiable Benefits

Business Function	Quantifiable Benefit	Source
Customer Service	Reduced wait times (from 11 to under 2 minutes); 2.3 million conversations handled by AI (work of 700 human agents); Repeat questions dropped by 25%.	Klarna
	Support agents handle 13.8% more customer inquiries per hour.	Nielsen Norman Group case study
Marketing	30% of marketing materials written by AI; Content costs cut by 30-50%; Clicks jumped 85% YOY; Cost per click reduced by 33%.	Bayer
	Ads with Google Gemini: 80% more clicks, 46% more engaged visitors, 31% less cost per purchase.	Monks used Google Gemini for Hatch
	Business professionals write 59% more business documents per hour with AI.	Nielsen Norman Group case study
Sales	AI agents automate lead generation; Sales teams move faster, eliminate repetitive tasks.	
Software Engineering	Developers using Gen AI: 10-30% productivity gains; 55% faster in general; 88% more productive; 96% faster with repetitive tasks; 85% more confident in code quality; 15% faster at code reviews.	ThoughtWorks, GitHub Copilot studies
	Programmers code 126% more projects per week with AI.	Nielsen Norman Group case study
Human Resources (HR)	89% of HR professionals report time savings/efficiency in recruiting with AI; 36% report reduced recruitment costs; 24% report improved ability to identify top candidates.	SHRM 2025 Talent Trends
	L&D programs with AI: 41% more effective, 39% reduced costs, 38% increased employee engagement.	SHRM 2025 Talent Trends
Finance & Accounting	95% of accountants leverage automation; 46% use AI daily; 8 out of 10 report AI boosts productivity and eases mental load.	2025 Intuit QuickBooks Accountant Technology Report
	AI-driven predictive analytics: Reduces forecasting errors by at least 20%.	IBM research

(*Contd.*)

TABLE 14.2 AI's Impact on Key Business Functions: Quantifiable Benefits (*Contd.*)

Business Function	Quantifiable Benefit	Source
Supply Chain	Logistics costs reduced by 15%; Inventory accuracy improved by 35%; Service level enhancements up to 65%.	McKinsey research
	Eliminated 350,000 unnecessary container moves annually; Improved truck servicing times by 20%.	DP World's Jebel Ali Free Zone (CARGOES TOS+ system)
	Achieved 100% order fulfillment rate during COVID-19 pandemic.	IBM (cognitive supply chain)

This table provides crucial quantitative evidence of AI's impact, moving beyond qualitative descriptions to measurable business benefits. It directly supports the argument that AI delivers tangible value, which is vital for managers and decision-makers. By consolidating data from various sources, it offers a powerful summary of AI's transformative potential in terms of productivity and efficiency across key business functions.

ESSAY QUESTIONS

Question 1: Discuss the core capabilities of Generative AI and how its ability to produce novel content fundamentally shifts the value proposition of AI from mere efficiency to innovation and augmentation. Provide examples of diverse content types Gen AI can create.

Hints for Answer: Define Generative AI as a type of AI that learns from existing data to produce new, original, and realistic content that reflects the characteristics of its training data without merely replicating it. Contrast this with earlier forms of AI focused on classification or prediction. Explain how this capability moves AI beyond simply optimizing existing processes to truly augmenting human creativity and enabling autonomous ideation. Provide examples of diverse content types Gen AI can create, such as text, images, video, music, speech, software code, and product designs.

Question 2: Analyze the economic implications of Generative AI, moving beyond traditional cost savings to driving new revenue and growth opportunities. Support your answer with projected economic impact figures and examples of how Gen AI unlocks new value.

Hints for Answer: Begin by citing the significant global economic impact projections, such as IDC's prediction of $22.3 trillion by 2030, representing approximately 3.7% of global GDP, and the $4.9 multiplier effect for every dollar spent on AI solutions. Mention McKinsey's projection of an annual economic impact of $6.1-$7.9 trillion and Goldman Sachs' prediction that Gen AI alone could boost global GDP by 7% ($7 trillion). Explain how Gen AI enables new growth opportunities through faster creation of new products (e.g., drugs, materials), worker augmentation (e.g., drafting, editing, summarizing content, coding), process improvement (e.g., reducing errors, accelerating decision-making), and risk mitigation.

Question 3: Describe the concept of "AI-native" organizations and explain their key characteristics and advantages compared to traditional businesses integrating AI. How does this shift impact competitive dynamics?

Hints for Answer: Define "AI-native" organizations as those fundamentally designed with AI at their core, where AI is engineered intrinsically from the ground up as a pervasive component of operations and services, rather than merely integrating AI functionalities into pre-existing systems. Detail key characteristics such as foundational AI integration, a data-driven and knowledge-based ecosystem, continuous adaptation and innovation, and a focus on trust and fairness. Discuss the advantages these organizations gain, including enhanced efficiency and performance, the ability to enable new business models (e.g., in banking, healthcare, telecom), cost savings through automation, superior scalability and flexibility, and improved security. Explain how this creates a new competitive divide, positioning AI-native firms as leaders in innovation and adaptability.

Question 4: How is Generative AI transforming the customer service function? Detail specific applications and quantifiable benefits, and discuss the evolving role of human agents in an AI-powered customer service environment.

Hints for Answer: Discuss the revolution in customer service through AI-powered assistants, citing examples like Klarna's AI handling 2.3 million conversations in one month (equivalent to 700 human agents), drastically reducing wait times from 11 minutes to under 2 minutes, and decreasing repeat questions by 25%. Explain the capabilities of voice-based AI assistance for 24/7 support and seamless transitions between channels. Describe the impact of AI translation for multilingual communication. Detail how hyper-personalization, driven by AI, analyzes customer data to deliver tailored experiences, potentially generating up to 40% more revenue for retailers. Conclude by explaining how this transformation redefines the human role in customer interactions, shifting human agents to focus on more complex, empathetic, and exception-handling tasks.

Chapter 15

Understanding Generative AI to Impact Innovation Processes, Models, and Targets

At the end of this chapter, we will learn:

- How Gen AI helps in idea generation and strengthening the Innovation Funnel?
- How to Optimize Product and Process Design?
- How humans should collaborate with AI?
- Overview of innovation models driven by Generative AI

15.1 ACCELERATING THE INNOVATION FUNNEL WITH GEN AI

Generative AI is not merely an additive tool in the innovation process; it is a transformative force that fundamentally accelerates and reshapes every stage of the innovation funnel, from initial ideation to product launch and beyond.

15.1.1 Rapid Ideation and Concept Generation

The initial stage of innovation, ideation, traditionally relies on human brainstorming and creative synthesis. Generative AI dramatically accelerates this phase. Gen AI models can rapidly ideate and generate novel concepts, solutions, and prototypes across various domains, significantly speeding up the "front-end" of the innovation funnel. This capability allows organizations to explore a much wider range of possibilities than previously feasible. AI systems excel at coming up with new ideas through semantic search and predictive modeling, generating hundreds of potential solutions by mixing existing knowledge in surprising ways. They are particularly adept at exploring the "adjacent possible"—ideas that are new but still feasible given current constraints—by systematically searching through vast solution spaces that human teams might miss due to cognitive biases or limited attention.

The ability of Gen AI to generate a vast quantity of diverse ideas shifts the challenge in ideation from simply generating enough ideas to effectively *filtering* and *evaluating* the deluge of AI-generated concepts. This implies a need for more sophisticated AI-powered evaluation tools and a refined human role in curating and prioritizing ideas. Human innovators, augmented by AI, can then focus on selecting the most promising concepts, refining them, and imbuing them with strategic context and human empathy.

15.1.2 AI-Assisted Design and Prototyping

Generative AI is revolutionizing the design and prototyping stages by enabling rapid iteration and visualization, drastically reducing the time and cost associated with these critical phases. Gen AI can be used for the procedural generation and iteration of product designs, manufacturing processes, and other complex systems. This capability enables rapid experimentation, helps identify optimal configurations, and uncovers novel design approaches that might not be apparent through traditional methods.

AI tools can rapidly visualize ideas and create preliminary designs, accelerating the creative process and minimizing costly physical prototypes. For example, Siemens engineers use AI to generate dozens of design options overnight, resulting in redesigned parts that are 75% lighter and projects completed 30% faster. Stable Diffusion, a latent diffusion model, facilitates image generation from text prompts, video and animation creation, and image super-resolution, aiding artists and media studios in digital media creation and apparel/product design. This moves prototyping from a costly, time-consuming physical process to a rapid, iterative virtual one. This implies a significant reduction in design cycle times and R&D costs, enabling more frequent product updates and a higher rate of design innovation. Physical prototyping may transition from an early exploration tool to a later-stage validation step.

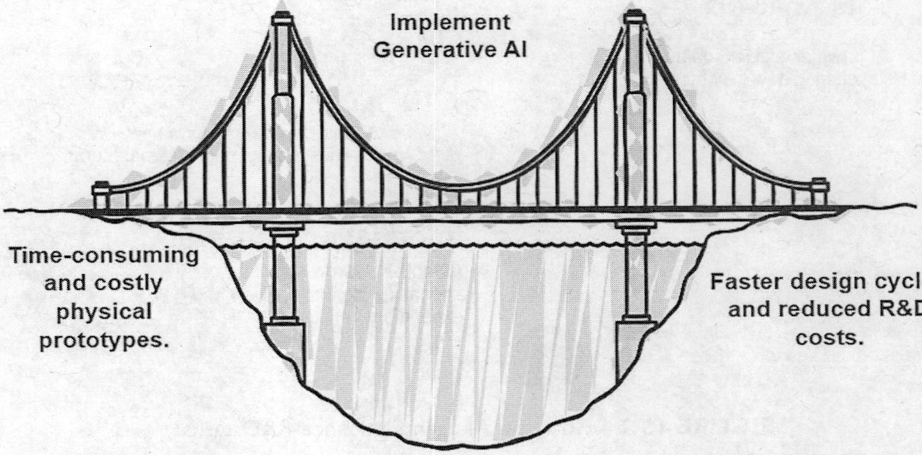

FIGURE 15.1 Generative AI transforms design and prototyping, accelerating innovation and reducing costs.

15.1.3 Accelerating Research and Discovery

Generative AI is poised to fundamentally transform scientific research and discovery, accelerating the pace of breakthroughs in various fields. Gen AI can expedite scientific research, drug discovery, and materials science by generating and evaluating hypotheses, models, and experiments. This capability can lead to breakthroughs that would be extremely challenging or time-consuming for humans to achieve alone.

AI agents are increasingly specialized for critical R&D tasks

- **Information Retrieval and Synthesis:** Tools like Crow (formerly Paper QA) are designed for retrieving and summarizing information in scientific literature, while Owl (formerly Has Anyone) helps researchers determine if specific experiments or hypotheses have already been explored.
- **Hypothesis Generation:** AI can assist in forming new theories or predictions by analyzing vast datasets and identifying patterns that humans might miss.
- **Experimental Design:** AI can enhance the planning and structure of experiments, streamlining complex R&D workflows. Phoenix, an AI agent, uses specialized tools to assist researchers in planning chemistry experiments.
- **Data Analysis:** AI empowers R&D professionals to gain new levels of efficiency and insight from their data, by analyzing research data and automating data-driven discovery in fields like biology (e.g., Finch agent).

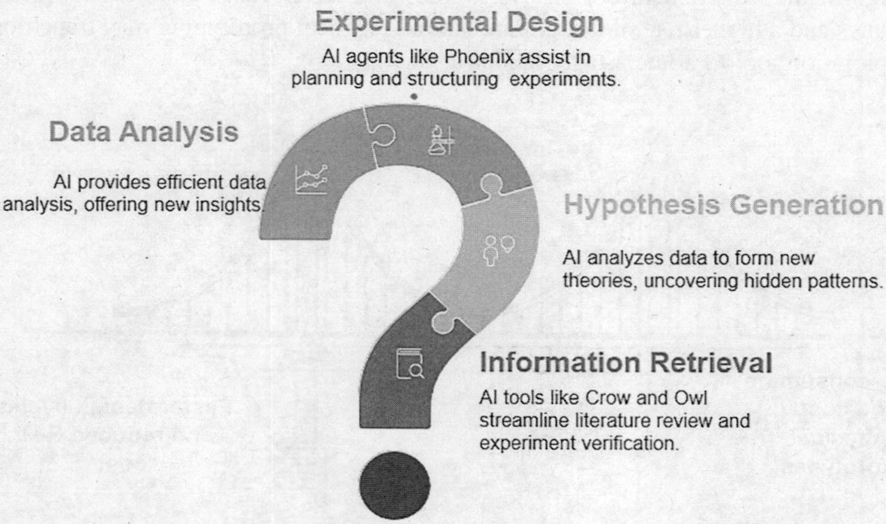

FIGURE 15.2 How can AI agents enhance R&D tasks?

AI's ability to generate and evaluate scientific hypotheses fundamentally transforms the scientific method from a human-centric, iterative process to a potentially AI-driven, parallel exploration of scientific knowledge. This could lead to an exponential increase in the pace of scientific discovery, with profound implications for industries reliant on R&D, such as pharmaceuticals (where AI is predicted to systematically discover over 30% of new drugs and materials by 2025) and materials science. It also raises questions about the human role in scientific creativity, the validation of AI-generated insights, and the very nature of scientific authorship.

15.4.4 Optimizing Product and Process Design

Generative AI offers unprecedented capabilities for optimizing both product and process design, moving beyond incremental improvements to potentially radical re-imagination. Gen AI can be used to procedurally generate and iterate on product designs, manufacturing processes, supply chains, and other complex systems. This enables rapid experimentation, helps identify optimal configurations, and uncovers novel design approaches that might not be apparent through traditional methods.

The optimization capabilities of Gen AI shift design and process improvement from human-led refinement to potentially radical, AI-driven re-imagination. AI can explore a much larger design space than humans, identifying truly optimal or revolutionary designs and processes that human intuition might overlook due to cognitive biases or limitations in processing vast amounts of data. For example, in manufacturing, AI can optimize warehouse layout, inventory placement, and workflow, leading to significant efficiency gains. In supply chains, Gen AI can simulate various scenarios to design innovative models, optimizing stock levels and reducing waste. This implies that competitive advantage will increasingly stem from a firm's ability to leverage AI to discover non-obvious optimal solutions, leading to superior products and more efficient operations.

15.2 ENHANCING HUMAN CREATIVITY AND COLLABORATION WITH AI

The rise of Generative AI is not leading to a future where machines replace human creativity, but rather one where AI acts as a powerful augmentation tool, fostering a new era of human-AI collaboration.

15.2.1 AI as an Augmentation Tool, not a Replacement

The prevailing narrative often focuses on AI taking jobs, but a more practical and beneficial perspective is emerging: AI functions as an intelligent assistant, enhancing human performance rather than supplanting it. AI excels at tasks that are repetitive, data-intensive, and rule-based, such as data entry, report generation, and invoice processing.This capability frees up human workers from tedious chores, allowing them to focus on activities that require uniquely human attributes: creativity, critical thinking, emotional intelligence, complex problem-solving, and interpersonal communication.This shift not only makes the work environment more stimulating but also boosts job satisfaction and sparks innovation.

By automating mundane tasks, AI creates a strategic opportunity for organizations to reallocate human capital towards higher-value, more creative, and strategic initiatives. The strategic value of

AI is not just in direct cost savings but in unlocking latent human potential within the workforce. This implies a shift in workforce development priorities from task-specific skills to uniquely human capabilities, suggesting that future education and training must emphasize creativity, critical thinking, and emotional intelligence to prepare individuals for symbiotic collaboration with AI.

15.2.2 Human-AI Symbiosis in Creative Workflows

Generative AI can act as a powerful assistant to human creatives, generating content, visuals, and ideas to complement and inspire their work. This augmentation of human creativity can lead to more original, impactful, and differentiated innovations. When AI systems and human innovators team up, several benefits emerge:

- **Parallel Processing of Ideas:** Ideas can be processed in parallel rather than one at a time, accelerating the ideation phase.
- **Avoiding Groupthink:** Teams can avoid groupthink and status-based filtering, as AI can introduce diverse perspectives and challenge conventional thinking.
- **Connecting Knowledge Areas:** AI can identify connections between different knowledge areas that humans might miss, fostering interdisciplinary insights.
- **Rapid Idea Testing:** Teams can test ideas quickly without building costly physical prototypes, using AI tools for rapid visualization and simulation.

This human-AI symbiosis in creative workflows implies a fundamental redefinition of "creativity" itself. It moves from an individual human endeavor to a collaborative process between human and machine, potentially leading to unprecedented levels of creative output and novel solutions that neither could achieve alone. This new dynamic requires a shift in the skills of human participants, emphasizing prompt engineering, critical evaluation of AI-generated outputs, and the ability to effectively integrate AI tools into their creative processes. It also raises philosophical questions about the nature of artistic and intellectual originality in an AI-augmented world.

15.2.3 Automating Repetitive Tasks to Free Human Innovators

A significant impact of AI is its ability to automate repetitive and data-intensive tasks across various business functions. Robotic Process Automation (RPA) and other AI-driven tools can automate tasks like data entry, report generation, and invoice processing. This automation not only increases efficiency and reduces human error but, more importantly, enables employees to dedicate their time to more engaging and impactful work.

By offloading mundane tasks to AI, organizations create a strategic opportunity to reallocate human capital towards higher-value, more creative, and strategic initiatives. This fosters job satisfaction and sparks innovation within the workforce. For example, in customer service, AI handling routine inquiries frees human agents to focus on complex, empathetic interactions. In HR, AI automates resume screening and job description generation, allowing HR professionals to focus on strategic talent acquisition and relationship building. In finance, AI automates invoice processing and account reconciliation, enabling finance teams to shift their focus to strategic planning and value creation.

This strategic reallocation of human effort implies that AI's return on investment extends beyond direct cost savings. It includes increased human engagement, enhanced creativity, and expanded strategic capacity within the organization. By embracing AI to automate the routine, businesses can unlock latent human potential, fostering a more innovative and fulfilling work environment for their employees.

15.3 NEW INNOVATION MODELS DRIVEN BY GENERATIVE AI

Generative AI is not merely optimizing existing innovation processes; it is enabling entirely new innovation models that redefine how organizations conceive, develop, and deliver value.

15.3.1 Autonomous Innovation Processes

With advancements in self-supervised learning and few-shot adaptation, Generative AI holds the potential to handle end-to-end innovation workflows with limited human intervention. This signifies a move towards truly autonomous innovation processes, where AI systems can independently identify problems, generate solutions, and even test them. This capability has the potential to revolutionize the speed, scale, and adaptability of the innovation process itself.

The potential for "autonomous innovation processes" implies a future where AI systems can independently explore vast possibilities for new products, services, or scientific discoveries. This challenges the traditional human-centric model of innovation management, necessitating new governance frameworks for AI-driven innovation. It raises questions about human control, accountability, and the ultimate direction of AI-driven innovation, as the "innovator" increasingly becomes an AI system. This profound shift requires organizations to rethink their innovation strategies, risk management, and the very definition of creative ownership.

15.3.2 Agile Innovation Processes and Design Thinking with Gen AI

The rapid idealization, prototyping, and iteration cycles enabled by Generative AI demand more flexible and adaptive innovation processes. Agile methodologies and design thinking, already recognized for their iterative and human-centered approaches, become indispensable for capitalizing on AI's speed. These methodologies should be deeply embedded throughout the entire innovation lifecycle.

In an "AI-Centered Design Thinking" framework, AI tools are integrated at each stage of the traditional design thinking process:

- **Empathize:** AI analyzes customer data to identify unstated needs and pain points.
- **Define:** AI clusters problems to reveal core challenges.
- **Ideate:** Generative AI produces diverse solution concepts.
- **Prototype:** AI tools rapidly visualize ideas and create virtual prototypes.
- **Test:** Machine learning identifies patterns in user feedback, providing insights for refinement.

This integration means that AI is not just compatible with agile and design thinking; it makes them *imperative*. The acceleration of iteration cycles by Gen AI forces a deeper adoption of these flexible methodologies. Organizations that are not culturally or structurally agile will struggle to fully leverage AI's speed in innovation, highlighting the critical importance of organizational readiness and continuous transformation to foster a truly adaptive innovation environment.

15.3.3 AI-Enabled Open Innovation and Ecosystem Collaboration

Generative AI's capabilities are fostering a shift towards more open, ecosystem-driven innovation models, enabling rapid and secure collaboration across organizational boundaries. This moves beyond traditional bilateral partnerships to a more fluid, dynamic "innovation network" where AI acts as a connector and accelerator.

AI facilitates frictionless partner integration, data and intellectual property sharing (within defined governance frameworks), and co-innovation workflows to maximize collective innovation potential. AI tools can scan vast external datasets, including patents, research papers, and social media, to identify complementary technologies, emerging solutions, and potential partners more efficiently. This capability allows firms to identify and integrate external AI advancements rapidly, making open innovation a competitive necessity.

The proliferation of open-source AI models and accessible AI platforms further democratizes AI capabilities, allowing firms to leverage pre-trained models and APIs from a wide array of external sources. This challenges traditional notions of firm boundaries and intellectual property, necessitating new legal and governance models for collaborative AI development. AI-enabled open innovation implies a need for new legal frameworks for data and IP sharing within AI-driven collaborations, and a shift in strategic focus from individual firm capabilities to the collective capabilities of the innovation network.

15.3.4 Personalization and Customization at Scale

Generative AI is fundamentally redefining the target of innovation, moving from broad market segments to individual consumers. It can create highly personalized products, services, and experiences tailored precisely to individual user needs and preferences. This capability enables "mass personalization," fostering deeper customer engagement and loyalty, and driving innovative business models.

The ability to personalize and customize at scale fundamentally shifts the target of innovation from broad market segments to individual consumers. This implies a profound transformation in marketing, product development, and customer relationship strategies. Instead of designing for an average customer within a segment, businesses can now design and deliver unique offerings for each individual. This requires hyper-granular understanding of customer data, leading to new data collection, analysis, and ethical considerations around individual privacy. The innovation process itself becomes more focused on understanding and responding to individual desires, creating a competitive advantage through bespoke experiences that are difficult for competitors to replicate without similar AI capabilities and data insights.

15.4 MEASURING AI-DRIVEN INNOVATION SUCCESS

Measuring the success of innovation in an AI-driven environment presents unique challenges that necessitate a departure from traditional metrics.

15.4.1 Metrics beyond Traditional ROI

Traditional Return on Investment (ROI) metrics often fall short for AI initiatives because AI's impact compounds over time, and its biggest value comes from efficiency, innovation, and risk reduction, which are hard to quantify in direct dollar terms. Focusing solely on ROI can lead to short-term thinking, causing organizations to prematurely pull the plug on AI initiatives before they have had a chance to iterate, optimize, and deliver real value.

The limitations of traditional ROI for AI highlight a deeper challenge in organizational performance measurement: how to quantify the value of strategic, long-term, and transformative initiatives that do not fit neatly into existing financial models. This necessitates a shift towards a more adaptive and multifaceted measurement framework. AI's value often manifests in non-traditional ways, such as freeing up human potential, enabling new opportunities, and mitigating unforeseen risks. This means that traditional, siloed performance metrics are inadequate, requiring a more integrated and forward-looking approach to measuring success that captures the strategic and transformative impact of AI.

15.4.2 Tracking Operational Efficiency Gains, Adoption, and Business Impact

Instead of chasing a single ROI number, organizations should track a broader set of metrics across four key areas to truly capture AI's value:

- **Operational Efficiency Gains:** This category quantifies the direct benefits of AI in streamlining operations. Key Performance Indicators (KPIs) include time and effort saved by the team, reduction in manual tasks, faster decision-making due to real-time insights, and overall employee productivity improvements through AI-assisted workflows. For example, a marketing team using AI to automate reporting and content generation may not see immediate direct revenue increases, but they save hundreds of hours, freeing them for higher-value work.
- **Adoption and Usage Metrics:** These metrics are crucial for ensuring that AI tools are actually being utilized effectively within the organization. KPIs include the adoption rate (how many employees actively engage with AI tools), usage patterns (whether AI is used for strategic work or just basic tasks), and employee AI fluency (whether skills are improving over time). If AI solutions are not adopted effectively, their potential value remains unrealized. Measuring engagement, AI literacy, and the evolution of strategic use ensures the development of a strong, AI-enabled workforce.
- **Business Impact and Innovation:** This category measures AI's contribution to top-line growth and strategic differentiation. KPIs include revenue growth directly attributable to AI-driven insights, improvements in customer experience (such as faster response

times or enhanced personalization), and the successful creation of new business models or product innovations. Companies leveraging AI strategically are not just cutting costs; they are creating new revenue streams and differentiating themselves from competitors in ways that go beyond simple financial formulas.

- **Risk Reduction and Compliance:** AI plays a significant role in protecting the business from avoidable risks. KPIs in this area include a reduction in compliance violations through automated monitoring, improved decision-making leading to fewer costly errors, and enhancements in cybersecurity through AI-driven threat detection. AI's value in risk mitigation contributes to long-term stability and protects brand reputation.

These measurements provide feedback for continuous improvement, helping organizations refine their AI innovation approach over time. By embracing a multifaceted measurement framework, businesses can gain a more accurate and holistic understanding of AI's value, ensuring that AI initiatives are strategically aligned and deliver long-term, compounding benefits.

ESSAY QUESTIONS

Question 1: Explain how Generative AI accelerates the innovation funnel, specifically focusing on rapid ideation, AI-assisted design, and prototyping. Provide examples to illustrate these accelerations.

Hints for Answer: Explain how Generative AI dramatically accelerates the ideation phase by rapidly generating novel concepts, solutions, and prototypes across various domains, allowing organizations to explore a much wider range of possibilities than previously feasible. Mention how AI systems can generate hundreds of potential solutions by mixing existing knowledge in surprising ways and exploring the "adjacent possible". For AI-assisted design, provide examples like Siemens engineers using AI to generate dozens of design options overnight, resulting in redesigned parts that are 75% lighter and projects completed 30% faster. Discuss how AI tools facilitate rapid visualization of ideas and virtual prototyping, minimizing costly physical prototypes and accelerating testing.

Question 2: Discuss the concept of human-AI symbiosis in creative workflows. How does Generative AI act as an augmentation tool for human creativity, and what new skills are required for human innovators in this collaborative environment?

Hints for Answer: Explain that AI functions as an intelligent assistant, enhancing human performance rather than replacing it, particularly in creative domains. Detail how AI excels at repetitive, data-intensive tasks, freeing human workers to focus on uniquely human attributes like creativity, critical thinking, emotional intelligence, and complex problem-solving. Describe the benefits of human-AI teaming in creative workflows, such as parallel processing of ideas, avoiding groupthink, identifying connections between different knowledge areas, and rapid idea testing without physical prototypes. Discuss the new skills required for human innovators, including prompt engineering, critical evaluation of AI-generated outputs, and the ability to effectively orchestrate AI tools to drive the innovation process.

Question 3: Analyze how Generative AI is enabling new innovation models. Focus on autonomous innovation processes, AI-enabled open innovation, and personalization/customization at scale.

Hints for Answer: For autonomous innovation processes, discuss how advancements in self-supervised learning and few-shot adaptation enable Gen AI to handle end-to-end innovation workflows with limited human intervention, revolutionizing the speed, scale, and adaptability of the innovation process itself. For AI-enabled open innovation, explain how Gen AI facilitates frictionless partner integration, data and intellectual property sharing (within defined governance frameworks), and co-innovation workflows to maximize collective innovation potential. Mention how AI tools can scan external sources like patents and research papers to identify complementary technologies and potential partners more efficiently. For personalization and customization at scale, describe how Gen AI creates highly personalized products, services, and experiences tailored precisely to individual user needs and preferences, fostering deeper customer engagement and loyalty, and driving innovative business models.

Chapter 16

Generative AI and Related Technology Adoption in a Business

It'll be unthinkable not to have (Artificial) intelligence integrated into every product and service. It'll just be an expected, obvious thing.

— Sam Altman, co-founder and CEO, OpenAI

At the end of this chapter, we will learn:

- What are the recommended adoption frameworks for Generative AI?
- How to ensure Data Governance?
- How to adopt Ethical AI Principles and Practices?
- How to build Technical Expertise and Cross-Functional Teams?
- Addressing regulatory requirements while AI adoption

16.1 STRATEGIC ADOPTION FRAMEWORKS FOR GENERATIVE AI

The adoption of Generative AI (Gen AI) in a business context requires a strategic and systematic approach that goes beyond mere technological implementation. It involves critical decisions about how to acquire, integrate, and scale AI capabilities to align with overall business objectives. Like any technology which always starts from the height of inflated expectation and leads to trough of disillusionment before it reaches plateau of productivity, Gen AI is no different.

16.1.1 Build vs. Buy vs. Partner in the AI Era

The traditional "build vs. buy" decision for technology acquisition is significantly complicated by the unique characteristics of Generative AI. For Gen AI, a "partner" option has become increasingly prevalent and often strategic.

- **Building In-House:** Developing Gen AI capabilities from scratch involves significant investment in R&D, specialized talent (e.g., machine learning engineers, data scientists), and computational infrastructure (e.g., high-performance GPUs, TPUs). This approach allows for full control over the technology, customization, and the potential to develop proprietary, AI-native systems that offer deep competitive advantages. However, it is costly, time-consuming, and carries high risk, especially given the rapid pace of AI advancements.

- **Buying (Acquisition):** Acquiring AI startups or companies with established Gen AI capabilities can provide immediate access to talent and technology. This is a faster route than building but can be expensive and carries integration risks, particularly in merging organizational cultures and technology stacks.
- **Partnering (Leveraging External Services):** This has emerged as a dominant strategy for Gen AI adoption. Businesses can partner with major cloud providers like AWS (Amazon Bedrock) and Microsoft (Azure OpenAI Service, Microsoft 365 Copilot) to access powerful, pre-trained foundation models and managed AI services. This approach offers several advantages:
- **Reduced Cost and Risk:** It lowers the massive upfront investment and specialized talent burden associated with building in-house.
- **Accelerated Deployment:** Firms can quickly integrate cutting-edge AI capabilities via APIs, accelerating time-to-market for AI-driven products and services.
- **Scalability:** Cloud platforms provide scalable infrastructure, allowing businesses to easily scale their AI workloads up or down as needed.
- **Access to Expertise:** Partners gain access to the deep AI expertise and continuous innovation of the cloud providers.
- **Focus on Core Business:** By leveraging external AI services, firms can focus their internal resources on their core business and unique value propositions.

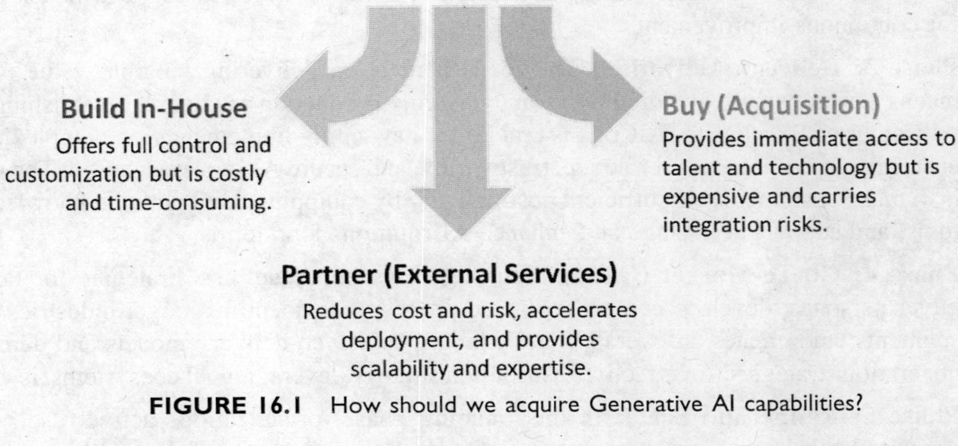

FIGURE 16.1 How should we acquire Generative AI capabilities?

However, partnering also introduces considerations such as vendor lock-in, data sovereignty (where sensitive data is processed by external models), and the long-term strategic control over core AI capabilities. The choice depends on the firm's strategic position, AI maturity, risk appetite, and the specific use case. For many, a hybrid approach combining strategic in-house development for core differentiators with extensive partnering for commoditized or foundational AI capabilities is proving effective.

16.1.2 Phased Implementation and Scalability

Implementing Generative AI effectively requires a structured, phased approach that prioritizes tangible value and allows for continuous learning and refinement. A "think big, start small, scale fast" methodology is often recommended.

A typical phased workflow for establishing a Gen AI practice includes:

- **Phase 1: Technical Activation:** This initial phase focuses on building foundational capabilities. It involves investing in employee training, streamlining internal processes with expert guidance, and hands-on enablement with AI technology. The goal is to showcase Gen AI's practical applications to internal stakeholders and customers through real-world examples. This phase emphasizes people (strong leadership, clear vision, inclusive employee involvement, persona-based training), process (leveraging AI adoption frameworks like AWS CAF-AI), and technology (integrating AI/ML services, serverless offerings, robust data foundations).
- **Phase 2: Solutions and Offering Development:** This phase is crucial for crafting innovative AI solutions tailored to specific client needs. It involves selecting high-value use cases, defining clear problem statements in collaboration with clients, and developing a Gen AI solution statement with identified KPIs and metrics for success. This also includes defining the solution architecture (ensuring scalability, availability, security), preparing and curating data (upholding data integrity and regulatory adherence), selecting and training appropriate AI models, and rigorous deployment and testing (unit, integration, user acceptance tests). This phase is iterative, necessitating a feedback loop for continuous improvement.
- **Phase 3: Delivery Activation:** The focus here is on delivering tangible value. This means starting small, avoiding hype, and ensuring production readiness. Establishing an AI Center of Excellence (AICoE) is crucial for navigating implementation complexities, ensuring responsible, cost-effective, trustworthy, and secure AI implementation. The goal is to make customers self-sufficient post-delivery by equipping them with the knowledge, tools, and support to manage and enhance AI solutions long-term.
- **Phase 4: Go-To-Market (GTM) Planning:** This phase defines strategies for target buyer personas, develops compelling value propositions, identifies target industries and segments, and creates an overall plan including co-sell/co-delivery models and demand generation strategies. An effective distribution strategy, leveraging AI ecosystems, is vital.
- **Phase 5: Refine and Scale:** In this ongoing phase, organizations actively sell and deliver Gen AI services, continuously refining their GTM strategy based on customer feedback. This involves an "AWS flywheel approach" to accelerate identifying high-value opportunities, creating products/experiences, and scaling rapidly. Continuous monitoring and improvement are key to long-term success.

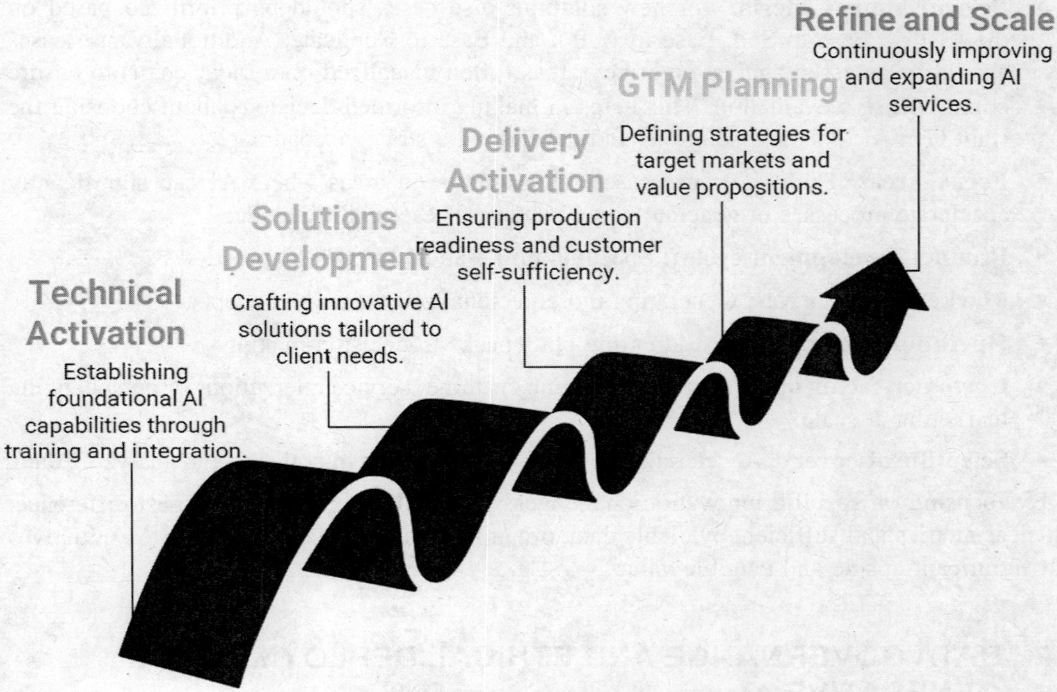

FIGURE 16.2 Building a Gen AI Practice

Scalability is a critical consideration when selecting Gen AI platforms and tools. Organizations must choose solutions that can handle increased volumes and complexity as their AI use cases grow, ensuring seamless integration with existing technology stacks and data systems.

16.1.3 Identifying High-Value Use Cases

Identifying the right Generative AI use cases is paramount for successful adoption and maximizing business value. It requires a clear understanding of organizational needs, strategic alignment, and a realistic assessment of AI's capabilities.

- **Clearly Defined Needs and Goals:** The foundation for successful Gen AI implementation is setting clear implementation goals and objectives. Organizations must articulate what they aim to achieve with Gen AI, whether it's cost reduction, increased customer satisfaction, enhanced productivity, or improved marketing ROI. These initiatives should be adopted in such a way that it supports overall business strategy.
- **Opportunity Identification:** Businesses should identify opportunities where Gen AI can innovate, differentiate, and enhance current offerings. This involves collaborating with clients or internal stakeholders to clearly define the problem and target use case through a "working backwards" approach, understanding their challenges, requirements, and desired outcomes.

- **Prioritization Criteria:** For new solutions, use cases should be prioritized based on the "3E's": Ease to Sell, Ease to Build, and Ease to Replicate. Additionally, use cases should be assessed against eight key areas (often visualized on a radar chart) to ensure comprehensive evaluation. This helps in making informed decisions about choosing the right Gen AI tools and solutions and developing a strategic roadmap.
- **Focus Areas:** High-value use cases often emerge in areas where AI can significantly accelerate processes or generate novel content. These might include:
- **Product development cycles:** Speeding up iteration and design processes.
- **Marketing initiatives:** Generating more personalized creative concepts.
- **Operational workflows:** Addressing bottlenecks in decision-making.
- **Customer-facing operations:** Automating customer service interactions or personalizing marketing at scale.
- **Scientific discovery:** Accelerating research by generating hypotheses and analyzing data.

By focusing on specific innovation challenges where AI can make the biggest difference, with clear metrics and sufficient available data, organizations can ensure their Gen AI initiatives yield significant upside and tangible value.

16.2 DATA GOVERNANCE AND ETHICAL DEPLOYMENT OF GENERATIVE AI

The effective and responsible deployment of Generative AI is critically dependent on robust data governance and a strong ethical framework. AI models are only as good and as fair as the data they are trained on, and their flexible interfaces introduce new vulnerabilities.

16.2.1 Ensuring Data Quality and Mitigating Bias

Generative AI models are heavily reliant on large amounts of data for training, and the quality of that data significantly influences the output.If the training data is inaccurate, unrepresentative, or contains biases, the Gen AI outputs will also be biased, potentially perpetuating harmful stereotypes or discriminatory results. This makes data quality and bias mitigation paramount.

- **Rigorous Data Preparation:** Companies must ensure their data is accurate, unbiased, and reflects real-world scenarios. This involves thorough data cleaning and formatting, identifying outliers, filling in missing values, and carefully selecting relevant features.
- **Bias Identification and Mitigation:** It is crucial to conduct thorough data analysis to identify and mitigate potential biases in training data. This involves implementing processes for testing, monitoring, and refining models to promote fairness and inclusivity. Fairness in machine learning typically involves three phases: pre-processing of data to identify and remove biases, applying fairness constraints during model testing, and post-processing adjustments to the model's decision-making.
- **Hidden Vulnerabilities:** Sensitive information can inadvertently become embedded in neural networks when models are trained on large datasets, creating vulnerabilities that

standard security audits might miss. This necessitates metadata labeling to flag sensitive data before it enters training pipelines and automated classification tools to identify personal information or regulated content.

- **Exponential Data Complexity:** The complexity of managing AI data grows exponentially with increasing AI adoption, making comprehensive testing for edge cases prohibitively expensive and outputs potentially chaotic. This emphasizes the need for continuous monitoring and improvement of data governance practices.

16.2.2 Ethical AI Principles and Development Practices

Establishing formalized responsible AI principles is crucial for aligning everyone in an organization to a shared vision of ethical AI. These principles guide the development and deployment of AI systems to ensure they are responsible, fair, and aligned with ethical principles and societal values.

Key ethical principles, often summarized from guidelines like those by the European Commission, include:

- **Human agency and oversight:** AI should augment human decision-making, uphold human rights, and have mechanisms for human oversight.
- **Technical robustness and safety:** AI systems should be secure, resilient, safe, accurate, and reliable, with contingency plans to prevent unintentional harm.
- **Privacy and data governance:** Systems must fully respect privacy and regulate the quality, privacy, and legitimate access to data.
- **Transparency:** Systems must be traceable and transparent, clearly marked as AI, with their capabilities and limitations communicated effectively. This includes being open about how and when Gen AI is used within the organization.

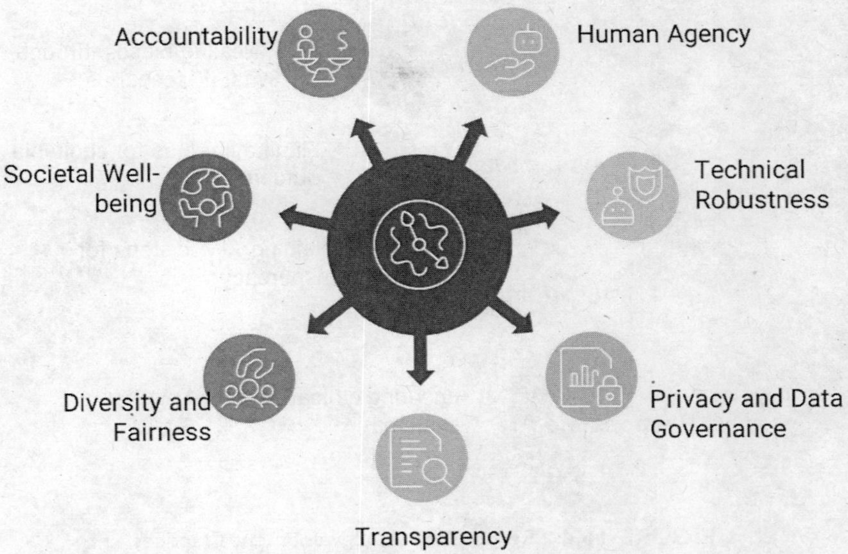

FIGURE 16.3 Ethical AI Principles.

- **Diversity, non-discrimination, and fairness:** AI should avoid promoting bias, support diversity, ensure equal accessibility, and involve stakeholders in the development process.
- **Societal and environmental well-being:** AI systems should benefit all human beings, including future generations, be sustainable, and environmentally friendly.
- **Accountability:** Mechanisms should be put in place to ensure responsibility and accountability for AI systems and their outcomes, including auditability and accessibility.

Responsible AI development practices involve:

- **Assessing Model Training Data:** Having diverse datasets helps represent various cohorts, improving the robustness and inclusiveness of the AI system. Understanding the data used to train models is necessary for uncovering or mitigating issues like AI bias.
- **Causal Analysis:** Understanding how cause-and-effect relationships work in AI models aids in ethical decision-making about how to deploy them, or if they should even be deployed at all.
- **Counterfactuals Analysis:** This process improves model fairness and decision-making by using "what-if" queries to reveal AI biases and logic problems.
- **Fairness in Machine Learning:** Eliminating AI bias is critical to ensuring systems treat different groups or individuals equitably.
- **Model Interpretability:** Developers must be able to interpret and explain why their models make specific decisions and demonstrate certain behaviors to promote trust and transparency.

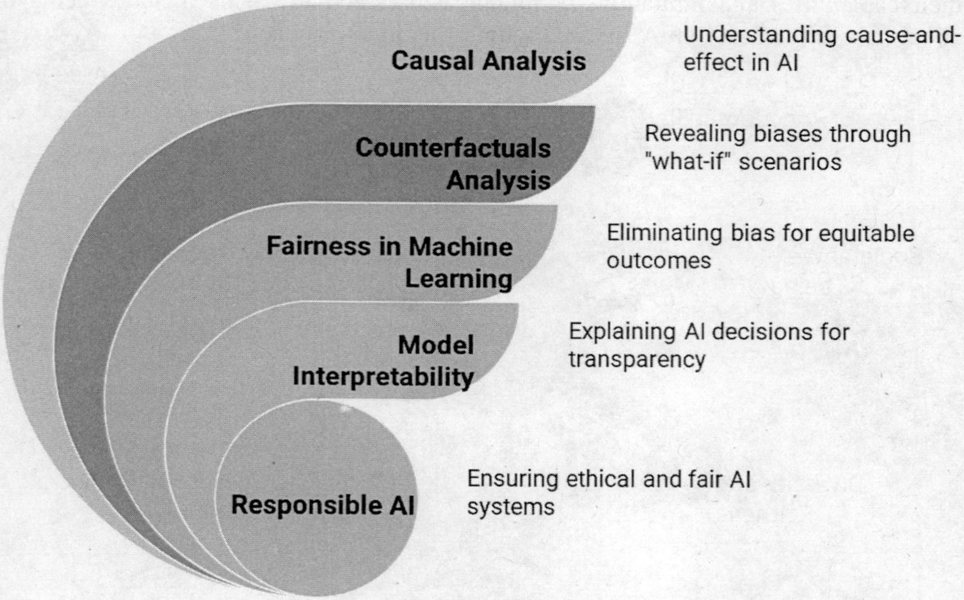

FIGURE 16.4 Responsible AI Development Practices.

By prioritizing these ethical considerations, enterprises can ensure that Gen AI applications are fair, inclusive, responsible, and generate long-term value for the organization and its stakeholders.

16.2.3 Security and Privacy in AI Workflows

The flexible nature of AI interfaces, particularly those that allow users to interact through natural language, introduces new attack vectors like prompt injection and accidental data exposure. Sensitive information can inadvertently become embedded in neural networks when models are trained on large datasets, creating hidden vulnerabilities that standard security audits might miss. This necessitates robust security and privacy measures specifically designed for AI workflows.

Best practices for securing AI data and ensuring privacy include:

- **Data Security Measures:** Implementing strict data security measures to protect sensitive or personally identifiable information used within Gen AI models. This involves following best practices for data encryption (both at rest and in transit) and access controls.
- **Privacy and Consent:** Safeguarding user data according to privacy standards, obtaining informed consent where necessary, and prioritizing anonymization techniques.
- **Access Controls:** Enforcing strict access controls for sensitive data, limiting access on a need-to-know basis and following the principle of least privilege.
- **Data Minimization:** Deploying data minimization practices specifically designed for AI workflows, ensuring that only necessary data is used for training and inference.
- **Input/Output Safeguards:** Implementing safeguards that scrub sensitive data from input logs and reject prompts that could compromise security. The design philosophy should minimize use cases that could introduce sensitive information while maintaining AI functionality.

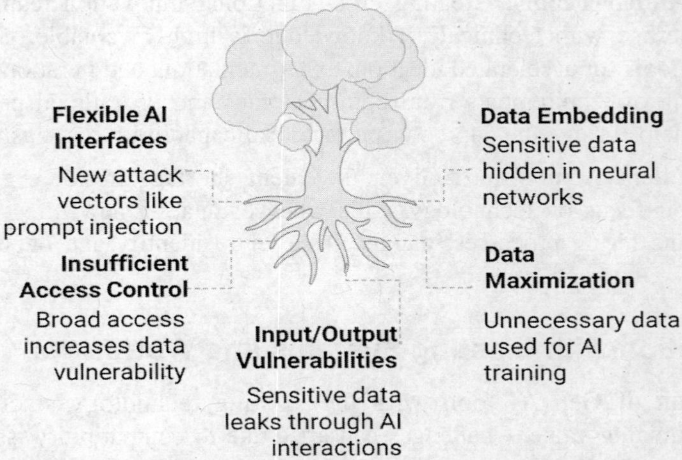

FIGURE 16.5 Securing AI Workflows and Data.

- **Continuous Monitoring and Auditing:** Tracking data lineage, model performance, and potential vulnerabilities through continuous auditing. This includes building flagging capabilities for users to report concerning AI outputs and establishing output contesting systems for error correction. Regular audits of data usage and Gen AI model performance are essential to detect anomalies, potential breaches, or unintended biases.

These measures are critical for ensuring responsible, secure, and compliant data management throughout the entire AI lifecycle, from training to deployment. They address unique challenges that traditional data management approaches cannot fully tackle, fostering trust in AI systems.

16.3 ORGANIZATIONAL READINESS AND CHANGE MANAGEMENT FOR AI ADOPTION

Successful AI adoption is not solely a technical challenge; it is fundamentally an organizational and cultural transformation. Preparing the workforce, adapting existing systems, and fostering a supportive environment are crucial for maximizing AI's benefits.

16.3.1 Building Technical Expertise and Cross-Functional Teams

Effective Gen AI implementation requires a certain level of technical expertise within the internal team or through strategic partnerships with external specialists. This includes skills in machine learning engineering, data science, and prompt engineering.

- **Upskilling the Workforce:** Organizations must invest in employee training and upskilling programs to build AI literacy across all job levels and departments. This is critical, as two-thirds of organizations report not being proactive enough in training employees to work alongside AI technologies, leading to underutilization and potential vulnerabilities. Role-based upskilling paths and hands-on workshops are crucial for practical experience.
- **Cross-Functional Teams:** Creating cross-functional innovation teams that combine domain expertise with technical AI knowledge is highly valuable. These teams can leverage AI tools for accelerated ideation, experimentation, and iteration, fostering better understanding of requirements from both customer and operational perspectives. This integration helps bridge the gap between technical capabilities and business needs.
- **Strategic Talent Acquisition:** Given the talent shortage in AI, organizations must intensify their focus on technology skills when evaluating new hires. AI-driven tools can streamline hiring processes, making it easier to identify and onboard talent more efficiently.

16.3.2 Integration with Existing Systems and Workflows

Seamless integration of Gen AI tools with the existing technology stack is crucial for efficiency and maximizing value. Challenges can arise due to compatibility issues or complex data flows.

- **Strategic Architecture:** Organizations need to define solution architectures that align with well-architected principles (e.g., scalability, availability, security). This involves using appropriate services for integration and deployment.
- **Data Strategy:** A robust data strategy is pivotal for Gen AI solutions, encompassing data preparation, ingestion, storage, and transformation. Upholding data integrity and regulatory adherence is key for developing trustworthy, ethical Gen AI solutions.
- **Workflow Adaptation:** Existing workflows must be adapted to incorporate AI functionalities. This involves initial training and fine-tuning of models, integrating them with existing systems, and carefully managing the change within the organization. The goal is to move from static, rule-based systems to dynamic, learning, and adaptive AI-native applications.

16.3.3 User Training and Fostering an Innovation Culture

Successful Gen AI implementation is not just about technology; it's about people and culture.

- **Prepare Employees:** Organizations must prepare employees for the changes and opportunities presented by Gen AI technology.This includes clearly communicating AI's role as an augmentative tool, not a replacement.
- **Tailored Training Programs:** Provide tailored training programs that teach users not only the mechanics of Gen AI tools but also how to differentiate high-quality output from lower-quality ones and how to provide feedback to refine models over time. This ensures employees can effectively leverage AI's capabilities.
- **Emphasize Collaboration:** Highlight the collaborative role of human experts in overseeing Gen AI processes and the potential for increased efficiency and productivity through human-AI symbiosis.
- **Continuous Learning and Experimentation:** Encourage continuous learning and experimentation with Gen AI models, as the technology rapidly evolves. This fosters a culture of innovation where employees are comfortable exploring new possibilities with AI.
- **Executive Sponsorship:** An executive sponsor is vital for effective Gen AI adoption, championing the vision, addressing concerns, implementing risk mitigation strategies, and driving continuous improvement. This leadership commitment helps foster a company-wide sustainability culture and ensures strategic alignment.
- **Metrics and Improvement:** Set clear metrics to evaluate the impact of AI-driven innovation initiatives, including idea volume/quality, time-to-market acceleration, success rates, and resource efficiency. These measurements provide feedback for continuous improvement and help refine the AI innovation approach over time.

By prioritizing these aspects, enterprises can ensure that Gen AI applications are fair, inclusive, responsible, and generate long-term value for the organization and its stakeholders.

16.4 REGULATORY LANDSCAPE AND FUTURE OUTLOOK FOR AI ADOPTION

The rapid evolution of AI technologies has created a dynamic and often fragmented regulatory landscape globally. Businesses adopting Gen AI must navigate these complexities while also considering the broader environmental implications and future trends.

16.4.1 Navigating Evolving Regulations

The AI regulatory landscape is rapidly evolving, with countries like China, Singapore, Italy, the U.S., Canada, India, the U.K., and the EU shaping their regulatory environments. The EU AI Act, for instance, aims to address all AI applications within a cohesive framework, categorizing AI systems into "risk tiers" (unacceptable, high, limited, minimal risk) with different regulatory burdens. In contrast, the U.S. regulatory environment is more fragmented, consisting of specific federal regulations and a growing "hodgepodge" of state regulations.

- **Challenges of Fragmentation:** While a fragmented landscape can lead to regulatory complexity for businesses, the breakneck speed of AI advancement makes it difficult to create a single, comprehensive regulatory regime that adequately addresses all applications or predicts all eventualities. This inherent variability of AI necessitates an approach that emphasizes flexibility and specificity over breadth.
- **Proactive Compliance:** Companies need to take a proactive approach to capitalizing on opportunities while continuously monitoring and complying with regulations now and in the future. This includes understanding contract and legal implications.The lack of comprehensive federal AI policy in the U.S. means businesses must be prepared to work with a patchwork of policies that are regularly updated.
- **Board Oversight:** Corporate boards face a crucial responsibility in overseeing AI deployment risks and ensuring management implements appropriate controls. Adopting Responsible AI practices is critical for consistent, well-informed decisions and executing AI strategy at speed. Boards must understand management's approach to regulations and compliance, and discuss contract and legal implications.

  The "breakneck speed of technological advancement in AI" creates a fundamental tension with the inherently slower pace of legal and regulatory development. This implies that AI regulation will likely remain dynamic and adaptive, focusing on outcomes and risk tiers rather than rigid prescriptive rules, requiring continuous legal and ethical vigilance from firms.

16.4.2 The Environmental Impact of AI Adoption

As discussed in Chapter 11, the adoption of AI, particularly Generative AI, comes with a significant environmental footprint.

- **Energy Consumption:** AI computing is far more power-intensive than traditional computing, with AI server racks consuming significantly more electricity. The energy demands of AI are rapidly increasing and outpace current efficiency gains, with global data centers projected to consume up to 1,000 TWh of electricity in 2026.

- **Water Consumption:** AI data centers require extensive cooling systems, leading to high water consumption. For instance, generating a 100-word email with ChatGPT-4 consumes approximately 519 milliliters of water.
- **Electronic Waste:** The AI boom increases demand for specialized hardware, resulting in more discarded processors and server parts. Organizations must align their AI strategies with sustainability goals and implement strategies for reducing AI's environmental impact:
- **Optimized Hardware and Cloud Computing:** Transitioning to more energy-efficient hardware (e.g., TPUs) and choosing data centers powered by clean or renewable energy sources significantly reduces emissions.
- **Efficient Training Mechanisms:** Optimizing training algorithms through techniques like model pruning and knowledge distillation can reduce emissions by up to 88 times.
- **Sustainable Vendor Partnerships:** Partnering with AI and cloud platforms committed to renewable or carbon-free energy and publishing sustainability metrics is crucial.
- **Company-Wide Sustainability Culture:** Educating employees on emissions, energy demands, and water use related to AI operations, and fostering a culture of sustainability, helps drive internal change.

16.4.3 Future Trends in AI Adoption

The future of AI adoption is characterized by continued explosive growth and deepening integration across all sectors.

- **Continued Growth:** AI is a rapidly growing industry, with projections showing an annual growth rate of 37.3% between now and 2030. McKinsey projects[1] an annual economic impact of \$6.1-\$7.9 trillion from AI. Half of surveyed organizations have increased investment in Generative AI in the last 10 months, with 44% piloting programs and 10% in production.
- **Increased Demand and Digital Transformation:** The rapid adoption is driven by increased demand in various sectors (healthcare, finance, retail), advancements in generative AI, big data availability, and the shift towards digital transformation and remote work.
- **Human-AI Collaboration:** The future of work is increasingly centered on a powerful and symbiotic relationship between AI and human collaboration. AI is poised to augment human capabilities, automate mundane tasks, and create new opportunities, leading to a more productive, innovative, and fulfilling work environment.
- **Evolving Skill Requirements:** There is an increasing need for AI literacy and the ability to work alongside AI systems. Educational institutions are adapting curricula to prepare the workforce for a future where AI is central to many professions.

[1]https://www.mckinsey.com/capabilities/mckinsey-digital/our-insights/the-top-trends-in-tech accessed 09082025

- **Ethical and Regulatory Maturity:** While challenges in reliability and bias persist, there is a growing public expectation for AI to be regulated. The regulatory landscape will continue to evolve, with a focus on responsible AI development and deployment, including principles of transparency, fairness, and accountability.

The future of Gen AI promises a more innovative, efficient, and sustainable world where human creativity and AI-driven precision coexist. Organizations that strategically embrace AI, manage its risks, and foster a culture of continuous learning and adaptation will be best positioned to thrive in this transformative era.

16.5 SUMMARY

The comprehensive revision of this book on Technology and Innovation Management reveals a profound truth: Artificial Intelligence, particularly Generative AI, is not merely another technology to be managed, but a fundamental force reshaping the very foundations of business and society. The insights gleaned from this analysis underscore several critical conclusions for managers, strategists, and policymakers navigating this new era.

Firstly, the **pace of technological change has accelerated to an unprecedented degree**. Generative AI adoption has outstripped that of personal computers and the internet, compressing traditional technology S-curves and demanding a continuous state of organizational agility and reinvention. This acceleration means that traditional, slower strategic planning cycles are no longer sufficient; instead, continuous learning and rapid adaptation become paramount for competitive survival.

Secondly, AI is **redefining competitive advantage** by enabling hyper-personalization at scale and simultaneously driving significant cost efficiencies. This capability transcends traditional trade-offs in generic strategies, allowing leading firms to pursue a "best of both worlds" approach. The ability to offer unique, tailored experiences to individual customers, alongside optimized, automated operations, fundamentally alters the competitive landscape, making AI a strategic imperative rather than a mere efficiency tool.

Thirdly, the rise of **"AI-native" organizations** signals a new competitive paradigm. These organizations, built from the ground up with AI at their core, possess an inherent advantage in adaptability, efficiency, and innovation. For legacy firms, this implies that digital transformation is no longer sufficient; a deeper, AI-centric organizational redesign is necessary for long-term competitiveness, impacting everything from IT architecture to talent strategy.

Fourthly, AI is **transforming innovation processes, models, and targets**. It accelerates the entire innovation funnel, from ideation and design to research and discovery, by augmenting human creativity and enabling autonomous processes. This human-AI symbiosis redefines creativity itself, but also necessitates new models for open innovation, where leveraging external AI capabilities becomes a competitive necessity. The target of innovation shifts from broad market segments to individual consumers, demanding hyper-granular understanding and tailored offerings.

Finally, the widespread adoption of AI necessitates a deep and proactive engagement with **ethical, social, and environmental considerations**. The potential for algorithmic bias, new privacy and security vulnerabilities, and a significant environmental footprint (energy, water, e-waste) demands robust data governance frameworks and a commitment to Responsible AI principles. The future of work will be characterized by human-AI collaboration, requiring a redefinition of job roles and a focus on uniquely human skills. The evolving regulatory landscape, driven by AI's rapid advancement, will likely remain dynamic and outcomes-based, compelling firms to maintain continuous legal and ethical vigilance.

In essence, AI and Generative AI are not just technologies; they are catalysts for a fundamental re-imagination of business, work, and society. Successfully navigating this transformation requires a holistic, integrated approach to Technology and Innovation Management that embraces agility, prioritizes responsible development, and fosters a symbiotic relationship between human ingenuity and artificial intelligence.

ESSAY QUESTIONS

Question 1: Discuss the critical importance of data governance and ethical deployment when adopting Generative AI. Explain how organizations can ensure data quality, mitigate bias, and address security and privacy concerns in AI workflows.

Hints for Answer: Emphasize that Gen AI models are heavily reliant on data quality, and inaccurate or biased training data can lead to biased or harmful outputs. Discuss best practices for **data quality and bias mitigation**: rigorous data preparation (cleaning, formatting, identifying outliers), and thorough data analysis to identify and mitigate biases (e.g., through fairness in machine learning phases like pre-processing, applying constraints, and post-processing adjustments). For **security and privacy concerns**, explain how flexible AI interfaces introduce new attack vectors (e.g., prompt injection, accidental data exposure) and how sensitive information can be inadvertently embedded in neural networks. Detail best practices such as implementing strict data security measures (encryption, access controls), safeguarding user data according to privacy standards, enforcing data minimization, implementing input/output safeguards, and conducting continuous monitoring and auditing (e.g., tracking data lineage, flagging capabilities, output contesting).

Question 2: Analyze the evolving regulatory landscape for AI globally. What are the key challenges in regulating AI, and how are different regions (e.g., EU, US) approaching this, particularly concerning "risk tiers"?

Hints for Answer: Begin by noting that the rapid evolution of AI technologies has outpaced the development of regulatory frameworks, leading to a complex and fragmented global landscape. Identify key challenges in regulating AI: the breakneck speed of technological advancement, the heterogeneity of AI (not a single technology), and the bitter disagreement among AI experts and policymakers regarding risks and approaches. Contrast the EU AI Act's approach, which pioneers a model sorting AI applications into "risk tiers" (unacceptable, high, limited, minimal risk), each bearing different regulatory burdens. Compare this with the US regulatory environment, described as more fragmented, consisting of specific federal regulations and a growing "hodgepodge" of state regulations, with a comprehensive federal law considered unlikely in the near future. Discuss the inherent tension between flexibility and breadth in AI regulation, and how a patchwork of flexible, regularly updated policies might be more effective than a broad, comprehensive one.

Chapter 17

Strategic Adoption Frameworks for Generative AI

A Comprehensive Enterprise Guide

It'll be unthinkable not to have (Artificial)intelligence integrated into every product and service. It'll just be an expected, obvious thing.

— Sam Altman , co-founder and CEO, OpenAI

At the end of this chapter, we will learn:

- How to steer between different AI alternatives and tools?
- Overview of various well-known adoption frameworks
- Why Strategic Alignment is Essential for Gen AI Adoption?
- How to ensure Organizational Readiness and Change Management?
- How to identify Generative AI Risks and Mitigate them?

17.1 INTRODUCTION

The emergence of Generative Artificial Intelligence (Gen AI) marks a pivotal moment in technology management, presenting both unprecedented opportunities and complex challenges for enterprises. Moving beyond nascent experimentation to achieve scalable, sustainable value from Gen AI necessitates a structured, strategic approach. This report synthesizes insights from leading institutions—including McKinsey, Harvard Business Review, and MIT Sloan—to outline comprehensive frameworks for Gen AI adoption.

The analysis reveals that successful Gen AI integration hinges on a multi-faceted strategy encompassing

- foundational technology evaluation,
- a clear understanding of adoption stages,
- robust organisational capability building,
- meticulous attention to strategic alignment,
- data governance,
- ethical considerations, and
- change management.

Many organisations face a typical "valley of death" situation, which is described as a situation where a promising concept or prototype does not transition into large-scale operational use. To overcome such challenges while scaling Gen AI adoption, organization should

- Ensure responsible AI guardrails as innovation enablers,
- Attempt Simultaneous development of human capital in AI maturity,
- Develop a strong operational backbone,
- Use an "inside-out" adoption approach where an organisation depends on internal capability before looking at anything else,
- Develop a broadened definition of Gen AI's return on investment,
- Recognise the transformative power of comprehensive AI literacy, and
- Bring AI and people together following the "augmentation imperative[1]" principle of empowering them through better visibility, smarter suggestions, and clearer reasoning.

By leveraging these strategic frameworks and addressing the identified considerations, enterprises can navigate the complexities of Gen AI, transform potential resistance into widespread adoption, and unlock profound competitive advantages.

17.2 INTRODUCTION: NAVIGATING THE GENERATIVE AI LANDSCAPE

Generative AI, with its capacity to create novel content across various modalities—from text and images to code and designs—is rapidly reshaping industries and redefining the future of work. Its transformative potential extends across diverse enterprise functions, promising enhanced productivity, accelerated product development, and revolutionised customer experiences. However, the path to realising this potential is fraught with complexities, including technological immaturity, ethical dilemmas, data governance challenges, and significant organisational shifts. Without a structured, strategic adoption framework, organisations risk falling prey to the hype cycle, investing in isolated experiments that fail to scale, or encountering unforeseen risks that erode trust and value.

This chapter is a strategic guide for enterprise leaders, drawing upon established technology management frameworks and expert perspectives from McKinsey, Harvard Business Review, and MIT Sloan. It aims to provide a comprehensive roadmap for navigating the Gen AI landscape, moving beyond ad-hoc implementations to a systematic, enterprise-wide integration that delivers measurable and sustainable business impact. The subsequent sections will delve into foundational evaluation tools, delineate stages of adoption, detail essential organisational capabilities, and articulate critical strategic pillars for successful Gen AI deployment.

[1] HYPERLINK "https://www.syntaxia.com/post/the-augmentation-imperative" \l ":~:text=We%20call%20this%20the%20Augmentation,smarter%20suggestions%2C%20and%20clearer%20reasoning" Accessed 09082025

17.3 FOUNDATIONAL FRAMEWORKS FOR EMERGING TECHNOLOGY EVALUATION AND ADOPTION

This section introduces core frameworks that offer a structured methodology for evaluating, adopting, and maturing emerging technologies like Generative AI within an enterprise context. These frameworks provide a systematic lens through which to assess the potential, risks, and strategic fit of Gen AI before significant investment.

17.3.1 The Emerging Technology Analysis Canvas (ETAC): A Visual Assessment Tool

The rapid pace of technological innovation necessitates a disciplined approach to evaluating new technologies. While organizations frequently make annual decisions regarding technology adoption, a universally accepted framework for the systematic evaluation of emerging technologies has historically been less prevalent. The Emerging Technology Analysis Canvas (ETAC)[2] addresses this need by offering a systematic, visual methodology to dissect complex technologies into manageable components for comprehensive analysis.

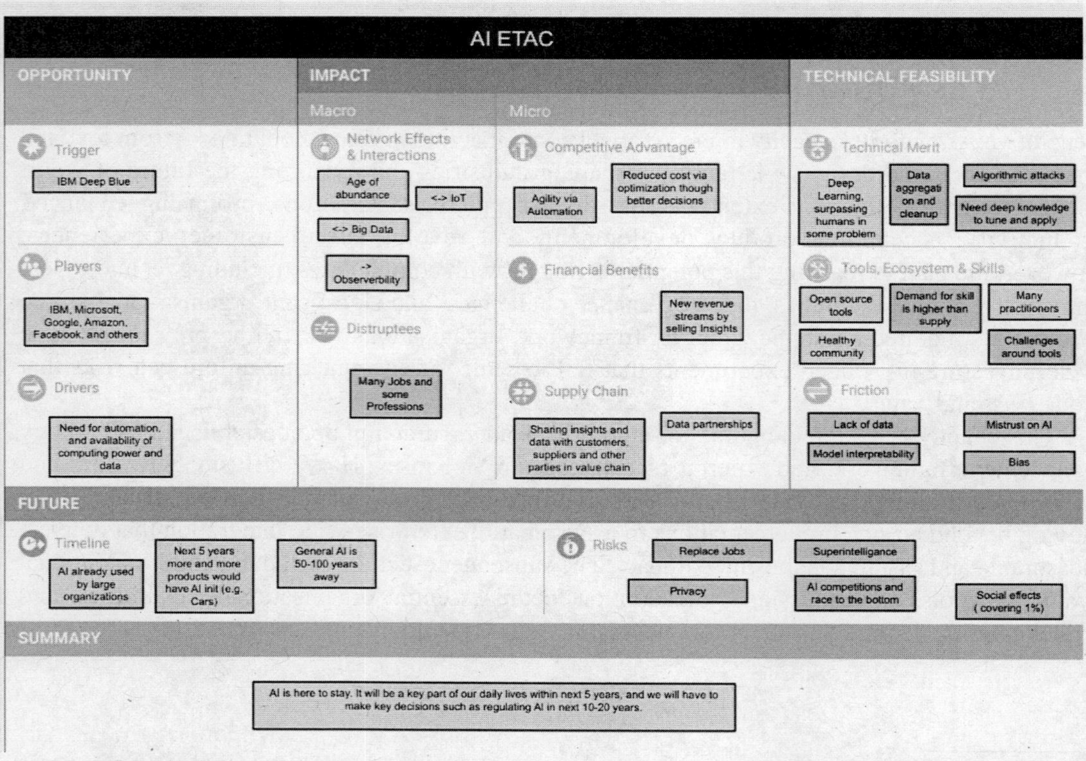

FIGURE 17.1 ETAC for AI (*Source* https://wso2.github.io/ETAC/) accessed 09082025.

---

[2] https://www.researchgate.net/publication/332369758_Emerging_Technology_Analysis_Canvas_ETAC accessed 09082025

A one-page, Visual Canvas for Emerging Technology Evaluation, in the style of 'the Business model Canvas' is how ETAC is described. This single-page, graphic style was purposefully created for quick comprehension and facilitates collaborative discussions among diverse stakeholders. It functions as a logical framework to assess, teach, learn, and discuss various facets of a technology, serving as a valuable brainstorming tool when attempting to understand emerging technologies. The canvas incorporates a series of probing questions, organised around a logical narrative, ensuring a concise, compact, and readily comprehensible representation of the technology's implications.

For Generative AI, ETAC provides a structured mechanism to transcend mere hype and conduct a rigorous assessment of its potential, inherent risks, and strategic alignment before substantial capital allocation. It fosters cross-functional understanding and dialogue, enabling stakeholders to visually map out Gen AI's implications across multiple dimensions, from technical viability to business impact.

While ETAC acts as a technical evaluation tool, its application encourages a holistic view essential for strategic Gen AI adoption. The "logical narrative" and "set of questions" embedded within ETAC, when applied to Gen AI, naturally prompt considerations of overarching business goals, necessary operational changes, and the human element.

Many researchers emphasise the importance of starting with "well-defined problems" and aiming for "measurable outcomes" for successful AI adoption. For example, McKinsey's focus on "value creation" in its technology strategy underscores the need for a comprehensive understanding of how a technology will contribute to the enterprise.[3]

By forcing a structured inquiry into various facets of the technology's potential application and integration, ETAC becomes an effective initial filter for strategic fit, ensuring that Gen AI initiatives are grounded in demonstrable business value rather than solely technological curiosity.

Furthermore, ETAC's visual and discussion-oriented nature makes it an excellent instrument for bridging the technical-business divide often encountered in Gen AI adoption. The framework is designed to "teach, to learn, and to discuss different aspects of the technology"[4], and its visual, single-page format, akin to the Business Model Canvas, is inherently suited for collaborative brainstorming and communication. In the context of Gen AI, which frequently involves a wide array of stakeholders—including IT, business units, legal, human resources, and operations—a shared visual tool can effectively remove communication gaps and cultivate a common understanding. Involving a cross-functional AI leadership team ensures alignment. It is not advisable to build any AI use cases from the top down, but rather to emerge from a recommendation from cross-functional AI discovery workshops. By providing a structured, accessible means to discuss complex technological implications, ETAC helps ensure that all parts of the organisation are aligned on the potential and challenges of Gen AI.

17.3.2 McKinsey's Technology Adoption Stages: Charting the Enterprise Journey

McKinsey's Technology Adoption framework offers a crucial perspective for comprehending the typical progression of a technology within an enterprise, from its initial exploration to full

[3] https://www.mckinsey.com/capabilities/mckinsey-technology/overview accessed 09082025

[4] https://wso2.github.io/ETAC/ accessed 09082025

integration. For Generative AI, a technology still undergoing rapid evolution, this staged approach is invaluable for managing expectations, allocating resources efficiently, and anticipating potential challenges.

McKinsey delineates five distinct stages of enterprise-wide technology adoption, categorized by the level of investment and application:

1. **Frontier innovation:** At this nascent stage, the technology is largely unproven in a business context, with minimal organizational investment or application.
2. **Experimentation:** Organizations begin testing the technology's functionality and viability through small-scale prototypes, typically without an immediate focus on Return on Investment (ROI). Few companies have initiated or completed scaling efforts.
3. **Piloting:** The technology is deployed in its initial business use cases, via pilot projects or limited implementations, to assess its feasibility and effectiveness.
4. **Scaling in progress:** Organizations are actively engaged in deploying and adopting the technology across the entire enterprise.
5. **Fully scaled:** The technology has been completely deployed and integrated throughout the enterprise, becoming a standard and widely utilized solution, with its value and benefits fully recognized.

This framework is particularly relevant for Gen AI, as it helps organizations identify their current position in the adoption lifecycle and understand the capabilities required to advance. It shifts the organizational focus from isolated experiments to a structured, enterprise-wide adoption journey.

McKinsey identifies several overarching themes impacting technology trends, which are highly pertinent to Gen AI:

- **Rise of autonomous systems and new human-machine collaboration:** Autonomous systems, encompassing both physical robots and digital agents, are transitioning from pilot projects to practical applications, demonstrating abilities to learn, adapt, and collaborate. Human-machine interaction is evolving with more natural interfaces and adaptive intelligence, fundamentally shifting the paradigm from human replacement to augmentation.
- **Scaling challenges:** The escalating demand for compute-intensive workloads, particularly driven by Gen AI, imposes new pressures on global infrastructure. This manifests as data centre power constraints, physical network vulnerabilities, and increased compute demands. Beyond technical hurdles, scaling efforts are hampered by supply chain delays, labour shortages, and regulatory friction.
- **Regional and national competition:** Global competition over critical technologies has intensified, prompting countries and corporations to prioritise sovereign infrastructure and localised chip fabrication.

McKinsey's broader technology strategy approach emphasises three core priorities:

- reimagining the role of technology by developing a tech-forward business strategy and an integrated approach;

- reinventing technology delivery through agile methodologies, next-gen infrastructure, engineering excellence, and strategic partnerships; and
- future-proofing the foundation by establishing business-backed architecture, ensuring data ubiquity, leveraging advanced analytics, and fortifying cyber and data privacy defences.

Common pitfalls observed in Gen AI programs include a "failure to innovate," often stemming from process constraints, rework, and delays in compliance, and a "failure to scale," characterised by pervasive risk concerns and cost overruns that can derail entire initiatives.

To mitigate these issues, McKinsey advocates for the development of a centralised platform comprising validated services—such as ethical prompt analysis, Large Language Model (LLM) observability, preapproved prompt libraries, multi-cloud automation, and access controls—and reusable assets, including application patterns, reusable code, and training materials.

Successful Gen AI platforms, based on McKinsey's experience, typically integrate four core components:

- **Self-service portal** enables secure, scalable access to Gen AI tools, accelerating solution development with validated capabilities and centralized dashboards for observability and budget control.
- **Open, modular architecture** supports integration and reuse of Gen AI services, reducing total cost of ownership and enabling common patterns like chatbots and Retrieval-Augmented Generation.
- **Automated responsible AI guardrails** ensure compliance and ethical use by auditing code, prompts, and outputs for risks like hallucinations, bias, or data leakage.
- **Centralized AI gateway** enforces these guardrails across the development lifecycle, promoting safe, transparent, and scalable Gen AI adoption.

Crossing the Valley of death: This transition often presents a "valley of death" where underlying infrastructure, talent, and governance deficiencies become prohibitive. The McKinsey framework highlights several scaling challenges such as

- compute-intensive workloads, especially from gen AI,
- data centre power constraints,
- supply chain delays,
- Skilled labour shortages, and
- regulatory friction.

Many Gen AI programs failure to scale due to risk concerns and cost overruns derailing the entire initiatives. The enterprises must proactively invest in scalable infrastructure, reusable components, and robust governance from the outset, rather than treating scaling as an afterthought. Without this forward-looking approach, initial successes may lead to costly dead ends and missed opportunities for widespread value creation.

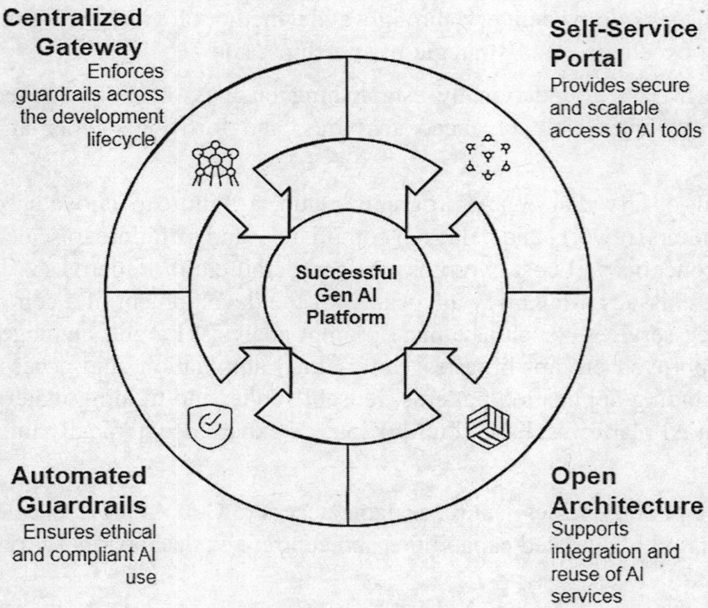

FIGURE 17.2 Components of Successful Gen AI Platforms.

Further, establishing responsible AI guardrails is not merely a compliance or ethical consideration; it is a fundamental enabler of enterprise-scale Gen AI adoption.

McKinsey explicitly identifies "Automated, responsible AI guardrails" as one of the three core components of successful Gen AI platforms, designed not just for risk mitigation and compliance but also to "foster innovation while managing risk". These guardrails involve proactive measures such as reviewing code for responsible AI, auditing LLM prompts and responses for data policy violations, hallucinations, and ethical biases, and tracking cost implications. The underlying rationale is that without these safeguards, security and reputational risk concerns if handled individually, become too large and expensive to overcome, leading to program shutdowns.

Gartner also heavily underscores the critical need for policies and controls to address risks like lack of transparency, accuracy, bias, and intellectual property. This suggests that building automated, responsible AI guardrails into the platform from the outset transforms risk management from a reactive, costly bottleneck into a proactive, scalable capability. This directly impacts an organization's ability to confidently progress from "piloting" to "scaling" stages, elevating responsible AI from a desirable feature to a core architectural and strategic requirement for Gen AI success, ensuring that innovation can proceed safely and efficiently.[5]

The following table summarizes McKinsey's Generative AI Adoption Stages, outlining typical activities, strategic focus areas, and key challenges at each phase, providing a practical, stage-gated roadmap for leaders.

[5] https://www.gartner.com/en/topics/generative-ai accessed 09082025

TABLE 17.1 McKinsey's Generative AI Adoption Stages and Strategic Focus Areas

Stage	McKinsey Description	Typical Generative AI Activities/Focus	Key Challenges for Gen AI at this Stage
1. Frontier Innovation	Technology is nascent; few organizations invest or apply it; largely unproven in a business context.	Educating the workforce on AI; setting up acceptable use policies; making data accessible; experimenting with AI technologies to get comfortable with automated decision-making.	Unproven business context; high uncertainty; lack of immediate ROI focus; limited internal expertise.
2. Experimentation	Organizations test functionality and viability with small-scale prototypes, typically without an immediate focus on ROI. Few companies are scaling.	Building pilots and capabilities; beginning to simplify and automate processes; creating initial use cases; sharing data via APIs; leveraging LLMs to augment work; tracking value created in pilots.	Lack of clear ROI; "proof-of-concept purgatory"; data fragmentation; talent shortage for scaling; organizational resistance to change.
3. Piloting	Organizations deploy the technology in first few business use cases via pilot projects or limited implementation to test feasibility and effectiveness.	Expanding process automation efforts; changing to a more test-and-learn way of working; architecting for reuse; incorporating pretrained models and investigating proprietary AI models; exploring autonomous agents.	Integration with legacy systems; data quality and bias concerns; privacy and security risks; initial scaling challenges; securing executive buy-in for broader investment.
4. Scaling in Progress	Organizations actively scale deployment and adoption across the enterprise.	Building a scalable enterprise architecture (AI platform); making data and outcomes transparent; developing a pervasive test-and-learn culture; implementing automated, responsible AI guardrails; developing reusable Gen AI services.	Compute-intensive workloads; data center power constraints; supply chain delays; labor shortages; regulatory friction; risk concerns (IP, bias); cost overruns; organizational resistance to widespread change.
5. Fully Scaled	Technology is fully deployed and integrated across the enterprise, becoming standard and used at large scale, with recognized value and benefits.	Continuous optimization and iteration of Gen AI models; pervasive use of autonomous agents; deep integration into core operations; continuous monitoring of performance, ethics, and compliance; driving new revenue channels and product development.	Maintaining ethical oversight; managing evolving cyberthreats; ensuring continuous talent optimization; adapting to new regulatory changes; sustaining innovation and competitive advantage.

17.3.3 MIT Sloan's Innovation and AI Maturity Models: Building Core Capabilities

MIT's contributions provide both a macro-level understanding of how innovation ecosystems thrive and a micro-level roadmap for enterprise AI maturity. These frameworks extend beyond mere technology adoption to encompass the critical organizational and cultural shifts required for sustained success.

The MIT framework[6] broadly defines "Innovation" as "the process of taking new-to-the-world ideas from 'inception to impact'". This impact can extend beyond commercial profits to include environmental, social, medical, or security outcomes. The framework highlights two critical "capacities" that serve as the "twin engines" of innovation ecosystems: Innovation Capacity (I-Cap) and Entrepreneurship Capacity (E-Cap), both underpinned by foundational institutions.

- **Innovation Capacity (I-Cap)** focuses on the ability of a place (city, region, or nation) to develop new-to-the-world ideas and translate solutions into useful products and services. This includes basic science and research (R&D) as well as the practical application of those findings.
- **Entrepreneurship Capacity (E-Cap)** emphasizes creating a favorable "business environment" and enabling the successful scale-up of all enterprises, including innovation-driven startups.

Five critical dimensions provide inputs into the I-Cap/E-Cap production function: **Human Capital** (talent, education, mobility policies) and **Funding** (R&D spending, tax policies, investment policies, public-listing requirements). A crucial observation from this framework is that simply adopting new technologies will not yield the expected ROI if not accompanied by fundamental changes to individuals' behavior, institutional leadership, and resulting incentive structures, all of which must become more agile and adaptive.

Complementing this macro perspective, the **MIT CISR Enterprise AI Maturity Model**[7] describes four stages of enterprise AI maturity, identified through a survey of 721 companies. This model demonstrates a strong correlation between higher maturity stages and significantly superior financial performance.

- **Stage 1: Experiment and Prepare (28% of enterprises):** The focus is on educating the workforce on AI, establishing acceptable use policies, making data accessible, ensuring data-driven decision-making, and identifying where human intervention is necessary.
- **Stage 2: Build Pilots and Capabilities (34%):** Enterprises begin to simplify and automate processes, create use cases, share data via APIs, adopt a coaching and communication-oriented management style, and leverage LLMs (both traditional and generative AI models) to augment work.
- **Stage 3: Develop AI Ways of Working (31%):** This stage is characterized by expanding process automation efforts, transitioning to a more test-and-learn operational approach,

[6]https://innovation.mit.edu/assets/BuddenMurray_An-MIT-Approach-to-Innovation2.pdf accessed 09082025

[7]https://cisr.mit.edu/publication/2024_1201_EnterpriseAIMaturityModel_WeillWoernerSebastian accessed 09082025

architecting for reuse, incorporating pretrained models (and investigating proprietary AI models), and exploring autonomous agents.

- **Stage 4: Become AI Future Ready (7%):** This represents the highest level of maturity, implying advanced integration, continuous adaptation, and pervasive AI capabilities across the enterprise. Enterprises in stages 3 and 4 demonstrated financial performance well above the industry average.

Furthermore, the **MIT Sloan Digital Transformation Framework** highlights a common pitfall: "jumping head-first into digital transformation without first establishing the necessary foundation". It underscores the importance of having an "operational backbone and shared customer insights" in place *before* attempting to build a digital platform. This framework advocates for a holistic approach, encompassing organizational change (including leadership commitment, talent development, and agile methodologies) and ecosystem engagement (collaborating with partners) to fully capitalize on digital opportunities.

For Gen AI, these MIT frameworks collectively underscore that success is not merely about implementing models but about cultivating the organizational capacity—including talent, culture, funding, and foundational infrastructure—to innovate with AI and mature its utilization over time. This emphasizes the need for foundational readiness and a long-term strategic perspective that extends beyond initial pilot projects.

The following table provides a detailed overview of the MIT CISR Enterprise AI Maturity Model, outlining the characteristics of each stage, key Generative AI focus areas, and the associated financial performance. This serves as a clear, actionable progression for organizations to benchmark their current AI maturity and plan for future stages.

TABLE 17.2 MIT CISR Enterprise AI Maturity Model: Stages and Required Capabilities for Generative AI

AI Stage	Characteristics/Attributes	Key Generative AI Focus Areas	Associated Financial Performance
1. Experiment and Prepare	Educating the workforce on AI; setting up acceptable use policies; working on making data accessible; ensuring decision-making is using data; identifying where humans need to be in the loop.	AI literacy programs; establishing Gen AI usage policies; data accessibility initiatives; initial exploration of Gen AI tools for data-driven decision support; identifying human-in-the-loop requirements for Gen AI outputs.	Below Industry Average
2. Build Pilots and Capabilities	Beginning to simplify and automate processes; creating use cases; sharing data via APIs; leveraging a coach and communicate management style; using LLMs—both out-of-the-box traditional and generative AI models—to augment work.	Developing specific Gen AI use cases (e.g., content generation, summarization); piloting Gen AI solutions in controlled environments; improving data sharing via APIs for Gen AI models; fostering human-AI augmentation through LLMs; tracking value from pilot projects.	Below Industry Average

(*Contd.*)

TABLE 17.2 MIT CISR Enterprise AI Maturity Model: Stages and Required Capabilities for Generative AI (*Contd.*)

AI Stage	Characteristics/Attributes	Key Generative AI Focus Areas	Associated Financial Performance
3. Develop AI Ways of Working	Expanding process automation efforts; changing to a more test-and-learn way of working; architecting for reuse; incorporating pre-trained models into work and investigating the use of proprietary AI models; exploring autonomous agents.	Scaling Gen AI process automation; implementing iterative Gen AI development cycles; designing enterprise architecture for Gen AI model reuse; integrating pretrained/proprietary Gen AI models into workflows; exploring autonomous Gen AI agents for complex tasks.	Well above Industry Average
4. Become AI Future Ready	Implies pervasive, adaptive, and integrated AI capabilities	Continuous optimization and innovation with Gen AI; widespread deployment of autonomous Gen AI agents; deep integration of Gen AI across all business functions; proactive adaptation to evolving Gen AI technologies and regulatory landscapes; driving new business models with Gen AI.	Well above Industry Average

17.4 STRATEGIC PILLARS FOR GENERATIVE AI ADOPTION

This section delves into the critical strategic pillars essential for successful Generative AI adoption, drawing consolidated perspectives and best practices.

17.4.1 Strategic Alignment is Essential for Gen AI Adoption; Initiatives must Tie to Business Goals and Measurable ROI to Avoid Becoming Costly Experiments

- Start with well-defined problems like customer service delays or repetitive tasks, involving cross-functional stakeholders early for alignment.
- Only ~25% of AI projects meet ROI expectations; success requires linking use cases to KPIs, tracking metrics, and modelling ROI rigorously.
- Focus on "big value" initiatives and scale programs for maximum impact, as advised by McKinsey and Gartner.
- Inside-out approach is recommended: begin with internal use cases to build trust, refine models, and prove ROI before scaling externally.

- ROI for Gen AI should include indirect benefits—worker augmentation, process improvement, risk mitigation, and sustainability—not just cost savings.
- Measure broader outcomes like employee productivity, compliance, and long-term strategic value.
- A comprehensive ROI framework ensures Gen AI drives competitive advantage and operational resilience beyond immediate financial returns.

17.4.2 Data Governance, Ethics, and Responsible AI

Generative AI's dependence on vast, diverse datasets and its inherent capacity to generate new content introduce unprecedented challenges related to data quality, intellectual property, bias, transparency, and ethical use. Proactive and robust governance is paramount to mitigate risks and cultivate trust. There are several key oversight risks associated with Gen AI:

- **Lack of transparency:** Gen AI models are often unpredictable, and even their creators may not fully comprehend their internal workings.
- **Accuracy:** These systems can produce inaccurate and fabricated answers, necessitating rigorous assessment of all outputs before reliance or public distribution.
- **Bias:** Policies and controls are required to detect and address biased outputs in accordance with company policy and legal requirements.
- **Intellectual Property (IP) and Copyright:** Currently, there are no verifiable data governance and protection assurances for confidential enterprise information. Users should operate under the assumption that data or queries entered into public Gen AI tools may become public, and enterprises are advised to implement controls to prevent inadvertent IP exposure.
- **Cybersecurity and Fraud:** Malicious actors are leveraging Gen AI for sophisticated cyber and fraud attacks, such as deepfakes for social engineering, necessitating robust mitigating controls.
- **Sustainability:** Gen AI consumes substantial electricity, making vendor selection that prioritizes reduced power consumption and renewable energy sources crucial for mitigating environmental impact.

17.4.3 Organizational Readiness and Change Management

Technology adoption is fundamentally a human endeavor. Without adequate preparation, comprehensive training, and proactive cultural shifts, even the most advanced Generative AI solutions will encounter significant organizational resistance, leading to underutilization and a failure to deliver their full potential.

A significant pitfall is treating AI adoption as a purely technical exercise, neglecting the human dimension. Many leaders underestimate the importance of change management, communication, and training, which can lead to superficial AI use or employee opposition. A common mistake is insufficient investment in AI literacy. The effectiveness of Generative AI's output is directly proportional to the quality of the prompts it receives, and inexperienced employees are more prone to crafting poor prompts, resulting in frustration and disengagement.

Organizational resistance is a pervasive challenge in enterprise AI adoption. Employees may harbour fears of job displacement, while managers might express skepticism towards algorithms. Many AI pilot projects fail due to human factors such as a lack of trust or inadequate training.

Strategic solutions and best practices to address these challenges include prioritizing comprehensive AI literacy programs for executives, teams, and frontline workers. This training should encompass prompt engineering, understanding data privacy implications, and addressing anxieties and fears surrounding AI.

It is crucial to foster a culture of augmentation by conducting workshops that explicitly clarify how AI supports—rather than replaces—roles, thereby shifting the narrative from human replacement to human-machine collaboration.

Securing executive sponsorship and communicating a clear vision for AI adoption is paramount. Senior leaders must actively champion AI initiatives, articulate the rationale for AI adoption (e.g., improved customer service, simplified workflows), and align it with the company's broader mission.

Thoughtful redesign of processes and roles is necessary, involving teams in how work is done and clarifying that AI augments human effort. The MIT CISR Stage 2 explicitly mentions using LLMs to augment work.[8] Furthermore, building a strong and diverse multidisciplinary team with expertise in AI, data science, project management, and domain knowledge, fostering collaboration between technical experts and business stakeholders. This pillar ensures that the workforce is not only prepared for but actively embraces Generative AI, transforming potential resistance into widespread adoption and productivity gains through effective human-AI collaboration.

17.5 HOW TO MITIGATE THE RISKS

Establishing a robust AI governance and ethics frameworks, complete with committees or protocols for reviewing algorithms for fairness and accuracy, and conducting regular bias audits is the recommended way to mitigate the risks associated with use of Gen AI. This can be done using the following steps:

Develop a comprehensive responsible AI strategy entrusting accountability to designated teams with defining roles and decision-making authority for AI initiatives. Organizations should adopt responsible AI principles (e.g., Microsoft's six principles, which align with the NIST AI Risk Management Framework) as business objectives, integrating them into project planning and development processes. It is also critical to select appropriate responsible AI tools and processes that align with specific use cases and risk profiles, and to identify and continuously monitor compliance requirements for relevant local and international AI regulations.

A leading research firm Gartner provides specific ethical guidance[9] for using Gen AI :

- "Start inside" by testing extensively with internal stakeholders before deploying customer- or external-facing content to prevent "hallucinations" from harming the business.
- "Prize transparency" by clearly labeling machine interactions to users.

[8]https://innovation.mit.edu/assets/Framework-Ecosystem-Policy_Oct18.pdf accessed 09082025

[9]https://www.gartner.com/en/topics/generative-ai accessed 09082025

- "Do your due diligence" by establishing guardrails to track biases and continuously validate results.
- "Address privacy and security concerns" by ensuring sensitive data is neither input nor derived, and confirming data usage with model providers.
- "Take it slow" by keeping functionality in beta for an extended period to manage expectations for perfect results.

Gartner also recommends crafting a usage policy for Gen AI rather than an outright ban, including directives such as: avoiding input of Personally Identifiable Information (PII), sensitive information, or company IP; turning off history if using external tools; and closely monitoring outputs for errors or biases. This pillar is non-negotiable for building trust, ensuring compliance, mitigating legal and reputational risks, and achieving sustainable, ethical Gen AI deployment. Ignoring these aspects can lead to significant financial penalties, erosion of customer trust, and ultimately, project failure.

Organization should integrate automated, responsible AI guardrails as a core component of successful Gen AI platforms, not just for risk mitigation but also to foster innovation while managing risk. Generative AI, robust data governance and responsible AI frameworks are not merely regulatory burdens or reactive measures to avoid pitfalls. Instead, they are strategic assets that enable innovation by building a trusted, controlled, and predictable environment for experimentation and deployment.

Another critical consideration revolves around the evolving landscape of intellectual property (IP) and data ownership in the age of Generative AI. Gartner explicitly flags "Intellectual property (IP) and copyright" as a significant and rapidly evolving risk, stating, "There are currently no verifiable data governance and protection assurances regarding confidential enterprise information. Users should assume that any data or queries they enter into ChatGPT and its competitors will become public information". They strongly advise implementing controls to prevent inadvertent IP exposure.

The following table summarizes the key Generative AI risks and provides corresponding mitigation strategies, aligning them with responsible AI principles. This offers a practical guide for proactive risk management, fostering a more confident, secure, and ethically sound adoption environment.

TABLE 17.3 Generative AI Risks and Mitigation Strategies

Risk Category	Description of Risk	Mitigation Strategy/Best Practice	Responsible AI Principle Addressed
Data Quality and Bias	Poor-quality, incomplete, or historically biased data leads to unreliable, unfair, or inaccurate AI outputs, eroding trust.	Establish robust AI governance and ethics frameworks; invest in data preparation, augmentation, and synthetic data generation; implement continuous human oversight and feedback loops.	Fairness, Accuracy, Robustness

(Contd.)

TABLE 17.3 Generative AI Risks and Mitigation Strategies (*Contd.*).

Risk Category	Description of Risk	Mitigation Strategy/Best Practice	Responsible AI Principle Addressed
Intellectual Property (IP) and Copyright	Lack of verifiable data governance for confidential enterprise information; risk of sensitive data/IP exposure via public model inputs; unclear ownership of AI-generated content.	Implement strict usage policies (no PII, sensitive data, or company IP input); confirm data usage with model providers; turn off history for external tools; continuously monitor outputs for IP leakage.	Privacy, Security, Accountability
Cybersecurity and Fraud	Malicious actors use Gen AI for sophisticated attacks (e.g., deepfakes, complex scams, social engineering); new vulnerabilities introduced by AI systems.	Educate users to recognize AI-generated text/media; create helpdesk practices to counteract AI spoofing; leverage AI-powered devices for real-time monitoring; establish clear AI governance policies for threat response.	Security, Robustness, Accountability
Lack of Transparency	Gen AI models are often "black boxes," making it difficult to explain or understand their decision-making processes and outputs.	Improve AI transparency and explainability tools; clearly label machine interactions; implement processes and guardrails to track biases and validate results.	Transparency, Explainability
Accuracy (Hallucinations)	Gen AI systems can produce inaccurate, fabricated, or nonsensical answers ("hallucinations").	Rigorous assessment and human validation of all outputs; continuous learning loops to refine responses; keep functionality in beta for extended periods to manage expectations.	Accuracy, Robustness
Insufficient Proprietary Data	Data is fragmented, siloed, or insufficient to train effective AI models, hindering customization and performance.	Develop robust data strategy and architecture (centralized data lakes); leverage data augmentation and synthetic data; form strategic data partnerships; use federated learning.	Data Responsibility, Efficiency

(*Contd.*)

TABLE 17.3 Generative AI Risks and Mitigation Strategies (*Contd.*).

Risk Category	Description of Risk	Mitigation Strategy/Best Practice	Responsible AI Principle Addressed
Sustainability Impact	Gen AI consumes significant electricity due to compute-intensive workloads.	Choose vendors that reduce power consumption and utilize high-quality renewable energy; optimize model size and efficiency; consider AI-powered devices to offload workloads.	Environmental Impact, Responsibility

The following table summarizes common Generative AI adoption mistakes related to people and processes, along with actionable corrective actions. This serves as a practical guide for avoiding pitfalls and fostering a more receptive and productive environment for Gen AI.

TABLE 17.4 Common Generative AI Adoption Mistakes and Corrective Actions (People and Process Focus)

Mistake Category	Description of Mistake	Corrective Action/Best Practice
Overlooking People: Change Management and Training	Treating AI adoption as purely technical; underestimating change management, communication, and training; leading to employee pushback or performative use.	Introduce comprehensive AI literacy programs for all employee levels; run workshops explaining how AI supports, not replaces, roles; empower "AI champions" for peer-led guidance.
Lacking Leadership Ownership and Coordination	AI adoption falls between departments; no single executive ownership; fragmented efforts, stalled adoption, and wasted time.	Designate a cross-functional AI leadership team (executives, HR, IT, frontline managers); align AI strategy with broader business transformation objectives; equip HR and operations to support adoption (systems, training, monitoring, feedback).
Building Top-Down Use Cases	Leadership ideates use cases benefiting their workflows, overlooking needs/pain points of other teams; leads to low adoption and minimal impact on productivity/satisfaction.	Implement cross-functional AI discovery workshops/use case clinics; involve IT, business units, compliance, and frontline employees; strategically solve problems from the bottom up.
Overestimating AI Capabilities (AI Isn't Magic)	Expecting AI to perform tasks it's not built for; overconfidence in tools leads to misaligned expectations and disappointment.	Start small, pilot AI in one team/function before scaling; clearly communicate AI's limitations alongside benefits; involve humans in the loop for oversight (especially critical decisions); regularly evaluate and refine AI outputs.

(*Contd.*)

TABLE 17.4 Common Generative AI Adoption Mistakes and Corrective Actions (People & Process Focus)

Mistake Category	Description of Mistake	Corrective Action/Best Practice
Treating AI as Replacement, not Augmentation	Removing too many human touchpoints in rush to cut costs; leaving users frustrated and frontline employees overwhelmed with complex issues.	Use AI to automate repetitive tasks, triage tickets, surface knowledge; keep humans involved for high-empathy, complex cases; prioritize hybrid human-AI experiences where AI empowers agents.
Insufficient Proprietary Data Available	Data is fragmented, siloed, or insufficient to train effective AI models; preparing data is time-consuming and expensive.	Centralize data lakes; use data augmentation and synthetic data generation; form strategic data partnerships; leverage federated learning.
AI Talent Shortage	Lack of in-house expertise to design, deploy, and maintain AI systems.	Upskill and reskill existing workforce; leverage low-code/no-code tools; partner with AI vendors or consulting firms; hire strategically and prioritize retention.
Unclear ROI and Business Case	Difficulty proving financial value; making it hard to get stakeholder buy-in; projects stuck in "proof-of-concept purgatory."	Align AI with strategic business goals and KPIs; define clear metrics before starting; begin with quick wins; quantify cost of inaction; engage finance and leadership early.
Integration with Legacy Systems	Existing systems are outdated or incompatible with AI workflows; prevents AI from scaling beyond isolated experiments.	Conduct technology readiness assessment; use integration platforms (iPaaS) and middleware; favor AI solutions with pre-built connectors; architect for scalability and performance.

17.6 CONCLUSION AND RECOMMENDATIONS

The strategic adoption of Generative AI represents a profound opportunity for enterprises to redefine operations, innovate products, and enhance competitive positioning. This analysis, drawing upon frameworks and observations from McKinsey, Harvard Business Review, and MIT Sloan, reveals that successful integration is not merely a technological endeavor but a holistic transformation requiring deliberate planning across multiple dimensions.

A key conclusion is that organizations must move beyond isolated experimentation and navigate the critical "valley of death" that often separates successful pilots from enterprise-wide scaling. This requires proactive investment in foundational capabilities, particularly scalable infrastructure, reusable architectural components, and robust data governance. The integration of "automated, responsible AI guardrails" is not a compliance overhead but a strategic imperative that enables innovation by providing a secure and trusted environment for Gen AI deployment. Without these safeguards, risks related to bias, intellectual property, and cybersecurity can quickly escalate, hindering widespread adoption and value realization.

Furthermore, the human element emerges as central to Gen AI success. Building "Innovation Capacity," particularly through comprehensive AI literacy programs for all workforce levels, is directly correlated with advancing through AI maturity stages and achieving superior financial performance. This "AI literacy dividend" empowers employees, reduces anxiety, and fosters a culture where Gen AI is seen as an augmentation tool rather than a replacement. The "augmentation imperative" dictates that workflows and roles must be thoughtfully redesigned to maximize human-AI collaboration, ensuring that Gen AI enhances human capabilities and productivity.

Finally, strategic alignment and a broadened perspective on ROI are essential. Enterprises should adopt an "inside-out" approach, prioritizing internal use cases to build capabilities, demonstrate value, and gain trust before tackling external-facing applications. The measurement of Gen AI's impact must extend beyond immediate financial metrics to include qualitative benefits such as improved employee experience, enhanced decision-making, risk mitigation, and contributions to sustainability goals.

Recommendations for Enterprise Leaders

1. **Adopt a Phased, Platform-Centric Approach:** Leverage McKinsey's adoption stages to guide your Gen AI journey, focusing on building a centralized platform with self-service capabilities, open architecture for reusable services, and embedded automated guardrails from the outset. Prioritize investments in scalable infrastructure and data pipelines to bridge the "valley of death" between pilots and enterprise-wide deployment.
2. **Prioritize Responsible AI as an Innovation Enabler:** Integrate ethical AI principles and robust data governance frameworks into every stage of Gen AI development and deployment. Establish clear policies for data input, IP handling, and output validation. Proactively manage risks related to transparency, accuracy, and bias to build trust and ensure sustainable innovation.
3. **Invest Heavily in Human Capital and AI Literacy:** Recognize that talent development is a core component of Gen AI strategy. Implement comprehensive AI literacy programs across the organization, focusing on prompt engineering, ethical considerations, and fostering an augmentation mindset. Empower "AI champions" and redesign workflows to maximize human-AI collaboration.
4. **Ground Gen AI in Strategic Business Problems:** Begin with well-defined internal use cases that address specific pain points and offer measurable outcomes. Adopt an "inside-out" strategy to build internal capabilities and demonstrate tangible ROI. Expand the definition of success metrics beyond direct financial gains to include productivity enhancements, risk reduction, and qualitative improvements in employee and customer experience.
5. **Cultivate an Adaptive Operational Backbone:** Ensure that foundational digital transformation efforts, especially data accessibility, quality, and integration across legacy systems, are robust. A strong operational backbone is crucial for scalable and impactful Gen AI deployment, enabling seamless data flow and efficient model integration.

By embracing these strategic frameworks and recommendations, enterprises can confidently navigate the complexities of Generative AI, transforming its immense potential into tangible, sustainable business value and securing a competitive advantage in the evolving digital economy.

ESSAY QUESTIONS

Question 1: Discuss McKinsey's five stages of enterprise-wide technology adoption and how they apply specifically to the strategic integration of Generative AI.

Hints: Refer to the "Frontier innovation," "Experimentation," "Piloting," "Scaling in progress," and "Fully scaled" stages. Explain typical Gen AI activities and challenges at each stage as outlined in the report, such as initial experimentation with LLMs, developing specific use cases, and building scalable platforms.

Question 2: Explain the concept of the "valley of death" in scaling Generative AI initiatives. What are the primary challenges that contribute to this phenomenon, and what strategic measures can organizations take to overcome it, according to the report?

Hints: Discuss "failure to scale" due to "risk concerns," "cost overruns," and "compute-intensive workloads". Mention the need for scalable infrastructure, reusable components, and robust governance, such as a centralized platform with validated services and automated guardrails.

Question 3: How do "responsible AI guardrails" and robust data governance frameworks act as enablers of innovation rather than mere compliance burdens in Generative AI adoption? Provide examples of such guardrails.

Hints: Discuss McKinsey's identification of "Automated, responsible AI guardrails" as a core component of successful Gen AI platforms, designed to "foster innovation while managing risk". Provide examples of guardrails like auditing LLM prompts for data policy violations, detecting hallucinations, and tracking cost implications. Also, refer to Gartner's ethical guidance on transparency, bias, and IP.

Question 4: Describe the MIT CISR Enterprise AI Maturity Model, outlining its four stages and their correlation with financial performance. How does this model emphasize the importance of human capital development for AI maturity?

Hints: Detail "Stage 1: Experiment and Prepare," "Stage 2: Build Pilots and Capabilities," "Stage 3: Develop AI Ways of Working," and "Stage 4: Become AI Future Ready". Explain how later stages correlate with "financial performance well above industry average". Connect "Human Capital" from the broader MIT innovation framework (I-Cap/E-Cap) to the early stages of AI maturity, such as "educating the workforce on AI".

Question 5: The report highlights the "operational backbone" as a crucial, often underestimated, component for scalable Generative AI. Explain what constitutes this operational backbone and why it is foundational for successful Gen AI deployment, drawing on insights from MIT Sloan.

Hints: Discuss the MIT Sloan Digital Transformation Framework's emphasis on having an "operational backbone and shared customer insights" in place *before* building a digital platform. Relate this to robust data governance, integrated systems, streamlined processes, and data accessibility.

Question 6: Elaborate on the concept of the "AI literacy dividend." How does investing in comprehensive AI literacy programs for all organizational levels contribute to successful Generative AI adoption and productivity gains?

Hints: Discuss how "AI-literate employees are more likely to adopt AI than those who aren't". Explain the importance of training in prompt engineering, understanding data privacy implications, and addressing anxieties and fears around AI. Mention frameworks like SHI's MAILS for measuring AI literacy.

Question 7: Explain the "augmentation imperative" in the context of Generative AI adoption. Why is it crucial to position AI as a tool that enhances human capabilities rather than replaces them, and what are the implications for workflow and role redesign?

Hints: Refer to the common mistake of "treating AI as a replacement not a tool for augmentation". Discuss McKinsey's "new human–machine collaboration models" shifting from "human replacement to augmentation". Emphasize redesigning processes and roles thoughtfully, involving teams in how work is done, and prioritizing hybrid human-AI experiences.

Question 8: Discuss the strategic advantage of an "inside-out" approach to value realization for Generative AI. Why is it recommended to begin with internal, operational use cases before tackling more complex customer-facing applications?

Hints: Refer to Harvard Business Review's advice to "start with well-defined problems" like "customer service delays, repetitive data tasks, or team bandwidth constraints". Discuss the common mistake of "ignoring internal use-cases" and the recommendation to build use cases "from the bottom up". Explain how this approach builds internal capabilities, refines models, and gains employee trust in a controlled environment.

Question 9: Identify and explain three significant risks associated with Generative AI adoption, as outlined by Gartner. For each risk, propose a corresponding mitigation strategy.

Hints: Choose three from: "Lack of transparency," "Accuracy (Hallucinations)," "Bias," "Intellectual Property (IP) and Copyright," "Cybersecurity and Fraud," or "Sustainability". For each, provide a specific mitigation strategy, such as establishing guardrails, validating outputs, implementing usage policies, or selecting energy-efficient vendors.

Question 10: What are the common pitfalls related to people and processes in enterprise Generative AI adoption? Discuss at least three such mistakes and outline the corrective actions or best practices to avoid them.

Hints: Refer to mistakes like "Not investing enough in AI literacy," "Building AI use cases from the top down," "Overlooking People: Change Management & Training," "Lacking Leadership Ownership & Coordination," "Overestimating AI Capabilities," or "Treating AI as Replacement, Not Augmentation". For each, provide a corrective action, such as comprehensive training, cross-functional workshops, securing executive sponsorship, or starting with small pilots.

Appendix

Key Technology Impact in Select Industries

INTRODUCTION

The objective of this appendix is to expose students with key technologies impacting select industries such as retail, telecom, travel and transport, health care media, oil and gas and education. This will help the students in understating the role of technology in shaping the efficiency and effectiveness of these industries.

KEY TECHNOLOGIES IMPACT IN RETAIL INDUSTRY

Retail industry is highly diversified and growing industry in the world which is estimated to generate \$20,002 billion revenue in 2017. This sector is going through a phenomenal growth with a CAGR (compound annual growth rate) of 3.9% over the next six years (2012–2017). Retail industry is one of the most impacted industry as far as adoption of new technology is concerned. Internet has given rise to global sourcing and selling with e-retailing giants like Amazon giving tough competition to established players like Wallmart and others. The main products which retail industry sells is of house hold nature, apparels, merchandise and commodities for personal use, and also home use technology products like white goods, camera, televisions, mobile phones etc. Retail Industry is highly price sensitive and dependent upon the economic conditions of the country.

Some of major retail Industry emerging trends influenced by technology are as follows:

- **Access to multiple sales and access channel:** Retail industry is no longer organised through large or small retail stores. It also now includes m-selling through internet, mobile apps and also reaching out to customer through television and on line calling, thus providing Omni channel customer experience. Most big retailers have large on line presence and e-retailers own large supply chain logistics facilities. This is leading to the extensive use of technology across entire business processes. Many new variations like collection of money booking online and collection at store or cash on delivery are newer additions.

- **Use of mobile devices:** Mobile devices are extensively used to record the proof of home delivery and inventory while on the move in the store aisle using Wi-Fi facilities. Customers are using specially designed mobile apps for booking orders and browse delivery states through the booked order. In case they don't remember the product code they can just click a photograph and let the on line site suggest matching products by using image recognition. In order to reduce the queue at the checkout stage new technologies, such as mobile PoS, mobile wallet, mobile money to money transfers, etc. are being deployed.
- **Customer data analytics:** Retail industry have vast data of customer purchases which are now a source of understanding customer buying pattern and thus positioning new products and services. It also helps to manage inventory and predict demand levels. With customers highly active on social media to express good or bad opinion about the product and companies this data has become "Big". By using big data analytics tool retailers can improve merchandising and supply chain. The decisions regarding marketing and promotions, opening of new product lines or stores are now getting influenced by insights provided by big data analytics.
- **Improvement in the delivery time:** Technology is extensively used to track and deliver packages in record promised time by retail industry for some time now. Now the next generation leap is to also track conditions of the package such as temperature for critical supplies. Supply chain of the retail industry is becoming more and more agile using features such as cross docking and direct delivery to stores or delivery in the real time. With integration of 3rd party logistics the retail industry is able to provide real time view of orders, inventory, and supplier deliveries. This is helping to reduce inventory and reduce delivery time.
- **Within stores improvement:** Major technology impact can be seen within stores where suppliers are kept updated of how the products are moving from the shelf. Use of Virtual Kiosk for trying out new apparels are new additions. Retail stores features such as visual merchandising, tracking of expiry dates of food items or self-checking counters are accelerating the use of technologies within the stores.
- **Personalisation of customers:** With the ability to track the customer as he/she buys from various stores both on line as well as offline, the retail giants are able to offer personalized services to the customers.

KEY TECHNOLOGY IMPACT IN TELECOM INDUSTRY

Telecom Industry is fueling the development and growth of many national economy. Indian telecom Industry has made rapid progress after liberalisation in mid 1990. This is also the fastest growing telecom market in the world where almost 9 million subscribers are added every month. The number of mobile phones have reached 970M Total & 862M Active millions[1] users and will be the 3rd largest smartphone market in the world to have nearly 314 million mobile internet users by 2017. Mobile devices have become a must have for common masses who are using not only for voice calls but to do commercial transaction, internet access, social media and entertainment

[1]http://trak.in/tags/business/2015/05/14/indian-mobile-subscriber-stats-march-2015/accessed 10092015

as well. No doubt this sector has attracted the biggest and brightest companies of the world to come and work in India as telecom provider, network and equipment supplier apart from creating some of the very successful Indian entrepreneurs.

In the coming years the mobile user base will shift to 3G and 4G network. 3G user base will grow at a CAGR of 61.3% from 2013–17 and likely to reach 284 million by end of year 2017.

Telecom industry has a wide spectrum of technologies which can be broadly classified under three major categories:

(a) Equipment Technologies used by the sender and receivers of telecom signals: This includes technologies for handset receiver and equipment's such as modems, routers etc, which convert voice signals into electromagnetic waves or vice versa.

(b) Network Technologies for transmitting the signals across locations also called OSS technologies. Mobile communications, Broadband communications, Satellite communications and a combination of these. Terms such as GSM/CDMA, 3G/4G, etc. are all related to the network technologies.

(c) Business Technologies primarily related with supporting the business operations of the telecom provider. This is also called BSS layer of the telecom technologies.

Telecom companies will focus to improve Network Reliability using latest technology. Due to exponential need for supporting high volume data, video and images, the telecom companies would use virtualisation, automation and optical network technology such as 100G, 200G and LTE to improve network efficiency and reliability. In addition the following major telecom inititaves will be taken by most leading telecom majors.

1. **Adoption of Internet of things:** Telecom companies would adopt technologies and services related to IoT. Increased rigor on IoT cybersecurity will help lower complexity of Machine-to-Machine communication.
2. **Use of predictive analytics for big data:** Telecom companies generate very high amount of data that can be used to derive enhanced insights through predictive analytics.
3. **Accelerated usage of cloud:** Telecom companies would use cloud platform to support their business and data volume growth. Even mission critical work hitherto restricted to on premise server will gain more acceptance for cloud

KEY TECHNOLOGY IMPACT IN TRAVEL AND TRANSPORT INDUSTRY

Transportation of goods and passengers has been a major source of revenue and for promoting economic activity. The latest advancement of technology in transportation industry is making this sector smart, efficient and ready for meeting future demands. Digital disruptive technologies are helping establishment of new business model leading to phenomenal success of companies like Uber that has become a multi-billion-dollar global corporation without owning s single vehicle! As global population will reach 4 billion in urban areas the need of smart technologies will be further needed to support overpopulated cities, their commute and daily needs.

Some of the emerging technologies to watch would be

(a) **Technologies to support personalisation:** Using mobile phone applications the commuters will have more control to choose the time, mode and price of the transport avoiding endless wait and uncertainty. Uber, OLA and few others have successfully demonstrated that in-city commute can be more customised and made cheaper using mobile phone apps.

(b) **Transportation will become more intelligent and integrated:** Leading to better prediction of demand, reducing overheads such as unfulfilled capacity, fuel wastage leading to better management of Transportation assets and prolonging the useful life.

(c) **Improved energy efficiency across road, rail and air travel:** By improving the physical structure of a vehicle or its mechanical design better fuel efficiency will be achieved. Research is continuously going on to achieve, better fuel efficiency through reduced rolling and air resistance by improving aerodynamics and wheel/tyre performance. Use of lightweight materials will result in less energy requirement.

(d) **Intelligent Transportation Systems (ITS):** It will lead to faster, cheaper and safer transportation for everyone. This will include connected and autonomous vehicles, alternative fuels, keyless fleet management and traffic analytics to facilitate smooth operations of the transportation network. Intelligent vehicles will provide real time information for better traffic management. This will result into converting the entire city as one system. Such development will have a positive impact on quality of life and ease of business for residents and tourist and business travellers.

(e) **Vehicle to vehicle communication (V2V):** Using intelligent wireless system will improve safety, prevent accidents. Its variants such as vehicle-to-pedestrian (V2P) and vehicle-to-infrastructure (V2I) are collectively called V2X. This technology enable constant communicates to the nearby vehicles informing speed, heading and direction. These connected vehicles will alert drivers for a dangerous situations and better speed management.

(f) **Pricing and payments:** It will be dynamic and digital eliminating use of paper in any form. Payment of toll taxes through smart card is a reality in most developed countries leading less crowding at toll plazas and saving of fuel cost for better environmental protection. Common ticketing across all mode of transports using a multi-mode smart card is going to be a universal feature.

(g) **Increased safety on roads:** Using advance technologies like cognitive computing safety on roads will be improved leading to positive impact to insurance industry. Safety features such as collison detection, vehicle immobilisation in case of drunken driving, etc. will aid in this direction.

(h) **Shortest path travel:** Using predictive algorithm, the shortest and fastest path will be predicted leading to less travel time. Multi city, multi-mode travel will soon join to lead to one seamless travel path for travellers saving time and money.

(i) **Use of video conferencing:** It will reduce the need of travel for face-to-face business meeting.

(j) **Automatic sensors at traffic intersection:** Controlling traffic signals based on traffic volume in a dynamic mode will be reality everywhere.

Key Technology Impact in Media Industry

Media industry is one such industry which has largely benefitted due to proliferation of internet and also facing major challenges due to social media. Consumers are no longer restricting themselves with one format or one channel but they want everything to be available across the channels. Proliferation of new devices and new channels has led to disruptive impact on both production, distribution and viewing. Consumer now expect on-demand content across a variety of fragmented platforms including social media.

The rapid advancement of internet and convergence of IT and Communication Technology has made greatest impact on media industry in the way the content is created and distributed. In fact this impact is being seen in all the three major processes of media industry value chain, i.e. Content creation, bundling that content into a market-ready product and content distribution.

- The digitisation of media content is leading to a new phenomenon, where consumers are also co-creators in the value chain as well.
- New Business Models have emerged leading to new players and new competitive opportunities. For example mobile phone has virtually become a delivery vehicle for all kinds of media, be it TV content, social media or traditional internet.
- This is one industry where the new technology is quickly introduced and widely adopted leading to lower prices of access. Developments such as broadband internet is pushing the adoption of IPTV (Internet Protocol Television) and sooner the Video on demand (VOD) systems will be a widely adopted.
- In terms of Cable, digital and satellite television, the High Definition Television (HDTV) is getting popular by the day. Our old favourite Radio is becoming more adoptable due to the internet using a new technology called Digital Radio (DAB) which will make clear sound waves without much interference that is seen in AM/FM frequencies.
- Digital cinema distribution is reality and helping eliminate piracy and giving better quality of the picture.

KEY TECHNOLOGY IMPACT IN HEALTHCARE

Healthcare is going through a paradigm shift. It is not just healing the sick, but preventing the onset of disease, early warning, improving the quality of life an prolonging the life span. Healthcare no longer episodic, isolated patient care but electronic health record-centric or patient-centered care, which is providing end to end care with responsibility predictable outcome. Healthcare is increasingly using intelligent tools in information management and discharge of patient care duties. Some of the key technologies making impact in health are:

- **IBM, Watson technology** which has built in artificial Intelligence is helping physicians identify treatment options by narrowing options among a large group of treatment choices.
- **Voice recognition is being used for** better electronic health record implementations.
- **Mobility and Internet of Things (IoT):** Health care is more and more becoming

location independent where doctors can monitor and advice patients using mobile communications, mobile videos, monitoring equipments connected on the Internet etc. Many critical patients tend to deteriorate because they are not provided adequate care during emergency as doctors are far away and there is no way they can monitor or see the patients conditions. This can be reduced using mobility solutions. IoT will play a major role in making mobility a success.

- **Cloud-based access and management of data** is becoming a reality which allows controlled access for hospital and health networks requisite patient data.
- **Sensors and wearable technology.** Wearable medical devices and sensors are simply another way to collect data, which could be as simple as an alert sent to a care provider when a patient falls down or a bandage that can detect skin pH levels to tell if a cut is getting infected. Similar data on blood sugar, pressure and other conditions can be monitored in real time basis.
- **Pharmacogenomics/genome sequencing.** Personalized medicine will be soon a reality where tailored treatment plan for individuals can be developed. This will lead to diagnostic accuracy. Pharmacogenomics is the study of how variations in the human genome affect the response to medications. By choosing the right drug suited to a patient gene will prevent adverse drug reaction, misdiagnoses and unnecessary costs.
- **Robotics:** Use of robotics in precision operations are becoming more and more acceptable. Miniature cameras help doctors to see on large screen the details inside any organ and through robot the necessary procedure can be conducted with precision.
- **Nanobots in blood:** These tiny robots move in our blood stream like white blood cells and destroy bacteria and other pathogens. They have their own sensors, and propulsion mechanism and can deliver chemotherapy 1000 times more accurately than any using drugs. This will prevent many side-effects to patients like the current treatments do.
- **Robotic "Flight Simulator" surgery:** To reduce the years of training too conduct Surgical procedures such simulators have been built. RoSS (Robotic Surgery Simulator) is providing real-world views of actual surgeries to aspiring, practicing, or professional surgeons. It also gives surgeons the tools they need to get it right when they perform in real life situation.
- **Augmenting human capabilities:** Technologies are being developed to supplement human capability that get lost due to accidents, ageing or any diseases. Development of prosthetic arms with his mind alone is one such development. Johns Hopkins Applied Physics Laboratory is engaged in creating naturally controlled artificial limbs.

KEY TECHNOLOGY IMPACT IN EDUCATION

The massive need for educating billions of population b across the world is forcing educators to adopt technology to reach out to students. Shortage of teachers, classrooms and ever-changing curriculum is forcing educators to embrace technology alternatives. Some of the upcoming technologies in education are as follows:

- **Massively open online courses (MOOCs) and tablet computing:** MOOCs courses run by leading universities, including MIT (edX) and Stanford (Coursera), are becoming very popular. They are providing high quality, online learning at scale to people regardless of their location or educational background, Tablet computing is facilitating access of online courses and are being welcomed at many places.

- **Learning analytics:** Uses data from variety of disparate sources to help arrive at a better understanding individual students' need so as to help improve teaching and learning. Sophisticated Web tracking tools are used to track precise student behaviours, recording variables like clicks and time spent on a page etc. to gauge whether the progress of student is adequate.
- **3D printing:** 3D printing is being used in education for better exploration of objects. Practical applications of 3D printing in physics, engineering, biology, Geology and anthropology can enable students to do rapid prototyping and develop production tools. Students of x-ray crystallography can print out models of complex proteins and other molecules.
- **Wearable technology** such as Bluetooth necklaces, clip-on cameras and augmented reality devices are being used in lecture delivery as well as by students to warn for any unsafe conditions. For example, it could alert chemical engineering students to the presence of dangerous fumes. Google glass like devices can allow users to connect to the Internet through voice commands. Use of pendant projectors for faculty and smart gloves to give feedback to students handling scientific equipment are soon going to be used.
- **Virtual field trips:** Instead to visiting a location such as factory or museum, platforms for virtual trips will be used more regularly.
- **Online collaboration:** Students will be using technology daily for online collaboration such as games/simulations and social media to remain connected with other students and faculty.

KEY TECHNOLOGICAL IMPACT IN OIL GAS AND UTILITY INDUSTRY

Oil gas and Utility industry is supplier of energy needs of the world. However it came under severe criticism causing environmental pollution due to burning of fossil fuel. Now this industry needs massive adoption of technology to improve at efficiency as well as reduce environmental impact. Some of the major initiatives taken by these industries are:

Use of Artificial Intelligence across the value chain. AI applications in global oil and gas market will rise to USD 2.85 billion by 2022, at a CAGR of 12.66% as per estimates. AI is used to optimize processes and maximize the returns on investment. It is used in several areas such as

- Planning and forecasting throughout the Exploration and Production (E&P) life-cycle,
- Enhancing operational efficiency and reducing costs by real-time drilling optimization
- Land surveying and pipeline inspections
- Reducing risks using predictive maintenance

IoT (internet of things) is used for several applications for

- Creating a Collaborative Ecosystem
- Increasing Production and Capital Throughput

- Equipment and Asset Management
- Remote Performance Monitoring
- Preventive Maintenance

Automation, Robotics and machines bases sensors are used for Automated refuelling at gas stations, Intelligent management of gas stations, Online and offline integration to boost development of social platforms for gas stations and use of big data to enhance user operation capacity.

Basic Machine learning, AR/VR is used in upstream oil companies engaged in refining and exploration. The vast assets of geological data can be used by data-driven analytics and Machine Learning to help in exploration and building an effective drilling strategy. Upstream O&G companies are able to locate geological anomalies using Machine Learning capabilities.

Digital Twins, i.e. the virtual clones of the assets, are created using historical design data to model and evaluate the future performances of complex design, process, and equipment modifications. A significant savings can result by trying these changes in a software model and predict its performance in actual field.

Multiple Choice Questions

Chapter 1

1. Which amongst the following are the perspectives for understanding Technology and Innovation Management (choose as many as applicable)
   (a) In managing and improving business functions and society
   (b) Generating more profits
   (c) Manage technology and innovation within an enterprise
   (d) All the above

2. The word "technology" has its origin in the two Greek words, the second one is "ology" indicating "knowledge of", which is the first one
   (a) "technics" (b) "technikos"
   (c) "techno" (d) None of the above

3. Chandra and Zulkieflimansyah summaries that technology is a subtle mix of (choose that is not applicable)
   (a) Know-how (b) Material
   (c) Techniques and tools (d) IT

4. The current age of our world is called
   (a) Stone Age (b) Bronze Age
   (c) Iron Age (d) Information Age
   (e) Capitalistic Age (f) Digital Age
   (g) Technology Age

5. What amongst the following are not a characteristic of technology (choose as many as applicable)
   (a) Need (b) Appropriateness
   (c) Priced (d) Universality
   (e) Builds on the past achievements (f) Availability

(g) Many be disruptive or totally new
(h) Driver of social change and driven by social need
(i) Interdisciplinary in nature

6. According to Abernathy and Utterbach (A-U) model the phases of technology growth are (choose as many as applicable)
(a) Fluid stage
(b) Dominant design and transition stage
(c) Development stage
(d) Mature stage
(e) All the above

7. According to Thomas S. Kuhn's Model, the phases of technology development are called
(a) Pre-paradigm
(b) Anti-paradigm
(c) Paradigm stages
(d) Post-paradigm
(e) All the above

8. The only way the human race can survive is to use technology to decelerate the population growth and conserve the "WEHAB" resources, what are these? (choose from the list)
(a) Water
(b) Waste
(c) Environment
(d) Energy
(e) Health
(f) Horticulture
(g) Astronomy
(h) Agriculture
(i) Building
(j) Biodiversity

9. Nano Ganesh is the name of
(a) A Lord Ganesh temple in Satara District in Maharashtra
(b) New Vehicle launched by Tata Motors
(c) New smart phone by Apple
(d) An innovation to use SMS to start irrigation water pumps using modem
(e) None of the above

10. Which is not amongst the three basic forms of technology described by
(a) Unit or small-batch technology
(b) Computer Technology
(c) Large batch/mass production
(d) Continuous process

11. A well-developed technology management strategy without a successful commercial implementation cannot lead to desirable economic returns? True/False

12. Management of Technology (MOT) is necessitated due to three major drivers (choose from the following list)
(a) Business
(b) Profit
(c) Technology
(d) Timing
(e) Opinion of public
(f) Organization

13. The workplace adoption of generative AI has been as swift as which of the following technologies?
(a) The Internet
(b) The personal computer (PC)
(c) Mobile phones
(d) Television

Chapter 2

1. A firm is said to have competitive advantage over its rival if its products and services are of
   (a) Higher price (b) Better packaging
   (c) Greater value perceived by the customer (d) All the above
2. According to Michael Porter the three generic strategies by which a firm can gain competitive advantage are
   (a) Instant service, instant delivery, instant marketing
   (b) Low-cost leadership, differentiation and focus
   (c) Better price, better product, better packaging
   (d) More production, more sales outlet, more publicity
   (e) All the above
3. If the Generic strategy is Differentiation and Strategic action is Superior product technology then the enabling technology would be
   (a) Product and process technology (b) IT
   (c) Manufacturing (d) Marketing
4. If the Generic strategy is Focus and Strategic action is Products for niche market or custom made then the enabling technology would be
   (a) CAD, CAM, CAE (b) Research and development,
   (c) IT Knowledge management (d) Automation
   (e) None of the above
5. If the Generic strategy is low cost and strategic action is higher margin per item of product or unit of service then the enabling technology would be
   (a) CAD, CAM, CAE (b) Research and development,
   (c) IT Knowledge management (d) Automation
   (e) None of the above
6. Does technology has a necessary role to play in automation of value creating processes and bringing in efficiency in the value chain activities of both product manufacturing and in services delivery? True/False
7. Which amongst the following is not a distinctive management layers in any organization
   (a) Strategic layer (b) Tactical layer
   (c) Top management layer (d) Operational layer
8. It is not really wrong to assume that technology, such as internet and social media will help build awareness, dissimilate knowledge about the product; data analytics to identify the right customer segment? Right/Wrong
9. Who famously said that marketing and innovation create value, all the rest are costs
   (a) Abraham Lincoln (b) Peter Drucker
   (c) Shahrukh Khan (d) Henry Ford

10. Which amongst the following are the major forces are changing the way businesses are being conducted in almost all industries? (Choose as many as applicable)
    (a) Mobility of the workforce
    (b) Mobile phones
    (c) Use of powerful analytics tools
    (d) Use of social media
    (e) Internet based payment gateway
    (f) Rapid progress of cloud computing
    (g) Cyber intelligence
    (h) Cyber crime
    (i) Cyber squatting
11. The first step for Management of intellectual property is
    (a) Filing patent
    (b) Advertisement
    (c) Creating awareness among employees, designers, managers and researchers
    (d) Creating an IP management framework
    (e) Monetisation, legal protection for infringement
12. Which of the following is a new strategic action enabled by AI/Gen AI in marketing and sales?
    (a) Traditional mass advertising campaigns.
    (b) Hyper-personalization at scale.
    (c) Manual lead generation processes.
    (d) Static product catalogs.

Chapter 3

1. Technology selection is based on
    (a) Price of the technology
    (b) Brand of the vendor
    (c) The evaluation report, business needs and strategy
    (d) Implementing technology in actual processes or in the products
2. A good technology strategy seldom helps in reducing operating cost, increased reliability and serviceability of the product? True/False
3. The full form of VMI in the context of a manufacturing firm is
    (a) Variable measures of incidents
    (b) Various monetary institutions
    (c) Vendor managed inventory
    (d) Viral marketing of input material
4. A technology leader gains the first mover advantage and builds a brand loyalty with its users
    (a) Never
    (b) Sometimes
    (c) Occasionally
    (d) Always
    (e) No idea!
5. Unfortunately despite many efforts and so much of money most technology is not becoming efficient and eco-friendly. True/False
6. Technology management is generally isolated and does not require partnership between industry, academia and government. True/False

7. Ecosystem technology management is
   (a) Done by every firm
   (b) Not done usually by one enterprise unless that enterprise is the industry leader
   (c) Government does it
   (d) No one does it
8. If the Technology management perspective is Value Creating Technology and the role of the enterprise is decisive/driving and the impact on the enterprise is major, then the usual method investment required for new development is
   (a) Outsourced (b) Industry consortia
   (c) Government funded (d) In-house
   (e) All the above
9. If the Technology management perspective is Value enabling Technology and the role of the enterprise is evaluative and the impact on the enterprise is significant then the Usual method Investment required for new development is
   (a) Outsourced (b) Industry consortia
   (c) Government funded (d) In-house
   (e) All the above
10. If the Technology management perspective is ecosystem technology, and the role of the enterprise is observer and the impact on the enterprise is disruptive then the usual method Investment required for new development is
    (a) Outsourced (b) Industry consortia
    (c) Government funded (d) In-house
    (e) All the above
11. In the context of AI/Gen AI adoption, the "late-mover advantage" is more probable for:
    (a) Simple, commoditized technologies.
    (b) Technologies with well-defined functionalities from the start.
    (c) More complex technologies where functionalities are discovered over time.
    (d) Technologies with high upfront R&D costs for first-movers.

Chapter 4

1. According to legendry Steve Jobs innovation distinguishes between a
   (a) Haves and haves not (b) Genius and ordinary
   (c) Leader and follower (d) All the above
2. Contrary to the popular belief innovation and invention are
   (a) Same (b) Different
   (c) Both (d) Neither
3. Noted researcher Joseph Schumpeter proposed that technological change follows a trilogy process described as
   (a) Make-buy-sell (b) Design-Develop-Deliver
   (c) Investigation-Invention-Innovation (d) Invention-innovation-diffusion
   (e) None of the above
4. Finally, the stage of diffusion leads to a stage of the technology when further development slows down and the industry waits for new breakthrough technology.

What is this stage called?

(a) Commercialization
(b) Commoditization
(c) Competition
(d) None of the above

5. According to Franken, the ability to generate or recognize new ideas, alternatives, or possibilities that may be useful in solving problems, communicating with others and entertaining ourselves and others is called

(a) Research
(b) Invention
(c) Kaizen
(d) Innovation
(e) Creativity
(f) None of the above

6. Which amongst the following is not a goal of innovation (choose as many as applicable)

(a) Cost reduction
(b) Customer satisfaction
(c) Creativity
(d) Compliance and regulation
(e) Competitive pressure
(f) Common sense
(g) Climate protection

7. Incremental and disruptive are

(a) Not an innovation
(b) Scales of innovation
(c) Extent of innovation
(d) Just inventions
(e) None of the above

8. Does innovation also carries certain risks, such as failure to meet the anticipated benefits such as cost saving or improved customer's response? True/False

9. According to Professor Clayton M. Christensen Disruptive innovations never happen at the bottom of the market which start at the lower-end, but ultimately cover the whole market. True/False

10. One of the impediments of innovation in any organization is called action paralysis. This stage happens when the organization

(a) Have some natural calamity like flood
(b) CEO is changes
(c) Lacks follow up actions
(d) Competition becomes very intense
(e) Government puts more constraints.

Chapter 5

1. In case of technology, a trend represents

(a) The evolution of the technology and its likely maturity over time
(b) Latest technology which is very hot selling
(c) The increase in cost of buying a technology
(d) The new fashion label from Tata
(e) All the above

2. Which amongst the following is not amongst the five stages of the Gartner Hype cycle methodology (choose as many as applicable)

(a) Innovation Trigger
(b) Commercial Success
(c) Peak of Inflated Expectations
(d) Trough of Disillusionment

(e) Start production (f) Scope of Enlightenment
(g) Plateau of Productivity

3. Technology Forecasting methods can be further classed under
(a) Good and bad methods (b) External and internal methods
(c) Exploratory and normative methods (d) Simple and complex methods
(e) None of the above

4. The forecasting technique Delphi is a statistical method proven for its success True/False

5. Brainstorming or Brain Writing method is
(a) Analysis based (b) Scenario-simulation
(c) Field Anomaly Relaxation Method [FAR]
(d) Futuristic idea generation based (e) Explorative
(f) Visualization based

6. As per technology adoption S curve the early adopters who see potential in the technology and are willing to take risk are usually
(a) 5% (b) 50%
(c) 85% (d) 15%
(e) Can't say

7. Intel launching Celeron processor for PCs and laptops is an example of
(a) New marketing principle (b) Segment zero principle
(c) Higher capacity principle (d) Extreme inputs principle

8. According to Christensen, disruptive technologies do not offer different performance package and are able to satisfy the mainstream customers. True/False

9. Which amongst the following is not choices of technology acquisition strategy
(a) In-house R&D (b) Buying the firm possessing technology
(c) Joint development or Joint venture (d) Contract R&D
(e) Sourcing components from low cost countries like China
(f) Obtaining licensing to use
(g) Purchasing final product and doing the branding and marketing
(h) Making equity investment in the technology firm

10. Which amongst the following is not a choice to collaborate with each other
(a) Joint ventures (b) Licensing
(c) Outsourcing or contract manufacturing (d) Retailing
(e) Consortium or collective research

Chapter 6

1. Which amongst the following is not a stage of Product Life Cycle (PLM) (choose as many as applicable)
(a) Conception stage (b) Commercial stage
(c) Design and prototype stage (d) Manufacturing stage

(e) Creative stage
(f) Sell, serve and maintain
(g) Discard and dispose off

2. Two dimensional CAD or 3D CAID (computer-aided industrial design software) is very popular at
(a) Conception stage
(b) Commercial stage
(c) Design and prototype stage
(d) Manufacturing stage
(e) Creative stage
(f) Sell, serve and maintain
(g) Discard and dispose off

3. The tools Computational Fluid Dynamics (CFD); and Mechanical Event Simulation (MES) are regularly used at
(a) Conception stage
(b) Commercial stage
(c) Design and prototype stage
(d) Manufacturing stage
(e) Creative stage
(f) Sell, serve and maintain
(g) Discard and dispose off

4. Is it correct to say that NPD process cannot ensure that the product meets quality standards including build as well as use quality. Yes/No

5. Some of the following are not the challenges which the NPD process has to face: (choose as many as applicable)
(a) Lack of good understanding of customer real needs
(b) Not able to follow a family of product or product portfolio approach
(c) Not quickly identifying and then resolving performance issues
(d) Outsourced partner's inefficiency or ineffectiveness
(e) Improper process for managing product change
(f) Ability to quickly prototype and convert prototype into mass-manufactured product
(g) Proper estimation of market size, too small or overestimation
(h) Good product quality
(i) Market is not ready for accepting the product
(j) Poor execution of NPD process

6. Many researchers advocated that NPD should be more holistic in nature like
(a) A Soccer team
(b) A cricket team
(c) A tennis team
(d) A rugby team
(e) A kabaddi team

7. Motorola project IRIDIUM proved too costly to develop and finally failed where a less optimum technology succeeded in the telecom space. Which were those technology?
(a) VSAT
(b) CSAT
(c) GSM
(d) 3D printing
(e) NFC
(f) Bluetooth
(g) WiMax

8. Is it correct to say that a good NPD/IPD team has nowhere else to go to solve their problems and should be self-driven and empowered? True/False

9. WIPO is the name of organization that
   (a) Makes oil products
   (b) Develops software
   (c) Leads promotion of the protection of intellectual property
   (d) Watch maker from Switzerland
10. Indian Patents Act, was first enacted in
   (a) 1970
   (b) 1917
   (c) 1947
   (d) 1957
   (e) 2007
11. Protecting intellectual property in the age of Generative AI introduces new challenges, including:
   (a) Simplified copyright attribution due to AI's clear authorship.
   (b) Reduced risk of "deep fakes" and product copies.
   (c) Copyright infringement from training data and unclear ownership of AI-generated content.
   (d) Elimination of all privacy concerns in data governance.

Chapter 7

1. Peter Drucker, the legendary management author and consultant defined Business Model as
   (a) How an organization leadership team is set up
   (b) Which are the location of its factories
   (c) What products it makes
   (d) Assumptions about what a company gets paid
   (e) Design and prototype of product
2. Business model includes activities that the firm has to think and plan in order to deliver what it promises to the customer? Which activies does it include?
   (a) Only marketing and sales
   (b) Production and dispatch
   (c) Support and services
   (d) All
   (e) None
3. Can we use Business Model as new tool to beat competition?
   (a) Yes, we can
   (b) No, we cannot it is too risky
   (c) May be we should
   (d) None of the answers are correct
4. What % of earnings that General Motors makes from finance repayments, not from auto sales.
   (a) 16%
   (b) 26%
   (c) 60%
   (d) 46%
5. Baden-Fuller and Haefliger consider business model relationship with technology as
   (a) Integrated process
   (b) a two-way process
   (c) Complex process
   (d) Overlapping process
   (e) None of the above

6. Crowd sourcing is type of
   (a) Procurement strategy
   (b) Managing crowd strategy adopted by local police
   (c) Business model to gather funds and resources
   (d) All the above (e) None of the above
7. In Razor and blades model
   (a) Main product is sold cheap and money is made through supplies or complementary products
   (b) Blades are sold along with Razor
   (c) This is just to depict a hair grooming function
   (d) It does not matter what you buy first you will buy the other anyway, right?
8. In Freemium business model
   (a) Services are usually free for the first month always
   (b) Basic services are free advanced/special features are charged
   (c) You pay lower premium (d) It gives Insurance premium free
9. Osterwalder's Business Model Canvas has how many sections?
   (a) One (b) Two
   (c) Three (d) Nine
   (e) Five
10. While Reversing the Value Chain you always start with
   (a) Expand portfolio of products and service
   (b) Explore Customer needs
   (c) Make or buy decision
   (d) Identify multiple integrated channel to reach to the customer

Chapter 8

1. Which famous cricketer has said this "You can plan hundred things, but if you don't execute it well it does not look good in the field"
   (a) Sachin Tendulkar (b) Rahul Dravid
   (c) Mahinder Singh Dhoni (d) Yuvraj Singh
   (e) Sourabh Ganguli
2. In case of TIM implementation, the accountability as well as responsibility lies with
   (a) Chief Executive Officer (CEO) (b) Chief Marketing Officer (CMO)
   (c) Chief Technology Officer (CTO) (d) Chief Operations Officer (COO)
3. Is it correct to say that Technology adoption hardly has any legal angle where the creating, acquisition and use of intellectual property is involved? Correct/Incorrect
4. The timing of technology intervention or new innovative ideas is a
   (a) Simple decision (b) Complex decision
   (c) Good decision (d) Easy decision
5. Sometimes firms adopt new technology due to pressure from peers. True /false

6. Which of the following is NOT a recommended metric category for measuring AI success beyond traditional ROI?
   (a) Operational Efficiency Gains
   (b) Adoption and Usage Metrics
   (c) Direct short-term financial returns only
   (d) Business Impact and Innovation

Chapter 9

1. Executive Support Systems (ESS) are customized systems for this level of managers of the organization
   (a) Middle (b) Top
   (c) Operational (d) Clerical
   (e) Technical
2. Decision Support Systems (DSS), CAD CAM, Simulation and Modelling systems are specially developed to facilitate
   (a) Operational issue resolution (b) Strategic alternatives
   (c) Specific decision making (d) All the above
3. ERP software traces its origin in the manufacturing industry's
   (a) Production Systems (b) Operational system
   (c) MRP (material resource planning) Systems
   (d) Customer management system
4. SCM application serves the need of information exchange with the
   (a) Suppliers and partners (b) Customers and retailers
   (c) Company and its competitors (d) None of the above
5. The various stages of Supply chain cycle are
   (a) Commit, schedule, deliver, make (b) Ship, buy produce, install
   (c) Commit, schedule, make, deliver (d) Seek, source, supply, stabilize
6. Companies use CRM software to help in cross-selling (selling other products) upselling (selling higher version of the products) using CRM systems. True/False
7. Sales force automation module which covers the automation and information support to the sales force team who are on the ground meeting customers and soliciting business is part of
   (a) ERP (b) SCM
   (c) CRM (d) BPM
   (e) FMS
8. It is not correct to say that Data Warehouse (DW) keeps summarised data which are extracted from operating database and maintained along with certain predicted periodicity. True/False
9. M commerce and E Business are
   (a) Not related at all (b) The former is part of later
   (c) The later is part of former (d) Can't say

10. For getting updated information on frequently published contents like blog entries, news headlines, audio, video the feature used is
    (a) E-commerce
    (b) M-commerce
    (c) E-business
    (d) Really Simple Syndication (RSS)
    (e) None of the above
11. Big data generated on social media is not hundred per cent accurate. True/False
12. 3-D printing is also known as
    (a) New manufacturing
    (b) Additive manufacturing
    (c) Additional manufacturing
    (d) Sedative manufacturing
    (e) None of the above
13. The field of marketing research that studies consumers' sensorimotor, cognitive and affective response to marketing stimuli is called
    (a) Impulse marketing
    (b) Aggressive marketing
    (c) Viral marketing
    (d) Neuro-marketing
    (e) Brain marketing
14. Near field communication (NFC) is a wireless technology, typically working within a distance of
    (a) 4 meters
    (b) 4 cm
    (c) 4 km
    (d) 4 mm

Chapter 10

1. Technological determinism theory presumes that technology drives the society culture and structure. True/False
2. The acronym OSTA stands for
    (a) Original System Technology Analysis
    (b) Open Science and Technology Analysis
    (c) Open System Task Analysis
    (d) None of the above
3. The name of the robot used by Amazon, the leading e-commerce giant, across its 10 warehouses is
    (a) Kiya
    (b) Kiva
    (c) Krish
    (d) Kemo
4. The noted German social scientist Ortwin Renn defines term risk as the certainty that an undesirable state of reality (adverse effect) may occur as a result of natural events or human activities. True/False
5. One of the following is not the ethical principles adopted in technology and innovation management
    (a) Priority principle
    (b) Life principle
    (c) Social principle
    (d) Price principle
    (e) Safety principle

6. Toxicological or epidemiological approach is used for
   (a) Technology planning
   (b) Technology evaluation
   (c) Technology forecasting
   (d) Technology Risk assessment
   (e) All the above

Chapter 11

1. The acronym USEPA stands for
   (a) Union of Social and Empowered Professional Association
   (b) United States Environmental Protection Agency
   (c) Undersecretary of Environmental Policy Activity
   (d) Urban Sanitation Emission Prevention Agency
2. The National Green Tribunal was established under the National Green Tribunal Act, in
   (a) 2010
   (b) 2000
   (c) 2005
   (d) 1998
3. Till the time, Chief Green officer role emerges Developing a comprehensive EGTS requires a series of concerted efforts to be taken by the senior management. Who could be that person?
   (a) Any manager
   (b) Chief of security and services
   (c) CEO or MD
   (d) Marketing head
   (e) Operations chief
4. The level 5 of Green Technology Maturity Model is called
   (a) Informed
   (b) Leading and optimizing
   (c) Implementing and perfecting
   (d) Planning and developing
   (e) Unaware/unconcerned
5. Which are the standards recommended for buying Green technology products?
   (a) ESAT and Five star
   (b) EPEAT and ENERGY STAR
   (c) ISI mark
   (d) BSI mark
6. The process of optimization of transportation, storage and material waste during production is called
   (a) Green Production
   (b) Green CRM
   (c) Green ERP
   (d) Green SCM
   (e) None of the above

Chapter 12

1. Fourth revolution is driven by
   (a) Business Needs
   (b) Political development
   (c) Technology such as AI, ML, Big Data, Block chain iOT
   (d) All the above

2. According to which law we tend to overestimate the impact of a new technology in the short run, but we underestimate it in the long run
   (a) Moore's law (b) Amara's law
   (c) Gilder's law (d) Metcalf's law
3. Which law says that the total bandwidth of communication systems doubles every six months?
   (a) Moore's law (b) Amara's law
   (c) Gilder's law (d) Metcalf's law
4. Which law state that the impact of a telecommunications network is proportional to the square of the number of connected users of the system?
   (a) Moore's law (b) Amara's law
   (c) Gilder's law (d) Metcalf's law
5. The innovation of the eco system and society involving all stake holders is called
   (a) Innovation 1.0 (b) Innovation 2.0
   (c) Innovation 3.0 (d) Innovation 4.0

Chapter 13

1. One of the following is not a IDEO Design Thinking Stage
   (a) Empathise (b) Define
   (c) Ideate (d) Prototype
   (e) Develop (f) Test
2. One of the following is not a stage of Stanford Design School's Design Thinking stages
   (a) Discovery phase (b) Interpretation
   (c) Innovation (d) Ideation
   (e) Experimentation (f) Evolution
3. One of the following is not the stages of IBM Design Thinking stage
   (a) Engage (b) Observe
   (c) Reflect (d) Make
4. One of the following is not a technique of IBM Design Thinking
   (a) Hills (b) Valleys
   (c) Playbacks (d) Sponsor users
5. PepsiCo under the leadership of CEO Indra Nooyi inducted Mauro Porcini as chief Design officer to redesign PepsiCo's
   (a) Bottle (b) Soft drink formulation
   (c) User experience (d) Packaging

Chapter 14

1. Which of the following is a core capability of Generative AI?
   (a) Data classification and prediction
   (b) Creating entirely new, realistic content from existing data

(c) Optimizing existing processes without altering content
(d) Performing rule-based calculations

2. According to Goldman Sachs, Generative AI alone is predicted to boost global GDP by approximately what percentage?
(a) 3%
(b) 5%
(c) 7%
(d) 10%

3. An "AI-native" organization is primarily characterized by:
(a) Integrating AI functionalities into pre-existing legacy systems.
(b) Designing the entire system with AI intrinsically at its core from the ground up.
(c) Primarily focusing on AI for back-office efficiency.
(d) Outsourcing all AI development to third-party vendors.

4. Which of the following is a quantifiable benefit of AI in customer service, as demonstrated by Klarna?
(a) Increased customer wait times to ensure thorough responses.
(b) Reduction in repeat questions by 25%.
(c) Requirement for more human agents to handle complex queries.
(d) Elimination of all human interaction in customer support.

Chapter 15

1. Generative AI's impact on the innovation funnel primarily involves:
(a) Slowing down ideation to ensure thorough human review.
(b) Rapidly generating novel concepts and prototypes.
(c) Eliminating the need for any human input in design.
(d) Focusing solely on incremental improvements to existing products.

2. The concept of "human-AI symbiosis" in creative work implies that AI:
(a) Replaces human creatives entirely.
(b) Acts as an augmentation tool, generating content and ideas to inspire human work.
(c) Is limited to automating only the most mundane creative tasks.
(d) Operates independently without any human oversight.

3. Which of the following is NOT a new innovation model enabled by Generative AI?
(a) Autonomous innovation processes.
(b) AI-enabled open innovation.
(c) Mass production of standardized, undifferentiated products.
(d) Personalization and customization at scale.

Chapter 16

1. In the phased implementation of Generative AI, the "Technical Activation" phase primarily focuses on:
(a) Defining the solution architecture and integration.

(b) Building foundational capabilities through employee training and hands-on enablement.
(c) Developing a go-to-market strategy for new AI solutions.
(d) Continuously refining the AI strategy based on customer feedback.

2. A key challenge in data governance for Generative AI is:
(a) The simplicity of tracking data lineage across AI pipelines.
(b) The inherent transparency of AI models.
(c) The potential for sensitive information to be inadvertently embedded in neural networks during training.
(d) The lack of need for continuous monitoring of AI outputs.

3. The EU AI Act categorizes AI applications into different "risk tiers." Which of the following is NOT one of these tiers?
(a) Unacceptable risk
(b) High risk
(c) Moderate risk
(d) Minimal risk

Chapter 17

1. According to McKinsey's framework, which stage of technology adoption involves organizations actively scaling the deployment and adoption of the technology across the entire enterprise?
(a) Frontier innovation
(b) Experimentation
(c) Piloting
(d) Scaling in progress
(e) Fully scaled

2. What percentage of AI initiatives, according to the report, have achieved their anticipated Return on Investment (ROI)?
(a) Approximately 75%
(b) Less than 10%
(c) About 25%
(d) Over 50%

3. Gartner's ethical guidance for using Generative AI includes the directive to "Start inside." What does this primarily mean?
(a) Begin by developing AI models internally before using external vendors.
(b) Test Generative AI extensively with internal stakeholders and employee use cases before deploying customer-facing content.
(c) Focus on internal data governance before addressing external compliance.
(d) Prioritize internal cost savings over external revenue generation.

4. In the MIT CISR Enterprise AI Maturity Model, what is the primary focus of enterprises in "Stage 1: Experiment and Prepare"?

(a) Expanding process automation efforts.
(b) Architecting for reuse and exploring autonomous agents.
(c) Educating the workforce on AI and setting up acceptable use policies.
(d) Leveraging LLMs to augment work and creating use cases.

5. Which of the following is NOT identified by McKinsey as one of the three core components of successful Generative AI platforms?
(a) A self-service portal
(b) An open architecture to reuse Gen AI services
(c) Automated, responsible AI guardrails
(d) A dedicated, siloed data lake for each business unit

6. According to the report, what is one of the most widespread challenges in enterprise AI adoption, with nearly half of organizations surveyed expressing worries about it?
(a) Integration with legacy systems
(b) AI talent shortage
(c) Data Quality and Bias
(d) Unclear ROI and business case

7. The Emerging Technology Analysis Canvas (ETAC) is primarily characterized as:
(a) A detailed financial modeling tool for technology investments.
(b) A one-page, visual canvas for emerging technology evaluation.
(c) A framework for managing technology supply chain logistics.
(d) A software development methodology for agile teams.

8. Gartner categorizes revenue opportunities for Generative AI into which of the following areas?
(a) Product development, new revenue channels, and cost/productivity opportunities.
(b) Market research, customer acquisition, and brand building.
(c) Supply chain optimization, human resources, and legal compliance.
(d) Infrastructure upgrades, cybersecurity enhancements, and talent recruitment.

9. SHI suggests that to counteract the mistake of not investing enough in AI literacy, what percentage of efforts should be directed towards people and processes?
(a) 30%
(b) 50%
(c) 70%
(d) 90%

10. What term describes the phenomenon where Generative AI systems produce inaccurate, fabricated, or nonsensical answers?
(a) Overfitting
(b) Hallucinations
(c) Bias amplification
(d) Data leakage

Answers

Chapter 1

1. a, c **2.** b **3.** b, d **4.** d, f, g **5.** c, f **6.** a, b, d **7.** a, c **8.** a, d, f, h, j **9.** d **10.** c **11.** True **12.** b, c, f **13.** a

Chapter 2

1. c **2.** b **3.** a **4.** b **5.** d **6.** True **7.** c **8.** Right **9.** b **10.** a, c, d, f, g **11.** c **11.** b

Chapter 3

1. c **2.** False **3.** c **4.** d **5.** False **6.** False **7.** b **8.** d **9.** a **10.** b **11.** c

Chapter 4

1. c **2.** b **3.** d **4.** b **5.** e **6.** c, f **7.** b **8.** True **9.** False **10.** c

Chapter 5

1. a **2.** b, e **3.** c **4.** False **5.** d **6.** d **7.** b **8.** False **9.** e **10.** d

Chapter 6

1. b, e **2.** a **3.** c **4.** No **5.** f, g, h **6.** d **7.** c **8.** True **9.** c **10.** a **11.** c

Chapter 7

1. d **2.** d **3.** a **4.** c **5.** b **6.** c **7.** a **8.** b **9.** d **10.** b

Chapter 8

1. c **2.** c **3.** Incorrect **4.** b **5.** False **6.** c

Chapter 9

1. b **2.** c **3.** c **4.** a **5.** c **6.** True **7.** c **8.** False **9.** b **10.** d **11.** True **12.** c **13.** d **14.** b

Chapter 10

1. True **2.** c **3.** b **4.** False **5.** d **6.** d

Chapter 11

1. b **2.** a **3.** c **4.** b **5.** b **6.** d

Chapter 12

1. c **2.** b **3.** c **4.** d **5.** d

Chapter 13

1. e **2.** c **3.** a **4.** b **5.** c

Chapter 14

1. b **2.** c **3.** b **4.** b

Chapter 15

1. b **2.** b **3.** c

Chapter 16

1. d **2.** c **3.** c

Chapter 17

1. d **2.** c **3.** b **4.** c **5.** d **6.** c **7.** b **8.** a **9.** c **10.** b

Index